Perspectives on Behavioral Medicine

Proceedings of the
Academy of Behavioral Medicine
Research Conference,
Snowbird, Utah, June 3–6, 1979

KU-245-166

Edited by

STEPHEN M. WEISS

National Heart, Lung, and Blood Institute
National Institutes of Health
Bethesda, Maryland

J. ALAN HERD

Department of Psychiatry
Harvard Medical School
Boston, Massachusetts

BERNARD H. FOX

National Cancer Institute
National Institutes of Health
Bethesda, Maryland

ACADEMIC PRESS
A Subsidiary of Harcourt Brace Jovanovich, Publishers

New York   London   Toronto   Sydney   San Francisco

ACADEMIC PRESS, INC.
111 Fifth Avenue, New York, New York 10003

United Kingdom Edition published by
ACADEMIC PRESS, INC. (LONDON) LTD.
24/28 Oval Road, London NW1 7DX

Library of Congress Cataloging in Publication Data
Main entry under title:

Perspectives on behavioral medicine.

(Perspectives on behavioral medicine ; 1)
"Proceedings of the Academy of Behavioral Medicine
research conference, Snowbird, Utah, June 3-6, 1979"--
Pref.
Includes index.
1. Medicine, Psychosomatic--Congresses. I. Weiss,
Stephen M. II. Herd, J. Alan. III. Fox, Bernard H.
IV. Academy of Behavioral Medicine (U.S.) V. Series.
[DNLM: 1. Behavioral sciences--Congresses. 2. Medicine--
Congresses. W1 PE872C]
RC49.P42   616.08   81-2577
ISBN 0-12-532101-5   AACR2

PRINTED IN THE UNITED STATES OF AMERICA

81 82 83 84   9 8 7 6 5 4 3 2 1

*To the memory of my father, Harry,
whose ever-questioning mind intuitively understood
the biobehavioral perspective so well-expressed
in this volume.*

—SMW

Contents

INTRODUCTION

CARDIOVASCULAR DISEASE

NEOPLASTIC DISEASE

WORKING GROUPS

SPECIAL TOPICS

List of Contributors

Numbers in parentheses indicate the pages on which the authors' contributions begin.

ROBERT ADER (163), Department of Psychiatry, Division of Psychology, School of Medicine and Dentistry, University of Rochester, Rochester, New York 14642

A. BARNEY ALEXANDER (301), Psychophysiology Department, National Jewish Hospital/National Asthma Center, Denver, Colorado 80204

DAVID E. ANDERSON (307), Department of Psychiatry and Behavioral Sciences, Johns Hopkins School of Medicine, Baltimore, Maryland 21205

JAMES A. BLUMENTHAL (401), Center for Aging and Human Development, Durham, North Carolina 27710

JAMES C. BUELL (25), University of Nebraska Medical Center, and Veterans Administration Medical Center, Omaha, Nebraska 68705

THEODORE M. DEMBROSKI (321), Department of Psychology, Eckerd College, St. Petersburg, Florida 33733

RICHARD I. EVANS (261), Department of Psychology, University of Houston, Houston, Texas 77004

ROBERT S. ELLIOT (25), Cardiovascular Center, University of Nebraska Medical Center, Omaha, Nebraska 68105

THOMAS W. ELWOOD* (215), Cancer Control Program, Johns Hopkins Oncology Center, Baltimore, Maryland 21205

M. A. FITZMAURICE (371), Pacific Northwest Research Foundation, and The Fred Hutchinson Cancer Center, Seattle, Washington 98104

---

* *Present address:* American Public Health Association, Washington, D.C. 20005.

STEPHEN P. FORTMANN (89), Stanford Heart Disease Prevention Program, Department of Medicine, Stanford University, Stanford, California 94305

BERNARD H. FOX (101), National Cancer Institute, Bethesda, Maryland 20205

THOMAS F. GARRITY (67), Department of Behavioral Science, College of Medicine, University of Kentucky, Lexington, Kentucky 40536

LAWRENCE W. GREEN† (215), Division of Health Education, Department of Health Services Administration, School of Hygiene and Public Health, Johns Hopkins University, Baltimore, Maryland 21205

THOMAS HANEY (401), Behavioral Physiology Laboratory, Department of Psychiatry, Duke University Medical Center, Durham, North Carolina 27710

JANICE L. HASTRUP‡ (351), Department of Psychiatry, University of North Carolina Medical School, Chapel Hill, North Carolina 27514

ALLEN H. HENDERSON§ (261), Department of Psychology, University of Houston, Houston, Texas 77004

J. ALAN HERD¶ (55, 297), Laboratory of Psychobiology, Department of Psychiatry, Harvard Medical School, Boston, Massachusetts 02115

PETER C. HILL (261), Department of Psychology, University of Houston, Houston, Texas 77004

JIMMIE C. HOLLAND (235), Psychiatry Service, Memorial Sloan-Kettering Cancer Center, New York, New York 10021

STEPHEN B. HULLEY (89), Department of Epidemiology and International Health, University of California, San Francisco, San Francisco, California 94143

C. DAVID JENKINS (41), Department of Behavioral Epidemiology, Boston University School of Medicine, Boston, Massachusetts 02118

JOHN I. LACEY (293), Fels Research Institute, School of Medicine, Wright State University, Yellow Springs, Ohio 45387

ALAN W. LANGER (351), Department of Psychiatry, University of North Carolina Medical School, Chapel Hill, North Carolina 27514

KATHLEEN C. LIGHT (351), Division of Health Affairs, University of North Carolina, Chapel Hill, North Carolina 27514

† Present address: Department of Health and Human Services, 200 Independence Avenue, S.W., Washington, D.C. 20201
‡ Present address: Department of Psychology, State University of New York, Binghamton, New York 13901.
§ Present address: Department of Psychology, Texas Wesleyan College, Fort Worth, Texas 76105.
¶ Present address: Sid W. Richardson Institute for Preventive Medicine, The Methodist Hospital, 6565 Fannin, Houston, Texas 77030

NEAL E. MILLER (3), The Rockefeller University, New York, New York 10021

FLORENCE R. MORRISON (135), California Department of Health Services, Infectious Disease Section, Berkeley, California 94704

BENJAMIN H. NEWBERRY (329), Department of Psychology, Kent State University, Kent, Ohio 44242

PAUL A. OBRIST (351), Department of Psychiatry, University of North Carolina, School of Medicine, Chapel Hill, North Carolina 27514

RALPH S. PAFFENBARGER, JR. (135), Department of Family, Community and Preventive Medicine, Stanford University School of Medicine, Stanford, California 94305

BETTYE E. RAINES (261), Department of Psychology, University of Houston, Houston, Texas 77004

VERNON RILEY (183, 371), Department of Microbiology, Pacific Northwest Research Foundation, Seattle, Washington 98104

BARBARA RIMER (215), Johns Hopkins School of Hygiene and Public Health, Baltimore, Maryland 21205

JULIA H. ROWLAND (235), Psychiatry Service, Memorial Sloan-Kettering Cancer Center, New York, New York 10021

DARREL H. SPACKMAN (371), Pacific Northwest Research Foundation, and The Fred Hutchinson Cancer Center, Seattle, Washington 98104

GEORGE STONE (287), Department of Psychiatry, School of Medicine, University of California, San Francisco, San Francisco, California 94143

REDFORD B. WILLIAMS, JR. (401), Behavioral Physiology Laboratory, Department of Psychiatry, Duke University Medical Center, Durham, North Carolina 27710

Preface

An important goal of the first annual meeting of the Academy of Behavioral Medicine Research was to produce this publication, which we hope will be useful to a wide spectrum of readers. The meeting attempted to examine—critically and in-depth—research relevant to two biomedical areas, the cardiovascular and the neoplastic. In the first area, behavioral research is fairly well launched; in the second, it is in a more primitive stage. In each area, an overview paper and papers on various subtopics were prepared. Most of them were circulated in advance; they were all discussed at the meeting, and then revised and edited as a result of the discussion. In addition, working groups and special-interest groups discussed a variety of selected toics and prepared reports on them.

Special thanks are due to the authors of the papers in this volume and to the members of the Program Committee who, with such short notice, worked hard and effectively: Robert Eliot, Bernard Fox, Alan Herd, Stephen Weiss, and Redford Williams. We also wish to thank Dr. Jerome Singer, our Secretary-Treasurer, who handled the myriad administrative details associated with planning such a gathering. Finally, we are especially grateful for crucial financial support from Heart House, the International Stress Foundation, and The Rockefeller Foundation.

NEAL E. MILLER

Perspectives on
Behavioral Medicine

Introduction

An Overview of Behavioral Medicine: Opportunities and Dangers[1]

NEAL E. MILLER

Behavioral medicine is an interdisciplinary field concerned with the integration of biomedical and behavioral knowledge relevant to health and disease. As will be evident from the other chapters in this volume, behavioral medicine involves the integration of relevant components of epidemiology, anthropology, sociology, psychology, physiology, pharmacology, neuroanatomy, endocrinology, immunology, and the various branches of medicine as well as related professions such as dentistry, nursing, and social work. At present, I believe the main emphasis of behavioral medicine should be on basic research; it also should be concerned with the application of its knowledge and techniques to prevention, diagnosis, therapy, and rehabilitation. The evaluation of these applications must be an essential part of their development.

Factors Producing the Upsurge of Interest in Behavioral Medicine

Although behavioral medicine has various roots extending far into the past, the current upsurge of interest in this area appears to be due to a number of converging factors. As sanitation, vaccines, and antibiotics are controlling the ancient scourges of infectious diseases, other conditions with larger behavioral components are assuming relatively more importance on the medical scene.

---

[1] Based on Presidential address given at the meeting of the Academy of Behavioral Medicine Research, Snowbird, Utah, June 1979.

3

At the same time, evidence has continued to accumulate on the importance of the brain and its nervous and endocrine systems in regulating vital processes, such as breathing, heart rate, blood pressure, vasomotor responses, electrolyte balance, hormones, and in being the source of peptides such as the pain-inhibiting endorphins and enkephalins. Mechanisms are becoming understood through which the brain, via control of the corticosteroids as well as direct innervation of the lymph nodes and thymus, may influence the immune system and thus have additional wide-ranging biomedical implications. Although much more research is needed to tie specific neurophysiological mechanisms to specific psychosocial effects, new methods are being developed for investigating the myriad ways in which the mind affects the body. Possibilities for fruitful research in that area are being expanded by the development of powerful new techniques for studying the pathways and activities of the nervous system, the levels of and the receptors for hormones, peptides, and brain amines, and for manipulating and measuring behavioral variables [22].

Concurrently, evidence for the importance of behavioral factors in health and disease also is accumulating from clinical, epidemiological, and experimental studies. These studies indicate the importance of stress and of coping with stress, of unhealthy life styles such as Type A behavior, of smoking, of the overeating and underexercise that produce obesity, of the abuse of alcohol and drugs, and of noncompliance with medical prescriptions. It is also becoming evident that an important factor in rehabilitation from disease and medical emergencies, such as a heart attack, is the type of behavior elicited and reinforced during these conditions.

As a result of these and other developments, it is being recognized that some of the most promising opportunities for further improvement in the health of this nation lie in the area of prevention by avoiding health-damaging, and by encouraging health-maintaining, behavior [5,25].

Opportunities and Dangers

The increased interest in behavioral medicine provides exciting opportunities for research and for clinical application. It also poses certain dangers. Some of the problems we are being asked to solve—smoking, obesity, Type A behavior, abuse of alcohol and drugs, compliance with prescriptions—are extremely recalcitrant. We must not lead our medical colleagues and the general public to believe that behavioral solutions to these problems will be easy. If we allow unrealistic expectations to be raised, these will inevitably result in disillusionment that will cause people to say, "We've tried behavioral approaches and they were worthless." This could set the field back for another generation. We need to restrain the sincere but naive individuals who sense an opportunity but, by making impossible promises, are likely to destroy it.

The Need for Understanding of the Time-Consuming but Cost-Effective Role of Basic Research

We need to educate the general public, via cooperation with science writers and via reforms in our own introductory courses, toward a better understanding of the time-consuming role of basic research that eventually leads, in ways that often are unpredictable, to practical applications that can repay the entire investment in research several times over. There is no reason to expect behavioral medicine to be an exception to the kind of history described in Lewis Thomas's report to the President's Biomedical Research Panel in 1976:

> It can be agreed that the development of antibiotics, starting with penicillin, represents one of the major triumphs of biomedical science, but when the history of that event is examined it becomes clear that Fleming's observation of his famous mold-contaminated agar plate in 1929 was not at all the beginning of that research. In fairness to the facts, the initial experiments were started around 1875, and it required over a half-century of meticulous, painstaking, and occasionally brilliant work, involving hundreds of European, British, and (later in the day) American microbiologists, before the experiments of Fleming could even have been contemplated. The groundwork that had to be laid was the astonishing knowledge, in the first place, that there *were* such things as pathogenic bacteria, and that certain bacteria, with their own properties and taxonomic labels, were responsible for particular human diseases. . . . If this early basic research had not been done, there would have been no place for antibiotics; they could have come along in labeled bottles but no one would have known what to do with them. . . . It is interesting that most of the research on infectious disease during those years was what we would today be calling "basic" science. There was, to be sure, an acute awareness among the investigators that they were studying the agents of important human diseases, and there must have been a shared hope that the ultimate outcome would be useful for humanity. However, the work continued, slowly but steadily, without much in the way of what we would today be calling a "pay-off." It took a long time. We tend to forget how many generations of talented scientists, beginning with Pasteur, worked out their lives on the problems of infection before the stage was set for the era of antibiotics [34, p. 6].

The Need for Developmental Research

In addition to the need for basic research, there is a need for developmental research. The principles of physical science involved in the development of a new model automobile have long been well known and the industry has a backlog of years of engineering experience. Yet no manufacturer would go into mass production of a radically new model without extensive empirical road-testing. And even then, some defects may slip by and have to be corrected by recalls during the first year of mass production and use. Yet many large social and behavioral programs are initiated without similar phases of pilot testing and rigorous evaluation. These often have produced costly failures, such as certain aspects of urban renewal and housing. To avoid such failures in behavioral medicine, we need to educate our students and the public concerning the need for a series of carefully evaluated pilot tests on progressively larger samples. Such evaluation is expensive, but not nearly as costly as the large-scale failures that may occur without it.

Some of the foregoing points will be illustrated in the discussion of a few selected topics; I cannot hope to sample the entire range of behavioral medicine.

Stress and Coping

Observations in combat and in the clinic, as well as in epidemiological and life-change studies show that conditions loosely described as stressful can produce a wide range of medically adverse effects such as ulcers, increased susceptibility to a wide range of chronic and infectious diseases, accidents, and mental illness [4, 12, 13, 14, 20, 27]. Subsequent chapters will emphasize adverse effects on the cardiovascular system, and some considerably weaker evidence on the development of malignancies. Because of confounding factors, such as diet, sanitation, and exposure to pollution, it is hard to use such evidence conclusively to prove a causal effect. But the foregoing observations are, as you will see, supported by an increasingly impressive body of carefully controlled experiments, especially in the area of cardiovascular effects.

To date, the evidence suggests that stress has a generally predisposing effect increasing the risk of a wide range of medically adverse effects rather than any specific one. But most of the studies, especially the experimental ones, have investigated the effects of only one type of stressor or of only one type of outcome. We need studies with the more efficient and powerful design of studying in a comparable way the effects of a number of stressors on a number of outcomes in order to determine whether some of the former can specifically predispose to some of the latter [22].

In a related field, we know that one behavioral profile known as "Type A" behavior is related to increased risk for cardiovascular disease [6]. But we do not know whether this behavioral profile increases the risk also for other conditions, such as ulcers. We need far more evidence to determine whether one such behavioral constellation predisposes to cardiovascular disease whereas another predisposes toward ulcers.

Looking at the other side of the problem, there is considerable clinical, epidemiological, and experimental evidence that in a stressful situation, strong protective effects can be exerted by a variety of social supports and also by the individual's own behavior in coping with sources of stress [15]. This evidence provides hope for eventual preventive measures. Today, average students in college can be taught principles of mathematics and physical science that enable them to solve problems that for centuries baffled some of the brightest minds of earlier times. With sufficient research, we should some day have hope of teaching pupils in school better principles and techniques for solving social and emotional problems [7].

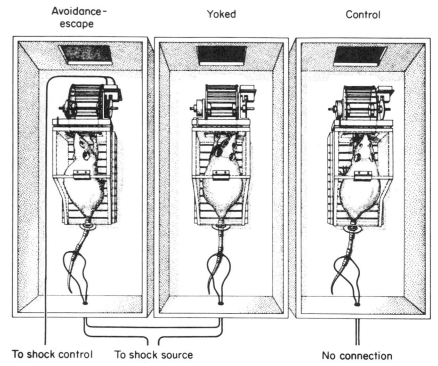

FIGURE 1. *This apparatus is used to measure the effects of ability to perform a coping response. The two rats to the left receive exactly the same shock because the electrodes on their tails are wired in series. The avoidance–escape ("executive") rat can perform the coping response of turning off the shock by rotating the wheel, but his yoked partner has no control over the shock. (Adapted from Weiss)* [36]

Complexities Increase the Danger
of Premature Applications

I have emphasized some of the opportunities for research on stress; now for some of the dangers. Figure 1 shows an apparatus that one of the colleagues in my laboratory, Jay Weiss, has used to study the effects of being able to perform an avoidance coping response on the development of stomach lesions. Electrodes on the tails of the first two rats are wired in series so they receive electric shocks that are exactly the same physical strength. These shocks are signaled by a tone. The rat on the extreme left can *avoid* the shock by rotating the wheel promptly after the tone; if he does not do this quickly enough, he can *escape* from the shock by turning the wheel. His yoked partner, in the middle, has access to a similar wheel, but it is not connected to any control over the shocks; he is at the mercy of his partner. The rat to the extreme right serves as the control, being exposed to the other conditions but without any electric shocks. As you can see from the left side of Figure 2, the "executive" rats who have a coping response available to control the shock develop considerably fewer stomach lesions than do their helpless, yoked partners. Since the rats in the two groups receive exactly the same physical strength of shock, the marked difference must be due to the purely psychological factor of the availability of a simple coping response.

In another part of the experiment, the conditions are changed. When the "executive" rat rotates the wheel, he delivers a shock to both himself and his partner; he is placed in an avoidance–avoidance conflict in which he has to give himself a shock in order to avoid or turn off a longer train of shocks. Under these conditions, as you can see from the right side of Figure 2, the results are exactly reversed; the "executive" rats with the avoidance coping response available have far more stomach lesions than their helpless, yoked partners. The change in one aspect of the situation has dramatically reversed the results [35].

The literature of stress is full of examples of such opposite effects. Both understimulation and overstimulation can produce adverse effects [9]. Sometimes fear produces tachycardia, as when the heart beats wildly with fear; at other times it produces bradycardia, as when the heart "stands still" or skips a beat with fear. In experimental studies, exposure to stress often increases susceptibility to disease and tumor genesis. But under other circumstances, it can have the opposite effect of decreasing susceptibility. You will see other examples in succeeding chapters of this volume.

Since stress can sometimes produce one kind of effect and sometimes its opposite, it obviously is hazardous to generalize widely from a given experimental result to a recommended practical application; the results may

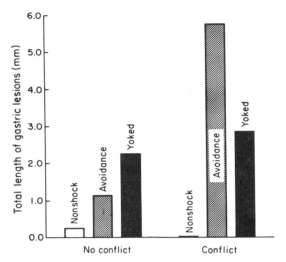

FIGURE 2. *Being able to learn an avoidance coping response to turn off the electric shock reduces the amount of stomach lesions when that response is simple and clear-cut, but it has the opposite effect when the task involves conflict. See text for details. (From data in Weiss)* [35]

turn out exactly opposite to what was intended. Before considering practical applications, we obviously need more definitive knowledge, such as that which may be supplied by dose– and time–response studies and by studies of the effects of various interactions [22].

Some of the complexities that baffle us now may result from imperfect knowledge or conceptualization. Let us hope that with increased knowledge the effects will look simpler, just as the motions of planets became easier to understand as soon as the change was made from the complex cycles and epicycles of the Ptolemaic system to the simpler orbits of the heliocentric one.

Predictability of Human Behavior

It is said that the human behavior is unpredictable. What odds would we want to bet our lives many times in order to get to a dinner or a meeting? But all of us do exactly that. When we fly, we bet our lives that the pilot will not decide to dive his plane directly into the ground. We bet our lives that the many drivers we meet on undivided portions of the highway will not choose to plunge their cars or trucks head-on into us. If human behavior were not highly predictable, a complex civilization such as ours would be utterly impossible. Even the rare examples of unpredictability that produce accidents are themselves statistically predictable from conditions such as unclear vision, fatigue, or alcohol ingestion.

Value of Simple Ideas

The simple idea that problems of human behavior do not have to be resolved by intuition or polemics but are subject to solution by empirical scientific techniques is itself extremely powerful in many situations. Sometimes a simple application of this idea can be very effective. When it was first decided to observe the behavior of people in museums, it was found that the curators arranged an exhibit, such as the evolution of the horse, so that it could best be understood by going from left to right. But when people enter a symmetrically laid-out room, the vast majority turn to go around it from right to left. Once these behaviors were observed, it was possible to put in simple devices to guide the public to the left. Their behavior was judged to be more easily modifiable than that of the curators.

During World War II, psychologists studying the transmission of verbal information and commands under noisy conditions were able to determine empirically that some words were confused much more frequently than others and to devise for important communications standardized phrases that greatly minimized possibilities for catastrophic confusion.

A Formula for Success

In a new field such as behavioral medicine, one of the first things to do is to look for simple, clear-cut situations to which well-verified principles apply. A general formula for success, which is much simpler to state than to apply, is

(a) Find something that is needed.

(b) Find something that you know you can do.

(c) Be sure it is of such a nature that you are able to prove to yourself and to others that you have done it.

Learning from the Advertising Profession

The problems inherent in overcoming addictions to smoking and alcohol and habits of eating unhealthy types and amounts of food are compounded by the skillful efforts of the powerful industries who have a strong economic interest in maintaining these harmful types of behavior. An example is the use of a behavioral technique, said to have been suggested by John B. Watson, to double the market for cigarettes. Formerly, the belief was widely held that it was immoral for women to smoke—that only prostitutes would do so in public. The feeling was so strong that any attempt to include a woman in a cigarette advertisement would have produced a reaction of general public outrage. But this moral tradition was systematically broken down through advertising that deliberately applied the behavioral principle of "crowding the threshold." In an advertisement depicting men smoking, a woman was first included so far in the irrelevant background that she was below the threshold for eliciting any adverse reaction. As the public became habituated to this inconspicuous inclusion, the female figure was moved by imperceptible degrees over a period of years through the next-to-last step depicting a wholesome, beautiful, stylishly dressed girl standing beside a handsome man, saying, "Blow some my way." There is no reason, except perhaps financial support, why we cannot study some of the behavioral techniques of the advertising profession and apply them to uses that benefit instead of harm the public. Some steps in this direction are illustrated in the chapter by Hulley.

Value to Behavioral Science of Exposure to Medicine

I have dealt briefly with how behavioral scientists, trained to observe behavior and to deal with it scientifically in complex situations, can contribute to medicine. But exposure to the problems of medicine can also make seminal contributions to the science of behavior. The hospital and clinic provide an excellent opportunity for the natural-history observation of human behavior in a significant life situation. They provide special opportunities for observing reactions to fear and other forms of stress and for observing coping responses. By exposing the behavioral scientist to variables that might not otherwise be encountered in the laboratory or in the experimental literature, they are a source of new problems and ideas. Clinical observations suggest new lines of experimental work such as those you will read about in subsequent chapters.

My own scientific career is an example of ideas that came from trying to build bridges between the laboratory and the clinic. Early instances are studies of frustration and aggression, and experiments on fear, conflict behavior, and displacement [17]. It was observations of the effects of tumors and of shell particles bouncing about in the third ventricle that first directed the attention of others to the role of the hypothalamus in hunger and emotion. I followed up some of this earlier work with studies of behavioral effects of lesions and of direct electrical and chemical stimulation of specific sites in the hypothalamus [16, 18]. The attempt to apply principles of learning to the etiology and therapy of neuroses was involved not only in the earlier work [7] but also helped to lead on to studies of visceral learning [19, 21].

Difficulties Inherent in Interdisciplinary Work

The preceding sections concerned the intellectual hybrid vigor produced by interdisciplinary work, but there also are considerable difficulties inherent in such work. I mention these in the hope that those who want to encourage such work will consider them and take special steps to counteract them. Academic bureaucracy has a strong tendency to reward disciplinary conformity. The people in the heartland of a discipline are not likely to understand or appreciate the work of those on the boundaries. Thus, the interdisciplinary worker is likely to find himself in the dilemma described by Stephen Leacock: "The humorists consider me to be a political scientist while the political scientists consider me to be a humorist." In times of austerity, the core members of any department are unlikely to waste their rewards on anyone who has strayed from the fold or is trying to come in from the outside.

Interdisciplinary work also involves overcoming difficulties in communication. Each partner needs to learn the other's terminology; similar words may mean different things. Each needs to know something of the other's concepts and principles. Such new learning requires considerable additional time and effort.

The ideal is two or more skills in one skull. But it is impossible for anyone to know everything he or she needs to know to be on the forefront of all the fields involved in behavioral medicine. Therefore, as programs develop in this field, there is a danger that they will try to teach each student too much of all fields and hence end up with graduates whose knowledge is so broad that it must inevitably be too shallow to serve as the basis for creative discoveries in any area. In my opinion, the broad field of behavioral medicine needs to be covered by different individuals, each learning in considerable depth different functionally useful combinations of interdisciplinary knowledge and skill. The variety of such individuals will be enough collectively to cover the entire field. The most important thing is to give the students the tools, experience, and confidence to embark on a lifetime of continued interdisciplinary learning.

Factors Leading to Overestimates of Therapeutic Effectiveness

The therapeutic application of behavioral techniques to conditions of biomedicine is a promising area. Unfortunately, it is an area in which dangerously overoptimistic claims already have been made, especially by certain enthusiasts using biofeedback training to elicit alpha waves.[2]

Caution must be used in evaluating the effectiveness of any new therapeutic technique because there are a number of factors that almost inevitably lead to overestimation. These are (a) the marvelous ability of the body to heal acute illnesses; (b) the tendency of most chronic illnesses to fluctuate, which can lead to a double selective error because patients generally come for treatment when they are feeling worse than usual and are discharged when they are feeling better than usual; (c) the extra enthusiasm, talent, and effort that innovators usually contribute to a new form of treatment; and (d) the powerful placebo effect.

Figure 3 shows a progressive improvement of blood pressure over a series of weeks. This apparently excellent therapeutic result was shown by one of the control patients receiving sugar pills in a double-blind test of the effectiveness of an antihypertensive medication. Such improvement in an objectively measured physical condition produced by a placebo treatment is not uncommon [1, 11, 29]. Although presenting formidable difficulties in the evaluation of new therapeutic techniques, placebo effects do

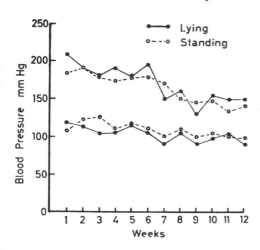

FIGURE 3. *This reduction in blood pressure was observed in a patient receiving placebo pills for 12 weeks as part of a double-blind test of an antihypertensive drug. (From Pickering et al. [26]. Reproduced with permission.)*

---

[2] For summaries of the status of therapeutic applications of biofeedback, see [19, 28, 32].

dramatically demonstrate the power of purely psychological factors; they deserve considerably more scientific investigation than they have received, as important phenomena in their own right.

Because of the factors exaggerating apparent effectiveness, the natural history of a new therapy tends to be, first, overenthusiasm and acceptance, followed by the opposite reaction of disillusionment and rejection, after which there may be a return to acceptance of some aspects of the treatment being considered truly beneficial for certain conditions. In the early part of this century, osteopaths and naturopaths were purporting to treat many different conditions with massage, heat, and applications of high-frequency electric current traveling to the patient impressively through fluorescent tubes. They were denounced as quacks. Certain useless aspects of their treatment have been abandoned, but others have been found useful and have been incorporated into physical therapy.

Rigorously designed evaluative studies are useful in weeding out useless or harmful therapeutic techniques and in speeding the acceptance of unconventional but useful ones. As larger proportions of medical expenses are paid by third parties—insurance companies and government agencies—and as consumer protection movements gain strength, there will be increasing demand for the evaluation of therapeutic techniques. Behavioral medicine will be wise to take a firm stand for the rigorous evaluation of all therapies developing in its domain and to organize efficient cooperative studies.

Role of Learning

I believe that the application of principles of learning is a particularly fruitful approach across a wide range of the activities involved in behavioral medicine. In conclusion, I will cite two examples of work from my own laboratory, each of which illustrates an application of learning, a behavioral scientist getting a new idea from collaborating with biomedical colleagues, and the unpredictable turns that research often takes.

Barry Dworkin and I were working on hypertension when Saran Jonas, our internist collaborator, suggested that electromyographic feedback might be applied to scoliosis, a lateral S-shaped curvature of the spine, the more benign treatment of which requires preadolescent girls to wear a physically restraining and cosmetically disfiguring brace like the one illustrated in Figure 4. The EMG approach ran into difficulties but, after a considerable period of development, facilitated by access to patients provided by Gordon Engler, Dworkin, and I devised the much less restrictive and conspicuous posture-training device illustrated in Figure 5. A nylon fishline sliding in a Teflon tube measures the circumference around the ma-

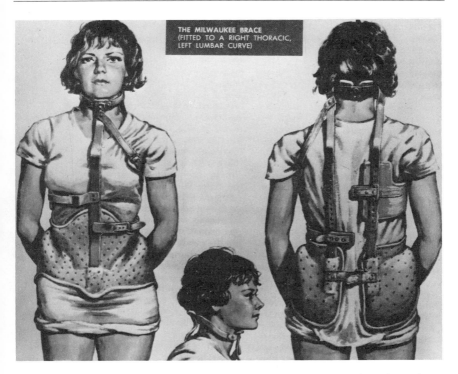

FIGURE 4. *This type of brace is used as the conservative treatment for idiopathic scoliosis. (Illustration by Frank H. Netter, M.D. in the CIBA Clinical Symposia Series, Vol. 24, No. 1 on scoliosis. Reproduced with permission.)*

jor axis of the body, which is lengthened as the spine is straightened. The distance can be lengthened also by expanding the chest, so a similar line around it measures that expansion and the device substracts the proper amount to yield a pure measure of spinal lengthening—standing tall. If the girl has been out of good posture for more than 20 seconds, a barely audible tone sounds. If she does not straighten up within a further 20 seconds, a louder tone sounds. Correcting her posture turns off either tone immediately. A calendar digital watch measures the total time out of correct posture.

Although basically simple, this device involves a number of subtleties that represent applications of principles of learning that are important for behavior that it elicits [8]. One of the attractive aspects of this project is the possibility of securing objective evidence of therapeutic effects by measuring the curvature of the spine via X-rays. At present, the device is working mechanically and is eliciting the desired type of behavior, but it is too

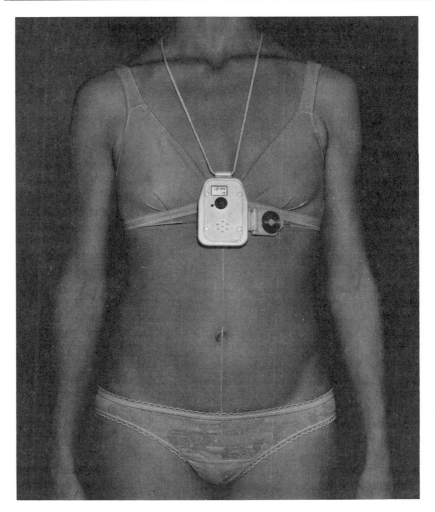

FIGURE 5.   *This posture-prompting device was developed by Barry R. Dworkin and Neal E. Miller. A nylon fishline sliding in a Teflon tube measures the circumference of the major axis of the body. A similar harness around the chest measures the circumference of the minor axis. The device subtracts a suitable fraction of the second measure from the first to yield a pure measure of straightening the spine by "standing tall." A digital calendar watch measures total time out of correct posture. The device yields signals to prompt the wearer to adopt a better posture.*

early in the treatment of too few cases for any statement about its therapeutic value. It does illustrate, however, a model for a new generation of devices that may greatly increase the power of therapeutic applications of feedback and learning through expanding the use of such technology from the brief, narrow confines of the clinic to full-time use during the patient's daily activities.

Role of Electronic Advances in Facilitating Applications of Learning

A considerable amount of behavior in the form of specified exercises and training plays an important role in conventional physical therapy. But the requirement for careful attention from a skilled therapist makes it economically difficult to train patients with recalcitrant disorders to achieve their full level of potential recovery. Imagine a therapist hour after hour patiently scrutinizing a girl with scoliosis and saying, "straighten up" whenever her posture becomes worse and "good" whenever it becomes better! However, the increased availability of more sophisticated instruments to measure desired changes in single elements and in complex patterns of both skeletal and visceral behavior, along with increasingly sophisticated possibilities for electronically programming the shaping of behavior by the use of rapidly advancing technologies such as microprocessors, yield the possibility of automating much of the therapist's work. These technical advances, plus the idea that learning may be applicable to the treatment of a wider range of conditions than has previously been considered possible, should facilitate radical advances in therapeutic applications.

Correcting a Homeostatic Defect in Patients with High Spinal Lesions

In the second example, a group was working at Goldwater Memorial Hospital on the ability of patients extensively paralyzed by polio to learn to make changes in blood pressure. This work yielded only modest results. But a patient whose spinal cord had been transected by a gunshot wound at T4 had been frustrated for over 2 years in his attempts to learn to walk with crutches and braces because he suffered from orthostatic hypotension that caused him to faint whenever he was helped into an upright position. This problem could not be corrected by conventional means. Hearing about our work on blood pressure, he asked Bernard Brucker, a staff member who was collaborating with us, to help him to learn how to increase his blood pressure. He was helped by training sessions during which he was promptly informed and praised whenever his blood pressure increased. To everyone's surprise, he rapidly learned to produce large increases. He also learned to perceive these increases so that he could dispense with the measuring equipment and practice by himself. The results are shown in Figure 6. When he was helped to an upright position and instructed not to try to control his blood pressure, the systolic level fell within 2 minutes to the dangerously low reading of 50 mm Hg, after which he was helped to sit down. But, when he was asked voluntarily to increase his blood pressure, he raised it 130 mm Hg and, despite being helped to stand up, kept it at a safe level for more than 5 minutes. This training transferred to the life situation so that he could walk with crutches and braces and maintain an adequate blood pressure with only marginal attention.

Brucker [2] secured similar results with other patients. Figure 7 illustrates results on a patient paralyzed from the neck down by a lesion at C4/5. For over 2 years, orthostatic hypotension had condemned her to remain in a reclining position with her feet elevated to approximately the level of her head. After learning to control blood pressure, she was able to remain in a normal sitting position for hours without danger of fainting, so that she could ride in a car and attend concerts, movies, and plays. Figure 7 shows that once she had acquired this control, she was able to dispense with the measuring equipment. Figure 7 also shows that the initial learned increases in blood pressure were accompanied by increases in heart rate. But with additional extensive practice, the response became specific to that component, increased blood pressure, that was useful in correcting her homeostatic defect, orthostatic hypotension. It has long been known that,

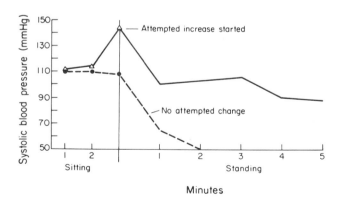

FIGURE 6. *The use of a learned response can correct a homeostatic defect. When a patient with his spinal cord severed at T4 is helped to stand up, his systolic blood pressure falls to a dangerously low level. But, if he uses his learned skill to produce a voluntary increase, he can maintain an adequate pressure. (From Brucker and Ince [3].)*

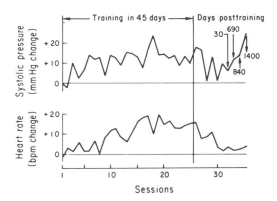

FIGURE 7. *Increased specificity of the learned skill of increasing blood pressure helps the patient, during extensive post-training experience, to use that skill to overcome severe orthostatic hypotension. The patient is paralyzed from the neck down by a spinal lesion at C4/5. (From Brucker [2] with additional data from Miller and Brucker [23].)*

with extensive practice of motor skills, the useless responses drop out so that the final performance becomes specific to the functionally useful ones.

Tests on these patients have ruled out the most obvious ways of indirectly influencing blood pressure via the skeletal responses of changes in breathing that affect p_{CO_2}, of muscular tension, or even of commands to paralyzed muscles. The eventual specificity of the response also makes such interpretations more difficult. But even with the limited repertoire of these patients, it is hard to prove with absolute certainty that no skeletal response is involved [23].

Wider Role of Visceral Learning in Homeostastis

The results with these patients raise a number of fascinating scientific problems. Treatment of these patients has demonstrated unequivocally the role of learning in correcting a severe visceral homeostatic defect, orthostatic hypotension. Why did not these patients learn such a correction by themselves? One patient apparently did. He reported asking the nurse to lower his feet gradually until he began to feel faint and then fighting off the faintness. As he succeeded, he had the nurse lower his feet further. He could not learn in an inconspicuous, automatic way because he was dependent on the nurse to lower his feet. The other patients did not learn because they were similarly dependent on outside help to change their posture. How many cases are there in which learning plays a significant role that has not been detected because conditions allow it to progress so smoothly and automatically that it is not obvious and because nobody has looked for it carefully enough?

Nonparalyzed patients taking medication that produces orthostatic hypotension report feeling faint and dizzy if they stand up too quickly and arresting such unpleasant feelings by sitting down and then standing up much more slowly. Eventually, they cease to be bothered as much. Are they learning increases in blood pressure motivated by the unpleasantness of feeling faint and rewarded when it occurs by the termination of such aversive feelings?

Working with patients with Raynaud's disease Surwit et al. [33] showed that, during a brief series of spaced cold-stress tests, patients given specific training in vasodilation showed improvement in resistance to vasoconstriction while those without such training did not show improvement.

Siegel [30, 31] has shown that the progressive decrease in the analgesic and hyperthermic effects of repeated small doses of morphine are produced by the acquisition of the compensatory responses of hyperalgesia and hypothermia, which appear if the rat is injected with a placebo instead of with the drug. He has also shown that the habituation produced by these responses varies with the stimulus context and hence must have a learned component, instead of being a purely pharmacological effect.

In a considerable number of other situations, the conditioned response (CR) is not similar to the unconditioned one (UCR), as would be expected from the traditional theory of response transfer or stimulus substitution; instead, the CR is opposite to the UCR as if it were a compensatory effect. Often, the UCR to an electric shock is tachycardia whereas the CR is bradycardia, the UCR to atropine is dry mouth whereas the CR is salivation, the UCR to mild doses of insulin is hypoglycemia whereas the CR is hyperglycemia. It remains to be determined whether these paradoxical conditioned responses are the classical conditioning of some automatically elicited compensatory effect, in which case that type of learning would be involved in the maintenance of homeostasis. On the other hand, these paradoxical CRs could be instrumental visceral responses reinforced by the compensatory effect that they produce. The second of these possibilities would have even more interesting implications as a mechanism for homeostasis [24].

You have seen some samples of work in behavioral medicine. You will see many more in subsequent chapters. In this new area, let us be bold in what we try but cautious in what we claim.

Acknowledgments

Work from the author's laboratory reported in this paper was supported by USPHS Grants HL 21532 and MH 28145, and by Grant 6-137 from the National Foundation, and by a grant from the Harry and Beatrice Renfield Foundation.

References

1. Beecher, H. K.: Surgery as placebo. *Journal of the American Medical Association* 176: 1102–1107, 1961.
2. Brucker, B. S.: Learned voluntary control of systolic blood pressure by spinal cord injury patients. Ph. D. Dissertation, New York University, 1977.
3. Brucker, B. S.; and Ince, L. P.: Biofeedback as an experimental treatment for postural hypotension in a patient with a spinal cord lesion. *Archives of Physical Medicine and Rehabilitation* 58:49–53, 1977.
4. Cassel, J.: The relation of the urban environment to health: Implications for prevention. *Mt. Sinai Journal of Medicine* 40:539–550, 1973.
5. *Daedalus:* Doing better and feeling worse: Health in the United States. *Daedalus* 106 (1):1–276, 1977.
6. Dembrowski, T. M. ed.: Proceedings of the Forum on Coronary-Prone Behavior. Publication No. (NIH) 78-1451. U.S. Department of Health, Education and Welfare, Washington, D.C., 1978.
7. Dollard, J.; and Miller, N. E.: *Personality and Psychotherapy.* New York: McGraw-Hill, 1950.
8. Dworkin, B. R.: Incorporation of learning principles into treatment systems. In *Proceedings of the XXII International Congress of Psychology.* Leipzig, 1980. p. 513.
9. Frankenhaeuser, M.: The role of peripheral catecholamines in adaptation to understimulation and overstimulation. In *Psychopathology of Human Adaptation*, ed. G. Serban, pp. 173–191. New York: Plenum, 1976.
10. Franz, S. I.: Cerebral–mental relations. *Psychological Review* 28:81–85, 1920.
11. Grenfell, R. F.; Briggs, A. H.; and Holland, W. C.: Antihypertensive drugs evaluated in a controlled double-blind study. *Southern Medical Journal* 56:1410–1415, 1963.
12. Jenkins, C. D.: Epidemiological studies of the psychosomatic aspects of coronary heart disease. *Advances in Psychosomatic Medicine* 9:1–19, 1977.
13. Klerman, G. L.; and Izen, J. E.: The effects of bereavement and grief on physical health and general well-being. *Advances in Psychosomatic Medicine* 9:63–104, 1977.
14. Levi, L., and Andersson, L.: *Psychosocial Stress—Population, Environment and Quality of Life.* New York: Spectrum, 1975.
15. Levine, S. and Ursin, H. eds.: *Coping and Health.* NATO Conference Series. New York: Plenum Press, 1980.
16. Miller, N. E.: Experiments on motivation; studies combining psychological, physiological, and pharmacological techniques. *Science* 126:1271–1278, 1957.
17. Miller, N. E.: Liberalization of basic S-R concepts: Extensions to conflict behavior, motivation and social learning. In *Psychology: A Study of a Science*, ed. S. Koch, study 1, vol. 2. pp. 196–292. New York: McGraw-Hill, 1959.
18. Miller, N. E.: Chemical coding of behavior in the brain. *Science* 148:328–338, 1965.

19. Miller, N. E.: Biofeedback and visceral learning. *Annal Review of Psychology* 29:373–404, 1978.
20. Miller, N. E.: Effects of learning on physical symptoms produced by psychological stress. In *Guide to Stress Research*, ed. H. Selye. New York; Van Nostrand Reinhold, 1980.
21. Miller, N.E.: Applications of learning and biofeedback to psychiatry and medicine. In *Comprehensive Textbook of Psychiatry*, eds. H. I. Kaplan, A. M. Friedman, and B. J. Sadock, 3rd ed., pp. 468–484. Baltimore: William & Wilkins, 1980.
22. Miller, N. E.: A perspective on the effects of stress and coping on disease and health. In *Coping and Health*, eds. S. Levine and H. Ursin, pp. 323–353. NATO Conference Series. New York: Plenum Press, 1980.
23. Miller, N. E.; and Brucker, B. S.: Learned large increases in blood pressure apparently independent of skeletal responses in patients paralyzed by spinal lesions. In *Biofeedback and Self-Regulation*, N. Birbaumer and H. D. Kimmel, pp. 287–304. Hillsdale, N.J.: Lawrence Erlbaum Associates, 1979.
24. Miller, N. E.; and Dworkin, B. R.: Homeotasis as goal-directed learned behavior. In *Neurophysiological Mechanisms of Goal-Directed Behavior and Learning*, eds. R. F. Thompson, L. H. Hicks, and V. B. Shvyrkov, New York: Academic Press, 1980. In press.
25. Nightingale, E. O.; Cureton, M.; Kalmar, V.; and Trudeau, M. B.: *Perspectives on Health Promotion and Disease Prevention in the United States*. Publication 78-001. Washington, D.C.: Institute of Medicine, 1978.
26. Pickering, G. W.; Cranston, W. I.; and Pears, M. A. *The Treatment of Hypertension*. Springfield, Ill.: Charles C Thomas, 1961.
27. Rahe, R. H.: Subjects' recent life changes and their near-future illness susceptibility. *Advances in Psychosomatic Medicine*, 8:2–19, 1972.
28. Ray, W. J.; Raczynski, J. M.; Rogers, T.; and Kimball, W. H.: *Evaluation of Clinical Biofeedback*. New York: Plenum Press, 1979.
29. Shapiro, A. K.: A contribution to a history of the placebo effect. *Behavioral Science* 5:109–135, 1960.
30. Siegel, S.: Morphine tolerance acquisition as an associative process. *Journal of Experimental Psychology: Animal Behavior Processes* 3:1–13, 1977.
31. Siegel, S.: Tolerance to the hyperthermic effect of morphine in the rat is a learned response. *Journal of Comparative and Physiological Psychology* 92:1137–1149, 1978.
32. Stoyva, J. ed.: Task force reports of the Biofeedback Society of America. *Biofeedback and Self-Regulation* 3:331–455, 1978.
33. Surwit, R. S.; Pilon, R. N.; and Fenton, C. H.: Behavioral treatment of Raynaud's disease. *Journal of Behavioral Medicine* 1:323–335, 1978.
34. U.S. Department of Health, Education and Welfare: *Report of the President's Biomedical Research Panel*. Appendix A: The place of Biomedical Science in Medicine and the State of the Science. DHEW Publication No. (OS) 76–501. Washington, D.C., 1976.
35. Weiss, J. M.: Effects of punishing the coping response (conflict) on stress pathology in rats. *Journal of Comparative and Physiological Psychology* 77:14–21, 1971.
36. Weiss, J. M.: Psychological factors in stress and disease. *Scientific American* 226(6):104–113, 1972.
37. Wolf, S. G.; and Goodell, H.: *Behavioral Science in Clinical Medicine*. Springfield, Illinois: Charles C Thomas, 1976.

Cardiovascular Disease

Environmental and Behavioral Influences in the Major Cardiovascular Disorders

ROBERT S. ELIOT
JAMES C. BUELL

The current interest in the relationship between behavioral and environmental circumstances in cardiovascular disease stems from a sizable body of evidence implicating psychosocial conflict, emotions, and behavioral patterns in the pathogenesis of coronary heart disease, sudden "coronary" death, cardiac arrhythmias, and systemic hypertension. This interest has been heightened by the observation that the traditional risk factors of elevated serum cholesterol, high blood pressure, and cigarette smoking are absent in more than half of the new cases of coronary heart disease encountered in clinical practice in the United States [24]. Indeed, it is difficult to separate the role of behavior and environment from the aforementioned risk factors in every instance. Each risk factor, in and of itself, is a composite of genetic, environmental, and behavioral components as well. Each risk factor can be provoked or sustained by influences which are beyond single simplistic metabolic etiologies or pathophysiological mechanisms. Thus, in view of our incomplete knowledge of the pathogenesis of coronary heart disease, and the likelihood that additional key factors are operating, it is not surprising that preventive measures confined to these new factors have met with limited success to date [39].

Despite these inadequacies, consistent and persuasive evidence links coronary and hypertensive heart disease with prolonged emotional stress, behavioral patterns, sociocultural mobility and changing life events. These disease states appear to be the major epidemic afflictions of industrialized communities in the twentieth century. Indeed, the prevalence of coronary heart disease and hypertension parallels the increasing complexity of social systems and social order whether we are speaking of animals or mankind. For these reasons, behavioral factors and environmental factors are the

PERSPECTIVES ON
BEHAVIORAL MEDICINE

25

subject of much current interest and investigation. To date, the field remains controversial and is littered with confusing terminology and imperfect methodology. Yet, this is to be expected at its relatively early stage of development. The purpose of this chapter is to review the multifaceted aspects of psychosocial and behavioral elements in human and animal studies that improve our current understanding of the aforementioned major cardiovascular disorders.

Psychosocial Stress in Animals

Whereas demographic evidence indicting stress in the pathogenesis of human cardiovascular disease remains circumstantial, data from animal experiments are direct and unmistakably link psychosocial disruptions to pathological changes in the cardiovascular system. Work summarized by Mason has shown that psychosocial stimuli can elicit either of two neuroendocrine responses [31]. One involves arousal of the pituitary-adrenal cortical system and the other that of the sympathetic-adrenal medullary system. In general, social interactions resulting in downward displacement in the social hierarchy lead to stimulation of the pituitary-adrenal cortical system with mental depression, decreased gonadotropin levels, enhanced vagal activity, gluconeogenesis, and pepsin production. The sympathetic-adrenal medullary system is called into play as agonistic or competitive behavior is invoked in an attempt to maintain status and prevent threatened loss of esteem and/or related objects of attachment.

Either of these responses can have pathophysiologic consequences. This dichotomy of "stress response" patterns is illustrated in the report of investigators who confined pairs of squirrel monkeys to chairs for eight hours a day during which one had to turn off a light once a minute or both would receive tail shocks. The animal responsible for avoidance of the shock had evidence of sympathetic arousal as shown by hypertension of 150/110 mm Hg and eventually developed myocardial fibrosis and degeneration. This animal did, however, maintain physical activity and outlasted the helpless partner that was incapable of controlling or coping. Five of the six helpless monkeys collapsed with bradycardia and four died in asystole [8]. The effects of stimulation in this study were manifested by two different response patterns (alarm or playing dead) associated with the two distinctly different responses of the neuroendocrine system. Furthermore, it is known that such neuroendocrine responses may be elicited singularly, sequentially, or in concert. These responses are mediated on the effective integrative level through two major loci.

The first is the limbic striatal system which is involved with social, emotional, and self-preservation behavior. The second is the brainstem–hypothalamic system which is concerned with sex, hunger, thirst, and sleep drives. It is, however, at the level of cognitive integration where species differences become most apparent. This process involves the frontal association cortex and parietal and temporal cross-modal association areas, termed the sociocultural brain. Only in man do these structures attain such overwhelming proportions when compared to the rest of the brain [21].

A separate but additionally important contribution from animal investigation by Stout and co-workers demonstrates the naturally occurring incidence and extent of atherosclerosis in a variety of animal species [41]. The *sine qua non* appears to be intimal trauma and damage, with or without the antecedent insudation of cholesterol or other lipid material. Predisposition to intimal trauma is based upon complex hydrodynamic factors [42].

Vascular vulnerability to sympathomimetic arousal is well demonstrated by experiments of Von Holst in adult male tree shrews [44]. In these experiments, a subordinate animal was introduced to another male that was an experienced fighter. The dominant male immediately attacked while the intruder submitted. The two were separated before injury could occur, but the subordinate was placed so that he could see the dominant animal without being attacked by him. The emotionally aroused subordinate lay still watching the other animal's movements more than 90% of its waking time. Its tail hair remained erect indicating a sustained sympathetic arousal. Within 2 to 16 days, despite eating and drinking, the subordinate animal would fall into a coma and die in association with a rising blood urea nitrogen and histologic evidence of renal insufficiency. These features point to acute renal vascular change as the cause of death. Hoff and colleagues observed the development of renal cortical necrosis following stimulation of the frontal cortex of the cat [22]. Knapp and his colleagues have demonstrated that continuous infusion of norepinephrine into the renal artery of the dog for 2 hours leads to irreversible renal failure [27].

Considering adverse neuroendocrine, hydrodynamic, and vascular catecholamine effects, prolonged provocation which arouses any combination of the aforementioned factors may influence the development of a variety of cardiovascular disorders. Some of the most intriguing of the laboratory investigations of chronic psychosocial stimulation are the reports of Lapin and Cherkovich [28]. They were among the first investigators to demonstrate successfully the pathogenetic potential of sustained agonistic social interaction. Their work involved changes in the social situation of dominant Hamadryas male baboons. The male of this particular species adopts its females when they are still immature and develops an intense attachment for them. When the dominant male was separated from the female and another male was put into the female's cage in full view of the former consort, the displaced male showed intense agitation. After several months, hypertension and other evidence of chronic cardiovascular disease developed in the original consort. While some of the studies were aimed at developing experimental neurosis rather than deliberate cardiovascular disease, the authors encountered 16 cases of hypertension, 19 cases of coronary insufficiency, and 6 cases of acute myocardial infarction.

Ratcliffe, in studies at the Philadelphia Zoo, observed that deaths in animals and birds from arteriosclerotic coronary heart disease increased from an incidence of less than 1% in 1948 to more than 10% in 1968 [36]. Diet and mean age at death were no different. He did, however, note that in 1948 the zoo began an attempt to assemble family groups. This contrived social grouping resulted in conflicts, breeding failures, and abnormal behavior within the "family groups." He eventually concluded that the increase in coronary heart disease resulted from behavioral responses to chronic social situations.

He then did an experimental follow-up, studying the psychological response of swine to separations occurring after the primary social bonds of grouped animals had been formed [37]. At the end of a year, the separated animals showed a significantly greater incidence, extent, and severity of coronary atherosclerosis. Whereas the grouped and paired swine responded to human visitors with friendly grunts and squeals for a handout, those swine that had been separated, especially the normally friendly females, failed to respond to visitors and even refused offers of added corn. The results of this quantitative study suggested that a sustained chronic emotional disturbance was significantly associated with chronic cardiovascular changes.

Henry has demonstrated that fixed hypertension with increased heart weight, progressive arteriosclerosis, myocardial fibrosis, and renal failure can be induced in socially deprived mice by subjecting them to social interaction [20]. An important observation in addition to the impact of social manipulation is the fact that different genetic strains of mice have different levels of blood pressure and different potentials for synthesizing adrenal catecholamines. They also have different temperaments responding differently in degree to the same social paradigm. Thus, the physiologic consequences of psychosocial provocation are largely engrafted upon a foundation of cultural and genetic predispositon. Nevertheless, psychosocial and behavioral factors are important in eliciting observable physiologic responses which indisputably eventuate in pathology. Such controlled and objective studies are impossible in the clinical arena; yet, the mechanisms and physiologic consequences are undoubtedly similar in many respects.

Considering the previous discussion concerning neuroendocrine responses, hydrodynamic factors, and catecholamine effects operating upon a genetic substrate, it is reasonable to suspect that psychosocial and behavioral factors might be linked to clinical cardiovascular disease through similar mechanisms in man.

Psychosocial and Behavioral Factors in Human Cardiovascular Disease

The clinical observations linking environmental and behavioral factors with cardiovascular disease, arrhythmogenesis and sudden death are too extensive to permit a comprehensive discussion within the confines of the space allowed. The reader is referred to a number of comprehensive reviews of the literature [30, 25, 14, 11, 4]. Here, we will briefly review some observations regarding psychosocial and behavioral factors as they relate to sudden death, coronary heart disease, and hypertension.

Sudden Death

Few folklore notions have enjoyed as widespread and persistent popularity as those that ascribe sudden death to emotional shock. Far back in recorded history people are described as dying suddenly while in the throes of fear, rage, grief, humiliation, or joy. Almost 2000 years ago, Celsus [7] recognized that emotional states could influence the heart when he commented that bathing, exercise, fear and anger and any other other state of the mind may often be apt to excite the pulse. In 1628, William Harvey reaffirmed the observation by stating that every affection of the mind that is attended with either pain or pleasure, hope or fear is the cause of an agitation whose influence extends to the heart [19]. In more recent times it has been implicitly recognized from Hunter's prediction of the circumstances of his death [23] to Cannon's observations on voodoo death [6] that the human psyche and circulation are somehow interrelated. Nevertheless, with the advent of scientific medicine in the late nineteenth century, these observations fell into disrepute as physicians began to embrace the more rational and objective view that the cause of death should be established at the necropsy table and in the the laboratory.

As an epidemiologic phenomenon, the incidence of sudden death at the Kennedy Space Center during the mid-1960s strongly suggested the influence of psychosocial and behavioral factors [38]. Although traditional risk factors were not remarkable, the sudden death rate among men at the Kennedy Space Center was nearly 50% higher than that of age and sex matched control groups. The divorce rate was three out of four marriages, and this microcosm led the nation in per capita consumption of alcohol. Some of the recognized factors contributing to the aberrant behavior in this society were (a) the perceived national urgency of putting a man on the moon by the end of 1969, (b) the great national and international visibility of the Center in which a dramatic failure would have adverse occupational consequences, (c) the problems of interpreting and coordinating the work of approximately 300 different major industrial subcontractors, particularly for administrators and managerial personnel engaged in interorganizational liaison, (d) the progressive decline in budget and employment, and (e) the threat of loss of employment and income from lack of demand for overspecialized and highly trained skills inappropriate in the common marketplace. In short, the project demanded an ever increasing if not frenzied pace of production with the ultimate reward of nearly inevitable dismissal. There were findings of an unusually high percentage of abnormal resting ECGs. In addition, there was a remarkable incidence of psychoneuroticism, anxiety, and depression within the population [45]. Post-mortem histologic features of victims of sudden death demonstrated the existence of myocardial contraction bands. This same histologic picture of hyperfunctional necrosis can be quickly induced in animals by the administration of boluses of catecholamines [12]. The abilities of catecholamines to facilitate rhythm disturbances, increase myocardial oxygen demand, augment vascular reactivity, and mobilize glucose and free fatty acids are well-established facts. The results of animal experimentation have demonstrated the protective effect of beta blockade [27], and recent studies suggest that beta blocker administration is also having a beneficial impact upon the incidence of coronary heart disease in some countries [2].

A large number of experimental animal studies have been reported which strongly implicate psychological stress in the precipitation of arrhythmias and sudden death, and several studies have recently appeared in the literature documenting the effects of psychological stress in lowering the threshold for ventricular fibrillation not only in animals but also in man [30, 14, 29].

Although it is difficult to conduct controlled human studies comparable to those readily obtained in animals, electrocardiographic monitoring during a variety of psychologically stressful tasks in humans has documented significant and potentially fatal rhythm disturbances in direct association with episodes of emotional stress. Thus, it appears that continuous electrocardiographic monitoring can provide previously unavailable physiologic data on the process of dying and the events preceding it. Such data is not accessible at the necropsy table. These findings are beginning to illuminate pathophysiological processes thereby offering prospective guidance as to which factors may lead to lethal consequences and what techniques are suitable for their control. Of perhaps equal importance is the fact that animal experimentation has taught us that the same experimental environments may produce different results in different species or, by altering time frames or options, produce different results in the same species, indicating that the impact and countenance of a psychosocial stimulus is highly selective and individual.

Whether an event elicits an adverse physiological response depends also upon a complex amalgam of factors including genetic predisposition, early social experience, and a life-long process of conditioning and cultural factors. The resultant perception constitutes the psychological prism through which daily events are uniquely and individually refracted.

Therefore, ambulatory monitoring as a measure of physiological response should also be correlated with aspects of cognitive behavior. The influence of psychosocial and behavioral factors is becoming increasingly well substantiated in the clinical area of arrhythmias and sudden death. Many physiological mechanisms contributing to this clinical phenomena are being discovered and examined. The aspects of cognitive integration eliciting such responses remain an important frontier for further investigation.

Coronary Heart Disease

Whereas the link between observed environmental provocation and physiological response is relatively immediate and direct in studies of arrhythmogenesis and sudden death, the role of psychosocial and behavioral factors in coronary heart disease is far more complex and elusive. Considering the slow evolution of clinical coronary heart disease and our incomplete knowledge of the pathophysiology of coronary atherosclerosis and the mechanism of its sequelae, one can hardly expect more proof than guilt by association. In truth, we really do not know for sure the mechanism whereby any heretofore commonly accepted coronary risk factor may effect arterial damage. We still have to find out what the intrinsic biophysical, metabolic, and neurochemical processes are by which such factors lead to the onset of clinical coronary heart disease. When such fundamental mechanisms are understood, it should not be too difficult to track down the precise cardiopathic mechanisms which might be fostered by psychosocial and behavioral factors.

Nevertheless, there is considerable evidence suggesting that coronary disease is often associated with psychosocial and behavioral phenomena including anxiety, depression, psychophysiological complaints, sleep disturbances, fatigue, and emotional drain. The association between life change indices and myocardial infarction is provocative, but a stronger association exists between cardiovascular disease and anxiety or depression. Such data suggests that environmental provocation cannot be viewed in isolation. It is reasonable to expect that such spheres of investigation might be highly interrelated yielding similar correlations because of a common denominator. The pivotal point of this common denominator might well be the ability of the individual to cope with life changes and dissatisfactions from the perspective of personal success or failure in dealing with his or her environment. As such, the multitude of adaptive resources and mechanisms at the disposal of an individual and one's subjective interpretation of their suitability to outcome are probably equally important factors [4].

A recent conference sponsored by the National Heart, Lung, and Blood Institute was designed to appraise the role of behavior as a predictor of potential coronary heart disease [32]. The role of behavior as a significant factor in the pathogenesis of coronary heart disease was recognized long ago by Osler [33] and focused upon by John Hunter [23] in his self-fulfilling prophecy: "My life is at the mercy of any scoundrel who chooses to put me in a passion." The Review Panel convened by the National Heart, Lung, and Blood Institute accepted the available body of scientific evidence as demonstrating that Type A behavior (as defined by the structured interview used by Rosenman and Friedman in the Western Collaborative Group Study, the Jenkins Activity Survey, and the Framingham Type A Behavioral Scale) was associated with an increased risk of clinically apparent coronary heart disease in middle-aged U.S. citizens. The risk was found to be beyond that imposed by age, elevated systolic blood pressure, serum cholesterol, or cigarette smoking, and appeared to be at least the same order of magnitude as the relative risks associated with the latter three of these factors.

Type A behavior was defined as "an aroused state superimposed on a complex underlying substrate of interrelated factors" [32]. Metaphorically it can be viewed as an iceberg with a small portion apparent above the surface. Unfortunately, situational (environmental) determinants, individual perceptive or cognitive differences, and other psychological components such as anxiety, depression, psychosocial problems, and physiological variations, pathophysiological aging mechanisms and genetic susceptibility are not easily assessed by these tests. Clearly, the most diagnostic of these tests in the assessment of Type A behavior is the structured interview of Rosenman and Friedman. None, however, was considered satisfactory with regard to prognostic sensitivity, specificity, and selectivity in predicting the advent of coronary heart disease. The Panel did, however, recommend that the structured interview be considered the most suitable as a "gold standard" at this time [32]. The Type A behavior as evaluated by the structured interview is manifested by behavioral styles of loud, explosive, rapid, and accelerated speech with short response latency, hostility, and a tendency toward verbal competition. Speed, impatience, hostility, competitive drive, and a sense of an effort-oriented person caught up in a joyless struggle constitute the fully developed Type A behavior pattern.

Glass's [16] observations that the Type A personality is vulnerable to depression are in accord with the study by Thomas, Ross, and Duszynski [43] of physicians with myocardial infarcts who readily became depressed, even as students; and likewise with a study by Bruhn and colleagues [3] of the coronary prone as an effort-oriented person whose achievements give him little satisfaction.

The mechanisms through which Type A behavior operates as a risk factor, or how it facilitates the progression of coronary heart disease, remain largely conjectural. Obviously, this weakness is shared with all risk factors until the pathogenesis of coronary atherosclerosis is more fully understood. However, the prevalence of certain biochemical and physiological phenomena are highly associated with the fully developed Type A behavior. These include elevated serum cholesterol, elevated pre- and postprandial serum triglycerides, increased platelet aggregation, faster clotting time, higher excretion of norepinephrine (particularly provoked by emotional challenge), a higher average serum level of corticotropin, a greater insulinemic response to glucose, a decreased growth hormone response to arginine, and greater lability and magnitude of blood pressure response under time demand tasks [10].

We believe it is important to make the distinction between Type A behavior as a circumscribed constellation of psychomotor manifestations defined by Rosenman and Friedman and the ill-defined, but constantly evolving, concept of coronary prone behavior. Indeed, many individuals manifesting Type A behavior survive unscathed into old age, attending the funerals of their younger Type B counterparts. Thus, the association is incomplete. It is obvious that genetic, perceptive, and other coping factors operate to counterbalance predisposing behavioral effects in many individuals. Furthermore, the cognitive integrative aspects of behavior and their link to pathophysiological responses remain largely unknown.

If, by behavior, one means the actions or reactions of man or animals under specified circumstances, a recent study by Dembroski [9] illustrates the distinction between Type A and B coronary patients and normal subjects. During a structured interview and an American history quiz, he noted an increase in systolic blood pressure during the history quiz in Type

B coronary patients but not in Type B controls. Indeed, the greatest increment of blood pressure change in either Type A or B groups was evoked in Type B myocardial infarction patients during the American history quiz. Work from our own laboratory, using similar but different techniques, tends to confirm and support Dembroski's observations, especially with regard to psychophysiologic behavior as a valuable adjunct in studying coronary prone behavior patterns [5]. Although the small sample size prohibits anything more than speculation at this time, it does suggest that we must attempt to examine and integrate the multifaceted aspects of overt, cognitive, and physiologic behavior if we are to gain further insight into our understanding of how behavioral facets translate into coronary proneness within both Type A and B behavior patterns.

Hypertension

Hypertension can be traced to an identifiable cause in less than 10% of cases and the condition affects approximately 35 million Americans. Yet, despite the widespread popular conception that an inner feeling of nervous tension is in fact hypertension, we know from objective evidence that such equivalency is incorrect.

On the other hand, a sizable and diverse number of scientific observations strongly suggest that psychosocial and behavioral factors participate in the pathogenesis of hypertension. The ability of adverse psychosocial situations to evoke chronic hypertension was alluded to earlier in the work of Henry [21, 20]. While the strength of evidence in the clinical arena is less than that for objective controlled animal experiments, psychosocial factors have been incriminated in terms of socioeconomic level, crime rate, residential change, and overcrowding.

Harburg and colleagues [18] have shown that blacks living in areas of Detroit with low ecological stress had less hypertension than their counterparts living in high stress areas. Gampel and co-workers [15] have reported that there was less hypertension among rural than urban Zulus; and of the latter, more of those who clung to traditional cultural practices and seemed unable to adapt successfully to the demands of urban living were hypertensive. Indeed, a remarkable contrast can be found between industrialized and primitive societies that demonstrates the relative absence of hypertension in the latter. Yet, immigrants from primitive societies to urban communities develop hypertension with equal or greater incidence, facility, and severity [15]. Apropos to these observations is the comment of Ostfeld and Shekelle [34]:

> There has been an appreciable increase in uncertainty of human relations as man has gone from the relatively primitive and more rural to the urban and industrial. Contemporary man, in much of the world, is faced every day with people and with situations

about which there is uncertainty of outcome, wherein appropriate behavior is not prescribed and validated by tradition, where the possibility of bodily or psychological harm exists, where running or fighting is inappropriate, and where mental vigilance is called for.

In reality, the agonistic society of Henry's animal experiments is tantamount to the society of urbanized industrialized man. However, just as different genetic strains of the same species manifest different temperaments and potential for developing hypertension, it is likely that similar modifiers are operative in the clinical setting. Thus, whatever provocation or stress may emanate from an agonistic society, genetic predisposition and cognitive integration are equally important factors in the equation resulting in hypertension. The mosaic theory of pathophysiology proposed by Page [35] seems appropriate, wise, and useful. From this vantage point, the socioenvironmental association with hypertension seen in a variety of epidemiologic studies suggests that social or emotional stress may play a role in the pathogenesis of hypertension. Controversies concerning the term aside, we find it more understandable and, therefore, more useful to recognize stress by its effect upon the organism in question; that effect being strain. Therefore, we know stress by the company it keeps—namely strain. We recognize that these concepts differ from Selye's concepts of good stress and bad stress. However, it seems necessary for the cognitive process to determine whether outside forces represent, for that individual, a strain-inducing phenomenon. Obviously, there is no other apparent explanation for the old adage, "One man's meat is another man's poison."

Beyond considerations of environmental provocation, psychological and behavioral aspects are also worthy of note. Notably, work by Alexander [1] suggests that the hypertensive personality may be described as one who frequently manifests inhibited and poorly expressed rage and anger. It has been proposed that this inhibited rage or "anger turned inward" results in stimulation of the autonomic nervous system and release of significant amounts of norepinephrine, leading to acute and eventually chronic hypertension. Observed behavior indicates that such individuals may be withdrawn, not easily communicative, and tend to avoid confrontation with people even when rage is justified, at times even seeming obsequious in their efforts to avoid conflict and to please those individuals with whom they are involved in interpersonal relationships.

On the other hand, it may be somewhat naive to transpose personality patterns into events influencing the autonomic nervous system and eventuating in hypertension. Others have suggested that this behavior may be a manifestation of an "awareness" by hypertensives of their hyperreactive cardiovascular system resulting in attempts to withdraw from confrontation lest by becoming involved they evoke excessive and potentially harmful responses [26, 46]. Work by Sapira [40] suggests that hypertensive patients deny the difference between a neutral and an overtly confrontational movie drama as if in some manner they had managed to avoid perceiving what was an obvious confrontation.

Whether observations linking personality and behavior with hypertension constitute valid clues to its pathogenesis or a protective response to genetic vulnerability, or even a functional defect as a consequence of the disease process, remains to be seen.

Suffice it to say, if behavior does not influence the inception of hypertension, the successful use of biofeedback in the control of hypertension is a behavioral factor of face validity. Green [17], among others, has demonstrated the remarkable ability of biofeedback techniques to control hypertension through the appropriate use of this nonpharmacologic technique. Perhaps the key to Green's success (over less successful investigators) is the utilization of biofeedback instrumentation to promote patient self-mastery and self-control rather than to use the machines to maintain therapist dominance. By fostering the element of self-mastery, Green's techniques offer powerful patient motivation and perhaps contribute strongly to the consequent success in lowering blood pressure.

In conclusion, and taken together, the studies relating psychosocial and behavioral factors to cardiovascular disease phenomena provide justification for the conclusion that such factors are importantly involved. We would conclude by emphasizing the need to study and evaluate the interaction of environmental and biological factors in laboratory studies of pathogenesis as well as clinical studies of management. Indeed, upon careful scrutiny, even the accepted so-called "nonbehavioral" risk factors such as hypercholesterolemia, hypertension, cigarette smoking, obesity, and sedentary lifestyles are each composite manifestations rather than single pathogens whose identities are powerfully impregnated and bolstered by varieties of behavioral and psychosocial underpinnings. Therefore, in reviewing the awesome impact of contemporary cardiovascular disease both in terms of its increasing socioeconomic importance and its biologic devastation, we may not be long able to afford comprehensive public health programs without increased and improved attention to powerful psychosocial and behavioral interactions.

References

1. Alexander, F.: *Psychosomatic Medicine. Its Principles and Applications.* New York: W. W. Norton and Company, 1950.
2. Berglund, G.; Sannerstedt, R.; and Andersson, O.: Coronary heart disease after treatment of hypertension. *Lancet* 1:1–5, 1978.

3. Bruhn, J. G.; Paredes, A.; Adsett, C. A.; and Wolf, S.: Psychological predictors of sudden death in myocardial infarction. *Journal of Psychosomatic Research* 18:187–191, 1974.
4. Buell, J. C.; and Eliot, R. S.: Stress and cardiovascular disease. *Modern Concepts of Cardiovascular Disease* 48:19–24, 1979.
5. Buell, J. C.; and Sime, W. E.: Quantitation of physiological response to emotional stress. *Journal of the South Carolina Medical Association,.* 75:555–561, 1979.
6. Cannon, W. B.: Voodoo Death. *Psychosomatic Medicine* 19:182–190, 1957.
7. Celsus, A. C.: *De Medicina*, Liber III, 6, circa 30 A.D. Quoted in East, C.F.T. *The Story of Heart Disease*. London:William Dawson and Company, 1957.
8. Corley, K. C.; Mauck, H. P.; and Shiel, F. O.: Cardiac responses associated with "yoked-chair" shock avoidance in squirrel monkeys. *Psychophysiology* 12:439–444, 1975.
9. Dembroski, T. M.; MacDougall, J. M.; and Lushene, R: Interpersonal interaction and cardiovascular response in type A subjects and coronary patients. *Journal of Human Stress,.* 5:28–36, 1979.
10. Dembroski, T. M.; MacDougall, J. M.; and Shields, J. L.: Physiologic reactions to social challenge in persons evidencing the type A coronary-prone behavior pattern. *Journal of Human Stress* 3:2–9, 1977.
11. Eliot, R. S.: Stress and cardiovascular disease. *European Journal of Cardiology* 5:97–104, 1977.
12. Eliot, R. S.; Clayton, F. C.; Pieper, G. M.; and Todd, G. L.: Influence of environmental stress on the pathogenesis of sudden cardiac death. *Federation Proceedings* 36:1719–1724, 1977.
13. Eliot, R. S.; Todd, G. L.; Clayton, F. C.; and Pieper, G. M.: Experimental catecholamine-induced acute myocardial necrosis. In *Advances in Cardiology*, Vol. 25, eds. V. Manninen and P. I. Halonen, pp. 107–118. Basel: S. Karger, 1978.
14. Engel, G. L.: Psychologic stress, vasodepressor (vasovagal) syncope and sudden death. *Annals of Internal Medicine* 89:403–412, 1978.
15. Gampel, B.; Slome, C.; Scotch, N.; *et al.*: Urbanization and hypertension among Zulu adults. *Journal of Chronic Disease* 15:67–70, 1962.
16. Glass, D. C.: *Behavior Patterns, Stress and Coronary Disease*. Hillsdale, New Jersey: Lawrence Erlbaum Associates, 1977.
17. Green, E. E.; Green, A. M.; and Norris, P. A.: Preliminary report on a new non-drug method for control of hypertension. *Journal of the South Carolina Medical Association,* 75:575–582, 1979.
18. Harburg, E.; Schull, W. J.; Erfurt, J. C.; *et al.*: A family set method for estimating heredity and stress. I. A pilot survey of blood pressure among Negroes in high and low stress areas, Detroit, 1966–1967. *Journal of Chronic Disease* 23:69, 1970.
19. Harvey, W.: Quoted in Eastwood, M. R. and Trevelyan, H. Stress and coronary heart disease. *Journal of Psychosomatic Research* 15:289–292, 1971.
20. Henry, J. P.: Understanding the early pathophysiology of essential hypertension. *Geriatrics* 31:59–72, 1976.
21. Henry, J. P.; Ely, D. L.; Watson, F. M. C.; and Stevens, P. M.: Ethological methods as applied to the measurement of emotion. In *Emotions: Their Parameters and Measurement*, ed. L. Levi. p. 469–482, New York: Raven Press, 1975.
22. Hoff, E. C.; Kell, J. F.; Hastin, N.; Sholes, D. M.; and Gray, E. H.: Vasomotor cellular and functional changes produced in kidney by brain stimulation. *Journal of Neurophysiology* 14:317–332, 1951.
23. Home, E.: A short account of the author's life. In *A Treatise on the Blood, Inflammation and Gun Shot Wounds*, ed. J. Hunter. Philadelphia: T. Bradford Publishers, P. I., 1796.
24. Jenkins, C. D.: Psychologic and social precursors of coronary disease. Part I. *New England Journal of Medicine* 284:244–255, 1971.

25. Jenkins, C. D.: Recent evidence supporting psychologic and social risk factors for coronary disease. Part I. *New England Journal of Medicine* 294:987–994, 1976.
26. Kalis, B. L.; Harris, R. E.; Sokolow M.; and Carpenter, L. G.: Response to psychological stress in patients with essential hypertension. *American Heart Journal* 53:572–578, 1957.
27. Knapp, R.; Hollenberg, N. K.; Busch, G. J.; and Abrams, H. L.: Prolonged unilateral acute renal failure induced by intraarterial norepinephrine infusion in the dog. *Investigations in Radiology* 7:164–173, 1972.
28. Lapin, B. A.; and Cherkovich, G. M.: Environmental change causing the development of neuroses and corticovisceral pathology in monkeys. In *Society, Stress and Disease: The Psychosocial Environment and Psychosomatic Diseases*, ed. L. Levi, Vol. 1, 266–279. London: Oxford University Press, 1971.
29. Lown, B.; DeSilva, R. A.; and Lenson, R.: Roles of psychologic stress and autonomic nervous system changes in provocation of ventricular premature complexes. *American Journal of Cardiology* 41:979–985, 1978.
30. Lynch, J. J.; Paskewitz, D. A.; Gimbel. K. S.; and Thomas, S. A.: Psychological aspects of cardiac arrhythmia. *American Heart Journal* 93:645–657, 1977.
31. Mason, J. W.: A review of psychoendocrine research on the pituitary adrenal cortical system. *Psychosomatic Medicine* 30:576–607, 1968.
32. National Heart, Lung, and Blood Institute. *Proceedings of the National Heart, Lung, and Blood Institute Panel on Coronary Prone Behavior and Coronary Heart Disease*. Amelia Island, Florida, 1978.
33. Osler, W.: The Lumleian lectures on angina pectoris. *Lancet* 1:697–702, 839–844, 1910.
34. Ostfeld, A. M.; and Shekelle, R. B.: Psychological variables and blood pressure. In *The Epidemiology of Hypertension*, ed. J. Stamler, R. Stamler and T. N. Pullman, pp. 321–331. New York: Grune and Stratton, 1967.
35. Page, I. H.: Pathogenesis of arterial hypertension. *Journal of the American Medical Association* 140:451–457, 1949.
36. Ratcliffe, H. L.: Environment, behavior and disease. In *Progress in Physiological Psychology*, eds. E. Steller and J. M. Sprague, pp. 161–228. New York: Academic Press, 1968.
37. Ratcliffe, H. L.; Luginbuhl, H.; Schnarr, W. R.; and Chacko, K.: Coronary arteriosclerosis in swine: Evidence of a relation to behavior. *Journal of Comprehensive Physiology and Psychology* 68:385–392, 1969.
38. Reynolds, R. C.: Community and occupational influences in stress at Cape Kennedy: Relationships to heart disease. In *Stress and the Heart*, ed. R. S. Eliot, pp. 33–49. Mt. Kisco, New York: Futura Publishing Company, 1974.
39. Russek, H. I.; and Russek, L. G.: Etiologic factors in ischemic heart disease: The illusive role of emotional stress. *Geriatrics* 27:81–86, 1972.
40. Sapira, J. D.; Scheib, E. T.; Moriarity, R.; and Shapiro, A. P.: Differences in perception between hypertensive and normotensive populations. *Psychosomatic Medicine* 33:239–250, 1971.
41. Stout, L. C.; and Bohorquez, F.: Significance of intimal arterial changes in non-human vertebrates. In *Symposium on Atherosclerosis*, ed. M. D. Altschule, vol. 58, pp. 245–255. Philadelphia: W. B. Saunders Company, 1974.
42. Texon, M.: Atherosclerosis, its hemodynamic basis and implications. In *Symposium on Atherosclerosis*, ed. M. D. Altschule, Vol. 58, pp. 257–268. Philadelphia: W. B. Saunders Company, 1974.
43. Thomas C. B.; Ross, D. C.; and Duszynski, K. R.: Youthful hypercholesterolemia: Its associated characteristics and role in premature myocardial infarction. *John Hopkins Medical Journal* 136:193–208, 1975.

44. Von Holst, D.: Renal failure as the cause of death in Tupaia belangeri (tree shrews) exposed to persistent social stress. *Journal of Comprehensive Physiology and Psychology* 78:236–273, 1972.
45. Warheit, G. J.: Occupation: A key factor in stress at the Manned Space Center. In *Stress and the Heart*, ed. R. S. Eliot, pp. 51–65. Mt. Kisco, New York: Futura Publishing Company, 1974.
46. Weiner, H.; Singer, M. T.; and Reiser, M. F.: Cardiovascular responses and their correlates. A study in healthy young adults and patients with peptic ulcer and hypertension. *Psychosomatic Medicine* 24:477–498, 1962.

Behavioral Factors in the Etiology and Pathogenesis of Cardiovascular Diseases: Sudden Death, Hypertension, and Myocardial Infarction

C. DAVID JENKINS

In order to focus precisely on the assigned topic, I consulted *Dorland's Medical Dictionary*. It defined etiology as the sum of knowledge regarding causes of disease, and pathogenesis as the development of morbid conditions or of disease. Much of our knowledge of etiology of the major cardiovascular diseases comes from epidemiological studies. The only way to avoid overlapping with the chapter on epidemiology is to write of causes of disease in terms of precise relationships to the development of morbid conditions (pathogenesis), but this in turn would overlap with the topic of the next chapter, "physiological mechanisms of disease." Thus the writer on "etiology and pathogenesis" is left with very little to say unless he sees his role as trespassing bravely on both adjacent topics and trying to serve a bridging function between epidemiological and experimental research on the one hand and physiologic and anatomic studies on the other.

Cardiovascular diseases are of many types, with different causes, different signs and symptoms, and different kinds of unhealthy changes in the function and structure of the heart and blood vessels. The behavioral aspects of each type of cardiovascular disease are also quite different. It is thus necessary to broach the assigned topic in separate sections: one for the atherosclerotic diseases including myocardial infarction and sudden coronary death, and a second for hypertension.

Atherosclerotic Diseases

A noted medical historian is quoted as saying: "Each civilization creates its own diseases." Arteriosclerotic heart disease (ASHD) is the epidemic of modern Western civilization. It has flourished in urbanized, industrialized nations of the twentieth century to an extent never before seen in the history of mankind. More than any other disease endemic to our civilization, ASHD has been created from a confluence of modern behaviors. Conquest of infectious diseases and improved nutrition permitted many more people to live to middle and old ages and, hence, become susceptible to ASHD. The habit of cigarette smoking which took a quantum jump after World War I is a behavioral habit which has contributed greatly to ASHD. Similarly, revolutions in food production and a shift in preference to fattier meats and processed foods in greater quantities has changed eating habits. Together with the mechanization of both farming and industry and the replacement of walking by the automobile, the total amount of heavy physical activity has been sharply reduced. This, with the changes in food habits, has made obesity the most prominent nutritional problem in the United States and many countries of Europe. The social and cultural changes during the century have led to substantial changes in the usual daily behaviors of most citizens and this, in turn, has raised what have come to be known as the standard risk factors for ASHD: cigarette smoking, elevated serum lipids, and obesity. Elevated blood pressures are the remaining major standard risk factor, and this, too, seems to be elevated in urbanized, industrialized countries more than in simpler, agrarian communities—as will be discussed later.

Not only have social and behavioral changes been the prime forces in raising the standard risk factors to ASHD, but it has now been demonstrated to the satisfaction of most leading authorities that social and behavioral factors also raise the risk of ASHD, including myocardial infarction, in ways independent of the standard risk factors, through mechanisms which are not yet clearly identified [31].

Several families of social and behavioral variables have been implicated in the scientific literature as being risk factors for ASHD. The following categories, while somewhat arbitrary in definition, have proved useful in summarizing the literature: (a) indices of social position and social change; (b) environmental stressors such as work overload, chronic conflict situations, and life changes; (c) personal responses to external or internal circumstances including life dissatisfactions, anxiety, depression, neuroticism, emotional drain, and sleep disturbance; and, finally, (d) a personal style of outward action (as contrasted to inner feeling) in response to the environment—the aggressive, competitive, irritable, hurried, Type A, coronary-prone behavior pattern.

As one reviews the broad array of published articles dealing with psychosocial variables and their relation to ASHD, a rather clear pattern emerges. Those psychosocial and behavioral factors which most consistently and most intensely involve sustained overstimulation of the central nervous system (CNS), have the most consistent positive associations with risk of ASHD. Those psychosocial factors which only at some times or only in certain persons imply chronic agitations of the CNS have weaker relationships to increased ASHD risk, and, finally, those variables most removed from universally strong CNS involvement have the weakest associations.

To illustrate this more specifically, one finds that the strongest, most consistent correlates of ASHD risk across a variety of research circumstances are long-endured, troubling emotions such as anxiety, depression, and sleep disturbance, and the habitual everyday struggle of the Type A coronary-prone behavior pattern. Having somewhat less strength and consistency as predictors of ASHD, are such variables as work overload, life dissatisfactions, chronic conflict situations, social mobility, and status incongruity. Finally, such social structural variables as are less certain to be uniformly a cause for behavioral arousal or emotional distress are concomitantly less consistently and less strongly associated with risk of ASHD across the full array of recent studies. Thus, except for behaviors that influence standard risk factors and those sociocultural variables which influence environmental exposures, it appears from this gradient that all the remaining psychosocial risk factors operate through the central nervous system to generate changes in autonomic nervous functioning and endocrine activity which, in turn, have a cumulative impact upon the cardiovascular system.

Social Deprivation

An apparent exception to the above generalization emerges when one considers a variety of recent reports all of which implicate social deprivation as a correlate of risk for ASHD in modern urban environments. Dohrenwend's research [6] indicates that persons in lower social strata encounter more negative life changes than those at higher levels. A sufficiently rewarding and secure occupation is required to generate income to buy the necessities of life. Persons with inadequate education are not prepared to hold a secure job at a skill level that can supply their needs. In addition, such persons may often be limited in interpreting the complexities of urban life and resolving potential problems before they grow to distressing proportions. Thus, persons in socially deprived situations may not only encounter a higher frequency of stressful events but may also be more likely to have inadequate abilities to deal with such threats. Studies using standardized psychological tests suggest that persons in lower social strata feel greater depression, despair, and anxiety.

Being in the lowest social class does not carry with it increased risk to ASHD in all circumstances. The relation of economic factors to ASHD seems to be very different at the several stages of industrialization. Thus, in developing countries such as India, Chile and, Taiwan, persons with higher income, higher level occupations, and higher education seem to be at elevated risk of ASHD [13]. This same finding was generated in the Israeli study of government employees [21]. As recently as the 1950s, studies in the rural south of the United States (Evans County, Georgia), showed that persons of middle and higher social status had much higher ASHD rates than those at the lower levels. But, by 1970, in the same county, lower status males had increased their ASHD rates to the point of nearly equaling the risks of their more advantaged middle-class neighbors [3]. For most urban states in the United States, this reversal of the social level at highest ASHD risk occurred in earlier decades. The same is true for the ASHD mortality rates from England and Wales. Thus, later in the cycle of industrialization, the lower social strata surpassed middle and upper level persons in risk of ASHD.

By way of illustrating the emerging role of social deprivation and social disorganization as a risk factor in industrialized areas, Table I presents data from 1972 and 1973 for Massachusetts. Using the age and sex composition of 39 administrative areas determined by the 1970 U.S. Census, and death certificate data from 1972 and 1973, an age–sex standardized mortality ratio for ASHD was calculated for each area based on the overall mortality experience of the state. The standardized mortality ratios were then correlated with 130 social and demographic indicators derived from the census for these same areas using Kendall's rank-order correlation as a conservative measure of association. We were greatly surprised that 53 variables correlated significantly at the $p < .05$ level with excess ASHD death, since only 7 would be expected by chance if the 131 variables were independent. Even though many of the indices are highly correlated with one another, this number of significant findings is far beyond expectations. Among the highest of all correlates with excess ASHD mortality are low occupational status, low education, unemployment, substandard housing, overcrowded housing and the percent of persons over age 65 with incomes below the poverty level.

These findings are not unique. Kitagawa and Hauser [17] have performed careful compilations of the association between overall mortality, mortality for specific causes and a variety of social and demographic indicators. They point out that educational level is less likely to be altered by illness in adults than are income or occupational level, and then proceed to show strong associations between low educational status and excess mor-

TABLE I
Social Correlates of Excess Mortality from Ischemic Heart Disease
(Age–Sex Adjusted Death Rates in Massachusetts, 1972–1973)

Factor	τ with excess mortality
EDUCATION	
High Education:	
Percentage Persons with	
4+ years of college	-.52
Median School Years Completed	-.47
Low Education:	
8 years or less (White)	.37
OCCUPATIONAL STATUS AND UNEMPLOYMENT	
High Occupational Status: Males	-.49
Low Occupational Status: Males	.39
Low Occupational Status: Females	.47
Percentage Unemployed	.37
HOUSING	
Median value of owner-occupied	
housing (white)	-.44
Median monthly rental (white)	-.48
Median monthly rental (black)	-.33
Percentage persons in overcrowded housing	.45
INCOME	
Median Income	-.20
Percentage families below poverty level	.28
Percentage persons aged 65+ below poverty level	.40

$\tau \leq .37$ is significant at $p < .001$
$\tau \leq .22$ is significant at $p < .05$

tality due to arteriosclerotic and hypertensive heart diseases in epidemiologic studies both of individuals and of geographic areas.

Insight into one possible etiological mechanism linking social deprivation with ASHD mortality is offered by the recent report from the Health Insurance Plan of New York by Weinblatt and colleagues [24]. This study revealed that low education (8 years of school or less) more than doubled the risk of sudden coronary death. In addition, low education interacted multiplicatively with the presence of complex ventricular premature beats (VPBs) in such a way that the presence of both these risk factors raised the rate of sudden death to 7.2 times the rate of men of comparable age who had high school or more education and were without complex VPBs. The mechanisms behind this phenomenon may have been expressed in a summary of animal research published by Lown and colleagues: "Environmental stressors of diverse types can injure the heart, lower the threshold of cardiac vulnerability to ventricular fibrillation, and in the animal with coronary occlusion, provoke potentially malignant ventricular arrhythmias [18]."

Chronic Disturbing Emotions

We turn now to evidence that sustained intense disturbing emotions might be risk factors for ASHD. The sheer number of such positive findings from many social settings, despite the wide variety of psychological measurements and clinical ratings used, argues that this is a robust association particularly in terms of angina pectoris. The overall implication of most studies is that the time sequence of the relationship of disturbing emotions to ASHD is prospective for angina pectoris but not for myocardial infarction. Both of these clinical manifestations, however, raise the levels of anxiety, depression, and emotional problems, thus affecting retrospective findings. The differential elevation of painful emotions in the period immediately after the acute myocardial infarction may have important implications for prognosis, as the work of Bruhn suggests [2].

New evidence published in the last decade extends earlier findings particularly with regard to psychophysiological complaints (hypochondriasis or somaticizing) and symptoms such as fatigue, emotional drain, and sleep disturbance [14]. Wardwell and Bahnson [28] found patients with myocardial infarction to score much higher than two control groups (other hospitalized patients and healthy community members) on a scale of somatic complaints. Appels in the Netherlands has found fatigue and emotional drain to be very commonly attributed to the 1-month period prior to myocardial infarction [1]. The prospective Israeli studies found persons scoring high on a brief anxiety scale or on indicators of life dissatisfaction to have 2.0 to 2.5 times the risk of future angina pectoris [22]. Their future risk of myocardial infarction, however, was not elevated [20]. A prospective study in Sweden by Floderus found the self-report of "nervous disease" was predictive of higher rates of death due to coronary disease and to total death rate excluding coronary disease [7]. This suggests that this family of variables may relate generally to poor health and not specifically to risk of ASHD.

Sleeping problems have recently been identified as precursors to ASHD, both angina pectoris and myocardial infarction. This has now been found in two retrospective studies with control groups and three prospective studies [15]. Among the latter is the finding of Floderus from Sweden that difficulties in falling asleep and restlessness during sleep are more common in individuals who later developed angina or who suffered fatal heart attacks [7]. Friedman and associates in the Kaiser-Permanente study in Oakland, California report similar findings predictive of myocardial infarction [8]. Finally, among Thomas's sample of medical students, those who reported consistently being tired upon awaking were heavily represented among those who many years later suffered myocardial infarction [25].

It has been argued that symptoms such as hypochondriasis, emotional drain, and sleep disturbances may be unrecognized or subclinical symptoms of cardiovascular disease rather than risk factors that truly precede the disease [8]. Whether or not this be the case, it might be of value to use these "psychological symptoms" as signals of the prodromal phase of myocardial infarction even if they cannot be considered true predictors.

A competing argument is that intense disturbing emotions may lead more to complaints about chest pain and, hence, to the discovery of ASHD, particularly angina, than actually relating to the disease process itself. Evidence from a study of patients undergoing coronary angiography for clinical reasons speaks to this hypothesis [32]. Coronary angiography is a procedure which allows x-ray visualization of coronary arteries and the rating of the amount by which they are obstructed by atherosclerotic deposits. An angiographic study of 95 men showed that the scores on anxiety and depression scales completed before the angiogram were associated with the severity of vessel obstruction even after the reported intensity of anginal pain was controlled statistically. These two scales were not related to such indices of cardiac disability as ejection fraction or number of hospitalizations for congestive heart failure; nevertheless they were associated with extent of atherosclerosis. If this finding can be replicated it would provide a strong argument that intense emotions such as anxiety and depression relate to atherosclerotic disease itself and not merely to its probability of being discovered.

In summary, a broad consensus of published research seems to have adequately established that anxiety, depression, neuroticism, and, particularly, sleep disturbance are associated with ASHD, with more consistent findings emerging for the prediction of angina pectoris as opposed to myocardial infarction. The kinds of life dissatisfactions and conflicts that lead to sustained disturbing emotions also have been repeatedly found to be associated with elevated rates of ASHD [14]. More research is needed to delineate the mechanisms by which the psychological factors are linked to the pathogenesis of this disease.

Type A Behavior Pattern

Of all the postulated behavioral risk factors for ASHD, the coronary-prone behavior pattern—Type A—has thus far amassed the greatest amount of research evidence. This evidence fulfills many of the demands which the scientific method requires of a relationship which is to be considered "causal" in nature. The association between Type A behavior, or various of its components, and ASHD has been replicated by many teams of workers in several nations [15]. The strength of the association between Type A and ASHD is on the order of a relative risk ratio of two-to-one or greater, which is comparable to that of other standard risk factors for this disease. Prospective studies have established that the predictor actually precedes the outcome condition. Research thus far has shown Type A to be rather specifically associated with diseases involving atherosclerosis. A biological gradient has been demonstrated in that the more intense presence of Type A leads to a higher probability of new CHD than an intermediate level of Type A and this, in turn, has higher probability than relative absence of Type A characteristics. This "dose-response" relationship applies both to risk of new CHD among healthy persons and risk of recurrent myocardial infarction in CHD patients. Finally, the observed findings with regard to the physiological concomitants of Type A behavior are biologically plausible contributions to an understanding of the pathogenesis of ASHD.

Thus far, over 40 published reports prepared by many research teams in different nations have shown that one or more aspects of the Type A behavior pattern were related to ASHD in cross-sectional or prospective studies [15]. All but 2 or 3 of these 40 studies showed positive associations. Although many of these studies were done in the United States, additional supportive evidence has been obtained in studies conducted in the Netherlands, Sweden, Israel, Australia, Argentina, Belgium, Poland, and the Soviet Union. Most of these studies have been retrospective or cross-sectional with control groups, but a few have been prospective, and a few others have been based on angiographic findings. Review of these many studies is beyond the scope of the present chapter.

One may reasonably conclude that there is a well-established association between the kinds of behavior referred to in the coronary-prone behavior pattern and ASHD prevalence, incidence, recurrence, and underlying atherosclerotic pathology. The findings are unlikely to be spurious and unlikely to be secondary to any of the biologic or demographic variables traditionally used in epidemiological studies of ASHD. The findings are not in conflict with earlier knowledge about atherogenesis and, indeed, may provide a point of departure for increasing scientific knowledge in this general area.

Hypertension

Hypertension is the most common single form of major chronic disease in the United States today [27]. Its primary characteristic, high blood pressure, is known to be a risk factor for many diseases, including coronary heart disease, stroke, congestive heart failure, and certain renal complications. While we know what hypertension causes, we know very little about what causes hypertension, particularly the 90–95% of cases which are essential hypertension. An expert committee of the Inter-Society Commission on Heart Disease Resources recently concluded that not enough is known about the antecedents of high blood pressure to give an adequate basis for formulating programs for primary prevention.

A vast amount of research has been done in which blood pressure is measured while persons are exposed to social situations manipulated so as to create stress. These studies have generally shown substantial but short-term blood pressure elevations followed by return to baseline levels. Many attempts have been made to identify or discriminate hypertensive individuals with psychometric instruments. Ostfeld and Shekelle [23] document the unproductiveness of this procedure. Many earlier studies attempted in-depth evaluation of relatively few hypertensive subjects. The methods of data gathering were clinical in nature and, hence, hard to compare across studies. Many of these studies also lacked control groups, "double blinding," and other features of research design, which are less necessary for hypothesis-generating studies than for hypothesis-testing studies. The final and most critical problem, however, is that the hypotheses generated by these studies have found little convincing and replicable support in the larger scale empirical studies which followed them.

There are sharp differences among nations and races in their average blood pressures. The question is still unresolved as to how much of these differences may be due to genetic factors and how much to social–environmental factors. A U.S. Public Health Service Report summarizes studies of mean blood pressures and prevalences of hypertension which were performed in widely different populations. In Kenya, distributions of these conditions differed among occupations. In Jamaica, place of residence was associated with differences. In South Africa, migration made a difference, and in many settings, including the United States, low education and low income are associated with elevated blood pressure. The PHS publication concludes its discussion of the African and Jamaican studies by saying, "There are clear indicators in the data that hypertension in Negroes [sic] (and especially in Negro men) is related to environment [26, p. 10]."

In the white race, too, environment makes an important difference in the United States, with rates of white hypertension considerably higher (and black hypertension notably lower) in the Northeast than in the South or West. Among whites, divorced men and women appear to have lower than expected prevalence, as do white males with agricultural occupations. Professional persons generally have lower prevalences of hypertension regardless of race or sex [26]. These demographic differences are difficult to explain in genetic terms and further suggest that environment, particularly the social environment, may have an important but as yet poorly understood role in raising the risk of hypertension. These observations suggest that independently of genetic factors, environment may also play a strong role in the differences in mortality rates for hypertensive heart disease and in the prevalence of hypertension for the major races in the United States.

The relation of the social environment to excess mortality from diseases involving hypertension was recently investigated in Massachusetts by correlating demographic, social, and economic data with age–sex standardized mortality ratios for these diseases in the 39 mental health catchment areas of that state [16]. Of the 130 social indicators 79 had significant rank correlations with excess of mortality from hypertensive diseases (including malignant hypertension, essential benign hypertension, hypertensive heart disease, and hypertensive renal disease). A broader category of all hypertensive-related deaths correlated with 35 of the social indicators. Death rates were excessive in areas with low occupational status, low median education, widespread poverty, broken families, and substandard housing. This profile of community risk factors parallels closely those for ASHD, homicide, and deaths due to fire and flames. Quite different social indices are associated with excess mortality due to respiratory diseases and stroke, thus arguing for some specificity of association rather than a general force for all causes of mortality.

Partial correlation procedures indicated that low education and low occupational status may be the most potent statistically of all the community predictors of excess hypertensive mortality. These findings suggest specific directions for research into the social mechanisms leading to aggravation of this common condition. They also provide a means for identifying areas having highest needs for community programs of hypertension control.

Environmental stress was related to elevated blood pressure in Detroit in a study by Harburg et al. [10]. Higher socioecological stress areas were marked by low socioeconomic status, high crime, high population density, high residential mobility, high rates of marital breakup, high proportion of one-parent families, and a high percentage receiving various forms of public assistance. Low-stress neighborhoods had opposite readings on these conditions. Black males living in high-stress areas had significantly higher blood pressure levels than their counterparts living in low-stress areas, but the same relationship did not generalize to white males or females. The findings are provocative but factors of greater general validity are needed which apply to all races and both sexes.

An extensive psychiatric and psychological literature exists which relates to blood pressure elevations. (Comprehensive reviews of this literature have appeared periodically.) An important generalization from the review by McGinn and Harburg [19] is that sustained blood pressure is less often related to behavioral factors than is responsiveness of the blood pressure to stimulus situations. They conclude that most experimental interventions create only very brief rises in blood pressure and that such conclusions from the laboratory are of doubtful utility in explaining sustained hypertension. Subsequent to this review, however, laboratory procedures for inducing sustained hypertension have been developed in animal models.

Henry and Cassel [11] synthesized the wide variety of findings from animal experimentation and international epidemiological studies. They concluded that the social environment is an important determinant of sustained elevation in blood pressure. Henry and Cassel offer the beginnings of a psychosocial theory for population differences in hypertension, and argue that the "defense alarm reaction," frequently evoked, may be the psychophysiological mechanism leading to sustained high blood pressure.

The plausibility of the hypothesis that the "defense alarm reaction" may be an important psychophysiological mechanism leading to elevated blood pressure is supported by studies in two quite different settings. D'Atri [4] studied prison inmates, with the hypothesis that a crowded environment and continuous subjection to the dangers of that environment would be associated with elevated blood pressures. He found that male prison inmates housed in single occupancy cells had much lower blood pressures than similar inmates housed in dormitory rooms. (Average systolic blood pressures were 110 and 134, respectively; average diastolic blood pressures were 68 and 79, respectively.) When height, weight, age, and race were controlled statistically these differences were undiminished. The findings were then replicated in another prison setting.

In a very different social setting, Rose and colleagues [24] studied a group of dedicated and responsible men who are "in control" rather than subjected to an environment which they cannot leave. Men in this very responsible profession of air traffic controlling had a very high incidence of new hypertension, two to four times the rate of men of similar ages in community and other occupational samples. Men who entered the 3-year study as normotensives and subsequently became hypertensive did not differ from the remaining normotensives in weight or age. Their intake blood pressures, however, averaged significantly higher. In addition, future hypertensives were rated higher (better) on coping by psychologist interviewers, reported less interference by their careers with other aspects of their lives, reported much *less* life change distress and were more often selected as ideal team members by their peers [12]. One of the few things air traffic controllers have in common with the prison groups is that they, too, frequently invoke the defense alarm reaction as they manage congested patterns of air traffic either near airports or on heavily traveled air routes.

Gutman and Benson's extensive review [9] concluded that conditions which required continuous behavioral and physiological adjustments were associated with sustained elevations of arterial blood pressure. Gutman and Benson point out the effectiveness of operant conditioning schedules both in raising and lowering blood pressure. Patel, Datey, Benson, and others, in a variety of studies, have shown a prolonged therapeutic effect of regularly practiced relaxation responses. A strong case for the potency of social and psychological factors in hypertension is made in the critical review of 103 references by M. H. Davies, "Is High Blood Pressure a Psychosomatic Disorder?"[5]

Despite these promising leads regarding the relation of social and behavioral factors to hypertension, they must be placed in the historical perspective which acknowledges that many such promising leads have been welcomed with hope and discarded with dismay over the past thirty years. The currently popular hypotheses may fare no better. Herbert Weiner, in his book, *Psychobiology and Human Disease* [30] offers the most current and comprehensive review of the biochemistry, physiology, and psychobiology of hypertension. He points out that blood pressure regulation is a multistage process involving a variety of interlocking regulative mechanisms. The breakdown of any one of them can jeopardize the effectiveness of the entire system and lead to changes in blood pressure. Thus, essential hypertension is probably a variety of different disorders having a final common expression. In addition, quite different mechanisms may be involved in raising blood pressure initially than those which maintain blood pressure at an altered level. Weiner concludes his chapter on hypertension as follows:

> It would have been desirable, if possible, to have made a definitive statement about the role of psychological factors in essential hypertension: however, no such statement can

be made. Psychological factors clearly do not by themselves "cause" the syndrome. . . . Essential hypertension . . . is a disease that can be brought about by many different mechanisms, and social and psychological factors may play a different etiological, pathogenetic, and sustaining role in its different forms [p. 185].

Summary

The etiology and pathogenesis of most major cardiovascular diseases have social and behavioral impacts woven through them at several levels. Culture and society affect the environment and the agents of disease as well as the behavior and susceptibility of the host who experiences the disease. Different psychosocial and behavioral factors contribute to the various cardiovascular diseases through a variety of etiological mechanisms at different stages in their pathogenesis. Future research should focus on delineating the specifics of these complex causal chains.

References

1. Appels,A.; Pool, J.; Kazemier, M.; and van der Does, E.: Psychische prodromata van het hartinfarkt. *Nederland Tijdschrift Psychologie* 34:213–223, 1979.
2. Bruhn, J. G.; Paredes, A.; Adsett, C. A.; and Wolf, S.: Psychological predictors of sudden death in myocardial infarction. *Journal of Psychosomatic Research* 18:187–191, 1974.
3. Cassel, J.; Heyden, S.; Bartel, A. G.; Kaplan, B. H.; Tyroler, H. A.; Cornoni, J. C.; and Hames, C. G.: Incidence of coronary heart disease by ethnic group, social class, and sex. *Archives of Internal Medicine* 128:901–906, 1971.
4. D'Atri, D.: Psychophysiological responses to crowding. *Environment and Behavior* 7:237–252, 1975.
5. Davies, M. H.: Is high blood pressure a psychosomatic disease? *Journal of Chronic Disease* 24:239–258, 1971.
6. Dohrenwend, B. S: Social status and stressful life events. *Journal of Personality and Social Psychology* 28:225–235, 1973.
7. Floderus, B.: Psychosocial factors in relation to coronary heart disease and associated risk factors. *Nordisk Hygienisk Tidskrift.* supplementum 6, 1974.
8. Friedman, G. D.; Ury, H. K.; Klatsky, A. L.; and Siegelaub, A. B.: A psychological questionnaire predictive of myocardial infarction: Results from the Kaiser–Permanente Epidemiologic Study of Myocardial Infarction. *Psychosomatic Medicine* 36:327–343, 1974.
9. Gutman, M. C.; and Benson, H.: Interaction of environmental factors and systemic arterial blood pressure. A review. *Medicine* 50:543–553, 1971.
10. Harburg, E.; Erfurt, J. C.; Hauenstein, L. S.; Chape, C.; Schull, W. J.; and Schork, M. A.: Socio-ecologic stress, suppressed hostility, skin color, and Black–White male blood pressure: Detroit. *Psychosomatic Medicine* 35:276–296, 1973.
11. Henry, J. P.; and Cassel, J. C.: Psychosocial factors in essential hypertension: Recent epidemiologic and animal experimental evidence. *American Journal of Epidemiology* 90:171–200, 1969.
12. Hurst, M. W.; Anderson, L.; Jenkins, C. D.; Herd, J. A.; Rose, R. M.; Kreger, B. E.: Biopsychosocial precursors of hypertension as a function of diagnostic criteria. Submitted for publication.

13. Jenkins, C. D.: Psychologic and social precursors of coronary disease. *New England Journal of Medicine* 284:244–255, 307–317, 1971.
14. Jenkins, C. D.: Recent evidence supporting psychologic and social risk factors for coronary disease. *New England Journal of Medicine* 294:987–944, 1033–1038, 1976.
15. Jenkins, C. D.: Behavioral risk factors in coronary artery disease. *Annual Review of Medicine* 29:543–562, 1978.
16. Jenkins, C. D.; Tuthill, R. W.; Tannenbaum, S.; and Kirby, C.: Social stressors and excess mortality from hypertensive disease. *Journal of Human Stress* 5:29–40, 1979.
17. Kitagawa, E. M.; and Hauser, P. M.: *Differential Mortality in the United States: A Study in Socioeconomic Epidemiology.* Cambridge: Harvard University Press, 1973.
18. Lown, B.; Verrier, R. L.; and Rabinowitz, S. H.: Neural and psychologic mechanisms and the problem of sudden cardiac death. *American Journal of Cardiology* 39:890–902, 1977.
19. McGinn, N. F.; Harburg, E.; Julius, S.; and McLeod, J. M.: Psychological correlates of blood pressure. *Psychological Bulletin* 61:209–219, 1964.
20. Medalie, J. H.; Kahn, H. A.; Neufeld, H. N.; Riss, E.; Goldbourt, U.; Perlstein, T.; and Oron, D.: Myocardial infarction over a five-year period. I. Prevalence, incidence and mortality experience. *Journal of Chronic Disease* 26:63–84, 1973a.
21. Medalie, J. H.; Kahn, H. A.; Neufeld, H. N.; Riss, E.; and Goldbourt, U.: Five-year myocardial infarction incidence. II. Association of single variables to age and birthplace. *Journal of Chronic Disease* 26:329–349, 1973b.
22. Medalie, J. H.; Snyder, M.; Groen, J. J.; Neufeld, H. N.; Goldbourt, U.; and Riss, E.: Angina pectoris among 10,000 men: 5-year incidence and univariate analysis. *American Journal of Medicine* 55:583–594. 1973.
23. Ostfeld, A. M.; and Shekelle, R. B.: Psychological variables and blood pressure. In *Epidemiology of Hypertension.* J. Stamler, ed. pp. 321–331. New York: Grune and Stratton, 1967.
24. Rose, R. M.; Jenkins, C. D.,; and Hurst, M. W.: *Air Traffic Controller Health Change Study: A Prospective Investigation of Physical, Psychological, and Work-Related Changes.* M. A. Levin, ed. Boston: Boston University School of Medicine, 1978 (Reprinted by the Federal Aviation Administration, Washington, D.C.)
25. Thomas, C. B.; and Greenstreet, R. L.: Psychobiological characteristics in youth as predictors of five disease states: suicide, mental illness, hypertension, coronary heart disease and tumor. *John Hopkins Medical Journal* 132:16–43, 1973.
26. United States Public Health Service. *Hypertension and Hypertensive Heart Disease in Adults: United States—1960–1962.* PHS Publication No. 1000, series 11, no. 13, National Center for Health Statistics. 1966.
27. United States Public Health Service: *Fifth Report of the Director of National Heart, Lung, and Blood Institute.* Heart, Lung and Blood Research: Five Years of Progress: The Challenge Ahead, No. (NIH) 78–1415, 1978.
28. Wardwell, W. I.; and Bahnson, C. B.: Behavioral variables and myocardial infarction in the Southeastern Connecticut Heart Study. *Journal of Chronic Disease* 26:447–461, 1973.
29. Weinblatt, E.; Ruberman, W.; Goldberg, J. D.; Frank, C. W.; Shapiro, S.; and Chaudhary, B. S.: Relation of education to sudden death after myocardial infarction. *New England Journal of Medicine* 299:60–65, 1978.
30. Weiner, H.: Psychobiology and Human Disease. New York: Elsevier, 1977.
31. Weiss, S. M. ed.: *Proceedings of the National Heart Lung and Blood Institute Panel on the Coronary Prone Behavior Pattern.* Held at Jacksonville, Florida, 4–6 Dec., 1978.
32. Zyzanski, S. J.; Jenkins, C. D.; Ryan, T. J.; Flessas, A.; and Everist, M.: Psychological correlates of coronary angiographic findings. *Archives of Internal Medicine* 136:1234–1237, 1976.

Behavioral Factors in the Physiological Mechanisms of Cardiovascular Disease

J. ALAN HERD

Epidemiological and clinical studies have demonstrated an association between behavioral characteristics and cardiovascular disease. The best known example of this relation comes from the Western Collaborative Study [26]. In a group of approximately 3000 men studied prospectively for 8.5 years, those who displayed Type A behavior patterns had more than twice the risk of developing coronary heart disease as individuals who displayed Type B patterns. More recent studies have demonstrated there is also an association between behavioral factors and systemic arterial hypertension. A 3-year prospective study of approximately 400 air traffic controllers in New York and New England was carried out by Rose, Jenkins, and Hurst at Boston University Medical Center [24]. Among the group of 400 controllers, a group of 36 controllers developed sustained hypertension during the study. These men had higher levels of blood pressure at work and greater responses to workload than the group of controllers who remained normotensive. Results of these studies suggest there may be pathophysiological links between behavioral factors and cardiovascular diseases. Other experimental laboratory and clinical evidence suggests that behavioral factors not only contribute to the clinical manifestations of cardiovascular diseases but also contribute to the basic disease processes of hypertension and coronary artery disease.

The pathophysiological links between behavioral factors and cardiovascular diseases appear to involve sympatho-adrenomedullary (SAM) activity. Physiological concomitants of increased SAM activity are (*a*) increased blood pressure and heart rate, (*b*) increased myocardial oxygen utilization, (*c*) increased circulating levels of epinephrine and norepinephrine, (*d*) increased plasma concentrations of free fatty acids, and (*e*) increased plasma renin activity. All of these physiological factors predispose to cardiovascular disease and the clinical manifestations of cardiovascular disease.

The rationale for studying physiological mechanisms is to determine how behavioral factors might cause cardiovascular disease. By studying these mechanisms we narrow our search for etiological agents and pathogenic processes from all possible agents and processes to those which are compatible with our concepts of pathophysiology. We focus our efforts on factors which seem most likely to be related to our objectives. Also, we expect our study of physiological mechanisms will reveal additional behavioral and physiological characteristics which predispose individuals to cardiovascular disease. When we know which individuals are likely to be affected and the pathophysiological processes involved, we can establish a rational basis for prevention and treatment.

There are many pathophysiological processes known to cause hypertension, myocardial infarction, and sudden death. Table 1 illustrates relations between (a) predisposing factors, (b) disease processes, (c) precipitating factors, and (d) clinical manifestations. The basic disease processes do not cause signs or symptoms by themselves. Clinical manifestations occur only when complications are added to the basic disease processes. Behavioral factors may influence both the basic disease processes and the clinical manifestations.

Many of the factors listed as predisposing and precipitating are influenced by behavioral phenomena. Dietary factors, physical activity, and cigarette smoking as well as neurogenic and endocrine factors are under

TABLE 1

Predisposing factors	Disease process	Precipitating factors	Clinical manifestations
Inherited		Thrombosis	Peripheral vascular disease
Diabetes mellitus	Atherosclerosis	Embolism	Myocardial infarction
Dietary		Cigarette smoking	Angina pectoris Sudden death
Physical inactivity	Hypertension	Neurogenic Endocrine	Congestive heart failure
Neurogenic		Physical activity	Hypertensive cardiovascular disease
Endocrine		Dietary	Cerebrovascular accident

behavioral influences. Therefore, a discussion of physiological mechanisms related to behavioral factors could include all pathophysiological processes known to cause cardiovascular disease. However, I will focus on neurogenic and endocrine factors known to influence cardiovascular disease. These are shown in Figure 1.

Sympathetic nervous system activity stimulates adipose tissue to release free fatty acids (FFA), stimulates liver to release glucose, stimulates kidney to decrease excretion of sodium and water and to release renin, stimulates heart to increase rate and force of contraction, stimulates arterioles to increase peripheral vascular resistance and veins to increase venous return, and stimulates adrenal medulla to release epinephrine and norepinephrine. Endocrine secretions known to be influenced by central nervous system activity also are listed in Figure 1.

Free fatty acids released by lipolysis apparently play an important role in cardiovascular and metabolic function. Figure 2 illustrates relations between SAM activity, FFA release, and FFA utilization. Catecholamines are probably the most important factors promoting lipid mobilization [15]. They are effective in mobilizing lipid from adipose tissue [25] both by their liberation from noradrenergic nerve terminals in adipose tissue and by their secretion from the adrenal medulla into the blood and arrival in adipose tissue through the circulation [15]. Also, glucocorticoids promote lipid mobilization [15] and insulin opposes it [14]. Thus, lipid mobilization is promoted by SAM stimulation of adipose tissue, especially when levels of glucocorticoids in the blood are rising and levels of insulin are falling.

When triglyceride stores in adipose tissue are mobilized, they are hydrolyzed to FFA and glycerol [15]. These FFA are utilized by skeletal muscles and myocardium in the production of energy [39]. They both are stored in these tissues as triglycerides and are used directly. The FFA not stored or utilized in the production of energy are eventually taken up by the adipose tissues or by the liver [32]. FFA taken up by the liver are formed into triglycerides and secreted as a component of very low density lipoproteins (VLDL) [31].

The rate at which the liver secretes VLDL is determined partly by the rate it synthesizes FFA from carbohydrates and partly by the rate it receives FFA in the blood. In the fasting state, the secretion of VLDL by the liver is determined principally by the levels of FFA in the blood [2]. These levels, in turn, are determined principally by the effects of catecholamines on adipose tissue and rates of energy production.

The effects of neuroendocrine factors on cardiovascular diseases involve many components and mechanisms. These are listed in Table 2. Pathophysiological mechanisms leading to atherosclerosis include damage to vascular endothelium and proliferation of vascular smooth muscle cells

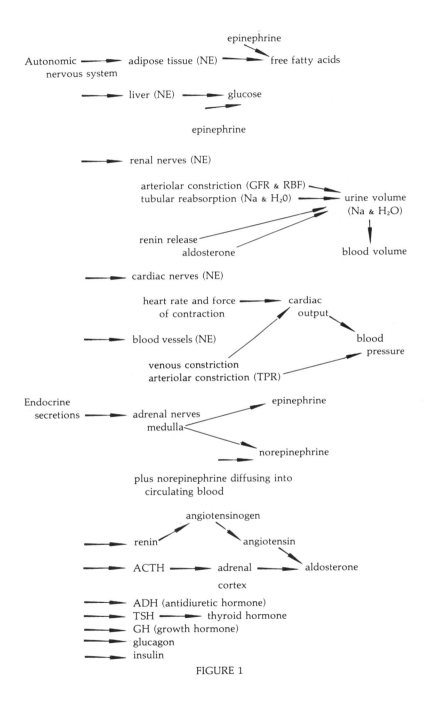

FIGURE 1

TABLE 2

Atherosclerosis	Hypertension
Components	Components
Cellular proliferation	Peripheral vascular resistance
Lipid deposition	Cardiac output
Vascular obstruction	Blood volume
	Renal function
Mechanisms	Mechanisms
Endothelial damage	Neurogenic
Platelet aggregation	Endocrine
Thrombosis	Cardiogenic
Vascular smooth	Renal
muscle proliferation	Vascular
Lipid accumulation	

[28]. Damage to vascular endothelium may be the result of hemodynamic factors such as high levels of arterial blood pressure or turbulence at bifurcations in large arteries. It also may be the result of chemical factors such as high blood levels of VLDL or other circulating substances [29]. Proliferation of vascular smooth muscle also may be influenced by several different factors. Tissue cultures of vascular smooth muscle cells proliferate most readily in the presence of VLDL [27]. Proliferation *in vitro* also is enhanced by the presence of insulin in the culture medium [16, 30]. These results from laboratory studies of atherogenic factors suggest mechanisms whereby physiological processes associated with neuroendocrine and metabolic factors may influence atherogenesis in humans and experimental animals [13, 14].

Pathophysiological mechanisms leading to arterial hypertension include increases in resistance to blood flow through arterioles, decreased excretion

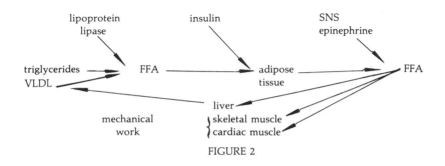

FIGURE 2

of sodium and water, and increased cardiac work in pumping blood at a higher arterial pressure. The relative contribution of each component differs in each patient. Some patients apparently have predominantly renal mechanisms, others endocrine mechanisms, and others predominantly neurogenic mechanisms. All mechanisms can occur without any other disease apparent as a primary cause. A large group of patients apparently have a predominance of neurogenic influences. They have high levels of circulating catecholamines in plasma, high plasma renin activity, and high cardiac output [8].

Several investigators have proposed specific pathophysiological processes as causes of cardiovascular disease. Taggart and Carruthers have studied the influence of behavioral factors on lipid metabolism [35]. Carruthers' hypothesis [5] is depicted in Figure 3. Taggart and Carruthers propose that stresses of modern living liberate catecholamines which mobilize FFA greatly in excess of metabolic requirements. They also propose that excess FFA may be taken up directly by arterial walls or converted to triglycerides which later are deposited in arterial walls.

Other hypotheses concerning development of arterial hypertension are depicted in Figure 4. All hypotheses are compatible with one another, but they emphasize different mechanisms. The Julius hypothesis [8] emphasizes neurogenic factors, the Folkow hypothesis emphasizes vascular factors [10, 11], and the Guyton hypothesis emphasizes renal factors. All these pathophysiological mechanisms could be influenced by behavioral factors.

The clinical manifestations of coronary heart disease may occur through several mechanisms (Table 1). These include the processes of thrombosis and embolism, increases in oxygen and substrate requirements of the myocardium, increases in cardiac rate, and disorders of cardiac rhythm. Each of these complicating mechanisms has been studied extensively. Results of these studies show that SAM function may contribute to several different mechanisms that may cause clinical complications.

One mechanism whereby SAM function may contribute to clinical manifestations of coronary heart disease is in production of ventricular arrhythmias and sudden death [21]. The underlying disease responsible for sudden death is usually coronary atherosclerosis [18], and it is probable that most individuals dying suddenly suffered ventricular fibrillation that was triggered by a series of premature ventricular contractions [34]. These premature ventricular contractions frequently occur in association with exercise and behavioral activities. Exercise testing often will expose ar-

emotional stress ⟶ NE ⟶ lipoproteins ⟶ FFA ⟶ atheroma

FIGURE 3. *Carruthers hypothesis.*

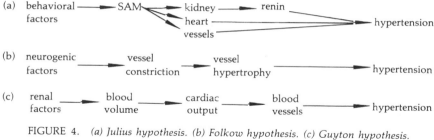

FIGURE 4. (a) Julius hypothesis. (b) Folkow hypothesis. (c) Guyton hypothesis.

rhythmias not observed while monitoring the electrocardiogram during normal daily activities [17]. Behavioral activities such as public speaking [37] and automobile driving [38] also have been reported to produce ventricular arrhythmias. In contrast, ventricular arrhythmias have been reported to occur much less frequently when subjects were asleep than when they were awake [20].

Increased levels of circulating catecholamines may predispose an individual to ventricular arrhythmias. These arrhythmias frequently occur during infusions of epinephrine or isoproterenol. Levels of exercise sufficient to provoke ventricular arrhythmias are associated with increased levels of catecholamines circulating in the blood. Levels of catecholamines in the blood also are elevated during behavioral activities such as public speaking [37] or driving a racing car [35]. As in physical activity, it is possible that at least part of the effects of behavioral activities on ventricular irritability are mediated by circulating catecholamines. Whatever the mechanism might be, prospective epidemiological studies have shown that ventricular arrhythmias were significantly associated with the presence of coronary heart disease and its complications including a high risk of sudden death [1, 9].

Results obtained recently from several laboratories also suggest that FFA may play an important role in the pathogenesis of cardiovascular disease. FFA may predispose to development of atherosclerosis and they may precipitate cardiac arrhythmias. Therefore, special efforts should be made to identify individuals who maintain high levels of FFA [23]. They may be at high risk for developing cardiovascular disease.

FFA levels in plasma have at least two important physiological effects. Increases in FFA levels increase intensity of platelet aggregation [3]. Since platelet aggregation plays a major role in evolution of atheroma, it influences the basic disease process. Increases in FFA levels also increase myocardial oxygen requirements [33]. Catecholamines sensitize the heart to FFA in such a way that FFA account for a major part of the increased myocardial oxygen requirement during SAM stimulation. In the presence of coronary artery disease, increases in FFA and increases in myocardial oxygen requirement or decreases in myocardial oxygen supply frequently may cause serious ventricular arrhythmias (Figure 5).

The physiological mechanisms linking behavioral factors to cardiovascular diseases are worthy of further research. Our hypothesis is that intense SAM activity elicited by behavioral factors is a cause of hypertension, myocardial infarction, and sudden death. However, SAM activity is essential for normal physiological function. Presumably, it is the excess SAM activity above that required for normal function that predisposes to cardiovascular disease and precipitates clinical manifestations.

Studies in several laboratories have suggested that individuals with high levels of SAM activity are at increased risk for developing cardiovascular disease. Dembroski et al. [6, 7] have shown that subjects displaying Type A behavior patterns have increased levels of blood pressure in response to challenge. Glass et al. and Friedman et al. [12] have shown that challenge elicits high levels of plasma catecholamines in subjects who display Type A behavior patterns. Herd et al. [24] have shown that air traffic controllers who develop sustained levels of arterial hypertension have exaggerated elevations in systolic blood pressure when exposed to high on-the-job workloads. These studies have all been conducted with subjects in good health. Further prospective studies must be carried out to determine if all subjects with exaggerated SAM activity have an increased risk for cardiovascular disease. In these studies, special attention should be paid to measurements of plasma FFA concentrations and plasma renin activity as well as elevations in heart rate, blood pressure, and serum concentrations of catecholamines.

This hypothesis of excessive SAM activity as a risk factor for cardiovascular disease provides a rationale for prevention and treatment of

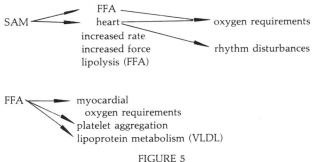

FIGURE 5

hypertension, myocardial infarction, and sudden death. The principal cardiac and metabolic effects of SAM activity can be suppressed by drugs such as propranolol, oxprenolol [36, 37], and practolol. These are "beta-blockers" and frequently are prescribed for treatment of patients with systemic arterial hypertension, coronary artery disease, and cardiac arrhythmias. Results of many clinical trials have demonstrated the efficacy of administering beta-blockers in prevention and treatment of cardiovascular disease [19, 22].

References

1. Adelson, L.; and Hoffman, W.: Sudden death from coronary disease related to a lethal mechanism arising independently of vascular occlusion or myocardial damage. *Journal of the American Medical Association* 176:129–135, 1961.
2. Basso, L. V.; and Havel, R. J.: Hepatic metabolism of free fatty acids in normal and diabetic dogs. *Journal of Clinical Investigation* 49:537–547, 1970.
3. Burstein, Y.; Berns, L.; Heldenberg, D., Kahn, Y.; Werbin, B. Z.; and Tamir, I.: Increase in platelet aggregation following a rise in plasma free fatty acids. *American Journal of Hematology* 4:17–22, 1978.
4. Butcher, R. W.; Baird, C. E.; and Sutherland, E. W.: Effects of lipolytic and antilipolytic substances on adenosine 3', 5'-monophosphate levels in isolated fat cells. *Journal of Biological Chemistry* 243:1705–1712, 1968.
5. Carruthers, M. E.: Aggression and atheroma. *Lancet* 2:1170–1171, 1969.
6. Dembroski, T. M.; MacDougall, J. M.; and Shields, J. L.: Physiologic reactions to social challenge in persons evidencing the Type A coronary-prone behavior pattern. *Journal of Human Stress* 3:2–10, 1977.
7. Dembroski, T. M.; MacDougall, J. M.; Herd, J. A.; and Shields, J. L.: Effects of level of challenge on pressor and heart rate responses in Type A and B subjects. *Journal of Applied Social Psychology.* 9:209–228, 1979.
8. Esler, M.; Julius, S.; and Zweifler, A.: Mild, high renin essential hypertension. Neurogenic human hypertension? *New England Journal of Medicine* 296:405–411, 1977.
9. Fisher, F. D.; and Tyroler, H. A.: Relationship between ventricular premature contractions on routine electrocardiography and subsequent sudden death from coronary heart disease. *Circulation* 47:712–719, 1973.
10. Folkow, B.; Grimby, G.; and Thulesius, O.: Adaptive structural changes of the vascular walls in hypertension and their relation to the control of the peripheral resistance. *Acta Physiologica Scandinavica* 44:255–272, 1958.
11. Folkow, B.; Hallback, M.; Lundgren, Y.; Sivertsson, R.; and Weiss, L.: Importance of adaptive changes in vascular design for establishment of primary hypertension, studied in man and in spontaneously hypertensive rats. *Circulation Research* 32/33 (suppl. 1):2–13, 1973.
12. Friedman, M.; Byers, S. O.; Diamant, J.; and Rosenman, R. H.: Plasma catecholamine response of coronary-prone subjects (Type A) to a specific challenge. *Metabolism* 4:205–210, 1975.
13. George, R.; and Ramasarma, T.: Nature of the stimulation of biogenesis of cholesterol in the liver by noradrenaline. *Biochemistry Journal* 162:493–499, 1977.

14. Gutstein, W. H.; Harrison, J.; Parl, F.; Kiu, G.; and Avitable, M.: Neural factors contribute to atherogenesis. *Science* 199:449–451, 1978.

15. Heindel, J. J.; Orci, L.; and Jeanrenaud, B.: Fat mobilization and its regulation by hormones and drugs in white adipose tissue. In *International Encyclopedia of Pharmacology and Therapeutics*. Pharmacology of Lipid Transport and Atherosclerotic Processes, ed. E. J. Masoro, sect. 24, pp. 175–373. Oxford: Pergamon Press, 1975.

16. Huttner, J. J.; Gwebu, E. T.; Panganamala, R. V.; Milo, G. E.; and Cornwell, D. G.: Fatty acids and their prostaglandin derivatives: Inhibitors of proliferation in aortic smooth muscle cells. *Science* 197:289–291, 1977.

17. Kosowsky, B. D.; Lown, B.; Whiting, R.; and Guiney, T.: Occurrence of ventricular arrhythmia with exercise as compared to monitoring. *Circulation* 44:826–832, 1971.

18. Kuller, L.; Lilienfield, A.; and Fisher, R.: Epidemiological study of sudden and unexpected deaths due to arteriosclerotic heart disease. *Circulation* 34:1056–1068, 1966.

19. Lambert, D. M. D.: Beta blockers and life expectancy in ischaemic heart disease. *Lancet* 1:793, 1972.

20. Lown, B.; Tykocinski, M.; Garfein, A.; and Brooks, P.: Sleep and ventricular premature beats. *Circulation* 48:691–701, 1973.

21. Lown, B.; Verrier, R. L.; and Rabinowitz, S. H.: Neural and psychologic mechanisms and the problem of sudden cardiac death. *American Journal of Cardiology* 39:890–902, 1977.

22. Multicentre International Study: Improvement in prognosis of myocardial infarction by long-term beta-adrenoreceptor blockade using practolol. *British Medical Journal* 3:735–740, 1975.

23. Nestel, P. J.; Ishikawa, T.; and Goldrick, R. B.: Diminished plasma free fatty acid clearance in obese subjects. *Metabolism* 27:589–597, 1978.

24. Rose, R. M.; Jenkins, C. D.; and Hurst, M. W.: Air Traffic Controller Health Change Study. FAA Contract No. DOT-FA73WA-3211, Boston University, 1978.

25. Rosell, S.; and Belfrage, E.: Adrenergic receptors in adipose tissue and their relation to adrenergic innervation. *Nature* 253:738, 1975.

26. Rosenman, R. H.; Brand, R. J.; Sholtz, R. I.; and Friedman, M.: Multivariate prediction of coronary heart disease during 8.5 year follow-up in the Western Collaborative Group Study. *American Journal of Cardiology* 37:902–910, 1976.

27. Ross, R.; and Glomset, J. A.: Atherosclerosis and the arterial smooth muscle cell. *Science* 180:1332–1339, 1973.

28. Ross, R.; and Glomset, J. A.: The pathogenesis of atherosclerosis. *New England Journal of Medicine* 295:369–377, 420–425, 1976.

29. Ross, R.; and Harker, L.: Hyperlipidemia and atherosclerosis. *Science* 193:1094–1100, 1976.

30. Stout, R. W.; Bierman, E. L.; and Ross, R.: Effect of insulin on the proliferation of cultured primate arterial smooth muscle cells. *Circulation Research* 36:319–327, 1975.

31. Schonfeld, G.; and Pfleger, B.: Utilization of exogenous free fatty acids for the production of very low density lipoprotein triglyceride by livers of carbohydrate-fed rats. *Journal of Lipid Research* 12:614–621, 1971.

32. Shapiro, B.: Triglyceride metabolism. In *Handbook of Physiology*, eds. A. E. Renold and G. F. Cahill, Jr., pp. 217–223. Washington D.C.: American Physiological Society, 1965.

33. Simonsen, S.; and Kjekshus, J. K.: The effect of free fatty acids on myocardial oxygen consumption during a trial pacing and catecholamine infusion in man. *Circulation* 58:484–491, 1978.

34. Smirk, F. N.; and Palmer, D. G.: A myocardial syndrome with particular reference to the occurrence of sudden death and of premature systoles interrupting the antecedent T waves. *American Journal of Cardiology* 6:620–629, 1960.

35. Taggart, P.; and Carruthers, M.: Endogenous hyperlipidaemia induced by emotional stress of racing driving. *Lancet* 1:363–366, 1971.
36. Taggart, P.; and Carruthers, M.: Suppression by oxprenolol of adrenergic response to stress. *Lancet* 2:256–258, 1972.
37. Taggart, P.; Carruthers, M.; and Somerville, W.: Electrocardiogram, plasma catecholamines, lipids and their modification by oxprenolol when speaking before an audience. *Lancet* 2:341–346, 1973.
38. Taggart, R.; Gibbons, D.; and Somerville, W.: Some effects of motor-car driving on the normal and abnormal heart. *British Medical Journal* 4:130–134, 1969.
39. Zierler, K. L.; Maseri, A.; Klassen, D.; Rabinowitz, D.; and Burgess, J.: Muscle metabolism during exercise in man. *Transactions of the Association of American Physicians* 81:266–273, 1968.

Behavioral Adjustment after Myocardial Infarction: A Selective Review of Recent Descriptive, Correlational, and Intervention Research

THOMAS F. GARRITY

Organization of the Review

The review presented in the following pages will be organized into in-hospital and posthospital phases of recovery. Within each division we will be summarizing trends in findings from research using the descriptive, correlational, and intervention approaches. The variables of interest will be primarily behavioral, though clinical and physiological variables are occasionally discussed. Because of the size and diversity of this literature, selectivity is exercised in an attempt to highlight areas in which there is now beginning to appear some mass and cohesiveness in the findings.

Recovery during Hospitalization

Descriptive Studies

SURVIVORSHIP

While only about half of the 1.3 million yearly myocardial infarction (MI) victims survive through the course of recovery, survivorship rates are considerably better for the young patients, especially those experiencing first attacks [101].

The experience of the Health Insurance Plan of New York indicates that only about 36% of their younger (less than 65 years), predominantly middle class subscribers with first MI succumbed during the first month [104]. It is typical that about half of those who do not survive die instantaneously or during the first hour or two after symptom onset [101]. Hospitalized MI patients divide almost evenly into those whose acute recovery courses may be considered relatively uncomplicated and those exhibiting more complicated courses characterized by severely impaired cardiac pumping efficacy and disturbances of normal rhythm [106].

The approach to in-hospital care for the MI patient has traditionally involved extended bedrest with stringent curtailment of activities requiring even moderate demand for cardiac work. Even uncomplicated MIs have recently averaged 4–5 days of intensive care monitoring and 21 days of hospitalization [107]. Extended bedrest however, may create its own problems for recovery because of the tendency of the body to "decondition" and develop other vascular problems, such as thromboemboli that may be traced to inactivity. Early ambulation will be discussed shortly as an intervention aimed at improved recovery.

EMOTIONAL STATUS

The psychological observations of Hackett and Cassem have provided a widely accepted view of emotional responses of MI patients under intensive care [40, 41]. These authors describe an acute course that involves elevated anxiety during the first day or two of care. This typically gives way, as denial ("the conscious or unconscious repudiation of part or all of the available meaning of an event to allay fear, anxiety or other unpleasant affects [40, p. 1367]") begins to operate. Hackett and Cassem argue that denial accounts for much of the apparent serenity often seen in coronary care patients. Depression then typically emerges as the dominant affect later in the coronary care unit (CCU) stay [43]. There is substantial agreement that a sizeable proportion of acute MI patients display emotional upset [14, 63]. There is also some support for the notions that anxiety tends to diminish after a few days of acute care [32, 75] and that denial is an important defense in this situation [32]. In the following section we will examine the often voiced contention that denial operates protectively for these patients.

The advent of the CCU brought with it decreases in mortality of MI patients estimated to range from 10% to 24% [16, 84]. This improvement is attributed to early diagnosis and management of potentially fatal rhythm disturbances. Despite the obvious advantages of the CCU for acute care, earlier reports of "intensive care psychosis," usually following open-heart surgery [40], raised questions about possible negative effects of the CCU environment on the patient. While organic factors appeared to play some part in this phenomenon [5, 34], environmental characteristics of the intensive care unit were also suspected. For example, presence of strange equipment and other seriously ill patients as well as disruption of diurnal cycles were viewed as possibly responsible for the occasional delirium [1, 65]. A spate of papers followed, aimed at examining the impact of CCU on patient recovery [10, 13, 22, 35]. Although one of these reported certain negative effects of witnessing a cardiac arrest [10], most revealed the tendency for patients to find the environment reassuring. Hackett and co-workers reported that even in the presence of arrest and resuscitation efforts, patient-witnesses were able to identify sources of comfort—for example, the efficiency and swiftness of the resuscitation team's response [40]. Although the design, conduct, and comparability of this research falls short of the ideal in several ways, the issue of the stress-inducing nature of the CCU environment has not recently been reopened. There presently seems to be agreement that the CCU, per se, elicits little emotional distress beyond that already present in response to a life-threatening illness.

Correlational Studies

SURVIVORSHIP AND CLINICAL STATUS

Not very far below the surface of most correlational research is the desire to uncover clues about possible causal links between variables of interest. In the case of the in-hospital experience of recovering coronary patients, the correlational literature seems intent on learning about links between emotional and clinical statuses. The general model supporting most of this work is the familiar psychosomatic framework that in this instance would link psychophysiological arousal and clinical complication of the MI recovery process. The potential usefulness of such information in acute care is evident.

As in the case in the animal and human stress literatures generally, studies of early recovery from MI describe associations between behavioral upset, especially anxiety, and alterations in certain indicators of autonomic arousal. In at least two studies, Klein and co-workers found associated elevations of anxiety and urinary catecholamine excretion levels [62, 63]; Miller and Rosenfeld had similar results [101]. Gentry and colleagues found an association between anxiety on the first day of CCU stay and urinary sodium/potassium ratios in their study of 16 patients [33]. Correlated changes in anxiety and systolic blood pressure were reported in MI patients after witnessing sudden cardiac death in a CCU [10]. Sczekalla described heart rate changes in similar patients within hours after witnessing resuscitation efforts [96]. Finally, Froese and colleagues found associations between anxiety and measures of the galvanic skin potential of MI patients in response to several questions about illness and CCU stimuli [26]. While the studies just cited are susceptible to a variety of methodological criticisms, the results prompt Doehrman to summarize as follows: "In general, there appears to be a positive association between physiological functioning and psychological functioning when both factors are assessed on hospitalized patients during a relatively narrow time span [21, p. 212]."

EMOTIONAL STATUS

A few studies have described associations between affective states in MI patients and physical complications of their recovery. In one of the Klein studies mentioned above [62] a series of patients ($N = 14$) facing transfer from CCU to general medical ward was monitored regarding biochemical indicators of arousal and incidence of cardiovascular complications. The correlation of these variables in this typically stressful change of environment was striking. Complications associated with catechol elevations included reinfarction, ventricular fibrillation, and death. While the replicability and causal ordering of these changes deserve to be questioned, these results suggest possibilities for interventions to lessen the strain of transfer. The approach of Klein's team is taken up in the following section on interventions. Two other groups have also linked extreme emotional upset with incidence of arrhythmias [38, 67].

Garrity and Klein [30] followed a larger group of MI patients ($N = 48$) from CCU to home at 6 months post-MI. A significant relationship was noted between the pattern of emotional adjustment during the acute phase and 6-month survivorship. Subjects showing a pattern of low or diminishing emotional upset were far more likely to survive to the 6-month point than those whose emotional upset failed to diminish. This result remained even when controls for severity of the MI and history of coronary events were introduced. These behavioral patterns had been previously associated with distinct catechol excretion patterns, albeit in a relatively small study group ($N = 38$) of MI patients [63]. Controlled studies that associate emotional state and cardiac death are rare. Anecdotes and case reports abound. Engel's collection of newspaper accounts and his accompanying literature review and commentary make for stimulating reading and may help to suggest the sorts of intervening psychophysiological mechanisms needing study in future work [24].

If indeed there are causal links between emotional upset, physiological arousal, cardiac complications, and possibly even death, then it would be logical that effective cognitive defenses might buffer the translation of anxiety, for example, into cardiac dysfunction. While the research is not extensive on this point, this view is widely held [26, 42, 81]. Hackett and coauthors [40] reported results that are the major source of the denial–survival hypothesis. "Major," "partial," and "minimal" deniers were defined in the sample of 50 post-MI patients on the basis of their willingness to report the presence of fear at any time during their hospital stay. While 20 of the 50 subjects fit the "major" denial category, none of these died during follow-up. Four subjects were labeled "minimal" deniers and two of these died. The other two deaths were in the "partial" denial group. Gentry and colleagues [32] reported similar findings in their group of 16 subjects. They found anxiety inversely related with denial. The only two deaths were among nondeniers (denial assessed using the same question as Hackett [40]).

Intervention Studies

PSYCHOTHERAPY AND PATIENT SUPPORT

Few studies of behavioral intervention during the acute recovery phase are presented in the literature. Two describe attempts to use individual psychotherapy to improve patient adjustment in the hospital phase. Lenzner and Aronson presented vignettes from the 100 MI patients treated individually in single sessions in the CCU [68]. The investigation did not employ controlled experimental design and did not collect standardized measures of outcome. The impression of the authors was that "pale, apathetic, depressed, and listless" patients became more "animated, alive, alert [and] responsive" during the sessions. Insights from the sessions were also thought to be useful to CCU staff responsible for patient care. Gruen presented findings from the study of 70 patients randomized into individual psychotherapy and no-treatment control groups [38]. The therapy involved daily, half-hour sessions aimed at facilitating coping and identifying areas of psychological strength. A number of benefits emerged; treated patients had fewer days in CCU, fewer supraventricular arrhythmias, less heart failure and a variety of advantages relating to affective states. This project is, in several ways, a model intervention study.

The paper by Klein and his colleagues, already partially described, included an intervention component [62]. Their experience, though not that of others [13], had shown that transfer from CCU was threatening and was often the occasion of behavioral and clinical disturbances. To counter this problem the transfer routine was modified to maximize patient preparation for and follow-up to transfer. Their comparison of seven patients pre- and seven patients postmodification of routine, supports the hypothesis that this treatment benefits patients behaviorally and clinically; signs of emotional distress, cardiac complications, and catechol elevations were fewer after the intervention.

EARLY MOBILIZATION AND DISCHARGE

Groden and Brown studied two groups of MI patients regarding the psychological effects of early ambulation after MI [37]. The early group was permitted out of bed at 14 days and was discharged at 21 days. The late group remained in bed for 25 days and was discharged at 35 days post-MI. The only effect observed was a lower Eysenck neuroticism measure in the early ambulation subjects at hospital discharge; the difference was not detectable one year later. Groden and others in an earlier study had compared the two approaches to the timing of ambulation and found no differences in mortality, development of hypotension, shock, or heart failure, episodes of chest pain or arrhythmia [36]. More recently, hospital stay for MI has become even shorter. The 1975 Professional Activities Study indicated that discharge occurred at an average of 17.4 days postadmission [17]. Hence, the findings of Groden and his colleagues may now be outdated.

Bloch and his colleagues in Geneva reported on a "strictly randomized controlled study" of 154 uncomplicated MI patients [6]. The early mobilization group began mobilization on Day 2 or 3 after the MI, whereas the control group was at strict bed rest for at least 3 weeks. Hospital discharge occurred at about Day 21 and 32, respectively. No differences in mortality or morbidity, either in-hospital or up to one year postdischarge, were detected. However, the early mobilization group experienced 98% return to work, whereas the late mobilization group experienced only 79% return to work. Other studies with less exacting experimental designs have also reported return to work advantages for early mobilization groups [44, 53].

Some suggest that, in concept, early ambulation and discharge should be advantageous [101]. Physically, they should lessen the deconditioning and risk of thromboemboli that follow from extended immobilization. Depression, a frequent concomitant of inactivity and deconditioning, should be less common. Other patterns associated with the passivity and dependence of extended convalescence should also be affected beneficially, including failure to return to work. But for the most part recent studies bearing on the spectrum of behavioral outcomes are not available.

There are several studies which tend to demonstrate the safety of early discharge [6, 44, 46, 53, 73]. Most recently, McNeer and his associates showed that patients selected for their lack of complications during 4 days of observation in a CCU could be discharged after 7 days in the hospital with no increase in subsequent mortality or morbidity, as compared with a nonrandom control group discharged at about 11 days [73].

A final intervention during the early phase of recovery after MI regards home care for uncomplicated infarct patients. Two British studies have drawn considerable attention [50, 69]. The more recent of these randomized 264 suspected and definite MI patients into home and hospital care at the time of first contact by an emergency medical team in the community [50]. An additional 85 patients were not randomized because of medical and social conditions clearly requiring hospitalization (e.g., complete heart block and housing unsuitable for home care). The investigators report no difference in mortality at 6 weeks post-MI, though there was a tendency for deaths in the home group to occur earlier after the MI than those in the hospitalized group. As was the case with early ambulation and discharge, studies to date have examined clinical endpoints to the exclusion of behavioral ones. But here, too, there is reason to suspect that home care might have advantages for behavioral adjustment.

Recovery after Discharge from Hospital

Descriptive Studies

Doehrman [21] provides a useful, recent summary of posthospital adjustment along the mortality, psychological, and vocational dimensions. We will use this trichotomization to guide our review of findings, since these are the areas of greatest research activity.

SURVIVORSHIP

As mentioned earlier, the largest portion of deaths occurs early after MI. If that period is survived, chances for long-term survival are good. Younger patients, having experienced their first MI, appear to have the greatest post-MI survivorship. More than 86% and 81% of first MI victims under 60 and 65 years of age, respectively, were reported to have survived to more than 4 years after the attack [78, 112]. Among older MI victims with first MI, the percentage drops but probably remains better than 60% [31, 110]. Long-term survival for those with a repeated MI is considerably lower.

EMOTIONAL STATUS

Emotional status after hospital discharge is difficult to characterize in terms of the proportions that experience favorable and unfavorable adjustment. Differences from study to study in the measurement of emotional status and the characteristics of the samples studied make overall numerical estimates quite inexact. There is, nonetheless, consistent comment about the common occurrence of "cardiac invalidism." This state is characterized by fear of sudden death, generalized health-related anxiety, and depression linked to loss of former wellness. There is also reluctance to return to higher activity levels, possibly because of an assumed connection between exertion and MI. Failure to return to work may be one manifestation of post-MI invalidism. Several studies found more than half of all MI patients emotionally upset in the early months after hospital discharge [74, 109, 111]. However, there is evidence that upset becomes an exception by 2 years after MI in those with no further complications of recovery [21]. Doehrman's review identified several studies of emotional adjustment using MMPI scales as criteria of outcome. The MI subjects tended to differ from test norms or control subjects on the depression, hysteria, and/or hypochondriasis scales [9, 11, 58, 76, 93].

VOCATIONAL ADJUSTMENT

Vocational adjustment after MI, especially return to work, has probably received more research attention than any other single outcome. Besides its ease of measurement, this outcome has been heavily studied because of its presumed link to emotional and economic well-being. (This assumption of the relationships of return to work, morale, and economic status has been questioned [71].) Estimates of *failure* to return to work within 1 year of MI range from 5% to 60% of those working before the attack; most estimates fall in the 10–30% range [15, 25, 29, 61, 79, 83, 99–101, 103, 107, 109, 111]. This extreme variability may be explained by differences in clinical and personal characteristics of the samples examined. Doehrman acknowledges the difficulties of estimating return to work, but on the basis of his review of 18 recent studies, ventures the guess that "for surviving patients previously employed, roughly 75% return to some type and amount of work within 6 months of acute incident, with 85% returning by 12 months [21, p. 210]." Although a high percentage appear to return to work, many individuals reduce their levels of productivity. In one study, 70% of those returning to work report not working as hard as before their MIs [99]. Another study reports a 30% reduction in work capacity after return to work [95]. Changing jobs and switching from full- to part-time work schedules are not uncommon [25, 28, 45, 74].

Although not examined in this review, the reader should be alerted to the existence of research reports on other aspects of the patient's personal and social adjustment after MI. Aspects of patient and spouse interaction have been studied to some limited extent. For example, return to a satisfying sexual relationship is beginning to become a subject of research interest [7, 48]. Reports have also appeared on the problems of husband and wife conflict [27, 61], the clarity of mutual understanding about recommended changes in life style [88], and the overbearing protectiveness of the patient's spouse [39, 109, 111]. In all of these problem areas, the role of the physician as manager of the patient's total recovery is beginning to be examined [61].

Correlational Studies

SURVIVORSHIP

Long-term survivorship after MI is most clearly related to age at onset, history of coronary disease, extent of myocardial damage, and the cardiac complications that it spawns. Several additional behavioral factors have been suggested as predictors of survivorship but are as yet only minimally studied. Three papers have described the Type A behavior pattern (measured by interview and Jenkins Activity Survey) as predictive of recurrent MI [56, 57, 92]. Factors related to social class, such as educational and occupational levels, have been found associated with mortality experience, with the more favorable social positions associated with better outcome [52, 98]. A study previously described in this paper reported an association between emotional status during the acute phase in CCU and 6-month survivorship [30]. It found that CCU patients showing greatest ability to cope with the early threat of MI had a distinct survivorship advantage.

EMOTIONAL STATUS

Depression after returning home from the hospital is common. This homecoming response has been linked to the physical deconditioning so usual in bed-confined individuals. The recovering MI patient newly at home experiences lack of energy, fatigues most easily, and tends to interpret these sensations as evidence of irreversibly impaired health. (This condition, of course, is reversible with gradually increased activity [109].) These early days at home are also times of minimal activity—providing more opportunity to dwell on values lost because of the MI.

Though the literature is quite limited in regard to empirical studies of correlates of long-term morale after MI, observations of several investigators appear to converge on the notion that personal assessment of health by the patient has a major influence on emotional status. One investigator found perception of health to be the best correlate of morale at 6 months post-MI, even when externally measured clinical status and several other sociobehavioral factors were statistically controlled [29]. This result fits the observations previously described that perceptions of lost stamina and susceptibility to sudden cardiac death may be linked with the syndrome of cardiac invalidism. As these perceptions undergo change for the better during later post-MI months, so, too, is there a decline in emotional disturbance [111].

It has been suggested that feelings of uncertainty and ambiguity are major cognitive–emotional problems for the postdischarge MI patient (and the spouse). Questions regarding what behaviors are recommended or proscribed are paramount in the minds of these people. How much activity, of which kinds, ought to be undertaken? Exactly which kinds of food are best? Must sexual activity be avoided? Such questions are typically dealt with in only the most cursory fashion before discharge [61, 70]. The limited literature, more hortatory than empirical, suggests that physician behavior may be a major determinant of emotional adjustment in this area. The explicit and detailed recommendation of the physician is generally said to be conducive to better patient adjustment [61]. The latter statement must be considered an hypothesis at this point, as no testing of the proposition has yet occurred.

VOCATIONAL ADJUSTMENT

As mentioned earlier, return to work has been the most plentifully studied of MI outcomes. We now have a fairly consistent picture of correlates of return to work. Clinical status of the patient as measured by severity of the MI [45, 66, 77, 79] and number of previous MIs [64] is related to return to work. As will be discussed shortly, these clinical factors may have their effects on return to work through the patient's appraisal of strategies for recovery based on the information about his health status.

The reviews of Croog et al. [18], Garrity [28], and Doehrman [21] all identify socioeconomic status, or its components, as being predictive of return to work. White-collar workers are more likely to return to work than blue-collar workers [45, 99, 105] and the latter are more likely to change jobs after first attack [97]. The upper class advantage may stem from working conditions and rewards that are more conducive to returning to work [90] and from employer attitudes and policies [91]. Younger age at MI is associated with likelihood of returning to work [25, 51, 64, 99]. This fairly consistent result may be partly explained by societal usages that encourage retirement by specific ages.

Finally, emotional factors may contribute to failure to return to work [49, 51, 79]. For example, Cay and colleagues [15] identified severe emotional upset as a correlate of failure to return to work within 4 months of MI. They also found that at 1 year most patients who had not returned to work were depressed and anxious. (Obviously, the direction of influence is unclear.) Patient opinions about their own level of physical handicap also seem influential in post-MI return to work. Those who estimated their handicap to be great more frequently failed to return to work. Another study reports quite similar results as regards individual perception of one's own level of health [28]. Both studies found patient perception of health to be predictive of return to work quite independently of clinical severity of the MI. Klein and his co-workers described a pattern of cardiac invalidism which linked fear of reinfarction and death, depression, preoccupation with physical symptoms, and failure to return to work [61]. Stern and associates described a similar picture in the minority of their patients who had failed to adjust after MI [100].

Intervention Studies

Attempts at intervening after hospital discharge in ways helpful for improving ultimate post-MI adjustment may be classified into two general approaches: personal or group psychotherapy and exercise reconditioning programs. While studies are few and generally not of the quality that would allow confident generalization, a brief review here might be suggestive of future directions.

PSYCHOTHERAPY

Among studies of group psychotherapy after hospital discharge, that of Ibrahim and his co-workers is perhaps the best designed [54]. They describe it as a "controlled clinical trial." Five psychotherapy treatment groups and five control groups, each containing about 12 MI patients, were compared on several behavioral and clinical outcomes. Although significant effects were not found in most of the emotional and physiological end points of the study, there was a slight tendency for the psychotherapy groups to experience improved survival rates (especially among the more seriously injured patients), report less social alienation, and experience briefer hospitalization during any rehospitalization in the surveillance period. These marginal effects are quite modest in relation to the many problems of adjustment the investigators hoped to affect. Moreover, these supportive psychotherapy groups met on a weekly basis for 50 sessions, each lasting 90 min. So major an investment of effort for such minor benefits must be termed disappointing.

More impressionistic results are described in two additional studies of group therapy. Adsett and Bruhn [2] ran 10 biweekly sessions for six male MI patients; parallel sessions were conducted separately for their wives. A group of matched control patients was also examined for adjustment status. Therapy was supportive and was organized around solutions to problems common to MI patients. The study and control groups of MI patients generally did not differ on physiological indicators of cardiovascular status, though patients in the psychotherapy group had significantly higher serum cholesterol and uric acid levels following therapy. The impression is reported that therapy subjects and their wives "achieved improved psychosocial adaptation." Rahe and his colleagues described a similar approach to group therapy, oriented to practical support and problem-solving for postdischarge MI patients [88]. Although no long-term follow-up of physiological effects was reported, several short-term behavioral benefits were apparent to the authors, including adherence to medical regimens and realistic planning for return to work.

Throckloth and associates [102] described a program of individual counseling done by a social-worker–occupational-therapist team with 50 MI patients who were eventually compared with 50 controls. The orientation of treatment was again decidedly pragmatic, with emphasis on facilitating return to job or preparation for a new, more appropriate one. Total numbers returning to work were not significantly different when groups were compared, but the rapidity of return was greater in the treatment group—72% returning in less than 4 months versus only 36% of the controls. Subjectively rated feelings of well-being were also greater in treatment subjects. Williamson [108] described a research plan to study the effects of "industrial rehabilitation" (not well detailed in the report) on vocational adjustment after MI. The results are not yet available.

The foregoing descriptions of studies of group psychotherapy for MI patients indicate that evaluation of effects are not yet far advanced. At this point no judgment can be made about their probable usefulness in affecting medical and behavioral outcomes.

EXERCISE RECONDITIONING

In the past 15–20 years, fairly intensive exercise training has been proposed as an approach to improving both physical and behavioral adaptation following MI. The presumption has been that systematically graduated exercise improves physical status by improving the body's ability to use oxygen and perform at higher work loads with less cardiovascular strain. There has also been the hope that development of collateral coronary vessels could be encouraged [23]. At the behavioral level, the hypothesis has been that successful physical training improves self-confidence and personal image of physical well-being. These, in turn, are expected to limit the tendency toward cardiac invalidism spawned by fear of imminent death.

At this point the literature appears to confirm the usefulness of exercise in raising post-MI cardiovascular work capacity. Bruce argues that this form of intervention, like any other form of effective therapy, is not free of risk [8]. However, he cites studies that tend to show that, under the proper circumstance, the risk of sudden cardiac death during training is small [86, 87]. Exercise training may even exert a protective effect against cardiovascular mortality in post-MI patients [8]. Blackburn [4] would reserve judgment on the latter issue and points to the randomized controlled trial in Goteborg, Sweden [94]. Although a mortality advantage was found among exercising subjects, Blackburn suggests that the difference may be explained by the fact that those with poorest physical status were forced to drop out of the exercise group.

At the physical level many questions about exercise training seem to remain. For example, which patients stand to benefit most from vigorous reconditioning programs? What should be the timing and progression of reconditioning? How vigorous should the program of exercise be? [4]

In relation to the behavioral effects of exercise training, there is great confidence that training improves morale among post-MI patients [59, 82], but less confidence-inspiring *evidence* that the relationship is real [21]. McPherson's comparison of normal and post-MI suggests that patients experience a greater sense of well-being, self-confidence, and optimism as physical fitness increases [72]. Naughton reports contrary results when MMPI scores are used as outcome measures [80].

Studies that report on return to employment after participation in an exercise program present results not greatly different from those of groups not vigorously exercised [12, 60]. Hence, it must be stated that, in spite of the *belief* in the behavioral and physical benefits of vigorous reconditioning programs, evidence in the literature is still equivocal. Only a study in the nature of a large clinical trial will provide solid information about the mortality, clinical, and behavioral effects, if any, of exercise programs for post-MI patients. Some of this information may soon be available from Rechnitzer and associates in their multicenter prospective study coordinated in Ontario [89].

Methodological Critiques of the Field

Several flaws of method have been consistently identified in the cardiac rehabilitation literature [18, 21]. A few stem from the nature of the medical condition being studied, but most are critiques commonly applied to many areas of scientific, especially behavioral, research.

Sample construction presents problems. A major problem here is that many of the reports in this literature are based on patient samples of convenience. Samples are typically far from being representative in terms of demographic, geographic, and clinical characteristics of the universe of MI victims. The criticism, then, involves the generalizability of findings derived from such samples. Even representative samples tend to grow less representative as attrition due to early mortality occurs. Acquisition of subjects may present challenging logistical problems because of the need for physician cooperation in gaining access to patients, but this is by no means insuperable.

In terms of study design, the lack of control groups is common. This flaw is most glaring in intervention studies in which patients often are made to serve as their own controls in comparing pre- and postintervention states. One study that looked at the effectiveness of exercise in lessening depression, for example, simply compared pre- and posttraining scores on the MMPI D scale in the same patient [47]. The obvious question remains about whether any improvement would have occurred without the intervention as a simple result of increasing time since MI. Another problem of design is a perennial one in illness research, namely retrospectiveness. This is most problematic when the researcher wishes to make statements about the effects of pre-illness characteristics on post-MI adjustment. Can subjects report on these without bias after the MI?

There are several familiar problems related to measurement. Different investigators who intend to study the same phenomenon often employ different measures of it. For example, denial in one study is measured by denial of the MI diagnosis [19] and in another denial of fear or anxiety since the MI [40]. With such discrepancies of measurement, comparison and consolidation of results is not possible. The goal of building knowledge by accumulating results is thwarted. Another aspect of this issue is the tendency of investigators to construct their own measures, typically with little effort to validate or assess reliability. While construction of an original measure is often necessary when no appropriate measure is available, failure to study psychometric properties of these measures is a clear weakness.

Recommendations for Future Research Activity

This review has divided the literature into descriptive, correlational, and intervention categories. The first of these, the descriptive, is now the most completely developed. It began developing earlier than the other two and has tended to draw attention to the variety of behavioral problems encountered by recovering MI patients. By now, this literature has identified a number of recurrent difficulties that tend to impair the quality of post-MI life for patients and their families. These descriptive studies have been useful in defining the areas needing better causal understanding so that rational ameliorative efforts could be designed, implemented, and evaluated.

This review has presented some of the more important fruits of these descriptive studies. At the behavioral level, the major problems appear to involve mastering the fear, anxiety, and depression created by this major change in health: early on, coping with fear of death and anxiety about necessary changes in life style; later, depression about values lost and withdrawal from an active, satisfying way of life. These issues are already fairly well-defined and are probably now in less need of further description.

Although descriptive studies have dealt extensively with adjustment difficulties at the conservative end of the continuum (i.e., those related to cardiac invalidism) their opposites have been almost ignored. I am referring here to the situation of MI patients who disavow the need for any change or limitation of life activities. Some might call such a person a "denier" [19]. It is surprising that the disciplines that have devoted enormous energy to studying patients who do not "comply" with medical recommendations regarding various medication regimens have neglected to study patient follow-through with physician recommendations after MI. The literature which emphasizes the problem of patient and spouse "overcautiousness" has little to say about the problem of "undercautiousness." While Croog and Levine [20] have reported that post-MI adherence to medical recommendations is more complete than it is in the presence of other illnesses frequently studied [3, 55], this issue needs further attention at even the descriptive level.

Another area still needing descriptive research efforts regards health worker–patient interaction. Some descriptive work has begun to suggest that what goes on between these two actors during recovery has important consequences for the quality of the patient's socioemotional adjustment [61]. But, as has been the case in other areas of health behavior (e.g., compliance), the major focuses of study have been away from treater–patient interaction. Careful observation of the nature of this interaction may well suggest both causes and solutions for some of the common problems of behavioral adjustment, such as failure to return to work, sexual relating, community involvement, and pre-illness morale.

Correlational studies are useful in providing clues about the causal structures within which important recovery outcomes are positioned. In this regard, they suggest experimental strategies that may lead to the testing of theoretically derived hypotheses and practical interventions. In sheer weight of numbers, correlational studies are second to the descriptive in this literature. Vocational adjustment, especially return to work, has been heavily studied in this way. The result has been a relatively stable picture of the factors associated with this outcome. While some of these factors hold little promise for manipulation as part of an ameliorative intervention, a few do. Factors, for example, related to *perception* of disability are alterable and may be reasonable targets for intervention.

Although additional correlational studies of return to work and other aspects of invalidism may be less needed, there still seems to be a need for correlational studies of behavioral factors in relation to changes in clinical status. Are there, in fact, coping strategies and emotional responses which promote physical well-being and, ultimately, survival? The studies of Type A behavior and recurrence of MI [56, 57, 92] provide examples of this kind of study. But several other studies discussed earlier also fit here, such as the studies of denial and mortality [32, 40], and studies of emotional disturbance and in-hospital complications [62]. Some of the findings in this limited literature are most exciting, but in great need of additional study.

Of the three categories of research reviewed in this discussion, the intervention study is found least frequently. In the logic of progression from simple descriptive, through correlational, to quasi-experimental manipulations of relevant factors, this paucity is to be expected. Even so, we sampled from a variety of intervention attempts aimed at improving some aspects of post-MI recovery. The interventions included early mobilization and nonhospitalization as alternatives to traditional CCU care, group and individual psychotherapy, and exercise reconditioning programs. To this point, clinical outcomes and survivorship have dominated evaluations. There is still need to examine outcomes indicative of quality of life, such as vocational and emotional adjustment. With their practical and theoretical benefits, carefully designed and imaginative intervention studies may represent the greatest potential for growth in the post-MI adjustment literature.

References

1. Abram, H.: Adaption to open heart surgery: Psychiatric study of response to threat of death. *American Journal of Psychiatry* 122:659–667, 1969.
2. Adsett, C.; and Bruhn, J.: Short-term group psychotherapy for post-myocardial infarction patients and their wives. *Canadian Medical Association Journal* 99:577–584, 1968.
3. Becker, M.; Drachman, R.; and Kirscht, J.: Predicting mothers' compliance with pediatric medical regimens. *Journal of Pediatrics* 81:843–853, 1972.
4. Blackburn, H.: Disadvantages of intensive exercise therapy after myocardial infarction. In *Controversy in Internal Medicine,* eds. F. Ingelfinger, R. Ebert, M. Finland, A. Relman, Philadelphia: Saunders, 1974.
5. Blachly, P.; and Kloster, F.: Relation of cardiac output to post-cardiotomy delirium. *Journal of Thoracic and Cardiovascular Surgery* 52:422–427, 1966.
6. Bloch, A.; Maeder, J.; Haissly, J.; Felix, J.; and Blackburn, H.: Early mobilization after myocardial infarction: a controlled study. *American Journal of Cardiology* 34:152–157, 1974.

7. Bloch, A; Maeder, J.; and Haissly, J.: Sexual problems after myocardial infarction. *American Heart Journal* 90:536–537, 1975.
8. Bruce, R.: The benefits of physical training for patients with coronary heart disease. In *Controversy in Internal Medicine*, eds. F. Ingelfinger, R. Ebert, M. Finland, A. Relman eds. Philadelphia: Saunders, 1974.
9. Bruhn, J.; Chandler, B.; and Wolf, S.: A psychological study of survivors and nonsurvivors of myocardial infarction. *Psychosomatic Medicine* 31:8–19, 1969.
10. Bruhn, J.; Thurman, A.; Chandler, B.; and Bruce T.: Patients' reactions to death in a coronary care unit. *Journal of Psychosomatic Research* 14:65–70, 1970.
11. Bruhn, J.; Wolf, S.; and Philips, B.: A psychological study of surviving male coronary patients and controls followed over nine years. *Journal of Psychosomatic Research* 15:305–313, 1971.
12. Carson, P.; Neophytou, M.; Tucker, H.; and Simpson, T.: Exercise programme after myocardial infarction. *British Medical Journal* 4:213–216, 1973.
13. Cay, E.; Vetter, N.; Philip, A.; and Dugard, P.: Psychological reactions to a coronary care unit. *Journal of Psychosomatic Research* 16:437–447, 1972.
14. Cay, E.; Vetter, N.; Philip, A.; and Dugard, P.: Psychological status during recovery from an acute heart attack. *Journal of Psychosomatic Research* 16:425–435, 1972.
15. Cay, E.; Vetter, N.; Philip, A.; and Dugard, P.: Return to work after a heart attack. *Journal of Psychosomatic Research* 17:231–243, 1973.
16. Christiansen, I.; Iversen, K.; and Skouby, A.: Benefits obtained by the introduction of a coronary care unit. *Acta Medica Scandinavica* 189:285–291, 1971.
17. Commission on Professional and Hospital Activities. Length of Stay in PAS Hospitals. Ann Arbor, Michigan, 1976.
18. Croog, S.; Levine, S.; and Lurie, Z.: The heart patient and the recovery process: a review of the literature on social and psychological factors. *Social Science and Medicine* 2:111–164, 1968.
19. Croog, S.; Shapiro, D.; and Levine, S.: Denial among male heart patients: an empirical study. *Psychosomatic Medicine* 33:385–396, 1971.
20. Croog, S.; and Levine, S.: *The Heart Patient Recovers*. New York: Human Sciences Press, 1977.
21. Doehrman, S.: Psycho-social aspects of recovery from coronary heart disease: a review. *Social Science and Medicine* 11:199–218, 1977.
22. Dominian, J.; and Dobson, M.: Study of patients' psychological attitudes to a coronary care unit. *British Medical Journal* 4:795–798, 1969.
23. Eckstein, R.: Effect of exercise and coronary artery narrowing on coronary collateral circulation. *Circulation Research* 5:230–235, 1957.
24. Engel, G.: Sudden and rapid death during psychological stress: folklore or folk wisdom? *Annals of Internal Medicine* 74:771–782, 1971.
25. Fisher, S.: Impact of physical disability on vocational activity. *Scandinavian Journal of Rehabilitation Medicine* 2:65–70, 1970.
26. Froese, A.; Cassem, N.; Hackett, T.; and Silverberg, E.: Galvanic skin potential as a predictor of mental status, anxiety, depression and denial in acute coronary patients. *Journal of Psychosomatic Research* 19:1–9, 1975.
27. Garrity, T.: Morbidity, mortality and rehabilitation. In *Psychological Aspects of Myocardial Infarction and Coronary Care*. eds. W. Gentry, and R. Williams, St. Louis: Mosby, 1975.
28. Garrity, T.: Vocational adjustment after first myocardial infarction. *Social Sciences and Medicine* 7:705–717, 1973a.
29. Garrity, T.: Social involvement and activeness as predictors of morale six months after first myocardial infarction. *Social Science and Medicine* 7:199–207, 1973b.

30. Garrity, T.; and Klein, R.: Emotional response and clinical severity as early determinants of six month mortality after myocardial infarction. *Heart and Lung* 4:730–737, 1975.
31. Geismar, P; Iversen, E.; and Mosbech, J.: Long-term survival after myocardial infarction: a national follow-up study on 642 patients in Denmark. *International Journal of Epidemiology* 2:257–263, 1973.
32. Gentry, W.; Foster, S.; and Haney, T.: Denial as a determinant of anxiety and perceived health status in the coronary care unit. *Psychosomatic Medicine* 34:39–45, 1972.
33. Gentry, W.; Musante, G.; and Haney, T.: State anxiety and urinary sodium/potassium as stress indicators on admission to a CCU. *Heart and Lung* 2:875–877, 1973.
34. Gilman, S.: Cerebral disorders after open heart operations. *New England Journal of Medicine* 272:489–498, 1965.
35. Graham, L.: Patients' perceptions in the CCU. *American Journal of Nursing* 69:1921–1922, 1969.
36. Groden, B.; Allison, A.; and Shaw, G.: Management of myocardial infarction—the effect of early mobilization. *Scottish Medical Journal* 12:435–440, 1967.
37. Groden, B.; and Brown, R.: Differential psychological effects of early and late mobilization after myocardial infarction. *Scandinavian Journal of Rehabilitation Medicine* 2:60–64, 1970.
38. Gruen, W.: Effects of brief psychotherapy during the hospitalization period on the recovery process in heart attacks. *Journal of Consulting and Clinical Psychology* 43:223–232, 1975.
39. Gulledge, A.: The psychological aftermath of a myocardial infarction. In *Psychological Aspects of Myocardial Infarction and Coronary Care,* eds., W. Gentry and R. Williams, St. Louis: Mosby, 1975.
40. Hackett, T.; Cassem, N.; and Wishnie, H.: The coronary-care unit: an appraisal of its psychologic hazards. *New England Journal of Medicine* 279:1365–1370, 1968.
41. Hackett, T.; Cassem, N.; and Wishnie, H.: Detection and treatment of anxiety in the coronary care unit. *American Heart Journal* 78:727–730, 1969.
42. Hackett, T.; Froese, A.; and Vasquez, E.: Psychological management of the CCU patient. *International Journal of Psychiatry in Medicine* 4:89–105, 1973.
43. Hackett, T.; and Cassem, N.: Psychological intervention in myocardial infarction. In *Psychological Aspects of Myocardial Infarction and Coronary Care.* eds. W. Gentry and R. Williams, St. Louis: Mosby, 1975.
44. Harpur, J.; Kellett, R.; Conner, W.; Galbraith, H.; Hamilton, M.; Murray, J.; Swallow, J.; and Rose, G.: Controlled trial of early mobilization and discharge from hospital in uncomplicated myocardial infarction. *Lancet* 2:1331–1334, 1971.
45. Hay, D.; and Turbott, S.: Rehabilitation after myocardial infarction and acute coronary insufficiency. *New Zealand Medical Journal* 71:267–272, 1970.
46. Hayes, M.; Morris, G.; and Hampton, J.: Comparison of mobilization after two and nine days in uncomplicated myocardial infarction. *British Medical Journal* 3:10–13, 1974.
47. Hellerstein, H.: Exercise therapy in coronary disease. *Bulletin of the New York Academy of Medicine* 44:1028–1047, 1968.
48. Hellerstein, H.; and Friedman, E.: Sexual activity and the post-coronary patient. *Archives of Internal Medicine* 125:987–999, 1970.
49. Higgins, A.; and Pooler, W.: Myocardial infarction and subsequent reemployment in Syracuse, New York. *American Journal of Public Health* 58:312–323, 1968.
50. Hill, J.; Hampton, J.; and Mitchell, J.: A randomized trial of home-versus-hospital management for patients with suspected myocardial infarction. *Lancet* 2:837–841, 1978.
51. Hinohara, S.: Psychological aspects in rehabilitation of coronary heart disease. *Scandinavian Journal of Rehabilitation Medicine* 2:53–59, 1970.

52. Hrubec, Z.; and Zukel, W.: Socioeconomic differentials in prognosis following episodes of coronary heart disease. *Journal of Chronic Disease* 23:881–889, 1971.

53. Hutter, A.; Sidel, V.; Shine, K.; and Desantis, R.: Early hospital discharge after myocardial infarction. *New England Journal of Medicine* 288:1141–1144, 1973.

54. Ibrahim, M.; Feldman, J.; Sultz, H.; Staiman, M.; Young, L.; and Dean, D.: Management after myocardial infarction: a controlled trial of the effect of group psychotherapy. *International Journal of Psychiatry in Medicine* 5:253–268, 1974.

55. Inui, T.; Yourtee, E.; and Williamson, J.: Improved outcomes in hypertension after physician tutorials. *Annals of Internal Medicine* 84:646–651, 1976.

56. Jenkins, C; Zyzanski, S.; Rosenman, R.; and Cleveland, G.: Association of coronary-prone behavior scores with recurrence of coronary heart disease. *Journal of Chronic Diseases* 24:601–611, 1971.

57. Jenkins, C; Zyzanski, S., and Rosenman, R.: Risk of new myocardial infarction in middle-aged men with manifest coronary heart disease. *Circulation* 53:342–347, 1976.

58. Kavanagh, T.; Shephard, R.; and Tuck, J.: Depression after myocardial infarction. *Canadian Medical Association Journal* 113:23–27, 1975.

59. Kellermann, J.: Rehabilitation of patients with coronary heart disease. *Progress in Cardiovascular Diseases* 17:303–328, 1975.

60. Kentala, E.: Physical fitness and feasibility of physical rehabilitation after myocardial infarction in men of working age. *Annals of Clinical Research* 4 (Supplement 9):1–84, 1972.

61. Klein, R.; Dean, A.; Willson, L.; and Bogdonoff, M.: The physician and postmyocardial infarction invalidism. *Journal of the American Medical Association* 194:143–148, 1965.

62. Klein, R.; Kliner, V.; Zipes, D.; Troyer, W.; and Wallace, A.: Transfer from a coronary care unit. *Archives of Internal Medicine* 122:104–108, 1968.

63. Klein, R.; Garrity, T.; and Galein, J.: Emotional adjustment and catecholamine excretion during early recovery from myocardial infarction. *Journal of Psychosomatic Research* 18:425–435, 1974.

64. Kjoller, E.: Resumption of work after acute myocardial infarction. *Acta Medica Scandinavica* 199:379–385, 1976.

65. Kornfield, D; Zimberg, S.; and Malm, J.: Psychiatric complications of open-heart surgery. *New England Journal of Medicine* 273:287–292, 1965.

66. Kushnir, B.; Fox, K.; Tomlinson, I.; Portal, R.; and Aber, C.: Primary ventricular fibrillation and resumption of work, sexual activity, and driving after first acute myocardial infarction. *British Medical Journal* 4:609–611, 1975.

67. Leigh, H.; Hofen, M.; Cooper, J.; and Reiser, M.: A psychological comparison of patients in "open" and "closed" coronary care units. *Journal of Psychosomatic Research* 16:449–457, 1972.

68. Lenzner, A.; and Aronson, A.: Psychiatric vignettes from a coronary care unit. *Psychosomatics* 13:179–184, 1972.

69. Mather, H.; Pearson, N.; Read, K.; Shaw, D.; Steed, G.; Thorne, M.; Jones, S.; Guerrier, C.; Eraut, C.; McHugh, P.; Chowdhury, N.; Jafary, M.; and Wallace, T.: Acute myocardial infarction: home and hospital treatment. *British Medical Journal* 3:334–338, 1971.

70. Mayou, R; Foster, A.; and Williamson, B.: Psychological and social effects of myocardial infarction on wives. *British Medical Journal* 1:699–701, 1978.

71. Mayou, R.; Williamson, B.; and Foster, A.: Outcome two months after myocardial infarction. *Journal of Psychosomatic Research* 22:439–445, 1978.

72. McPherson, B.; Paivio, A.; Yuhasz, M.; Rechnitzer, P.; Pickard, H.; and Lefcoe, N.: Psychological effects of an exercise program for the post-infarct and normal adult men. *Journal of Sports Medicine and Physical Fitness* 7:95–102, 1967.

73. McNeer, J; Wagner, G.; Ginsburg, P.; Wallace, A.; McCants, C.; Conley, M.; and Rosati, R.: Hospital discharge one week after acute myocardial infarction. *New England Journal of Medicine* 298:229-232, 1978.
74. McGrath, F.; and Robinson, J.: The medical social worker in the coronary care unit. *Medical Journal of Australia* 2:1113-1116, 1973.
75. Miller, W.; and Rosenfeld, R.: Psychophysiological study of denial following acute myocardial infarction. *Journal of Psychosomatic Research* 19:43-54, 1975.
76. Mordkoff, A.; and Rand, M.: Personality and adaptation to coronary artery disease. *Journal of Consulting and Clinical Psychology* 32:648-653, 1968.
77. Morris, J.: Occupation and coronary heart disease. *Archives of Internal Medicine* 104:903-907, 1959.
78. Mulcahy, R.; Hickey, N.; Graham, I.; and McKenzie, G.: Factors influencing long-term prognosis in male patients surviving a first coronary attack. *British Heart Journal* 37:158-165, 1975.
79. Nagle, R.; Gangola, R.; and Picton-Robinson, I.: Factors influencing return to work after myocardial infarction. *Lancet* 2:454-456, 1971.
80. Naughton, J.; Bruhn, J.; and Lategola,M.; Effects of physical training on physiologic and behavioral characteristics of cardiac patients. *Archives of Physical Medicine and Rehabilitation* 49:131-137, 1968.
81. Nixon, P.; and Bethell, H.: Preinfarction ill health. *American Journal of Cardiology* 33:446-449, 1974.
82. Nye, E.; and Poulsen, W.: An activity programme for coronary patients: a review of morbidity, mortality and adherence after five years. *New Zealand Medical Journal* 79:1010-1013, 1974.
83. Obier, K.; and Haywood, J.: Psychosocial problems of coronary care unit patients. *Journal of the National Medical Association* 63:425-428, 1971.
84. Panthridge, J.: Mobile coronary care. *Chest* 58:229-234, 1970.
85. Pranulis, M.: Coping with an acute myocardial infarction. In *Psychological Aspects of Myocardial Infarction and Coronary Care.* eds. W. Gentry and R. Williams, St. Louis: Mosby,1975.
86. Pyfer, H.; and Doane, B.: Exercise for the cardio-pulmonary patient. *Northwest Medicine* 68:129-134, 1969.
87. Pyfer, H.; and Doane, B.: Cardiac arrest during exercise training. *Journal of the American Medical Association* 210:101-102, 1969.
88. Rahe, R; Tuffli, C.; Suchor, R.; and Arthur, R.: Group therapy in the outpatient management of post-myocardial infarction patients. *International Journal of Psychiatry in Medicine* 4:77-88, 1973.
89. Rechnitzer, P.; Sangal, S.; Cunningham, D.; Andrew, G.; Busk, C.; Jones, N.; Kavanagh, T.; Parker, J.; Shepard, R.; and Yuhasz, M.: A controlled prospective study of the effect of endurance training on the recurrence of myocardial infarction. *American Journal of Epidemiology* 102:358-365, 1975.
90. Reeder, L.: Socioeconomic effects of heart disease. *Social Problems* 4:51-54, 1956.
91. Reeder, L.: Employment practices and the cardiac. *Journal of Chronic Diseases* 18:951-963, 1965.
92. Rosenman, R.; Friedman, M.; Jenkins, C.; Straus, R.; Wurm, M.; and Kositchek, R.: Recurring and fatal myocardial infarction in the Western Collaborative Group Study. *American Journal Of Cardiology* 19:771-775, 1967.
93. Ruskin, H.; Stein, L.; Shelsky, I.; and Bailey, M.: MMPI: comparison between patients with coronary heart disease and their spouses together with other demographic data. *Scandinavian Journal of Rehabilitation Medicine* 2:99-104, 1970.

94. Sanne, H.; Elmfeldt, D.; and Wilhelmsen, L.: The preventive effect of physical training after a myocardial infarction. In *Preventive Cardiology*, eds. G. Tibblin, A. Keys, and L. Werko, Stockholm: Almqvist and Wiksell, 1972.

95. Sanne, H.: Exercise tolerance and physical training of non-selected patients after myocardial infarction. *Acta Medica Scandinavica* 551 (supplement):1–112, 1973.

96. Sczekalla, R.: Stress reactions of CCU patients to resuscitation procedures on other patients. *Nursing Research* 22:65–69, 1973.

97. Sharland, D.: Ability of men to return to work after cardiac infarction. *British Medical Journal* 2:718–720, 1964.

98. Shapiro, S.; Weinblatt, E.; Frank, C.; and Sager, R.: Social factors in the prognosis of men following first myocardial infarction. *Millbank Memorial Fund Quarterly Bulletin* 48:37–50, 1970.

99. Shapiro, S.; Weinblatt, E.; and Frank, C.: Return to work after first myocardial infarction. *Archives of Environmental Health* 24:17–26, 1972.

100. Stern, M.; Pascale, L.; and McLoone, J.: Psychosocial adaptation following an acute myocardial infarction. *Journal of Chronic Disease* 29:513–526, 1976.

101. Task Force or Cardiac Rehabilitation of the National Heart and Lung Institute. Needs and opportunities for rehabilitating the coronary heart disease patient. DHEW Publication no. (NIH) 75–750, 1974.

102. Throckloth, R.; Ho, S.; Wright, H.; and Seldon, W.: Is cardiac rehabilitation really necessary? *Medical Journal of Australia* 2:669–674, 1973.

103. Weinblatt, E.; Shapiro, S.; Frank, C.; and Sager, R.: Return to work and work status following first myocardial infarction. *American Journal of Public Health* 56:169–185, 1966.

104. Weinblatt, E.; Shapiro, S.; Frank, C.; and Sager, R.; Prognosis of men after first myocardial infarction: mortality and first recurrence in relation to selected parameters. *American Journal of Public Health* 58:1329–1347, 1968.

105. Weinstock, M; and Haft, J.: The effect of illness on employment opportunities. *Archives of Environmental Health* 29:79–83, 1974.

106. Wenger, N.: The early ambulation of patients after myocardial infarction. *Cardiology* 58:1–6, 1973.

107. Wenger, N.; Hellerstein, H.; Blackburn, H.; and Castranova, S.: Uncomplicated myocardial infarction. *Journal of the American Medical Association* 224:511–514, 1973.

108. Williamson, J.: The value of industrial rehabilitation following cardiac infarction. *Proceedings of the Royal Society of Medicine* 70:656–657, 1977.

109. Wishnie, H.; Hackett, T.; and Cassem, N.: Psychological hazards of convalescence following myocardial infarction. *Journal of the American Medical Association* 215:1292–1296, 1971.

110. Woodhouse, S.: Subsequent mortality in patients surviving myocardial infarction. *New Zealand Medical Journal* 69:24–27, 1969.

111. Wynn, A.: Unwarranted emotional distress in meń with ischaemic heart disease. *Medical Journal of Australia* 2:847–851, 1967.

112. Zukel, W.; Cohen, B.; Mattingly, T.; and Hrubec, Z.: Survival following first diagnosis of coronary heart disease. *American Heart Journal* 78:159–170, 1969.

Clinical Trials of Changing Behavior to Prevent Cardiovascular Disease

STEPHEN B. HULLEY[1]
STEPHEN P. FORTMANN

Our topic is clinical trials directed at the role of life style in causing and preventing cardiovascular disease (CVD). The individual characteristics at issue include not only the behavioral risk factors themselves, such as cigarette smoking, sedentary life style, psychological stress, and Type A behavior pattern, but also physiological variables such as high blood cholesterol level, hypertension, and obesity. All of these factors can be attributed to habitual behaviors that characterize Americans of the twentieth century, and all are susceptible to intervention programs.

As associations between risk factors and CVD were discovered during the last several decades, scientists turned their attention to two related problems. First, do the associations represent cause and effect? And second, at a more practical level, will programs directed at altering the risk factors lead to a reduction in disease incidence? Of the many approaches to researching these questions, clinical trials offer the greatest potential for a clear answer. They are also especially costly and difficult to execute, and they are therefore usually undertaken as a last resort after other less expensive forms of research have been inconclusive [8]. Unfortunately, clinical trials are sometimes inconclusive, too. This is particularly true for trials of modifying habits and behavior, variables that are complex, diffuse, difficult to change, and not amenable to double blind designs.

In this report we will address the issue of how the *design* of such trials influences the quality of the resulting information. We will compare the advantages and disadvantages of two major trials that represent quite different approaches to the problem: the Multiple Risk Factor Intervention

[1]*Present affiliation:* Department of Epidemiology and International Health, University of California, San Francisco, San Francisco, California 94143.

PERSPECTIVES ON
BEHAVIORAL MEDICINE

Trial (MRFIT), a study of a clinic-based intervention program, and the Stanford 5-City Project (5CP), a test of a community-directed intervention program. Both of these life-style intervention studies will be contrasted with the Lipid Research Clinics (LRC) Primary Prevention Trial, an example of a conventional trial with an independent variable (the cholesterol-lowering drug cholestyramine) that is discrete and administered in a double-blind fashion.

The design features of all three studies are summarized in Table 1. Because the two life-style trials are pioneering efforts directed at behavior change, we will describe their methodology in some detail before turning to the comparative analysis of each design and the implications for behavioral medicine research and practice.

The Multiple Risk Factor Intervention Trial

The MRFIT is a randomized, collaborative trial to test the hypothesis that a 6-year program for lowering three major coronary risk factors will reduce mortality from coronary heart disease (CHD) among men at above average risk [2, 16]. Clinical centers in 22 communities began by recruiting men aged 35–57 who were initially free of overt CHD but judged to be at greater than average risk. Eligibility for the trial was based on a combined risk score calculated from the serum cholesterol level, the diastolic blood pressure, and the reported cigarette smoking history. The populations screened were not probability samples drawn from entire communities, but volunteers recruited from various industrial and residential groups who agreed to participate in a 6-year research program. By February 1976, after 2 years of recruitment, over 370,000 men had been screened and 12,866 men had entered the trial.

A series of three baseline examinations to determine eligibility culminated in randomizing the participants into two groups of equal size, termed Special Intervention (SI) and Usual Care (UC). Members of the SI group were instructed in a standard, fat-controlled eating pattern designed to lower serum cholesterol concentration, and weight reduction was sought among those who were overweight. Participants who smoked cigarettes were counseled in approaches to quitting, and those with hypertension entered a stepped-care program of weight reduction, sodium restriction, and conventional medications [17].

The intervention goals for the SI group were to achieve, on the average: (a) a 10% reduction in serum cholesterol level, (b) a 10% reduction in diastolic blood pressure, and (c) a 20%, 30%, or 40% reduction in cigarette smoking prevalence for heavy, moderate, or light cigarette smokers,

TABLE 1
Summary of Design Features of Three Current CHD Prevention Trials

I. The Lipid Research Clinics (LRC)
   HYPOTHESIS: Cholestyramine will reduce CHD incidence.
   DESIGN:
   1. *Subjects:* 3800 men aged 35–59 who have LDL cholesterol > 175 mg/dl, are free of overt CHD and are willing to be randomized into a 7-year trial.
   2. *Control:* stratified randomization
   3. *Independent variable:* cholestyramine versus placebo (double blind).
   4. *Dependent variables* (assessed by annual examination of entire cohort):
      (a) Intervening variable—plasma cholesterol
      (b) Endpoint—7-year incidence of all MI (blind)

II. The Multiple Risk Factor Intervention Trial (MRFIT)
   HYPOTHESIS: A clinic-based program for lowering three major risk factors will reduce CHD mortality.
   DESIGN:
   1. *Subjects:* 12,866 men aged 35–57 who have a risk factor score in the top 10–15% of the population, are free of overt CHD, and are willing to be randomized into a 6-year trial.
   2. *Control:* randomization
   3. *Independent variable:* Special Intervention versus Usual Care.
      The Special Intervention program is designed to:
      (a) Lower serum cholesterol (with fat-controlled diet and weight loss)
      (b) Treat hypertension (with low salt diet, weight loss, and drugs)
      (c) Encourage smoking cessation
   4. *Dependent variables:* (assessed by annual examination of entire cohort):
      (a) intervening variables—serum cholesterol, blood pressure, cigarette smoking
      (b) endpoints:
         (i). Primary—6-year incidence of fatal MI (blind adjudication)
         (ii). Secondary—6-year incidence of all MI, and of total mortality

III. The Five-City Project (5CP)
   HYPOTHESIS: A multifactor community-based health education program will reduce CHD morbidity and mortality.
   DESIGN:
   1. *Subjects:* all residents aged 12–74 in five northern California cities (total N = 130,000)
   2. *Control:* two treated versus three untreated cities (selected)
   3. *Independent variable:* a prevention program which provides mass media and promotes "face-to-face" intervention in order to lower prevalence of:
      (a) high plasma cholesterol
      (b) hypertension
      (c) smoking
      (d) sedentary life style
      (e) psychosocial stress
   4. *Dependent variables:*
      (a) intervening variables—knowledge, attitudes, behavior, risk factor levels (assessed by a survey of a probability sample of households)
      (b) endpoints—7-year incidence of fatal and nonfatal MI, stroke, and total mortality (assessed by complete morbidity and mortality surveillance with blind adjudication)

respectively. The primary hypothesis of the trial was that this intervention program would reduce CHD death rates; secondary hypotheses were that it would also lower the total incidence of myocardial infarction (both fatal and nonfatal) and total mortality.

The MRFIT intervention program generally began with ten weekly meetings of eight to ten participants and their wives. The theme was an integrated, multifactor approach to risk reduction, and the sessions educated participants in the relationship between risk factors and CHD, provided them with skills needed for changing behavior, and supported their efforts to achieve these changes. After the initial phase, the intervention program was largely carried out through individual counseling that provided skills and support for preventing recidivism among those who had achieved their goals, and for enhancing further change among those who had not.

Recognizing the complexity of this effort to achieve long-term reduction in risk factors, each clinical center assembled a multidisciplinary team to guide the participants. Physicians, nutritionists, smoking cessation specialists, nurses, and persons trained in the behavioral sciences worked closely together. To achieve continuity and coordination over the years, a particular health counselor was designated for each participant to assist him in meeting and maintaining his goals. Because homemakers play key roles in achieving success, their involvement was encouraged.

Preliminary results of the MRFIT intervention effort are now being released. A review of the changes occurring during the first 2 years of the trial [18] has revealed success in achieving the risk factor goals. Information on disease incidence will become available in 1982.

Stanford Five-City Project (5CP)

In 1972, the Stanford Heart Disease Prevention Program launched a field study in three California communities to determine if risk behaviors could be changed in large heterogeneous populations using a variety of mass media supplemented by some face-to-face interventions [7, 11, 15]. The Three Community Study demonstrated that a mass media program can substantially reduce the risk factors for CHD, particularly when it is complemented by face-to-face education similar to that used in the MRFIT. Whether such public education programs can also reduce the rates of the disease events themselves remains uncertain.

The Stanford group has now launched a second community intervention project, the 5CP, that differs from the first in extending the outcome considerations to include disease incidence, and in having more effective technology. The two treatment and three control cities are relatively large, having a total population of 130,000 in the age range 30–70. A series of independent surveys of population samples is used to assess the true community impact of the public health program on knowledge, behavior, and risk factors. In addition, repeated surveys of longitudinal cohorts permits the use of correlational, network, and path analysis [5]. An epidemiologic surveillance system comprehensively monitors all cardiovascular disease events occurring in the five cities over the 8 years of the trial. The system is designed to apply uniform diagnostic criteria to information acquired from hospital records, death certificates, health professionals, and members of the community.

The education program includes messages delivered through a variety of media, including television, radio, newspapers, and direct mailings. Stanford personnel help existing community resources to provide interpersonal education for a high proportion of the community residents. The education program coordinates and guides health resources that already exist in the communities; this includes continuing education courses for physicians and other health professionals. The program also encourages organizations not primarily concerned with health to sponsor learning groups in such areas as nutrition, exercise, weight loss, smoking, and control of stress. Initially, Stanford personnel are available to lead groups; later they will help community members to assume leadership. Stanford coordinators provide kits of instructional materials packaged so they can be used by persons with no particular scientific or behavioral background.

With the cooperation of schools and youth groups, programs are introduced to help young people alter habits in the areas of smoking, diet, and physical activity. Since the youth program parallels the adult education campaign, it encourages entire families to adopt a healthier life style. The technology for life-style intervention developed at Stanford is described in further detail in several earlier reports [6, 12, 15, 19, 24].

Commentary

The evolution of study design to test public health programs that involve life-style intervention has been discussed in a collection of papers published recently as a symposium on CHD prevention trials [3, 5, 9, 20, 23]. The issues are examined further in Table 2, contrasting the designs of the two life-style intervention trials (MRFIT and the 5CP) with the more familiar design of the LRC drug trial.

Clinical trials of life-style intervention are generally not suitable for *testing etiologic hypotheses* such as the diet–heart hypothesis. This is because aspects of life-style do not lend themselves to the role of experimental variable; they are diffuse, hard to measure, complex, and confounded by other variables. Intervention magnifies these difficulties due to

TABLE 2
Consequences of the Choice of Design of the CHD Prevention Trials[a]

	LRC	MRFIT	5CP
I. Recap of Design Features			
A. Type of trial	Clinic-based drug	Clinic-based life-style	Community-based life-style
B. Experimental unit	Individuals	Individuals	Cities
C. Kind of control	Randomized	Randomized	Not randomized
D. Independent variable	Double blind	Not blind	Not blind
E. Dependent variable	Blind	Assessment not blind	Assessment not blind
		Adjudication blind	Adjudication blind
II. Consequences of the Choice of Design			
A. Main purpose			
1. Testing etiologic hypothesis	Yes	No	No
2. Testing efficacy of health program	No	Yes	Yes
B. Magnitude of impact on CHD risk			
1. of an individual	Low	High	Medium
2. of the nation as a whole	Low	Medium	High
C. Generalizability (external validity)	Low	Medium	High
D. Strength of causal inference (internal validity)	High	Medium	Low
E. Relative cost of the trial	High	High	Medium
F. Philosphical desirability of the intervention	(Low) Medium	Medium	High
G. Ethical suitability	Medium	Medium	Medium
H. Amount of "spin-off" information	Medium	Medium	High
I. Relevance to health policy	High	High	High

[a]The valuations are the judgments of the authors, and are explained in the text.

problems of standardization and adherence. Therefore, trials of modifying life-styles are more suited for the practical function of *testing* the *efficacy* of *programs* for improving health.

Drug trials, on the other hand, can be focused on a particular etiologic link by virtue of their single, discrete independent variable. The LRC trial of cholestyramine has its chief implications as a surrogate test of the diet–heart hypothesis, and is much less important as a test of medical policy regarding cholestyramine; a program to modify dietary habits has wider applicability than a drug regimen.

The disadvantage, insofar as etiologic hypothesis testing is concerned, of the multifactorial nature of life-style trials is offset by several advantages. The overall *magnitude* of the calculated *reduction in CHD risk* of the participants is greater, improving the power of the experiment and the importance of its conclusion. This has been particularly true of the clinic-based model, where larger reductions in risk factor values have been observed [18]. On the other hand, the projected impact of these trials on the risk of the entire U.S. population is greater for the 5CP because of the greater cost-effectiveness and wider impact of community-directed intervention. Another advantage of multifactor trials is the fact that the general knowledge of risk factors in this country has made it very difficult to carry out a trial of a single factor such as diet without influencing other habits such as exercise and smoking. Finally, the multifactor approach seems likely to produce the most relevant answer, as it tests the actual program of interest to practitioners of preventive medicine.

The *generalizability* of the 5CP exceeds that for either the LRC trial or the MRFIT. The study participants of the latter two trials are a select group of health-conscious individuals, so findings in these particular samples of the U.S. population may not be applicable to Americans generally. The generalizability of the LRC trial is lower than that of MRFIT because of uncertainty contributed by the surrogate nature of the independent variable; the MRFIT interventions are more directly relevant.

The strength of *causal inference* is weakest for the 5CP because of the multiplicity and low specificity of the independent variables, because the dependent variable is susceptible to more sources of bias in the absence of a defined cohort, and because statistical analysis of the results will consider the findings as derived from a sample of only five—the total number of cities involved. The LRC trial provides the strongest causal inference because its single, discrete, independent variable can be administered in double-blind fashion to minimize the potential for bias.

The *cost* of all three trials is great relative to conventional medical research studies, but small when one considers the potential magnitude of the impact of the results on the cost of CHD morbidity and mortality in the nation as a whole. Of the three trials, the 5-City Project is the most cost-effective, owing to reliance on mass media and on catalyzing existing community health resources for delivering the intervention and to the use of surveys and surveillance for assessing its results. The resulting efficiency has the further advantage of permitting the study to be carried out by a single group of scientists at Stanford, which streamlines the process of making scientific and administrative decisions.

The nature of the intervention used in the 5CP is also more desirable on a *philosophical* level. For one thing, self-care is preferred by many over the medical model approach. Also, this is the only test of primary prevention, with the potential for preventing risk factors from occurring in the first place. Thus, the healthy life-style being recommended to all people from an early age could ultimately eliminate the need for screening. Comparing the LRC with the MRFIT, the philosophical disadvantage of the attention to drugs in the former becomes a minor issue if one considers this trial a surrogate test of dietary intervention.

The *ethical* basis for randomized trials such as the LRC and MRFIT is the philosophy that persons may volunteer to receive either of two programs when the net benefit of one over the other is not established. This reasoning is sound unless, as is often the case, the investigator's assessment of the available evidence suggests that one of the programs is probably superior. In this event, the following question arises: Should not the participants receive the benefit of this judgment even in the absence of conclusive proof? The 5CP, on the other hand, has its own ethical dilemma. Is it appropriate to promote controversial health policy through mass media that reach citizens who have not requested the information or signed informed consent? Even if the program does reduce disease rates, the distinction between informing, persuading, and coercing remains difficult. None of these trials is entirely free of ethical concern.

All three of these trials have enormous potential for providing *"spin-off" information*. For example, the selection of hypercholesterolemic participants for the LRC provided a superb data base for epidemiologic studies of the lipoproteins and their determinants in various populations. The MRFIT has great potential for examining previously unresolved natural history issues using correlational analyses (it is the first major study that includes assessment of all the major psychosocial risk factors in a single population) and for studying the influence of tobacco and diet on various cancers. The 5CP is widely recognized as a forum for developing improved methods for community-wide education, using mass media and face-to-face contact to assist individuals in achieving self-directed change. The 5CP will also be the first general application of community surveillance for cardiovascular morbidity and mortality over a period of years, permitting the critical issue of secular trends in cardiovascular case fatality rate to be examined. All three trials have involved scientists from such widely different disciplines as biochemistry, epidemiology, medicine, behavioral sciences, communication, and sociology, and this collaboration has resulted in new perspectives on both disease and research. These examples demonstrate the value of large trials above and beyond their specified *raison d' être*.

Conclusions

The bottom line of all medical research is its relevance to the development of *health policy*. For the three trials considered here, this issue is exemplified by considering a major controversy in behavioral medicine, the diet–heart hypothesis. Although previous research has strongly implicated the contribution of a cholesterol-raising diet to CHD [10, 21], implementation of national policy toward a fat-controlled diet has been hindered by the difficulty in proving beyond reasonable doubt that diet is a *cause* of coronary heart disease [13], and therefore that dietary intervention is beneficial. The residual uncertainty, and the counterpressure from financial and other interests, have hindered the development of a coherent national prevention effort promoting a fat-controlled diet.

While clinical trials are not the only approach to increasing scientific understanding of these issues [14], they may be an inescapable part of the process [1,4,8,20]. We have shown that each of three major kinds of clinical trials has its own particular advantages and disadvantages. What should be equally clear is the complementary nature of the various approaches, and the relevance of all three to life-style intervention policy and to the preventive medicine of the future.

References

1. Blackburn, H.: Multifactor preventive trials in CHD. In *Trends in Epidemiology*, ed. G. Stewart, pp. 212–230. Springfield, Ill.: Charles C Thomas, 1972.
2. Collaborating Investigators: The Multiple Risk Factor Intervention Trial (MRFIT). *Journal of the American Medical Association* 235:825–828, 1976.
3. Cornfield, J.: Randomization by group: a formal analysis. *American Journal of Epidemiology* 108:100–102, 1978.
4. Davis, C. E.; and Havlik, R. J.: Clinical trials of lipid lowering and coronary artery disease prevention. In *Hyperlipidemia: Diagnosis and Therapy*, eds, B. M. Rifkind and R. I. Levy, pp. 79–92. New York: Grune and Stratton, 1977.
5. Farquhar, J. W.: The community-based model of life style intervention trials. *American Journal of Epidemiology* 108:103–111, 1978.
6. Farquhar, J. W.: *The American Way of Life Need Not Be Hazardous to Your Health*. New York: Norton, 1978.

7. Farquhar, J. W.; Maccoby, N.; Wood, P. D.; Alexander, J.K.; Breitrose, H.; Brown, B. W.; Haskell, W. L.; McAlister, A. L.; Meyer, A. J.; Nash, J. O.; Stern, M. P.: Community education for cardiovascular health. *Lancet* 1:1192–1195, 1977.
8. Fredrickson, D. S.: The field trial: some thoughts on the indispensible ordeal. *Bulletin of the New York Academy of Medicine* 44:985–993, 1968.
9. Hulley, S. B.: Symposium on CHD prevention trials: design issues in testing life style intervention. *American Journal of Epidemiology* 108:85–86, 1978.
10. Hulley, S. B.; and Sherwin, R. S.: Epidemiology as a guide to clinical decisions: II Diet and coronary heart disease. *Western Journal of Medicine*, in press.
11. Maccoby, N.; Farquhar, J. W.; Wood, P. D.; and Alexander, J.: Reducing the risk of CV disease: effects of a community-based campaign on knowledge and behavior. *Journal of Community Health* 3:100–114, 1977.
12. McAlister, A. L.; Farquhar, J. W.; Thoresen, C. E.; and Maccoby, N.: Behavioral science applied to cardiovascular health. *Health Education Monographs* 4:45–74, 1976.
13. Mann, G. V.: Diet-heart: end of an era. *New England Journal of Medicine* 297:644–650, 1977.
14. Marmot, M.; and Winkelstein, W.: Epidemiologic observations on intervention trials for prevention of CHD. *American Journal of Epidemiology* 101:177–181, 1975.
15. Meyer, A. J.; Nash, J. D.; McAlister, A. L.; Maccoby, N.; Farquhar, J. W.: Skills training in a cardiovascular health education campaign. *Journal of Consulting and Clinical Psychology* 48:129–142, 1980.
16. MRFIT Research Group: Statistical design considerations in the MRFIT. *Journal of Chronic Disease* 30:261–275, 1977.
17. MRFIT Research Group: The MRFIT. *Annals of the New York Academy of Sciences* 304:293–308, 1978.
18. MRIFT Research Group: Primary prevention of heart attacks: the MRFIT. *American Journal of Epidemiology* 112:185–199, 1980.
19. Nash, J. D.; and Farquhar, J. W.: Community approaches to dietary modification and obesity. *Psychiatry Clinics of North America* 1:713–724, 1978.
20. Sherwin, R.: Controlled trials of the diet-heart hypothesis: some comments on the experimental unit. *American Journal of Epidemiology* 108:92–99, 1978.
21. Stamler, J.: Life styles, major risk factors, proof and public policy. *Circulation* 58:3, 1978.
22. The LRC Program: The Coronary Primary Prevention Trial: Design and Implementation. *Journal of Chronic Disease* 32:609–631, 1979.
23. Syme, S. L.: Life style intervention in clinic-based trials. *American Journal of Epidemiology* 108:87–91, 1978.
24. Taylor, C. B.; Farquhar, J. W.; Nelson, E.; and Agras, S.: Relaxation therapy and high blood pressure. *Archives of General Psychiatry* 34:339–342, 1977.

Neoplastic
Disease

Behavioral Issues in Cancer

BERNARD H. FOX

The research literature on behavior in medicine has, until very recently, been fragmented; the topic has been viewed either within the confines of behavior theory with medicine as the circumstantial milieu, or within medicine, behavior theory being dragged in as an afterthought. Only recently have the two coalesced, the close relationship having been observed and the need for knowledge about that relationship appreciated [4]. When this happened, various things were done about it. Among them, an American Psychological Association (APA) Section on Health Research was created in 1975, after a task force, formally organized in 1973, explored the area; this Academy held its first meeting in 1978; the Institute of Medicine, National Academy of Sciences (established 1970) created a Division of Mental Health and Behavioral Medicine in 1978; a new journal [50] was established in 1978; and a new APA Division of Health Psychology was formally created on January 1, 1979. A number of other related events, too numerous to describe, also took place.

A central theme leading to all of them, however, was the fact that medicine encompasses not only the biology of man and animals, but that it also must include their more molar reactions as individuals, their interindividual interactions, their group behavior—whether family, community, cultural, national, general societal, or that defined by circumstance or assigned category—and finally, the interactions among the biological and behavioral states and changes.

One would think that there would be no need to point to the importance of cancer as an area for behavioral medicine research within the whole group of human diseases and dysfunctions. But that has not been true in the past [93], or even now [4]. It is an important area. Some 16% of all deaths are due to cancer, and about one in four of all people will get cancer during their lifetime. The phenomena associated with the disease evoke the very depths of human emotion, with consequent behavior worthy of the most searching inquiry. Unlike most common diseases, the symptoms are not uniform and recognizable, for three reasons: First, cancer is not one disease but more than 100, so that a tumor at any site can provoke any of a number of different disruptions of function. Second, one of the most unusual aspects of the disease is that cancer cells are a kind of mutation; the exact genetic character of the altered cells varies enormously, and can mimic the function of many of the body's existing cells, including hormonal ones. Thus, for example, a stomach or liver or bone tumor can produce ACTH, with associated confounding of proper function in the pituitary–adrenal axis. Third, whatever effects a primary tumor produces by virtue of its location (e.g., a colon tumor may occlude the digestive tract, with its associated symptoms), such a tumor can produce a large variety of symptoms depending on where it metastasizes. The damage is in part defined by the new location. Such a colon tumor may cause blindness, for example, or intolerance to toxic substances, or psychosis, if it metastasizes to the eye, liver, or brain, respectively.

Partly because of the aforementioned facets of the disease, but also because of a number of other characteristics peculiar to cancer, it has many aspects that lead to the need to attack the research problems of this disease uniquely. To address some of them, the following categories, based on one of the many classifications of health behaviors, are suggested as a convenient framework for describing important areas of research in respect to cancer: epidemiology (descriptive and etiological), prevention, detection, diagnosis, treatment, rehabilitation, continuing care, terminal illness, and the posthumous phase.

Throughout the discussion, I shall refer to studies that are peculiar to cancer because of the nature of the disease, and to unsolved problems that are interesting in their own right, whether unique to cancer or not.

Epidemiology

This discipline offers broad opportunities for behaviorally related research. A number of behaviors are associated with incidence of cancer, and many increase the risk of getting it. In addition, many conditions or their associated behaviors, and many behaviors whose psychic precursors are not primarily at issue, are suspected of leading to cancer incidence or to changes in its progress. A sampling of these, listed in Table 1 (adapted from [33]), will serve to give their flavor. A personal view of confidence that

TABLE 1
Examples of Conditions That Have Been Associated with Altered Risk of Cancer or Changes in Its Prognosis[a]

A. WHAT PEOPLE ARE, OR WHAT HAPPENS TO THEM PERSONALLY.

1. **Demographic and social characteristics**
   Sex; age; socioeconomic level; marriage; race; religion; local culture; ethnicity; geographic location—world, country, region, urban–rural, rainfall, 1–4[b].

2. **Psychological characteristics**
   Life stress, both short and long term, 4; personality, inferred from both interview and test or scale items, 4; attitudes, 3–4; neurologic symptoms, 4; mental illness, 3–4; lack of knowledge, 3–4.

3. **Physical characteristics**
   Somatotype, 4; specific body dimensions—structure, 4; obesity, 2–3; height and weight, 3; breast size, 4; hair color, 4; complexion and eye color, 1–3; age-related balding, 4.

4. **Congenital and genetic traits**
   Age at menarche (suspected to be mostly nutrition-related), 3–4; age at menopause, 4; family history of cancer, 1–4; congenital deficiency or abnormality (e.g., villous polyps, immune deficiency), 1–4.

5. **Other diseases and pathology**
   Skin keratoses, 1–3; kidney or bladder stones, 4; traumata, scars, burns, 3–4; communicable diseases, 2–4; tissue irritation, 3–4; leukoplakia, 2–4; cell dysplasias, 2–4; various viral diseases, 4; trichomonas, 3–4; schistosomiasis, 3–4.

B. WHAT PEOPLE DO TO THEMSELVES

1. **Habits**
   Drinking, 2–4 (with smoking 1); tobacco (smoking, chewing, snuff), 1; coffee, 4; marijuana, 4; narcotics (reduced risk, cervical cancer?!), 4; tea, 4; betel with lime, 2.

2. **Customs and cultural behavior**
   a. *Cultural habits*
   Sun cult, 2; breast feeding, 4; age at marriage, 2–4; age at first intercourse (women), 1–2; number of sex partners, 3; wife has cervical cancer, 4; age at birth of first child, 2; circumcision, 2–4; certain sick pets, 4; eating habits, 4.

   b. *Hygiene*
   Washing, douching, 4; mouth cleanliness, 4.

C. DIET

1. **Natural components and lacks**
   Amount eaten, 2–4; cholesterol, 4; fats and beef, 3–4; vitamin deficiencies, 1–4; carcinogens (e.g., nitrosamine, aflatoxin), 1; tannin, 4; magnesium, iron, iodine, selenium deficiencies, 1–2.

2. **Processing effects**
   Refined foods and lost bulk, 3–4; preservatives and colorants, 4; water purification, 4.

D. WHAT IS DONE TO PEOPLE

1. **Environmental pollution**
   Pesticides, herbicides, 3–4; air pollution, 2–4; water pollution, 4; ionizing radiation, 1–4; nonionizing radiation or fields, 4.

TABLE 1 *(cont.)*

    2. Occupation

       X-ray, 1; uranium, 1; asbestos, 1; arsenic, 1; polyvinyl chloride, 1; benzene, 1–2; ben-z[a]pyrene, 1; other organic substances, 1–4; sun, 2; nonionizing radiation, 4. These must be coupled with dangerous nonbehaviors (i.e., failure to protect against the known presence of carcinogens), 1–4.

    3. Possible iatrogenic effects

       Drugs (e.g., for cancer treatment, for postmenopausal symptoms, to prevent miscar-riage), 1–4; X-ray for diagnosis, 3–4; for therapy, 1–4; irritation by prosthetics, 4; im-munosuppression (e.g., for transplantation), 1–2; errors in diagnosing precancerous states, 2–4; errors in diagnosing cancer, very few, but regularly occurring, 1; tonsillec-tomy, 4.

E. ANIMALS

    1. What they are

       Strain variations in susceptibility to both spontaneous and induced cancer, 1.

    2. What is done to them

       Animal feed variations, 1–2; animal bedding variation, 4; variations in stress of nor-mal environment, 3–4; abnormal stress riding on usual environmental stress, 1; prenatal stress to mother, 3–4; early versus late stress, 1; stress before carcinogenic treatment, early versus late, 1–2; stress before or after carcinogenic treatment, 1; condi-tioning of immune system, 1.

    [a]Adapted from [33].

    [b]My personal judgment of confidence or range of confidence that the condition cited is connected with the incidence or progress of various cancers: 1—certain; 2—high to moderate; 3—moderate to low; 4—suspi-cion or speculation, often based on only one study or several questionable ones.

there is a connection with incidence or prognosis is given on a scale of 1 (certain) to 4 (based only on suspicion, speculation, or a possibility stem-ming from theory). Many are cited with a range of confidence because the factor cited has been shown to have greater or lesser connection dependent on cancer site, sex, age, ethnic identity, or other contingent condition. For example, log of rate of total U.S. cancer incidence is an almost perfect linear function of age from about 10 years to about 60 years, after which the rate of increase slows, approaching zero at age 85 (incidence rate at that age was about 2100/100,000 per year in the interval 1973–1976 [97]). The confidence scale score would be 1 for incidence in those 50 years but 2–4 for disease progress. The confidence that stomach cancer differs among races by virtue of genetic characteristics is 3–4. This rating follows the find-ings of Haenszel *et al.* [43] that in Hawaii the rate of Nisei—second genera-tion Japanese—having more Western diets approached that of Hawaiian long-term natives, but the rate of Issei—first generation immigrants—re-mained close to that of their Japanese prefectures of origin, although the diet-related findings for Japan itself differed from that somewhat.

    In view of the aforementioned behavioral associations with cancer in-cidence and progress, what kind of behavioral research is possible? First, the actual seeking out of descriptive associations of behaviors with cancer incidence and progress is an important goal. For example, one such finding was that, in women, early intercourse and/or many partners are among the factors associated with increased risk of cervical cancer. This is a fairly broadly accepted view, having been verified in a number of population groups [e.g., 87]. Even here, however, there are muddy waters, and an interesting research problem is presented. One would expect that female prison inmates should have higher rates of positive Pap smears than the population, and so they do—about sixfold [75]. But women with presumably similar sexual histories—drug addicts, treated in the Public Health Service facility at Lexington, Kentucky—have about one-ninth the number of abnormal smears in prison inmates, and about one-eighth the number of malignancies [109], perhaps even fewer than the population. This unexpected finding has gone unremarked in the research community, but could be pursued, even if it is difficult logistically.

A number of factors in other cancers, however, are only tentatively connected with the incidence of cancer. Examples are presence of certain sick pets [13] (the relation does not hold for well pets); and, more demographically oriented, children living near high-current sources —transformer stations, high-tension lines—were at increased risk of cancer [111]. Repetition of the latter studies is needed to increase or decrease confidence in the tentative findings.

Another whole class of epidemiologic studies relates to personality and stress or precursors of increased cancer risk. A number of reviews of these studies have appeared [1, 3, 7, 15, 21, 34, 47, 60, 67]. Most of the past epidemiologic studies examining incidence of cancer (excluding mental disease) draw inferences from retrospective data in which the effects of the probably already existent cancer in the cases is either overlooked or downgraded. Such studies inspire little confidence. Prospective studies of this type in which measures were taken (more or less) clearly before the occurrence of cancer have been few [23, 44, 52, 60, 68, 72, 99, 106]. Of these studies, some have serious defects in design [e.g., 23], suffer from analytic problems [e.g., 44], are questionable on the basis of variables difficult to control [e.g., 52], or have unspecified controls [e.g., 68]. Ongoing studies by Paffenbarger [72] and Shekelle [99] have yielded provocative results [66, 10]. Because of their differing test measures they are not necessarily comparable. They point up, however, a major need in behavioral medicine research: in normals, resolving the role of psychological factors and stress as precursors to cancer, and further down the road, if they are found to be precursors, their role in etiology of cancer—causes or just associated variables.

The putative role of psychosis as a protector against cancer has been rehashed several times. Perhaps the best review of the issue is that of DuPan and Müller [29], but others have written on the subject [35, 51, 76, 91]. Although much of the evidence points to a negative answer, the exact state of affairs is still not completely settled, especially the open issue of whether paranoid tendencies in a psychotic yield excess risk of cancer, rather than protection—a suggestion from the data appearing in several believable papers. It is a problem worthy of challenge to our better investigators because of its complexity.

Epidemiology is not restricted to descriptive data and etiology of diseases. Studies of factors affecting disease progress, aside from treatment, evoke considerable interest, and are among the more feasible types of studies in cancer epidemiology. A number of studies on behavioral factors relating to cancer recurrence and survival have been done, but mostly paper and pencil measures. Almost all of them have yielded conclusions unsatisfactory to the critical observer, sometimes because of failure to control for certain variables, sometimes because of the number of cases was too small, sometimes because of faulty analysis. They have been epidemiological in the sense that they examine states in nature, rather than experimental in the sense of having deliberately altered such natural states. In this whole domain, one poorly explored research area cuts across the epidemiology of both disease initiation and disease progress—active behavior, as opposed to personality. Such behavior can be mostly externally initiated, as in stress, or self-initiated, as in smoking or drinking. A few examples will illustrate. There is a whole array of stressful occupations whose relation to cancer is unknown: ghetto school teachers, traffic controllers, social workers, cancer nurses, workers in high noise environments. There is a whole array of life-style components in this and other countries whose role is quite unexplored in relation to cancer incidence. These are of interest since the cross-national and cross-cultural statistics show major variations, which have led to some hypotheses. The data become heuristically very provocative when they show, as they have many times, that immigrants' cancer incidence approaches that of the new country, usually reaching it when full integration of newborns into the society and its mores has taken place. But stress changes could also be in the picture.

Epidemiologic interest in cancer has been focussed on animals for a very long time. The animal model forms one of the most promising resources for study of human cancer, provided that we can transfer the findings confidently. In the animal we have now found a place for conditioning as a mechanism for affecting the immune system, which is a vital element in animal cancer susceptibility [2]. The carcinogenicity of certain substances and the protective role of some bodily substances may be more easily explored using behavioral stimuli [12]. The role of stress in the postponement or hastening of cancer has been broadly examined, but because of the variety of results (not necessarily contradictory, but certainly confusing), the field cries out for clarification. Riley's observation alone [83] may require the redoing of scores of studies under better controlled conditions. The connection of the hypothalamus and the immune system [84, 102] yields a sizable body of work that must be joined with the stress work on immunity and on cancer incidence and mortality to form an integrated theoretical structure; simultaneously, we continue to ask and must examine how well the human state conforms to such an animal model structure.

A fascinating possibility in animal work is the application of signal detection theory, so heavily pursued during our recent wars. Swets' description [105] of ROC (receiver operating characteristic) in medical work is well known. It would be of great interest to apply ROC theory to the accuracy of animal pathologists' judgments about severity of dysplasia in the slides of different tissues following animal challenge with various substances being tested for carcinogenicity. This test situation would require different theoretical tactics in ROC analysis. For this problem, Fox [32] suggested the mean or median of a pathologists' panel, similar to a Delphic technique, as a first approximation. Together with that, he suggested associated confidence statements by the tested pathologists as an independent adjustor of certain ROC measures.

Lastly in the epidemiologic picture, we have moved very slowly from association to causation, and we may be able to create some more potent hypotheses by use of path analysis. This avenue has already been explored tentatively in respect to demographic and some social variables, but is wide open for further work [39].

Prevention

In a number of medical areas we are observing a convergence of interest and effort toward prevention. It has taken a long time, but the repeated and hoary calculations of those concerned with relative benefit in general health areas, almost all pointing toward more benefit from prevention than treatment, seem to be making an impact. Cancer prevention is no exception. I believe that one main reason for this rising interest is the appearance of a number of epidemiologic findings on which prevention efforts can focus. When we did not know what to attack in a prevention program, we could not carry it out. Now we do know some things, and the number of practical preventive actions is increasing as we do more research.

The problem of prevention is of prime interest to behavioral medicine researchers in all areas, since behavior is so critical to prevention. The investment in biology, chemistry, and other laboratory sciences in cancer treatment, however, has been much larger than in behavior.

We can divide prevention into three kinds: primary, which addresses the prevention of the initial appearance of cancer; secondary, which deals with catching the person who has cancer at as early a stage as possible—that is, detection; and tertiary, which is essentially the prevention of bad sequellae of disease and treatment after diagnosis. I shall discuss the latter two in later sections.

The cancer prevention researcher is confronted with a broad range of behavior types in primary prevention. If we look at the epidemiology of cancer, we quickly see various classes of behavior that might be changed to effect a lower risk of cancer. It must be pointed out, parenthetically, that a great deal of the risk of cancer is at present a matter of chance [62]. This point is important to make, lest anyone think that adopting currently available preventive behavior will reduce cancer incidence radically. It would reduce the risk some, but not eliminate it. Chance sources, for example, include background radiation, cumulative traces of carcinogens in foods, and exposure to ambient unavoidable carcinogens such as benz[a]pyrene in auto exhaust. These exposures interact with unknown personal susceptibility.

Many conditions cannot be altered at all by behavior change, even if it is known that they or things associated with them increase or decrease risk (e.g., somatotype, hair color, complexion, eye color, race, height, menarcheal age, menopausal age, family history of cancer, and congenital deficiencies). Other things are very hard to change (e.g., socioeconomic level, marriage, geographic location). Others might be changed, but one would hardly expect either the individual or society to change them for the sake of cancer prevention (e.g., age at marriage, age at first intercourse in women, number of sexual partners, and age at birth of first child).

But other conditions can be affected by behavior change, and that possibility hinges on a number of issues. We already know that many people are not beginning to smoke or are reducing or stopping smoking for whatever reason. What will it take to increase that number? We think of school education; home influence; change in peer pressure; the multitude of smoking cessation devices; laws (restaurant nonsmoking areas, air travel nonsmoking seat privileges, no smoking in government employee conferences or meetings, and the like); and more general communication efforts such as union education.

Fox [33] described classes of behavior change sources. They are susceptible to a broad range of research inquiry (see Table 2). Changes in laws, regulations, work situations, communication, social habits, attitudes, and the like require techniques and devices well known to some but not to

Conditions Associated with Personal Characteristics or Behavior That Could Be Changed by Various Agents[a]

Condition[b]		Behavior by			
		Individual	Physician	Government	Industry
Psychological characteristics					
0	Life stress, attitudes, emotional reactivity	×			×
Physical characteristics					
?		×			
Other diseases and pathology					
? +	Communicable diseases	×	×	×	
0	Tissue irritation	×			
Habits					
+	Drinking	×	×		
+	Smoking, chewing, snuff	×	×	×	×
0 ?	Marijuana	×	×		
Customs and culture					
+	Sun cult	×	×		
0	Age of marriage	×			
0	Eating habits	×	×		
0	Living habits	×			
?	Personal hygiene	×			
?	Intercourse, age of initiating, multiple partners	×			
Diet, natural components					
+	Amount eaten	×	×		
?	Fat, protein	×	×		
+	Severe vitamin deficiency	×	×		
?	Mineral deficiency	×	×		
0	Carcinogens (e.g., aflatoxin)			×	×
Diet, processing effects					
?	Refined foods and lost bulk	×	×	×	×
?	Preservatives and coloring			×	×
?	Water purification			×	×
Environmental pollution					
0 ?	Pesticides (home use, industry)	×		×	×
?	Air pollution (tires, exhaust, factories	×		×	×
?	Water pollution (tires, exhaust, factories, purification processes)	×		×	×
?	Excessive radioactivity			×	×

TABLE 2 *(cont.)*

		Behavior by		
Condition[b]	Individual	Physician	Government	Indust
Occupation				
+ Known carcinogens			×	×
+ Dangerous nonbehaviors (not wearing masks, careless contact with radioactive materials)	×		×	×
Possible iatrogenic effects				
+ Carcinogenic drugs		×		
+ X ray therapy and diagnosis		×		
? Prosthetics		×		
? Immunosuppression (e.g., from transplantation medication)		×		
+ Errors in detecting and diagnosing precancerous sites		×		

[a]All the entries, both categories and judgments, reflect personal views and are not necessarily official views. (Adap from [33]).

[b] + implies that a clear-cut improvement in cancer risk could be achieved;
　? implies that a questionable amount of improvement could be achieved;
　0 implies that behavior change would affect cancer risk little or not at all or that beh ior change is very difficult to bring about.

others. Some cannot be successful here in any case because our social structure differs from that of more authoritarian countries, democratic though they may be—Sweden, Germany, Canada, and Japan, for example. It is a difficult struggle to move population behavior in a given direction.

A whole set of research problems is posed by the ethical issues of prevention. If people are frightened by certain information on cancer prevention, what information and its outcomes are acceptable to the public, to the purveyors of the information, to the legislature, to the receiver of the information? Attitude or behavior on this whole topic is right now mostly at the stage of expressing that pious dictum—"we need to do research on that topic." The whole area of cost-effectiveness and cost–benefit forms part of the ethics issue. For example, if a preventive action will delay by 1 year the appearance of cancer in 0.1% of the population in their late 60s, how much fright or concern or behavior change or cost to how many people is worth such a delay? Since probability of lung cancer rises as the 4.5 power of the duration of smoking [28], and the median age of getting cancer involves a 40–50 year exposure, then delaying youthful smoking by 2 years involves about a 20–25% change in the proportion getting cancer after an average smoking history $[(42/40)^{4.5}$ or $(47/45)^{4.5}]$. How much is it worth to society to achieve such delay? Such issues have not been explored well or brought into the decision factories of industry, government, or private institutions.

Smoking, which is a major cause of cancer, has been the subject of much behavioral research, but a number of problems remain to be solved. Since 90% of all who stop smoking do so on their own, what is the natural history of smoking cessation? Can we identify the groups who will be most susceptible to each of the various approaches to cessation, to allow targeting of techniques? Is there a way of getting more accurate estimates of actual smoking in surveys, in view of the 10–40% discrepancies between reported smoking levels and those projected by consumption figures [108], as well as the 10–25% discrepancies when validating self-report by chemical means in cessation efforts [71, 112]?

Similar research in relation to drinking is indicated, although drinking is carcinogenic mostly in association with smoking, helping to produce oropharyngeal and esophageal cancers.

In respect to carcinogens in the workplace, there is a major research need. The agencies involved—industry, government, unions—and the individual's needs complicate the picture severely. Self-protection by the worker is often very uncomfortable (heat increase with protective clothing, interference with easy breathing by masks) and expensive (safe work behavior may involve reduced output). It is possible to change workers' behavior [49], but the road will be long and hard. Industry is often unwilling to reduce exposure to carcinogens, denying in many clearly dangerous cases, and in almost all merely suggestive cases, that there is a danger at all. Unions are mixed, some pushing hard for improvement, others very little. Government requires very convincing proof before it will take an official action. The social forces associated with the history of uranium miners' work safety are very instructive [73]. The miners' experience teaches much about potential improvement because of the extent of their problem, and is the basis for potential research because of the variety of human interactions involved.

Another facet of industrial carcinogenesis is the issue of how to deal with workers who have been exposed earlier and are now retired. Should one tell former asbestos workers they are at severe risk? How much effort do you put into trying to stop them from smoking? If continuing to smoke is one of their few pleasures, what of the guilt induced by not stopping? What psychotherapy is advisable for such people? What prevention could we devise that would avoid or solve the deep emotional problems associated with people at very high risk who want to stop smoking? Similar important questions can be asked about such high-risk workers and workplaces.

Akin to that problem is a general one that has been asked by some concerned people. When discoveries about cancer risk are made, should the distributors of information balance the effect of publicizing these discoveries with the associated alarm (and worse) for the many among us who fear cancer generally, and the few who are truly cancerophobic (see

[48]), against the effect of not releasing such information? The criteria are at best fuzzy, officialdom is imbued with zeal to "let the people know," and if the discovery is published in a journal, there is no way to prevent the press from broadcasting the news. Are there any ways of dealing with the problem of cancer fear other than the patently unsuccessful one of trying to withhold information?

Detection

What behaviors are involved in detection? The doctor does physical examinations, applies instruments and machines, analyzes body fluids, and looks at slides of possibly cancerous or precancerous tissue. In physical examination the doctor palpates the breast or prostate, for example, and looks at unusual tissue states on or in the person. Examples of such tissue are leukoplakia or other dysplasia in the mouth or throat, dysplasia on the cervix (colposcopy), polyps in the rectum (proctoscopy), both changing and static nevi or other unusual growths on the skin, or lumps or hyperplasia anywhere. Not many studies have been done on the error rates in such tissue examination; one such is on breast tumor detection by palpation [98]. Although most asymptomatic—the most frequent type—breast cancers are detected by the patient or sex partner by palpation, the doctor's role involves similar breast search during various examinations (e.g., Pap smear, birth, or routine physical). In most of these no mammography is given, and although the latter is considerably more efficient at discovering small, early tumors [46], palpation is still the major technique for discovering breast cancer.

The level of error depends on many things. For example, we know that when colposcopy accompanies a Pap smear, the false negative rate falls considerably [107]. On the other hand, in examining for suspected melanoma, the average physician who, after eyeball inspection, refers a patient to a department of dermatology, has a false positive rate of about two out of three [17]. This is quite good from one point of view, since the physician noted a suspicious growth to begin with, but poor from another point of view. Few dentists in the past have paid much attention to asymptomatic erythroplastic (red) lesions of the oral cavity, recently found to be more indicative of cancer (when they persist) than the previously emphasized white patches [58]. The research of interest in the above areas may not be welcomed by the medical fraternity as a whole but the field of medical education and professional practice is heavily involved here, and specifically that of psychophysical measurement. As in research on slides, signal detection theory in the form of ROC analysis is immediately useful.

Screening procedures are special detection procedures whose objective is a quick overview of certain important disease markers, usually planned for application to numbers of people. For cervical cancer screening, colposcopy is often not feasible. In that case the screener has only a Pap smear when investigating cervical status; it is under those conditions, for example, that ROC analysis can be extremely valuable in determining error sources. This is also true of palpation in breast examination.

Not only does the physician do physical examination, however. He is also involved in educating the patient in self-examination, and in teaching procedures for new physicians who are being indoctrinated into the newly popular prevention catechism. There is potential for behavior research on attitudes of doctors [45], training in screening procedures, and the like.

This field is likely to become extremely important as the number of partial cancer markers increases. One can do several tests, and the development and application of these tools for screening offers opportunity for much valuable study.

As for the target of the detection process, the potential cancer victim, there exists a substantial literature. It is true here, as in most fields, that where we are quite secure about the facts, little research is engendered. Where there is high variability, considerable uncertainty, and a wide-ranging distribution of characteristics or conditions, we will find persistent research. So it is in this field. There are classic papers on delay in going for a medical examination—with and without symptomatology [5, 42]. There is abundant work on attitudes toward various diseases [54, 104]; belief in having or not having cancer, usually when symptomatic, but sometimes when not; and a few papers on bringing about behavior change in respect to screening for cancer [e.g., 53].

Breast self-examination (BSE) cuts across both the above categories. For the behavioral scientist whose training has been focused on experimental areas, this topic is most challenging. It involves signal detection theory, but also experimental design, learning theory, and hardware design—artificial tumors of various sizes and densities in artificial breasts of various textures used for BSE training [103]. In these areas almost no work has been done. For those in other disciplines of behavior measurement and change, this area involves attitude measurement, psychometrics, compliance behavior, coping strategies, and cultural differences, to name only a few. In addition, cancer control agencies have a major interest in finding ways of stimulating population-wide BSE habits.

Some major problems remain to be explored. For example, in respect to behavior associated with screening, what differences are there among various cultures; gradients of education; races; other sociodemographic characteristics? In respect to the image of cancer and knowledge about it, can we change these to the point of screening response (some might ask whether we should)? An almost completely unexplored area is the understanding by people of the meaning of probabilities, rates, and frequencies in respect to cancer incidence, survival, and mortality. This bears both on reactions to screening needs and on the treatment area, to be dealt with below. The psychodynamics of delay in screening or personal medical examination is of great interest. How much delay is defensive? How many are aware of defenses? What kinds of defense are there? Who has them? Should they be breached? If so, how? If not, what advantage can be taken of them? Would one ever think of inducing them? Little or no work has been done on these questions. The delay issue, almost by definition, implies that the person has a symptom. What about "delay" in those who are non-symptomatic but have signs, pointed out by the doctor? Apply the same questions to them, and a whole new field of inquiry is opened up.

Diagnosis

At this point, we examine a major phase of behavior research in cancer: how the patient interacts with others. It is not entirely appropriate to separate phenomena occurring as a result of diagnosis from similar ones associated with treatment. For example, following (or preceding, in some cases, as will be shown below) diagnosis of cancer, we occasionally find depression. But such an event may well persist into the treatment phase; it may, indeed, be a continuation of the diagnosis-related depression, or it may not.

This topic and the kindred one of general psychiatric illness have shown a consistent connection with cancer. We expect the obvious symptoms associated with specific organs (e.g., an adrenal tumor sometimes produces hypo- or hyperplasia and consequent hypo- or hypersecretion of gluco- or mineralocorticoids). A pituitary tumor can provide hypersecretion of ACTH. However, any other tumor can also produce ACTH if the mutation leading to the cancer cell is of a specific kind (and lung cancer almost always does), together with all the symptoms associated with hypersecretion of ACTH by the pituitary itself. Such symptomatology is called a paraneoplastic effect because it comes from a different organ site. Many hormonal dysfunctions can be imitated, and more important—whether they come from hormonal, enzymatic, vascular, or other sources—many psychic symptoms can be seen [64]. Some preliminary work on frequency and type of psychic symptoms has been done, and although we know something about the descriptive association of these with tumors, our overall knowledge is very meager. For example, pancreatic tumors seem to have a strong (as such things go) relationship to depression [38], perhaps one-eighth of such tumors producing such symptoms before tumor diagnosis, sometimes years before. It has been suggested that when physicians encounter depression, they should consider as one possibility the existence of cancer [37]. In particular, such advice is appropriate for psychiatrists since clinical depression cases often wind up in their offices. Organic factors in cancer patients affect psychological adjustment in many ways and, both at the diagnostic stage and later, must be considered [24, 86]. Because the range of psychic symptoms is so broad [11], we have only scratched the surface in describing that class of paraneoplastic symptoms. A large field for research lies open to behavioral medicine investigators.

What was formerly a major issue is this country before the 1950s, for example, has gradually become a minor one in this country: Should the doctor tell the patient the nature of the disease? In Europe and elsewhere the practice of not telling the patient is widespread, but here almost all doctors now do tell the patient. What has not been settled, and may often be a major problem, is how and when to tell. The knowledgeable psychiatrist who has oncologic experience could advise the family physician or oncologist, but there are not very many psychiatrists with this kind of experience and usually neither the oncologist nor the family physicians will call on a psychiatrist for advice on this matter. Some research can be done, but at first it would probably be descriptive, and only later lead to improvements. In any case, an educational effort is needed. This should not be taken to mean that there are no insightful family physicians or oncologists; only that there are not enough.

The process of diagnosis and the events surrounding it probably have a potent effect on the patient's perceptions and reactions, both at the time of the events and later. Consider what happens. A person may feel sick or have an unusual symptom; or in a routine visit or during treatment of some other disease, the doctor discovers a suspicious sign or symptom; or the person has undergone a screening process and one of the findings is questionable. At this point, depending on how the findings were presented or what the self-noted symptoms were, the patient starts out with a potentially widely varying degree of suspicion that it is cancer. While it would be difficult research, a description of the range and character of beliefs and attitudes at such a point would be important in order to alert the people following up such cases to the variety of reactions possible, very probably not suspected by them. Once contact is made with the physician, a biopsy or other determining examination is suggested. Subtle cues and signs may well be conveyed by the doctor, who has, knowingly or not, already formed an estimate of the probability that the patient has cancer [34].

At the biopsy situation itself people are mostly worried, but sometimes not overtly. The large variety of defenses points to the need for contingent models of procedures with all patients—both prophylactic and therapeutic. The research to tell how to handle patients who display certain reactions has not been done. Indeed, we do not even have the tools to tell with great confidence what internal reactions they do have. The counsellor —psychiatrist, nurse, social worker, surgeon, oncologist, family physician—should be able to know what the patient thinks about or is worried about.

At the time of diagnosis, the word is either good or bad. While not particularly much research has been done on how to say that the word is bad, the subject has been examined; but I have never heard anyone even discuss how to handle the person for whom the word is good, let alone do research on the matter. Yet the risk of malignancy among those with certain benign tumors or unusual tissue such as polyps or cervical dysplasia or keratoses is greater than in the average person of equal age. Such knowledge should be made broadly available to physicians. We do not know how many do have it, and certainly we do not know how to give such information to the patient, to avoid excessive fear due to failure to understand the implications of a relative risk of two, or even three, for one particular tumor site.

Variations in coping capability during and after treatment have been well recognized for years. The questions raised by these variations, felt to be important by a number of workers, are whether one can identify beforehand those who, during treatment and rehabilitation, will handle the cancer and its treatment well or poorly; and if one can, what prophylactic or therapeutic procedures best deal with the poor responder. Recent papers give limited answers in regard to certain groups of cancer patients [65, 96, 110, 114] and a short review, prepared under contract with the National Cancer Institute on breast cancer patients, describes predictive assessments taken at various times after diagnosis and during treatment. The one immediately after diagnosis is relevant here. Some data have been tentatively analyzed but not yet written up [81]. Unfortunately, the preceding studies are weighted heavily toward breast cancer, and we have much less information on other cancers. Moreover, most of the data deal with prediction and almost none with evaluation, admittedly a far more difficult research task. A group in Sweden has been considering a study of combined prediction and evaluation [77], as is currently a group in Israel [78]. It seems that this area offers fertile soil for major research efforts.

Treatment

The treatment issue has many facets, and it will be possible only to mention some highlights here. Other sources give a more thorough view of the subject [22, 48, and as bibliographic sources, 22, 27, 70, 88]. A series of observations and relevant questions about breast cancer have been presented by Schain [90], many of which could form the basis for valuable research projects. Her point is that in much of the medical world's involvement with cancer patients, we have mostly clinical judgment, not research-based data, to provide guidelines for dealing with these patients.

After the biopsy confirms malignancy, the patient is often faced with a particularly difficult decision. Some doctors go ahead with the treatment they decide on, asking only whether the patient will accept it. For those who do, the decision is moot. Other doctors, however, may present the patient with options for treatment and ask that he or she make a choice. Almost all patients are completely unequipped to make such a choice. Even if the physician fills them in, they are usually not in any shape (partly because of their emotional state) either to apprehend the facts properly or to weigh them. The momentary criteria are quite different from what they might be under other conditions. Often the patient would not be able to make a reasoned judgment even without the emotional upset because the facts and issues are so foreign. But the most devastating situation, not at all uncommon, is the one in which the physician himself is quite in the dark as to the best course to follow, or what to tell a person. For example, the profession is now considering under what conditions a radical mastectomy, a total mastectomy, or a "lumpectomy" should be done. For some cases, this is quite clear. For others, it is not. Modern practice is tending toward fewer radicals in this country, but only during the last few years. Research by behavioral medicine workers might contribute to such judgments by detailing the quality of life and psychic changes associated with each. The physician can describe the physical sequellae of each procedure, but should their life-style consequences enter into the judgment [8, 9]?

Parallel to the issue of severity of ablative procedures, which appears in cases other than breast cancer, is that of one- or two-stage surgery. In the first, the surgeon operates, takes a biopsy sample for pathologic examination, and if it is cancerous, does the surgery, removing the malignant tissue. The patient has already agreed to the procedure if the finding is bad. In the second, after biopsy the patient wakes up and has time to reflect on the next decision, with possible options, after learning the biopsy outcome. The latter procedure is becoming much more common these days, due to at least two factors: Anesthesia and biopsy-taking have become safer over the years; and the efforts of behaviorally oriented professionals concerned with ethics, quality of life, and informed consent have finally borne fruit. To be sure, much of the research was clinical, but its yield was no less potent in this case than it would have been if controlled trials had been carried out.

It would be valuable to explore in greater depth, Schain [90] points out, the criteria for either explaining matters in detail to patients or only just enough to satisfy informed consent laws. Some people want and demand full disclosure of facts. Others act as deniers or repressers, and really do not want to dwell on unpleasant matters. Still others say they want to know, but act as if they do not. Identifying the various groups clearly and defining good practice toward them is an important research job, only a little of which has been done.

A varying amount of depression and anxiety is reported among patients under treatment. Some show moderately high levels [74] and some lower [79]. It is almost impossible to compare already published results in this area. Depression would be expected to be greater in those with more advanced disease, on grounds of anticipating earlier death or feeling less hope for a cure. But symptoms are also worse in advanced cases and depression has been shown to be a partial function of symptom severity [24] and treatment modality [20]. Add to these the variation in the measures used and differing ages of the patients (depression is a function of age), and the picture looks like a jigsaw puzzle whose pieces have been placed at random. We do not know much about emotional reactions to having cancer or being treated for cancer, and it would be valuable to know. The ironic aspect of the results of Cooper et al. [20], who showed that chemotherapy significantly improves survival over radiotherapy alone, is that at least in breast cancer [101], it also made patients feel worse than radiotherapy a year after treatment started (chemotherapy lasted a year, radiotherapy was over shortly after it started). The ethical problems again begin to emerge here.

When a patient learns the truth, many things go through his or her mind, all having a bearing on current and future emotional state. Among them are worries about pain, mutilation, body function loss, treatment effects, death, what will happen to the family, appearance, sex life, being a burden, and one's job. Counsellors should have some inkling of the dynamic processes of the patient, because many of these may lead to repression or denial, and they must decide under what conditions these psychological devices may be helpful to the patient.

Poor communication with the patient is very common, appearing not only in cancer treatment but also in the treatment of other diseases [55]. Uncertainty on the part of the physician may be at the root of some communication problems. Davis [25] specifies two kinds of uncertainty on the part of the doctor—clinical and functional. In the first, the doctor really does not know. In the second, the doctor knows, but acts as if he or she does not. Sometimes, moreover, although the doctor appears to be quite certain when telling the patient something, in the doctor's mind he or she is quite uncertain. In both cases, these things are done to manipulate the patient and family as the doctor thinks best. "Best," however, may involve keeping the patient from knowing that the doctor is uncertain, both for reasons beneficial to the patient and administrative management. It seems beneficial not to let the patient lose confidence in one of the few things he or she can hold onto at this bad time, namely, the doctor [61]. There are cases where a patient really wants to know and would achieve a desirable security from this knowledge. The doctor should be among the first to want to know how to distinguish those who would benefit from those who would not. This problem demands much work.

Very little research exists on why doctors, whose individual clinical experience leads them to act quite differently from one another, act the way they do in informing or not informing patients about projected survival, relapse, and side effects. Regarding side effects, which are fairly standard for many therapies, there is less variation in the communication. As to survival and relapse, they can be quite uncertain, although good normative figures are available for survival [6]. Relapse data are rather harder to come by, which may give a clue to part of the difficulty. The problem is that relapse has been much less investigated because of logistic impediments.

Communication with the patient is made difficult both because the doctor assumes that the patient knows the meanings of certain terms when he/she might not know them, but also because patients color the meanings of received messages according to subtle informal cues conveyed by the doctor and by their own hopes, wishes, and defenses. For an excellent discussion, see McIntosh [61]. This whole problem leads to many possibilities for research. What is well communicated? What is not? Why or why not? Under what clinical, personal, hospital, or demographic conditions do good and poor communication occur? How good are the perceptions of the doctor that this or that patient should be handled in one way or another? Perhaps more important, how do the communications and the way they are received affect the coping behavior of patients and their families?

The entrance of families into the picture complicates matters since they can be a source of telling, misinterpreting, not telling, and emotional reaction. Moreover, the doctor must deal with them as well as with the patient. The conspiracy of silence so often read about and seen is not an unusual event. The various aspects of the impact of the family on coping by the patient and of their own coping form a major set of research problems.

Some of the classic problems in treatment are well known, but have not been thoroughly addressed: effects of surgery, especially important to those with oropharyngeal or nasal cancer, which involves severe facial disfigurement; amputations, whether breast, leg, arm; organ removal with hormonal consequences (male or female castration, adrenal); physiologic effects (e.g., removal of intestinal organs with resulting effect on eating habits and bodily needs); and functional effects (e.g., colostomy, laryngeal dysfunction, nerve cutting leading to paralysis or anesthesia, impotence). Some of these effects have been worked on for a long time, and solutions have been approximated. To achieve good solutions, the problem is rather one of trying to get such information to where it is needed than to derive new techniques. We must thus deal with training research, information diffusion theory, public spending and priority issues, ethical issues, logistic problems, legal considerations, and sometimes politics, all researchable.

Many difficulties are encountered in preparation for and recovery from surgery, and are due to the side effects of various adjuvant therapies. In surgery, amputation involves a major psychic trauma, requiring fundamental readjustment of self-image [92]. The emotional upheaval is difficult to deal with by the patient, by the doctor and paramedical people, and by relatives. How to understand what is going on inside each patient and to determine what course is best form important research objectives that should be attacked diligently. Where there is no amputation the usual difficulties attending the postsurgery patient apply here, but in the case of cancer there is an added ingredient, fear for one's life. This produces more extreme and varied reactions in postsurgery patients than one usually finds, and puts a greater strain on the coping capabilities of the patient, medical community, and family than surgery unaccompanied by threat to life. Most research thus far has merely recounted and detailed the nature of such problems, but little research has addressed possible solutions to them [57].

The problems associated with adjuvant therapy are important. The most widely used therapies are irradiation, chemotherapy, and hormones. Irradiation can be whole-body or local and can come from various sources—x-ray, high energy particles (e.g., cyclotron), or radioactive implants. Side effects can include nausea, vomiting, hair loss, skin rashes, and loss of appetite. While very distressing the therapy is less threatening or damaging emotionally than chemotherapy because its duration is seldom longer than a month, and side effects are usually gone within another month (except hair loss, because of slow regrowth). Various hormone therapies can induce several disturbances—of temperature control, menstrual dysfunction, impotence, weight change, "moon face," loss of sexual desire, and edema, among others. Chemotherapy can last 2 years or longer, and is often accompanied by nausea, vomiting, loss of appetite, hair loss, and skin rashes. With some chemical agents neurological symptoms appear. With most, there is immunosuppression of various kinds and degrees—depression of bone marrow function, platelet, and white count are often found, and sometimes that of polymorphonuclear cells. Sometimes the gut lining is affected, with persistent diarrhea. Occasionally there is hemorrhage and obstipation. Moreover, chemotherapy is often not used until relapse or metastasis; the psychological effects of the latter interact with the physical and psychological effects of chemotherapy, and make for a difficult period for both the treated and treating.

Special treatment is needed and special problems arise during chemotherapy under some conditions. For example, usual chemotherapy tends to induce immune suppression of varying degree. When the suppression is severe, the patient may have to be physically isolated to prevent infection, since defense against infection has been virtually wiped out by the chemotherapy. Where patients agree to the isolation after having it explained to them, it is tolerable, although they complain of not being able to get comfort from touching [48]. When a child is thus isolated, it can be much more hurtful—even damaging, both because of the need for touching and the usually arbitrary imposition of the isolation without thorough explanation or personal involvement of the child in the decision.

All of these impose burdens on the patient, the doctor, and the family. Taking into account the discomfort, the fright, the anticipated social problems, and possible death, patient reaction can be strong. There may be failure of compliance (missed appointments), feelings of guilt, feelings of anger which may be displaced onto doctor or family, depression, anxiety, and in the extreme, psychosis. We need to evaluate ways to deal with undesirable reactions in various diseases, treatments, and groups.

Some of these reactions may be seen in research in responses to paper and pencil tests or interviews. It is small wonder that cancer patients are so often found to be different from noncancer patients [34]. I maintain that their recollections are probably also affected by the disease. Validation of these recollections has only been attempted through family questioning (e.g., [40])—itself subject to potential bias. Moreover, psychological tests given to prebiopsy patients are assumed to reflect their premorbid state. Research efforts to examine the validity of recollections and of premorbid status on tests would do much to determine the degree of confidence one should have in the many studies attempting to predict cancer susceptibility from personal history and personality.

As for the treatment responses themselves, evaluating ways of dealing with undesirable ones for various diseases, treatments, and groups defines a major research need. In fact, however, the very determination of possible changes in patient reactions over time is difficult because there is so much interpatient variation, and repeated measurements may involve considerable contamination due to faulty recollection. Perhaps behavior itself is the most valuable measure—employment [8], return to previous lifestyle, involvement with others, hobbies, etc. But the very use of the word "perhaps" indicates our uncertainty.

During treatment and especially shortly after surgery the patient needs support both from family and treatment team. At such a time the volunteer who has been through it can be of value: the mastectomee, the amputee, the colostomy wearer. However much help they may be, they have, in general, only the sketchiest of training, if any at all. Whom to train and how—these matters have not received much research attention. Moreover, however much we might hear that volunteers have been helpful, we do not have good measured data on how much or in what ways.

After diagnosis and through the whole treatment period, the role of faith and the clergy becomes important for many patients, since religion is to many a lifelong resource to be called on during times of stress. Little controlled research has been done on its potential value.

As new developments in treatment occur, their relationship to psychological medicine should be explored. For example, chronobiologic studies often show considerable differences in treatment efficacy or toxicity of chemotherapeutic agents according to the time of day they are given. These differences vary markedly among animals and also among people. Is there a behavioral measurement that might identify those who show such chronobiologic variation? For example, among patients who do show circadian variations, would it not be feasible to measure psychobiologic reactions such as sensitivity, reaction time, difference thresholds, thinking capability, evoked potential intervals and amplitudes, mood states, and the like? A positive finding could focus research on predictors.

Suicide is one extreme outcome that some therapists fear. However, it is, as Holland suggests [48], not really a very frequent event. In a study of all registered cancer patients in Connecticut from 1940–1973, Fox et al. [36] established that in 144,530 cases the overall age-adjusted annual suicide rate among men who had been diagnosed with cancer was about twice that of the population for equivalent person-years of risk, and just about the same as that of the population among women cancer patients. Since the rates range from 10 to 50 per 100,000 at various ages in men and 3 to 15 per 100,000 in women, the absolute numbers are not very large. Interaction of marital status, site, and disease severity with age, sex, and amount of time after diagnosis has not yet been analyzed in respect to suicide rate.

One of the most serious, pervasive, and potentially damaging problems is the personal involvement of medical groups, especially the young hospital worker—doctor, social worker, nurse—in the emotional issues of patients. Patients complain of the distinct, depersonalized behavior of medical personnel, but if medical workers do become deeply involved, they are soon torn apart by the repeated emotional traumata that follow this involvement. Just as with social workers, they can experience "burnout," a term defined as "loss of concern for people—an emotional exhaustion which involves cynicism and the dehumanized perception of patients" [16]. If they do get involved, do not want burnout, but cannot find a resolution, oncologic workers may change fields, going into other specialties. The turnover in young personnel in cancer work is higher than usual, but in those who have been in it for some time, it is lower than usual. Several devices have been suggested to handle the problem [59], but research is very scanty.

Rehabilitation

The main formal areas of this topic are adjustment to loss of body parts and functions, to prostheses, and reentry into family and societal functioning. Most cancer centers are equipped to handle all of them, but with different efficiencies. Where a patient is not near a cancer center, or is being treated by general physicians and/or surgeons, or cannot pay for rehabilitative treatment, things can get difficult. Involved in rehabilitation of any kind is the notion of relearning and, often, retraining. Some of this may be arduous and long-term, as in learning esophageal speech after laryngectomy. There are, throughout the country, many ostomy societies to help those with various ostomies. Loss of limb can be trying, as is the consequence of muscle section in radical mastectomy.

The most universal problem, however, is emotional adjustment—reentry into one's normal (if possible) or a new life-style. This may come with the altered view associated with loss of organ or function, but in addition, a further adjustment is needed with restoration or prosthesis—silicone implants, false leg, nipple grafting, facial reconstruction, etc. Particular problems of adjustment go with loss of emotionally important organs —hysterectomy, oophorectomy, castration, mastectomy.

Reaction of family members can involve resentment, worry, disgust, fear, all associated with rejection; or encouragement, help, reassurance, support, all associated with love. Exploration of these reactions and relationships is only at a very tentative stage, and it should be expanded and intensified.

One expects interruption of smooth sexual relationships during treatment. But after the major period of treatment is finished, the return to normal—or at least acceptable—sexual relations often does not take place. Among the psychological difficulties in the patient are altered self-image, worry about acceptability to the partner, reduced libido, and shame. Sometimes physical difficulties directly produce psychosexual problems, with reduced sex drive. For example, reduced desire has been shown after pituitary ablation [94], although later work was more equivocal [95]. In breast cancer, testosterone treatment markedly increases sexual desire [31]. The patient's partner may worry about forcing attention where it is not wanted—a frequent event with husbands—whether or not the patient actually does or does not want the attention. In any case the ramifications of the issue are broad, and offer scope for solution of many problems.

The whole matter of being able to go back to one's job concerns the rehabilitation worker. In Germany, for example, general rehabilitation centers exist, with cancer patients as one among the variety of disabled patients dealt with at each center [26]. Research in physical medicine of many kinds is needed because of the broad range of physical disabilities associated with cancer during and after treatment. Together with these, in the area of work, a similar broad range of jobs and disabilities must be matched in the rehabilitative process. Attempts have been made to predict return to work [96], and it is an area worth further study. There may be need for readjustment to the old job, learning a new job, retirement and home-adjustment, and the emotional adjustment generally. How best to achieve good adjustment on all levels is a challenging problem. In a comprehensive review, Barofsky [8] maintains that work measurement should be a major technique in evaluating treatment in clinical trials, as well as a general status evaluator.

Continuing Care

The cancer patient always has in mind the possibility of relapse. This is one of the main sources of worry and emotional stress, because a relapse—especially in the form of metastatic recurrence—has a depressing prognosis. During this phase the patient alternates between hope and fear. Feelings of resentment can emerge. When, or if, the doctor stops treatment after adjuvant therapy following relapse, the patient may feel that the doctor has given up hope, otherwise treatment would continue. Throughout this as well as earlier phases, one of the patient's major complaints is lack of information or communication from medical personnel. Much of our knowledge about continuing care comes from survey and interview data. New approaches to finding out about continuing care are needed, as well as achieving better continuing care.

During this time many patients experience a worsening or, in many cases where there has been none, the beginning of pain. The doctor's job is to decide on further treatment and, where symptoms are bad, what palliative approaches to use. It is also during this time that medical personnel experience their most difficult relationships with patients and their families. The outlook is bad, and negative emotions abound: depression, anger, fear, and worry. Patients react in many ways: There may appear displaced aggression, blatant denials, deep depression, intense appeal to the doctor to do something, and demand for support and reassurance from any source. It is during this time that so many patients and families turn to the so-called unproven methods of treatment [19]—Laetrile, vitamin C, various worthless machines. I place imaging [100]—trying to mobilize immune defenses by attempts to imagine them and their attack on cancer cells—in the class of unproven methods, but do not wish to couple it with Laetrile and vitamin C. The latter has had an unsuccessful clinical trial, [69], and Laetrile is now undergoing a trial, whereas for imaging, the literature shows no evidence that well-controlled trials have indeed been carried out [100]. Such imaging should be distinguished from the practicing of imaging of body parts and sensations suggested by Witkin [113] in his work on sex therapy in mastectomy patients. To be sure, the latter's criterion for success is more easily measured than Simonton's and deals with a different problem.

Holland [48] has described characteristic psychic states and behaviors under various conditions of treatment success and failure, including continuing care. Recent attempts to improve compliance and reduce emotional trauma point to intriguing research possibilities. These can be approached at any of the different stages and conditions outlined by Holland, with different needs and possible outcomes for the patient. Such research is essentially an attempt to describe and improve on coping behaviors of various types. While these have been looked at [18, 41, 63], much of the effort along these lines is at a beginning level.

Terminal Illness

This phase of cancer is the most fearsome of all. Death is imminent. Often the family and medical workers both turn their faces away from the patient, withdrawing support previously given. Pain episodes, if present, are likely to increase in number, duration, and severity. Demands on the family, if the patient is at home, and on the medical team, if he or she is in the hospital, become greater.

In the hospital, a major unsolved problem is the attitudes of both doctors and nurses toward pain-relieving medication. It is evident that "there is a large percentage of nurses in all services who possess inadequate factual information concerning narcotic analgesic drugs....Those nurses in the services most likely to care for cancer patients with chronic pain are those who are least charitably disposed toward the administration of adequate doses of narcotic analgesic drugs" [45]. Both detailed understanding of the existing state of affairs and approaches toward improved education are clearly needed.

In the terminal stage, both family and medical staff withdraw from the patient, physically and symbolically. To the doctor, the dying patient who is beyond help is a kind of threat, causing discomfort. In everyone, there is a certain amount of empathy, and confronting a terminal state creates a most uncomfortable empathetic reaction.

Handling the end stages of cancer is difficult, but the hospice concept seems to have had great success. The effort to establish hospices is gaining strength in this country [30], the concept having already proven itself in England [89]. Maintenance of dignity, understanding of reasonable care for pain, and regard for support needs characterize this kind of institution. A search for its success level compared with other milieux of terminal care would form an important baseline. Using this baseline, one could then explore and compare techniques, both those used in hospices now, and those used elsewhere. Despite the success of the movement, there are still problems with it [80] that research can help to solve.

Even at the terminal stage of cancer progression, information for family is poor, and they complain about that fact [85]. The repeated complaints, at whatever stage, about poor communication between medical worker and patient or family is a theme that should engender intensive research efforts to find means of improving that state of affairs.

As for special areas of research in terminal cancer, earlier work on psychedelic drugs in psychotherapy [82] has not been extended much. The recent work on enkephalins and endorphins, occupiers of pain receptor sites in the brain, might easily lead researchers in that field and others to use cancer patients as valuable sources of natural pain, perhaps for comparison with artificially induced pain or for basic research on mechanisms of pain induction and removal. Work on marijuana and its active principle to relieve nausea is still continuing and may expand with FDA approval and supply of the drug. Hypnosis has been an area of steady interest in pain and nausea control and provides much material for research.

Finally, in the hospital, the number of negative (by omitting life-extending actions) euthanasia episodes among cancer patients with febrile or "poor" status is relatively high, except with Catholic doctors and patients [14]. These consist of withholding life-prolonging orders after a hopeless prognosis statement, withholding antibiotics and no intravenous medication, evidence of intent to discontinue treatment, and the like.

Positive euthanasia is endorsed by not trivial proportions of medical workers [14]. Would they be even higher if the responses related to cancer only?

Research on attitudes and behavior in respect to euthanasia is very sparse. It is a difficult area because of religious, legal, and medicoethical considerations.

The Posthumous Phase

This topic has received almost no attention in the literature. Exceptions are found in accounts of the team approach and comprehensive cancer care [56]. But because the family's contact with the personality of the patient does not automatically cease with his or her death, research on posthumous adjustment should have some importance. The description of the slow, oscillating, phasic recovery of family members, especially mothers of children who died of cancer, is somewhat surprising at first glance [56]. But it should encourage research in an almost completely neglected area.

Conclusion

From this review it is evident that cancer, affecting all ages, encompassing many sciences, and involving many levels and modes of behavior, is susceptible to molar and molecular research at all stages of its potential and actual effects. The latter are multifarious. Whether such research is done by the anthropologist interested in attitudes toward delay in going to the doctor or toward the disease itself; or the psychologist asking whether personality traits predict susceptibility; or the physician exploring techniques of improving or bringing about compliance with his recommendations; or the labor relations negotiator struggling with the balance of present or reduced income against constant or decreased hazard of cancer—that is not the issue. The important matter is that whatever problems face those involved with trying to achieve better circumstances for those who might get cancer, already have it, or are involved as family, medical worker, volunteer, or religious counselor, the first step in solving such problems is knowledge about them. This implies good research. While clearly, such research will not necessarily solve the problems (how many stopped smoking or did not start, simply because we know something about failure of various approaches?), it is almost certain that they will not be solved without good prior knowledge about the problems. And generally, the best way to get such prior knowledge is through well-designed research.

The reader is encouraged to study the field, with its many possibilities for such exploration and study.

References

1. Abse, D. W.; Wilkins, M. M.; VandeCastle, R. L.; Buxton, W. D.; Demars, J. P.; Brown, R. S.; and Kirschner, L. G.: Personality and behavioral characteristics of lung cancer patients. *Journal of Psychosomatic Research* 18:101–113, 1974.
2. Ader, R.; and Cohen, N.: Behaviorally conditioned immunosuppression. *Psychosomatic Medicine* 37:333–340, 1975.
3. Aimez, P.: Psychophysiologie du cancer. Existe-t-il un terrain psychophysiologique prédisposant? Influence des facteurs psychique sur la relation hôte–tumeur. (Psychophysiology of cancer. Is there a predisposing psychophysiological area? Influence of psychological factors on the host–tumor relation.) *Revue de Médecine Psychosomatique* 14:371–381, 1972.
4. APA Task Force on Health Research: Contributions of psychology to health research: Patterns, problems and potentials. *American Psychologist* 31:263–274, 1976.
5. Antonovsky, A.; and Hartman, H.: Delay in the detection of cancer. A review of the literature. *Health Education Monographs* 2:98–128, 1974.
6. Axtell, L. M.; Asire, A. J.; and Myers, M. H.: *Cancer Patient Survival. Report No. 5.* DHEW Publication No. (NIH) 77-992, National Cancer Institute, Department of Health, Education & Welfare, Washington, D.C. 1976.
7. Baltrusch, H. J. F.: Ergebnisse klinisch-psychosomatischer Krebsforschung. (Results of clinical–psychosomatic cancer research.) *Psychosomatic Medicine (Solothurn)* 5:175–208, 1975.
8. Barofsky, I.: *Returning to Work: A Measure of the Efficacy of Medical Treatment.* Lexington: Lexington Press, 1980, in press.
9. Barofsky, I.; and Sugarbaker, P. H.: Quality of life assessment, cancer treatment and clinical trials. Paper presented at Annual Meeting, American Psychological Assn., Toronto, Ontario, 1978.
10. Bieliauskas, L.; Shekelle, R.; Garron, D.; Maliza, C.; Ostfeld, A.; Paul, O.; and Raynor, W.: Psychological depression and cancer mortality. *Psychosomatic Medicine* 41:77–78, 1979 (Abs.).
11. Bower, B. F.; and Gordon, G. S.: Hormonal effects of nonendocrine tumors. *Annual Review of Medicine* 16:83–118, 1965.
12. Boyd, S. C.; Sasame, H. A.; and Boyd, M. R.: High concentrations of glutathione in glandular stomach: Possible implications for carcinogenesis. *Science* 205:1010–1012, 1979.
13. Bross, I. D. J.; Bertell, Sister R.; and Gibson, R.: Pets and adult leukemia. *American Journal of Public Health.* 62:1520–1531, 1972.
14. Brown, N. K.; Brown, M. A.; and Thompson, D.: Decision making for the terminally ill patient. In *Cancer: The Behavioral Dimensions*, eds. J. W. Cullen, B. H. Fox, and R. N. Isom, pp. 319–329. New York: Raven Press, 1976.
15. Cagossi, M.: La variabile psychica nella ricerca oncologica. (Psychological variables in cancer research.) *Archivio di Psicologia Neurologia e Psichiatria* 32:323–337, 1971.

16. Cartwright, L. K.: Sources and effects of stress in health careers. In *Health Psychology* eds. G. C. Stone, F. Cohen, and N. E. Adler, pp. 419-445. San Francisco: Jossey-Bass, 1979.

17. Cassileth, B.: Personal communication. University of Pennsylvania Cancer Center, Philadelphia, Pa. 1979.

18. Cobliner, W. G.: Psychological factors in gynecological or breast malignancies. *Hospital Physician.* 13:38-40, 1977.

19. *Unproven Methods of Cancer Management.* American Cancer Society, Inc., New York, N.Y. 1979.

20. Cooper, A. F.; Hughson, A. V. M.; McArdle, C. S.; Russell, A. R.; and Smith, D. C.: Psychiatric morbidity after chemotherapy and radiotherapy for breast cancer. *British Journal of Cancer* 40:310, 1979.

21. Crisp, A. H.: Some psychosomatic aspects of neoplasia. *British Journal of Medical Psychology* 43:313-331, 1970.

22. Cullen, J. W.; Fox, B. H., and Isom, R. N., eds.: *Cancer: The Behavioral Dimensions.* New York: Raven Press, 1976.

23. Dattore, P. J.: Premorbid Personality Factors Associated with Neoplasms. An Archival Approach. Ph.D. dissertation, University of Kansas, Lawrence, 1979.

24. Davies, R. K.; Quinlan, D. M.; McKegney, F. P.; and Kimball, C. P.: Organic factors and psychological adjustment in advanced cancer patients. *Psychosomatic Medicine* 35:464-471, 1973.

25. Davis, F.: Uncertainty in medical prognosis, clinical and functional. In *Medical Care* eds. W. Scott, and E. H. Volkart, pp. 311-321. New York: Wiley, 1966.

26. Die Stiftung Rehabilitation Heidelberg. (The Heidelberg Rehabilitation Institute). D-6900 Heidelberg, Bonhoefferstrasse. Prof. Dr. med. E. Weidmann, Medical Director.

27. Dintruff, D.; Anderson, F.; Costello, K.; Botts, P.; Cook, M.; and Fotopoulos, S., eds.: *Psychological Aspects of Breast Cancer An Annotated Bibliography Relevant to Intervention Design.* Kansas City, MO.: Midwest Research Institute, 1976.

28. Doll, R., and Peto, R.: Cigarette smoking and bronchial carcinoma: dose and time relationship among regular smokers and lifelong non-smokers. *Journal of Epidemiology and Community Health* 32:303-313, 1978.

29. DuPan, R. M., and Müller, C.: La mortalité par cancer chez les patients psychiatriques hospitalisés (Cancer mortality among hospitalized mental patients). *Schweizerische Medizinische Wochenschrift* 107:597-604, 1977.

30. Edwards, C. H.: Implement hospice concept for terminal cancer patients. National Cancer Institute Contract No. CN75391, 1979-1980 to Riverside Hospital, Boonton, N.J.

31. Foss, G. L.: The influence of androgens on sexuality in women. *Lancet.* 1:667-669, 1951.

32. Fox, B. H.: Internal research proposal. National Cancer Institute. 1975.

33. Fox, B. H.: The psychosocial epidemiology of cancer. In *Cancer: The Behavioral Dimensions*, eds. J. W. Cullen, B. H. Fox, and R. N. Isom, pp. 11-22. New York: Raven Press, 1976.

34. Fox, B. H.: Premorbid psychological factors as related to cancer incidence. *Journal of Behavioral Medicine* 1:45-133, 1978.

35. Fox, B. H.: Cancer death risk in hospitalized mental patients. *Science* 201:966-967, 1978.

36. Fox, B. H.; Stanek, E. J.; Boyd, S. C.; and Flannery, J. T.: Suicide rates among cancer patients. *Proceedings of the Fifth World Congress of the International College of Psychosomatic Medicine.* Held in Jerusalem, Israel, 1979. In press.

37. Fras, I.; and Litin, E. M.: Comparison of psychiatric manifestations in carcinoma of the pancreas, retroperitoneal malignant lymphoma and lymphoma in other locations. *Psychosomatics.* 8:275-277, 1967.

38. Fras, I.; Litin, E. M.; and Pearson, J. S.: Comparison of psychiatric symptoms in carcinoma of the pancreas with those in some other intra-abdominal neoplasms. *American Journal of Psychiatry*, 123:1553–1562, 1967.

39. Goldsmith, J.R.; and Berglund, K.: Epidemiological approach to multiple factor interactions in pulmonary disease. The potential usefulness of path analysis. *Annals of the New York Academy of Science* 221:361–375, 1974.

40. Greer, S.; and Morris, T.: Psychological attributes of women who develop breast cancer: A controlled study. *Journal of Psychosomatic Research* 19:147–153, 1975.

41. Gullo, S. V.; Cherico, D. J.; and Shadick, R.: Suggested stages and response styles in life threatening illness: A focus on the cancer patient. In *Anticipatory Grief*. eds. B. Schoenberg, A. Carr, A. Kutscher, D. Peretz, and I. Goldberg, pp. 53–78. New York: Columbia University Press, 1974.

42. Hackett, T. P.; Cassem, N. H.; and Raker, J. W.: Patient delay in cancer. *New England Journal of Medicine* 289:14–20, 1973.

43. Haenszel, W.; Kurihara, M.; Segi, M.; and Lee, R. K. C.: Stomach cancer among Japanese in Hawaii. *Journal of the National Cancer Institute* 49:969–988, 1972.

44. Hagnell, O.: The premorbid personality of persons who develop cancer in a total population investigated in 1947 and 1957. *Annals of the New York Academy of Sciences* 125:846–855, 1966.

45. Hayes, D. M.: The impact of the health care system on physician attitudes and behaviors. In *Cancer: The Behavioral Dimensions*, eds. J. W. Cullen, B. H. Fox, and R. N. Isom, pp. 145–157. New York: Raven Press, 1976.

46. Henderson, I.C.; and Canellos, G. P.: Cancer of the breast. The past decade. Part I. *New England Journal of Medicine* 302:17–30, 1980.

47. Holden, C.: Cancer and the mind. *Science* 200:1363–1369, 1978.

48. Holland, J. C.; Psychological aspects of cancer. In *Cancer Medicine*, eds. J. F. Holland and Frei, E. III, pp. 991–1021. Philadelphia: Lea and Febiger, 1973.

49. Hopkins, B. L.: Behavioral procedures for reducing worker exposure to carcinogens. Nat. Inst. of Occup. Safety and Health Contract # CDC (NIOSH) 210-77-0400 to University of Kansas, Lawrence, KA 66045.

50. *Journal of Behavioral Medicine* 1 (1), 1978.

51. Katz, J.; Kunofsky, S.; Patton, R. E.; and Allaway, N. C.: Cancer mortality among patients in New York mental hospitals. *Cancer* 20:2194–2199, 1967.

52. Keehn, R. J.; Goldberg, I. D.; and Beebe, G. W.: Twenty-four year followup of army veterans with disability separations for psychoneurosis in 1944. *Psychosomatic Medicine* 36:27–45, 1974.

53. Kegeles, S.: A field experimental attempt to change beliefs and behavior of women in an urban ghetto. *Journal of Health & Social Behavior* 10:115–125, 1969.

54. King, S. H.: *Perceptions of Illness and Medical Practice*. New York: Russell Sage Foundation, 1962.

55. Korsch, B. M.; and Negrete, V. F.: Doctor–patient communication. *Scientific American* 277:66–74, 1972.

56. Lansky, S. B.; Lowman, J. T.; Gyulay, J. E.; and Briscoe, K.: A team approach to coping with cancer. In *Cancer: The Behavioral Dimensions*, eds. J. W. Cullen, B. H. Fox, and R. N. Isom, pp. 295–308. New York: Raven Press, 1976.

57. Mages, N. L.; and Mendelsohn, G. A.: Effects of cancer on patients' lives: A personological approach. In *Health Psychology*, eds. G. C. Stone, F. Cohen, and N. E. Adler, pp. 255–284. San Francisco: Jossey-Bass, 1979.

58. Mashberg, A.: Erythroplasia vs. leukoplakia in the diagnosis of early asymptomatic oral squamous carcinoma. *New England Journal of Medicine* 297:109–110, 1977.

59. Maslach, C.: Burned out. *Human Behavior* 5:16–22, 1976.

60. McCoy, J. W.: *Psychological Variables and Onset of Cancer.* Ph.D. dissertation, Oklahoma State University, 1976.

61. McIntosh, J.: Processes of communication, information seeking and control associated with cancer: A selective review of the literature. *Social Science and Medicine* 8:167-187, 1974.

62. Miller, D.: On the nature of susceptibility. *Cancer* 46:1307-1318, 1980.

63. Miller, C. L.; Denner, P. R.; and Richardson, V. E.: Assisting the psychosocial problems of cancer patients: review of current research. *International Journal of Nursing Studies* 13:161-166, 1976.

64. Mitchell, W. M.: Etiological factors producing neuropsychiatric syndromes in patients with malignant disease. *International Journal of Neuropsychiatry* 3:464-468, 1967.

65. Morris, T.; Greer, H. S.; and White, P. W.: Psychological and social adjustment to mastectomy. *Cancer* 40:2381-2387, 1977.

66. Morrison, F.; and Paffenbarger, R. S.: Personal communication, 1979.

67. Morrison, F.; and Paffenbarger, R. S.: Epidemiologic aspects of biobehavior in the etiology of cancer: a critical review. (This volume.) 1980.

68. Nemeth, G.: Prospective psychologic and somatic examinations of patients who later developed carcinoma. *Proceedings of the Third International Symposium on Psychobiologic, Psychophysiologic, Psychosomatic, and Sociosomatic Aspects of Neoplastic Disease,* 1978. In press.

69. New study denigrates vitamin C's value. *Oncology Times.* 1(2):7, 1979.

70. Nowak, G. D.: *Psychological Aspects of Cancer, April, 1973 through December, 1977.* Literature Search No. 77-17, National Library of Medicine. Department of Health, Educ. and Welfare, USPHS, NIH, Bethesda, MD 20205.

71. Ohlin, P.; Lundh, B.; and Westling, H.: Carbon monoxide levels and reported cessation of smoking. *Psychopharmacology.* 49:263-265, 1976.

72. Paffenbarger, R. S.: Psychosocial Factors in Students Predictive of Cancer. Grant No. R01 CA22574 Bethesda: National Cancer Institute, 1977.

73. Pearson, J. S.: *A Sociological Analysis of the Reduction of Hazardous Radiation in Uranium Mines.* Center for Disease Control, U.S. Department of Health, Education and Welfare. DHEW Publication No. (NIOSH) 75-71, 1975.

74. Peck, A.: Emotional reaction to having cancer. *American Journal of Roentgenology* 114:591-599, 1972.

75. Pereyra, A. J.: The relationship of sexual activity to cervical cancer: Cancer of the cervix in a prison population. *Obstetrics and Gynecology* 17:154-159, 1961.

76. Perrin, G. M.; and Pierce, I. R.: Psychosomatic aspects of cancer. *Psychosomatic Medicine* 21:397-421, 1959.

77. Personal communication. On request, the author will write to the relevant researcher for permission to name him/her.

78. Personal communication. On request, the author will write the relevant researcher for permission to name him/her.

79. Plumb, M. M.; and Holland, J.: Comparative studies of psychological function in patients with advanced cancer in self-reported depressive symptoms. *Journal of Psychosomatic Medicine* 39:264-276, 1977.

80. Potter, J. F.: A challenge for the hospice movement. *New England Journal of Medicine* 302:53-55, 1980.

81. *Psychological Aspects of Mastectomy, Final Report.* National Cancer Institute Contract N01-CN-55312 to Midwest Research Institute, Kansas City, MO, 1979.

82. Richards, W.; Grof, S.; Goodman, L.; and Kurland, A.: LSD-assisted psychotherapy and the human encounter with death. *Journal of Transpersonal Psychology* 4:121-150, 1972.

83. Riley, V.: Mouse mammary tumors: Alteration of incidence as apparent function of stress. *Science* 189:465–467, 1975.

84. Rogers, M. P.; Dubey, D.; and Reich, P.: The influence of the psyche and the brain on immunity and disease susceptibility: A critical review. *Psychosomatic Medicine* 41:147–164, 1979.

85. Rose, M. A.: Help for the cancer patient's family. *New England Journal of Medicine* 292:433, 1975.

86. Roth, J.: Die paraneoplastische Syndrome. (The paraneoplastic syndromes.) *Hippocrates* 44:18–38, 1973.

87. Rotkin, I. D.: A comparison review of key epidemiological studies in cervical cancer related to current searches for transmissible agents. *Cancer Research* 33:1353–1367, 1973.

88. Sands, R. G., ed.: *Psychosocial Aspects of Cancer: An Annotated Bibliography.* Louisville: University of Louisville, 1977.

89. Saunders, C.: The last stages of life. *American Journal of Nursing* 65:70–76, 1965.

90. Schain, W. S.: Guidelines for psychological management of breast cancer: A stage-related approach. In *The Breast,* eds. H. S. Gallager, H. P. Leis, R. Snyderman, and J. A. Urban, pp. 465–475. St. Louis: Mosby, 1978.

91. Scheflen, A. E.: Malignant tumors in the institutionalized psychotic population. *American Medical Association Archives of Neurology and Psychiatry* 66:145–155, 1961.

92. Schoenberg, B.; and Carr, A. C.: Loss of external organs: Limb, amputation, mastectomy and disfiguration. In *Loss and Grief: Psychological Management in Medical Practice,* eds. B. Schoenberg, A. C. Carr, D. Peretz, and A. H. Hutscher, pp. 119–131. New York: Columbia University Press, 1970.

93. Schofield, W.: The role of psychology in the delivery of health services. *American Psychologist* 24:565–584, 1969.

94. Schon, M.: Hypophysectomy as a psychological experience. *Diseases of the Nervous System.* 124:75–83, 1963.

95. Schon, M.: Psychological effects of hypophysectomy in women with metastatic breast cancer. *Dissertation Abstracts International* 33:2821B–2822B, 1972.

96. Schonfield, J.: Psychological factors related to delayed return to earlier life-style in successfully treated cancer patients. *Journal of Psychosomatic Research* 16:41–46, 1972.

97. Department of Health, Education, and Welfare: *SEER Program: Cancer Incidence and Mortality in the United States, 1973–1976.* Unpublished report by the National Cancer Institute, 1979.

98. Shapiro, S.: Evidence on screening for breast cancer from a randomized trial. *Cancer* 39:2772–2782, 1977.

99. Shekelle, R. B. A.: Prospective study of personality and risk of cancer. National Cancer Institute, Grant No. RO1 CA 22536, 1977.

100. Simonton, O. C.; Matthews-Simonton, S.; and Creighton, J.: *Getting Well Again.* Los Angeles: J. P. Tarcher, Inc. 1978. Distributed by St. Martin's Press, New York.

101. Smith, D. C.; Ross, D. J., Russell, A. R.; and McArdle, C. S.: Adjuvant chemotherapy in early breast cancer. *British Journal of Cancer* 40:310, 1979.

102. Stein, M.; Schiavi, R. C.; and Camerino, M.: Influence of brain and behavior on the immune system. *Science* 191:435–440, 1976.

103. Stephenson, H. S.; Adams, C. K.; Hall, D. C.; and Pennypacker, H. S.: The effects of certain training parameters on detection of simulated breast cancer. *Journal of Behavioral Medicine* 2:239–250, 1979.

104. Stone, G. C.; Cohen, F.; and Adler, N. E., eds. *Health Psychology.* San Francisco: Jossey-Bass, 1979.

105. Swets, J. A.; Pickett, R. M.; Whitehead, S. F.; Getty, D. J.; Schnur, J. A.; Swets, J. B.; and Freeman, B. A.: Assessment of diagnostic technologies. *Science* 205:753–759, 1979.
106. Thomas, C. B.: Psychological and familial precursors of cancer. National Cancer Institute Grant No. RI8 CA 24416, 1978.
107. Verschoof, K. J. H.: Resultate in der Frühdiagnostik des Zervixkarzinoms bei 6000 Frauen einer gynäkologischen Praxis. (Results of early diagnosis of cervical cancer in 6000 women in a gynecological practice.) *Mitteilungsdienst der Gesellschaft zur Bekämpfung der Krebskrankheiten.* 6:984–996, 1973.
108. Warner, K. E.: Possible increases in the underreporting of cigarette consumption. *Journal of the American Statistical Association* 73:314–318, 1978.
109. Weaver, J. M.; Dockery, J. W.; de la Puente, J.; Kevorkian, A. Y.; and Hnat, R. F.: Narcotic addiction and cervical carcinoma. *Acta Cytologica* 10:154–155, 1966.
110. Weisman, A. D.: Early diagnosis of vulnerability in cancer patients. *American Journal of Medical Science* 271:187–196, 1976.
111. Wertheimer, N.; and Leeper, E.: Electrical wiring configurations and childhood cancer. *American Journal of Epidemiology* 109:273–284, 1979.
112. Wilcox, R. G.; Hughes, J.; and Roland, J.: Verification of smoking history in patients after infarction using urinary nicotine and cotinine measurements. *British Medical Journal* 2:1026–1028, 1979.
113. Witkin, M. H.: Sex therapy and mastectomy. *Journal of Sex and Marital Therapy* 1:290–304, 1975.
114. Worden, J. W. and Sobel, H. J.: Ego strength and adaptation to cancer. *Psychosomatic Medicine* 40:585–592, 1978.

Epidemiological Aspects of Biobehavior in the Etiology of Cancer: A Critical Review

FLORENCE R. MORRISON
RALPH A. PAFFENBARGER, JR.

This review was made from an epidemiological point of view and had two objectives: (a) to assess studies of psychosocial variables and cancer against epidemiological principles generally applied to research on human subjects; and (b) to determine if the many biases which affect such research were eliminated or controlled by the study designs used. However, it was not our intent to produce a catalog of strengths or weaknesses of specific studies; others have done so recently [32, 47, 45]. Rather, we agreed with Kissen, who noted, "Methodology that may be open to criticism does not necessarily invalidate the findings [56]." Therefore, we adopted the following criterion: Only those methodological flaws which raised questions about the interpretation of results would be discussed. In identifying such flaws, we were impelled to propose a counterhypothesis and to adduce evidence to make it tenable [17].

Epidemiology is an integrative discipline, and, as such, it follows established principles to assess all environmental and host characteristics that influence the natural history of disease. Some of these principles, particularly applicable to retrospective studies that attempt to establish a causal relation between psychosocial variables and cancer are [15, 101]:

1. *Strength of association.* The disease (cancer) should be associated statistically with the attribute of interest (i.e., its frequency should be substantially greater or smaller in a group with the disease than in a comparable control group without the disease). (Comparability between case and control groups signifies that the groups are similar in

the frequency and distribution of characteristics that influence the incidence of the disease, except for the attribute of interest.)

2. *Temporal sequence.* The temporal sequence of events should support the hypothesis—the presumed cause should have occurred before onset of the disease.

3. *Reproducibilty.* The association should be shown to be repeatable (i.e., observed by different persons, in different places, at different times, and under different circumstances).

4. *Persistence.* The association should persist when other variables known to be risk factors for the disease are controlled or eliminated.

5. *Consistency.* The findings should be consistent with the generally known facts of the natural history and biology of the disease (cancer). Moreover, they should be consistent by age, race, and demographic characteristics.

6. *Dose–effect relation.* Where applicable, the risk of disease should be greater with increased exposure or "dose" of the attribute under study; that is a dose–effect relationship should be demonstrable.

7. *Specificity.* The suspected risk factor (attribute) should be specific for the disease under study. If the association is limited to a specific group and to particular sites and types of disease and there is no association between that group and other diseases, that is a strong argument in favor of causation.

8. *Biological plausibility.* The hypothesized relationship should be biologically plausible in light of knowledge about the disease.

No one of these eight principles verifies or invalidates a cause-and-effect hypothesis. As more of these principles are satisfied, the more likely a causal hypothesis becomes. What they can do then, with greater or less strength, is to help answer the fundamental question: Is any other answer more likely than cause and effect?

Behavioral scientists who have investigated the relationship between stress or psychosocial phenomena and cancer have generally supported either of two hypotheses: (*a*) basic (ingrained) personality traits or characteristics precede and in some way cause cancer, or (*b*) environmental circumstances or situational events that cause emotional upheaval or distress are antecedent to cancer. Distinctions between long-standing traits and more transitory states are often blurred and many investigators suggest some combination of personality traits and disastrous events as predisposing to cancer, but, for convenience, they are treated here as two separate groups. Both hypotheses attribute the behavioral characteristics of patients with cancer to antecedent personality or events; we suggest it is equally likely that the disease is responsible for the behavior observed.

Catastrophic Events and Cancer

An early, innovative attempt to link catastrophic events and cancer was made by LeShan and Worthington [71]. They used an indirect method to test the hypothesis that the loss of a major relationship (outlet for emotional energy) occurred in those who died of cancer more often than could be accounted for by chance. They predicted specific patterns of mortality by marital status and other demographic variables and concluded from an examination of older, incomplete data that their predictions were supported. However, Kraus and Lilienfeld examined U.S. national statistics for 1956 on the 20 leading causes of death by age, sex, race, and marital status. The pattern they found, different from that predicted by LeShan and Worthington, was that married people experienced lower mortality rates from all causes than did those who were single, widowed, or divorced for each age group and sex. Contrary to other predictions, the relative excess mortality in those who were single, widowed, and divorced was consistently greater in males than in females. The widowed experienced excess mortality for all 20 causes of death, but the greatest excess mortality among the widowed was found for cardiovascular–renal disease. The relative risks for malignant neoplasms (i.e., death rates for widowed individuals divided by death rates for married) were some of the lowest among the 20 causes of death. Several hypotheses that seemed equally plausible were suggested to explain the excess mortality observed among the widowed: (a) selection factors that return the healthiest widowed individuals to the married category; (b) homogamy—those less healthy tend to pick mates like themselves; (c) shared unfavorable environment; and, finally, (d) the effects of widowhood, which include grief; new worries and responsibilities; alterations in diet, work regime, and recreational life; frequently reduced economic condition; and other specific changes resulting from becoming widowed. Any of these possibilities might have influenced the risk of disease and death.

In Great Britain, studies of mortality in surviving spouses, particularly widowers, and in other close relatives, obtained results similar to those reported by Kraus and Lilienfeld [90, 97, 125]. Increased deaths occurred predominantly in the first 6 months to a year following the death of a spouse or relative. In one study which investigated cause of death, the greatest excess was due to heart disease [90].

In a later paper, LeShan reported on the emotional life histories of 450 adult cancer patients and 150 controls matched for age, sex, and social class [70]. Hypotheses were developed from interview and therapy material and tested against projective test material. Hypotheses were then refined and tested again, presumably on the total sample. The study identified a pattern of development that was present in 72% of cancer patients but in only 10% of controls. The pattern was one of emotional damage to patients' ability to relate to others; it had been initiated in childhood and was often accentuated by some event like the loss of a parent or death of a sibling. Since examination of the data led to the hypotheses, a test of the hypotheses based on the same data was sure to give significant results. Therefore, when a set of data has been used for exploratory analysis, replication on another set of data is needed for confirmatory analysis [63]. The results might have been due to differences in recall between those with and without cancer; patients with the disease make great efforts to find explanations for their illness while those who are well are not so motivated. Or the results might have been due to interviewer and therapist bias in eliciting past adverse events; apparently study staff were able to distinguish patients and controls. Finally, differences found might have been due to chance. Without replication, interpretation of the results remains questionable.

In a group of 102 patients with leukemia and lymphoma, Greene obtained results similar to those of LeShan [41]. Neither men nor women showed a consistent personality type, but both gave a history of various personal losses or separations for up to 4 years prior to the diagnosis of malignancy. The study included no control group, so it was not possible to conclude that the personal experiences reported by these patients would have differed from an otherwise similar group without leukemia or lymphoma. A later study of three sets of monozygotic twins led Greene and Swisher to conclude that leukemia had developed in each case in a setting of major psychological stress for the entire family, which affected the leukemic twin particularly [42]. The conclusion is questionable since it was made by investigators who knew which twin was leukemic. Though old records were searched, and high school counselors, local physicians, and relatives were interviewed, the responses of these individuals also were probably affected by knowledge of the disease [69].

Separation experience and cancer of the breast was studied by Muslin, Gyarfas, and Pieper [83]. Separation was defined as the permanent loss of a first-degree relative or other person who the subject stated was emotionally important to her. Information was collected from all women admitted for breast biopsy before surgery, so that neither the subject nor the assistant who administered the questionnaire knew if the breast lesion was malignant. A subsample of subjects was interviewed by a psychiatrist. Of 165 admissions, 74 were assigned to 37 matched pairs. The questionnaires were analyzed in pairs by a sequential statistical test. Each pair consisted of a patient with cancer and a patient with benign disease who were matched for race, age, marital status, and socioeconomic background. The investigator

who paired the subjects was furnished with the needed background information but knew nothing of the subjects' exposure to separations. Analysis
of separation data showed no differences between malignant and benign
groups in either early or recent separation experiences. Psychiatric interviews showed no differences between patients with malignant and benign
disease. The negative results might be attributed to the use of women with
benign breast disease as controls. Since benign breast disease is a risk factor
for breast cancer, it might be argued that the control group had not yet
developed or been diagnosed with the disease. But even with a substantially increased risk, the number of breast cancer cases expected in 37
women is negligible and unlikely to have produced the similarity in cases
and controls.

The relation between feelings of a hopeless type of "giving up" and
cancer of the uterine cervix was investigated by Schmale and Iker [102].
Feelings of hopelessness expressed by "giving up" were considered to be the
triggering mechanism for the clinical appearance of disease. The study
group consisted of 51 women admitted for excisional biopsy because of
repeated cervical smears which were graded Class III when stained by the
Papanicolaou method. Only women who were essentially healthy, had no
gross evidence of disease, and were under age 50 were included. Data collection and interpretation were made before the subject, her physician, the
pathologist, or the investigator knew the histologic results. Predictions of
cancer were based on reported responses of hopelessness to a life event
within the preceding 6 months. Other predictions related to three MMPI
scales. Investigators correctly identified 11 out of 19 women with cancer
and 25 out of 32 women without cancer ($p = .02$). No differences were
found in the MMPI scales. Since the investigators were aware that all study
subjects had had repeated Class III Papanicolaou smears, that knowledge
coupled with other information gleaned from disclosure or observation
during the interview (i.e., race, country of birth, socioeconomic level,
number of marriages and sex partners, and symptoms of cervical
pathology) might certainly have affected predictions [88].

The authors noted that since the cancer was present at the time of interview, the expressed hopelessness could not be exclusively related to the
prior significant life event. In fact, only one subject in each group reported
the acutal loss of a close relative. Threats of loss, which made up the majority of the recent, significant life events, were about equal in the two
groups.

Saxon Graham and his associates studied the relation of social trauma to
cancer of the cervix and breast [38, 39]. The studies were well designed and
controlled; sample sizes were large (350 to 450 cases and approximately
two controls per case). Traumatic events—death, divorce, unemployment

and economic want, residential and occupational mobility, and prolonged illness in the immediate and extended family—were assessed in cases and controls for 5 years prior to the cancer diagnosis. No differences in social trauma were found in those with cervical or breast cancer when compared with those without the disease. In both studies, control groups were composed of patients with other types of cancer and nonneoplastic diseases that did not involve the breast or genital organs. The proportion of each type of control was not specified in either study, and the authors did not state that both types of control were combined because of their essential similarity.

Carl and Stephanie Simonton attempted to effect a change in the progression of various cancers through the use of psychotherapy [107]. They attributed the onset and course of disease to both life history pattern and personality characteristics; the individual's state of mind, they believed, was responsible for bringing on his illness. In a study of 152 cancer patients who received radiation therapy for advanced disease, they found that response to treatment was directly related to attitude, regardless of type or extent of disease. Patients were taught a process of relaxation and visual imagery with components similar to biofeedback, meditation, autogenic training and self-hypnosis. Five staff members used patients' reports of their imagery to determine their attitudes toward the disease [108, 121].

The Simontons' work is difficult to evaluate: Little description of the patients, their disease status, or past and concurrent therapy are given in their publications. A recent, popular report indicated that about 10% of 180 patients treated by them were disease-free at time of publication; average survival for the other 90% has been over 2.5 times longer than the average for a terminal cancer patient who received only standard medical treatment. Such claims can neither be substantiated nor refuted without many more details than are available in these reports.

Animal Experiments

Much work with animals has explored the relation between "stress" and tumor formation. Personality characteristics presumably cannot be studied in animals, though "behavior types" in dogs are mentioned in the literature [24]. These experiments, on laboratory rats and mice primarily, expose the animals to various forms of stress, such as electric shock, food or water deprivation, crowding, excessive heat, cold or exercise, among others. Crisp has described the major findings of animal work to be the great variability of results that depend on the species and strain of animal, and the difficulty of accurately identifying the really relevant factors in producing disease [25].

La Barba found that rats and mice developed smaller tumors under conditions of exercise or excessive crowding. His review of the literature suggested that such results were found in both species and for different types of carcinomas. Shock or alterations in early handling produced varied results in tumor formation. Maternal separation had no real effect on the organisms' response to subsequent pathogenic stimuli. Electric shock led to early appearance of mammary tumors in mice, but avoidance conditioning and immobilization inhibited the growth of Ehrlich carcinoma. Natural stress, such as a natural enemy, produced tumor inhibition across a wide variety of species [66].

Riley found that mammary tumor incidence in mice could be modified from 92% under chronic stress to 7% in a protected environment [99]. Henry, Stevens and Watson found that forced breeding increased mammary tumors [49], but in another study, Cooley, Henry, and Stephens found that tumor rate was not elevated in animals that were force bred [23]. Newberry et al. found that stress induced by shocking rats for 35 to 40 days significantly reduced tumor formation [87].

Work reported by Good, Fernandes, Yunes et al. suggests that nutritional stress, especially protein and/or calorie deprivation, leads to many changes in the immune responses of mice, rats, and guinea pigs [37]. Chronic protein deprivation enhanced cell-mediated immune responses while humoral responses were usually depressed but sometimes unaffected; responses depended on the antigen used. Chronic protein deprivation improved tumor immunity by depressing production of B-cell blocking factors. However, when protein was limited to less than 5% of daily food intake, both cellular and humoral immunity were depressed.

Seifter demonstrated that moderate doses of vitamin A in the diet of mice reduced adrenal enlargement and thymic shrinkage in animals with skin grafts, tumors, and a variety of other stresses [104]. It also accelerated skin graft rejection. In sarcoma and mammary adenocarcinoma, vitamin A prevented or delayed tumor appearance and prolonged survival. Newberry demonstrated that stress induced through the use of forced restraint also significantly inhibited tumor development [86]. Inhibition of tumor growth has been reported in rats subjected to various kinds of stress or chemical induction of carcinogenesis [92, 96]. Cortisone administration and sound stress exposure significantly reduced tumor induction in DBA/1 mice and had little effect in A/Jax mice [81]. In several additional studies, stress did not significantly increase tumor incidence [10, 11, 53, 109]. Still other investigators have demonstrated enhanced tumor growth to various stresses, such as flashing or fluorescent light, rotary motion, or cold [100, 112, 117].

These experiments with animals do not allow broad generalizations, nor is any single conclusion more plausible than others. What investigators refer to as stress in rats, mice, guinea pigs, dogs, and other animals is so far removed from human experience that the appropriateness of extrapolations to human situations has been questioned [30]. Frequently, the "stress" is physical rather than emotional or it is unclear because of confounding in the experimental design [2, 74]. Most of the animal strains used in these experiments are bred for tumorigenesis, so that a good proportion of these animals develop tumors even in the absence of chemical, radiation, or viral carcinogens. Spontaneous tumors in mice of low-cancer strains are immunologically quite different from induced tumors [51]. Furthermore, humans and other species are not uniformly affected by known carcinogens [22]. Not all of the experiments reviewed were double-blind so results might have been affected by investigator bias. Finally, experiments often used only a small number of animals, so sample size might have contributed to the nonreproducibility of results.

Personality Traits and Cancer

Bacon, Renneker, and Cutler in 1952 made an early attempt to delineate the personality traits of women who developed breast cancer. Forty patients with breast cancer, but no controls, were interviewed for evidence of psychosomatic reactions. Evaluations were based on the psychiatric material elicited by recall and the interviewer's personal observations [5]. Patients under age 55 showed the following characteristics: masochistic; sexually inhibited; impulses of motherhood inhibited; inability to discharge or deal appropriately with anger; aggressiveness or hostility covered by a facade of pleasantness; unresolved hostile conflicts with mother handled through denial and unresolved sacrifice; and delay in getting treatment. Women over 55 did not exhibit this set of characteristics. The authors concluded that there was an internalized self-destructive drive in the cancer patient which was not a postcancerous reaction to cancer but a lifelong pattern of behavior.

Elsewhere, Renneker and Cutler outlined the emotional problems faced by women with breast cancer [98]. Patients had to adjust to mutilation as well as to a potentially deadly disease. Post mastectomy, they were filled with anxiety, feelings of worthlessness, and depression. The loss of the breast was seen as a loss of feminity and motherliness. The threat of cancer to the breast was so great the the first reaction of women was to protect the breast and only secondarily to protect life. Since the patients studied were aware of their illness, the results cannot be regarded as due to personality alone.

In a 1954 study of emotional factors and exacerbation of cancer symptoms by Blumberg, the MMPI, the WAIS, and the Rorschach Ink Blot test were administered to patients with inoperable tumors [13]. A group of 18 patients were studied by means of these tests, and the results were used to predict neoplastic growth rate in a second group of 32 patients. Statistically significant differences on the MMPI were found between patients with fast and slow growing tumors and some suggestive trends were found in the Rorschach results. Patients with fast growing tumors were described as more defensive, more motivated to appear good and less disturbed than they actually were.

Growth rates were determined by the speed with which recurrences and metastases were diagnosed, as well as reaction to treatment. But since these patients all had advanced disease they might already have been aware of the speed with which their illness had progressed. Under such circumstances, patients with fast growing tumors might will behave in a noticeably different manner from others not so afflicted. Anxiety, depression, defensiveness, and inability to reduce tension are all explainable by the threat of incurable malignancy and its rapid spread [78].

In a similar study, Klopfer examined three patients with fast growing tumors and three with slow growing tumors to determine the characteristics of patients with either type [62]. (Too many types and sites of cancer have been identified for a sample of six patients to be considered adequate.) In several predictive studies made after criteria had been established, the author achieved 70–80% accuracy in predicting rate of tumor growth. The same criticisms apply to this as to Blumberg's study; differences between cancer patients with fast and slow growing tumors are as likely to be due to the disease process and awareness of its progression, as to personality factors. Unless it can be demonstrated that the findings of such studies are *not* due to the disease, it cannot be concluded that the results are due to personality factors.

Among the leading proponents of the view that personality traits lead to cancer are Claus and Marjorie Bahnson. Their work has encompassed not only studies of individuals with and without malignant disease but an attempt to formulate a model, psychophysiological complementarity, which depicts how personality might lead to cancer [6]. The model postulates that cancer patients and the cancer-prone repress emotions related to lóss. These repressed emotions, probably mediated through the central nervous system, create a cellular situation conducive to neoplastic development. Why repressed traumatic emotions should have a greater effect on risk of developing neoplasia than unrepressed traumatic emotions is not discussed. Others have proposed that traumatic experiences alone (i.e., "life events") lead to illnesses which include cancer [52]. Rasmussen, by contrast, has suggested that stress, trauma, etc. may lead to stimulation of the immunologic system as well as to its depression [95]. Another assumption implicit in the Bahnsons' theoretical formulation is that people have certain "normal" reactions to stressful or disastrous events, particularly to the death of a near relative or spouse. Quite possibly those individuals who appear to repress "expected" emotions simply do not have them, or do not have them to the degree generally seen in others.

The Bahnsons' studies of cancer patients have produced results which tend to support the hypothesis that cancer patients, compared with other patients and normal individuals, make heavy use of denial and repression. In unstructured interviews with cancer patients (but no controls), it was found that all of a group of 24 had been unable to transcend their early dependence on a parent or parent substitute [8]. Conflicts generated by dependency needs led to the use of denial and repression by these patients which, in turn, resulted in a continual constriction of their life patterns.

In structured interviews, cancer patients denied to an unusual degree that they experienced feelings of defeat, failure, frustration, or lack of acceptance and love [8]. Rorschach protocols suggested similar personality structure, but, of greater interest, these patients gave overwhelming amounts of anatomical responses which reflected excessive concern and anxiety about the body, such as references to falling apart, being mutilated or cut up and "weird and paranoid references to death." Yet the authors stressed that almost all of these patients were unaware of their diagnosis. They noted also that several cancer patients gave rare responses to inside parts of the blots:

> Budding potatoes, bulbs, onions and flowers are perceived to unfold independently of other percepts in a bizarre and unusual way. Other responses depict the creation of new islands in the ocean or the appearance of clumps of organic matter in the white spaces of the Rorschach cards. On the level of Rorschach interpretation these rare phenomena seem to support the hypothesis suggested above, that cancer in some way represents a phylogenetically old and regenerative process—at least it does in the *unconscious fantasies* of these patients [Emphasis added].

The authors seem to be of two minds about cancer patients' knowledge of their disease.

In another experiment, the Bahnsons tested the hypothesis that persons with cancer make use of projective defenses to a lesser extent than do normal subjects [8]. Adjective checklist responses to clicks of "white noise"—a neutral environmental stimulus—indicated that patients with cancer were significantly different on two of five dimension-of-emotion scales as well as on two polarity-of-emotion scales, and all differences were in the expected direction. However, 12 statistical tests were made, so the p value required for significance on any one test at the $\alpha = .05$ level would have been .0042 by Bonferroni's inequality (the simplest test to calculate), and none of the differences found met that criterion [80].

In a replication of the study just described, 30 male patients with cancer, each under treatment but unaware of his diagnosis, were compared with 64 normal males selected by a street sampling technique [9]. Statistically significant results were obtained in seven out of ten comparisons. It is doubtful that controls chosen by a street sampling technique would be comparable to the study group for risk factors known to be associated with cancer. At any rate, the authors did not provide data which would make it possible to determine the comparability of cases and controls.

In a reanalysis of data presented in the 1969 paper, four groups of individuals were compared: cancer patients, patients who had a myocardial infarction, mixed sick controls, and normal controls [7]. Three-way analyses of variance, which took account of socioeconomic status and age, were performed. Mean scores for the groups were compared for 12 psychological scales. Results indicated that the cancer group was lowest in anxiety somatization, recent stress, stress at work, perception of external control, Pattern A, and alienation. (Pattern A relates to feeling pushed or controlled by external demands.) Cancer patients of high socioeconomic status saw themselves as healthier and physically stronger than controls. The cancer group was also highest in commitment to social norms and religiosity. Standard statistical techniques were not used to analyze the data, which were comprised of many measurements on the same individuals, nor was a global α level determined for all the comparisons made. Therefore, significance of the statistical tests cannot be evaluated.

Most of the studies done by David Kissen and his associates were attempts to validate the hypothesis that male lung cancer patients had a significantly diminished outlet for emotional discharge. In one study, this hypothesis was tested on 220 lung cancer patients, 204 chest clinic patients with diagnoses other than cancer, and 95 patients from other wards of the same hospital [57]. Outlet for emotional discharge was determined through interviews with patients while the interviewer (Dr. Kissen) and the patient were unaware of the diagnosis. All patients admitted to three chest clinics who were 25 and over were interviewed. Confirmation of the interview impression was obtained through the use of two other measures: (1) a lower incidence of childhood behavior disorders, and (2) the mean neuroticism (N) on the short form of the Maudlsey Personality Inventory.

Statistically significant differences were found in outlet for emotional discharge, as judged from the interview, between lung cancer patients and other patients approximately matched for age. Patients with lung cancer and a poor outlet for emotional discharge appeared to have more than 4.5 times the mortality rate for lung cancer when compared with patients who had a good outlet, and more than 2.5 times the rate of those cancer patients with a moderate outlet. These differences held up at all levels of smoking except for pipe smokers. Information on childhood behavior disorders as judged from the interview material was not included, nor was a test of the difference in mean Neuroticism scores between cancer and other patients.

Judgments of outlet for emotional discharge based on interviews were the most subject to bias—conscious or unconscious. The interviewer, Dr. Kissen, was a former chest physician who had seen many lung cancer patients over a period of years. The probability that he could guess the eventual diagnosis much of the time was high, especially since most lung cancer patients were probably diagnosed when their disease was far advanced. The End Results Study reports that for men diagnosed with lung cancer during 1955–1964 in the United States, only 19% had localized disease [3]. That pattern has not changed [106]. Furthermore, at diagnosis, patients show signs and symptoms of their condition, usually against a background of chronic bronchitis of variable degree [19, 36]. Many, if not most of the patients, undoubtedly knew or suspected their diagnosis [77, 78]. It was unlikely that the interview material was free of bias.

In a later paper, Kissen presented data on adverse events which presumably had psychological relevance for the development of cancer [58]. Only men aged 55–64 were included in the analysis. Differences were found between lung cancer and other medical and surgical patients on the following factors: before age 15—separation from or death of a parent; unhappy home due to either friction between parents or parental absence from the home and other breaks with parents. In adult life, main adverse events were related to work and interpersonal difficulties, particularly in marriage. Difficulties of more than 10 years' duration appeared to be more significant than those of shorter duration.

This study was subject to the same biases as the earlier one and, in addition, included multiple comparisons. If the number of comparisons had been taken into account, all the childhood differences would have failed to reach statistical significance. Of the adult difficulties, only work-related problems, one adult difficulty, and multiple adult difficulties would have retained significant status. Furthermore, though only men aged 55 to 64 were included in the analysis, patients with lung cancer were older than controls and more often of lower socioeconomic class. Other important differences may have existed between the groups, since attempts to ensure comparability of patients and controls were minimal. In this paper, Kissen considered the possibility that the disease process itself might in some way have influenced the findings, and suggested that only prospective studies could verify the validity of the reported results.

Two of Kissen's posthumous papers dealt with steroid excretion patterns and differences in personality test scores for lung cancer patients and controls [59, 60]. An examination of excretion levels of 17-ketosteroids and 17-hydroxy-corticosteriods for 48 cancer patients and 48 controls showed that patients with cancer had a *lowered* adrenal response to the stress of hospital admission than did controls. This study, like the previous one, did not deal appropriately with the problem of multiple significance tests; of the 14 tests made, none would have been significant if the required adjustment had been made. The authors noted that differences in steroid excretion in cancer patients might be the result of the disease and might not be related to the cause of the disease. Study results run counter to the hypothesis that stress is associated with cancer.

In a further sample of lung cancer patients and controls, mean neuroticism scores on the Maudsley Personality Inventory for lung cancer patients were found to be significantly different from age-matched controls ($\bar{x} = 4.57$ for those with lung cancer versus $\bar{x} = 5.34$). Similar results were obtained on the neuroticism scale of the Eysenck Personality Inventory. However, cancer patients and controls did not differ in their scores on the Eysenck Extraversion Scale, in adversities experienced before age 15 or as adults, and in the way in which they tended to report events other than deaths. In reporting the death of a loved one, lung cancer patients more often reported it incidentally rather than in direct response to questions about disturbing and worrisome events. A new 11-item scale—Awareness of Autonomic Activity—was constructed and administered to a subsample of cancer patients and controls. Cancer patients had significantly lower scores on this scale and this finding led the authors to conclude that perhaps the most important component of neuroticism they had measured in cancer patients all along was lack of awareness of autonomic activity. In this study as well, multiple significance tests vitiated many of the significant results; and aside from age, no attempt was made to assure comparability of cases and controls.

In a Hungarian study Levendel *et al.* attempted to utilize the Rorschach for early identification of lung cancer patients. Protocols were obtained from 125 histologically confirmed malignancies, 25 suspected lung cancer patients, 50 patients with different stages of pulmonary tuberculosis, and 50 healthy controls. Cancer patients could be significantly differentiated from the other samples on 17 of 26 criteria—particularly those which related to a sense of impending crisis [72].

Gotthard Booth studied the Rorschach responses of 93 cancer patients and 83 tuberculosis patients [14]. He found that tuberculosis patients were predominantly "genital types" who were dependent on sharing life with others and flexible in the pursuit of this objective. Cancer-prone individuals were characterized by the need for establishing unilateral control over certain chosen objects (e.g., they were predominantly "anal" types). Booth maintained that the perceptual tendencies of the cancer group were definitely unrelated to the presence or absence of disease since 13 records had been obtained by him up to 25 years before appearance of disease symptoms; 46 patients were sick when tested and 35 had undergone surgery for cancer. Since most of the protocols were known to have come from persons with cancer, it is hard to believe that that knowledge did not influence the investigator.

Mastrovito *et al.* studied 228 first admissions to Memorial Hospital [76]. Only women admitted for suspected or confirmed gynecologic malignancies—ovary, uterus, cervix, and vagina—were included. The adjective checklist was administered to each patient shortly after admission to hospital, in most cases prior to confirmed diagnosis. One hundred eighty women were found to have malignancies; the remaining 48 with benign lesions served as controls. Comparison of the two groups showed that cancer patients were more highly controlled, more conforming, and less adventurous, assertive, autonomous, and spontaneous than women in the control group. This personality configuration was drawn from seven scales on the adjective checklist which differentiated between the two groups at p levels ranging from .001 to .023.

Two groups of investigators in Europe reported that women with breast cancer differed from controls. The Swiss study found that fewer patients with breast cancer felt alone or unwanted as children and far fewer had fantasies about loss. These patients were also less realistic, had more defense mechanisms and tended to suppress evidence of conflict [12]. The German study found that women with breast cancer differed from controls on the following personality factors: hypochondriasis, depression, masculine-feminine interests, paranoia, and the exhibition of morbid anxieties, fears, and phobias [91]. Women in the German study were aware of their disease, and the authors felt their responses might have been affected by that knowledge. In the Swiss study, women with breast cancer differed from their controls in age (9-year difference in means), marital status, and backgrounds of broken homes.

Greer and Morris investigated 160 consecutive admissions for breast tumor biopsy by detailed structured interviews and standardized tests administered one day before operation and before the diagnosis was known. Information obtained from cases was verified by interviews with husbands or close relatives. Sixty-nine women in this group had cancer, and the remaining 91 had benign breast disease. This study was set up to measure psychosocial, hormonal, and immunologic variables in women with breast cancer before and after surgery [44]. The principal result was that breast cancer was significantly associated with abnormal release of emotions, and this was a behavior pattern which existed throughout adult life. The abnormality was primarily extreme suppression of anger and, in patients over 40, extreme suppression of other feelings. In addition, extreme expression of emotions, though much less common, also occurred in a higher proportion of cancer patients than controls. No significant differences were detected between cases and controls in psychiatric disorders, marital relations, interpersonal relations, work and leisure activities, or sexual adjustment. Nor were significant differences found in verbal intelligence, hostility or direction of hostility, extraversion, and neuroticism. Denial related to delay in seeking treatment was used by 38% of cancer cases and 32% of controls.

In another paper, Greer and Morris discussed the lack of comparability between patients and controls, and the possibility that those with breast cancer might have become aware of their diagnosis during medical and surgical consultations prior to the psychological examination [45]. Though they noted the difficulty of recall over long periods of time, they did not feel that recall might have been affected by awareness of disease.

Katz *et al.* examined the ratio of corticoid to androgenic steroids and psychological status in a group of 30 women hospitalized for breast biopsy. Both hydrocortisone and androgen values were unremarkable; in fact, the hydrocortisone levels were slightly lower than for normal women in their laboratory [54]. Defensive effectiveness scores showed women on the whole did surprisingly well under this threat, and the authors inferred from this, as did others, that it is not the stress situation per se that evokes psychic distress and adrenal corticosteroid response, but rather, these are dependent upon how the stress is perceived, interpreted, and defended against [54, 55, 67, 75]. Evaluation of the psychological measurements showed no correlation between a single emotion and hydrocortisone production. Elevated rates were associated with apprehension, worry, fear, dejection, discouragement, and despair. Low cortisone excretion rates were associated with hope, faith in God or fate, and pride in the ability to handle life-threatening situations.

Several investigators, among them Henderson [48], Cameron and Hinton [20], and Worden and Weisman [124], have studied the reasons for delay in seeking medical advice among cancer patients as a means of assessing personality characteristics. Henderson found that delay was associated with hysterical personality structure and utilization of denial and repression as defense mechanisms. In addition, among those who delayed, 50% gave a history of psychiatric illness, which varied from mild phobic states to acute or chronic psychotic illnesses. Cameron and Hinton found that those who delayed were no more or less neurotic than those who sought advice early, but introversion was significantly associated with delay, whereas education brought women with breast lumps in faster. Worden and Weisman found positive correlations with delay of 3 months or more; the belief that symptoms were not serious; poor relation with spouse, if married; rejection and/or isolation in childhood; greater denial; and powerlessness on the Vulnerability Index. Two inverse correlations were found with delay: few or no children, if married; and lower social introversion as measured by the MMPI.

Two prospective studies have been reported in the literature [46, 114–116]. Hagnell studied one parish in Sweden with a population of 2550 that had been classified on five personality variables in 1947. A review of the cancer experience of the parish population over the next 10 years demonstrated no personality differences in men with cancer as compared with those without the disease. Contrary to the results of other researchers, women with cancer were significantly more socially oriented, warm, hearty, concrete, and interested in people than women without the disease. One difficulty with this approach is that many of the cancers reported during the 10-year interval may have already existed in 1947 (at least in a subclinical state) and so might have contaminated personality classifications made at the time [46].

The second study, that by Thomas and her associates, followed a cohort of approximately 1200 Johns Hopkins medical students for up to 30 years [114–116]. At the time of the most recent report, 37 malignancies exclusive of skin cancers had been identified [115]. One of the study findings was that former students who developed malignant growths had significantly lower scores than did healthy controls on a scale which measured "closeness-to-parents." However, contrary to the author's conclusion and because of improper interpretation of multiple significance tests, no significant differences were demonstrated between students who ultimately developed cancer and their classmates who did not [114]. An additional difficulty with the reported findings is that no adjustment was made for known risk factors such as smoking.

How does this group of studies measure up to the epidemiological principles enumerated? Little evidence has been produced on the strength of the association between catastrophic events or personality traits and cancer. Ratios of mortality among those widowed compared with married individuals indicate that the relative frequency of death after loss is much greater for other diseases than for cancer.

The temporal sequence of psychosocial variables and cancer has been largely ignored in studies which examined catastrophic events; none considered the time required for a neoplasm to grow from initiation of the first cancer cell or cells to clinical recognition. Thus, the time for which significant psychosocial factors or stressful life events have been assessed is usually too short [31, 34, 110]. In many instances, cancer induction must have taken place prior to the period studied. Studies of personality traits avoided the problem of cancer growth rates but made invalid judgments of equivalence from current to past behavior. There is no evidence to support the view that behavioral expression of personality traits remains constant over long periods of time and unaffected by changes in life situations.

The association between psychosocial variables and cancer has not been shown to be reproducible. Several investigators, whose studies were well designed and executed, found no difference between cancer patients and controls. Differences in the various study results suggest that the results might have been influenced by bias due to recall, selection, or confounding. Alternatively, the results might have been due to chance.

The association has not been shown to persist when variables known to be risk factors for cancer were controlled; these factors were not generally considered in the design of most of the studies.

Interpretations of the data obtained in studies of catastrophic events are not consistent with what is known of the natural history and biology of cancer. Those studies ignore the long latency period required for initiation of the disease, the growth rates of malignant neoplasms at different sites, and the signs and symptoms of different malignancies.

No dose–effect relationship has been demonstrated in these studies but perhaps that principle is not applicable to psychosocial phenomena.

The work of LeShan and Thomas indicates that neither catastrophic events nor personality traits are specific for cancer [71, 114–116]. Other investigators have related stress or psychosocial variables to ulcers, heart disease, mental illness, dwarfism, and amenorrhea [27, 40, 68, 79, 111, 113].

The biological rationale of the hypothesized relationship has yet to be verified; the studies reviewed have not adduced results which deal with that issue. Several ways in which psychosocial variables might lead to cancer have been hypothesized: (a) elevated adrenocortical hormones brought on by emotional states [55, 89, 122]; (b) immunodepression brought on by emotional states [1, 33, 93]; (c) overstimulation of immune mechanisms [103]; (d) genetic predisposition through the mechanism of the histocompatability antigen system [4]; and (e) increased blood levels of free fatty acids [26]. None of these hypotheses suggest the precise pathways by which oncogenesis could be mediated. The view most widely held by investigators is that emotional states depress the immune system and thereby allow cancer cells to slip through the network of guardian cells and proliferate. This view is based on the theory of immunosurveillance postulated by Burnet [18].

For the theory of immunosurveillance to be proved correct, three major points must be substantiated [105]:

1. All or most of the tumor cells must behave as foreign antigens in the host of origin.
2. The antigenicity of the tumor cells must be present from the start of tumor growth and be able to invoke an immune response in the host.
3. Tumor incidence should vary inversely with the immunocompetence of the host.

These points have not been substantiated completely, and this has engendered a controversy in the literature [50, 65, 94, 103]. It has been demonstrated that virally and chemically induced tumors are antigenic, but spontaneous tumors are not [30, 51, 94]. Most human tumors arise spontaneously. Evidence suggests that induced tumors in animals have antigens at an early stage, but the ability of such tumor cells to evoke an immune response is questionable [105]. On the third point, the evidence is mixed. Supporting the theory is the finding that newborn animals are more susceptible to viral induction of tumors. However, newborns are relatively immunoincompetent so that evidence is not very supportive. Immunodeficient or immunodepressed humans do develop more cancers but these neoplasms are primarily leukemia, lymphoma, and reticulum cell sarcoma. Such individuals show no increase in the common cancers, as would be expected if the theory applied to cancer in general. Evidence that does not support the theory of immunosurveillance is found in thymectomized and in fully immunodeficient nude mice. Both types of animals show a lower incidence of tumors rather than the expected increased incidence [105]. So it appears that the theory of immunosurveillance has not been established, particularly for spontaneous tumors.

Perhaps a more promising theory is that of hormonal carcinogenesis recently postulated by Nandi [84]. To paraphrase him, hormones are elevated in patients with cancers of endocrine glands or their target tissues. Hormones regulate cell division in normal cells, and successful neoplastic transformation requires hormonal stimulation of cells that have received carcinogenic insult. Further, normal cells have finite divisional capabilities, whereas neoplastic cells possess infinite divisional capabilities. Normal cells, when present in a high ratio, inhibit the growth of neoplastic cells. Nandi considers hormones to be neither mutagenic nor carcinogenic. Instead, they play a dual role in carcinogenesis. First, hormones are thought necessary to fix the cell genome that has been neoplastically transformed by carcinogens. Second, hormones act to shorten the life span of normal cells by enhancing the rate of cell division. Thus hormones cause a reduction of the normal-cell to tumor-cell ratio in the endocrine gland or its target tissue and so facilitate tumor-cell growth. Recent experimental work and some epidemiologic observations support the hypothesis. If it can be shown that hormones released during emotional states or "stress" reactions act to increase the release of other hormones, and if the hypothesis of hormonal carcinogenesis can be verified, a specific mechanism for relating emotional states to carcinogenesis would be identified. This relationship, however, places psychosocial variables in the class of promotors rather than initiators of carcinogenesis [73].

Finally, we must ask if the results admit of no other interpretation. Do alternative hypotheses explain the results as well or better? Haney has suggested that anecdotal reports and studies which link diagnosed illness with disastrous events might well be due to changes in illness behavior brought about by those events [47]. Old adages support the same point of view: "There but for the grace of God go I," and "Our tears are not for others, but for ourselves." On a practical plane, people engaged in the care of relatives with serious illnesses may defer attention to their own symptoms. When freed of the obligations of care, they may seek medical consultation and so have illness diagnosed.

We suggest the following alternative hypothesis: the disease, its progression, and its associated symptomatology account for the personality characteristics found in patients with cancer.

The disease and its possible effects on patient response were not considered in the retrospective studies reviewed. Though generally unstated, the impression left by most studies was that responses obtained could not have been affected by the disease process or any of its symptoms so long as the patient and the investigator were unaware of the diagnosis. If that view is correct, how then do most cancers come to diagnosis? The disease might be identified by screening tests, routine checkups, or accidentally when patients are examined for other reasons. Screening tests and programs exist primarily for breast and cervical cancer but are not available for most other cancer sites [118]. For breast cancer, evidence indicates that 69% or more of breast lumps are found by women themselves [43, 77]. Screening tests for cervical cytology are available to a large portion of the population through private physicians, clinics, and screening programs [28]. Frequently, however, individuals who avail themselves of screening tests or programs do so because they have experienced symptoms. Clearly, the diagnosis of the overwhelming majority of cancers cannot be attributed to screening. The National Ambulatory Medical Care Survey in 1977 found that less than 10% of the population visited a doctor for a checkup, so that most cancer diagnoses cannot result from such examinations [85]. If determined efforts do not identify malignancies, it is unlikely that they come to light accidentally.

Most malignant disease is diagnosed because patients seek medical care for symptoms that are either immediately recognizable as dangerous or that persist over a long time without improvement. A lump in the breast brings women (occasionally men) to medical attention [43]; bleeding is a symptom of cervical or uterine malignancy [35] and of cancer of the colon or rectum [120]; growths on the skin which do not resolve, persistent cough, or any of the seven warning signs which have been so prominently advertised alert individuals to potential disease. For many malignancies, the symptoms are vague—becoming easily tired, malaise, and lethargy. Pain is usually absent in early disease. Though symptoms may be nonspecific, individuals may be aware of having felt poorly without improvement over a period of time [123]. Further evidence comes from statistics for 1970–1973 on the stage of disease at diagnosis. Of eight major sites, oral, stomach, colon and rectum, pancreas, lung, breast, uterus, and prostate, only for uterus and prostate are the majority of cases diagnosed when the disease is still localized [106]. (Pathological staging for cancer of the prostate, however, may differ substantially from clinical staging [61].) The End Results Study gives similar data for 1955–1969 [3].

These data support the belief that patients come to medical attention because they have persistent symptoms of disease. Investigations of reasons for delay in seeking medical care noted symptoms in the patients studied [20, 48, 124].

Are patients aware of their disease even though the diagnosis has not been mentioned? Several studies found that most of the patients interviewed and observed knew the nature of their illness: however, a prominent feature of cancer patients was denial of that awareness [29, 77, 78, 82]. Weisman reported that 10% of patients denied the diagnosis even after they had been informed of it [119]. The Rorschach responses of cancer patients reported by Bahnson—budding potatoes, formation of new islands—certainly suggest patient awareness of the disease process [8]. Differences in symptoms or their severity between benign and malignant disease and a host of other cues from medical and hospital staff, as well as other patients, provide information on the diagnosis to those with cancer [47, 78].

Additional clues that cancer affects behavior come from reports of malignant disease presenting as psychiatric illness [16]. This evidence supports the contention that patient awareness of malignancy distorts responses obtained at diagnostic workup and that those responses are due to the disease, not personality traits, though they may be exacerbated by catastrophic events. Additional support comes from a study of cancer patients who survived one, three, and six years after cancer diagnosis and treatment [21]. The investigators found that the most traumatic time for patients was at diagnosis when they reacted with shock, anxious distress, and emotional turmoil. Increasing survival was associated with changes in behavior which allowed for a return to family, work, and social activity.

Summary

Investigators of biobehavior in the etiology of cancer have given insufficient attention to those epidemiologic principles which would establish a causal relation between behavioral characteristics and human cancers. Many investigators have attempted to establish such a causal link but study designs frequently have not considered such concepts as the long time lag between neoplastic initiation and clinical recognition of most adult cancers. An additional concept often overlooked is that retrospective studies cannot adequately appraise characteristics of mood, thought, and behavior that existed before clinical recognition of the disease. As a group, these studies have failed to meet essential epidemiologic criteria such as strong association, consistency, reproducibility, and specificity.

We believe that an adequate test of the hypothesis that biobehavior either initiates or promotes cancerous growth requires a prospective approach which utilizes large samples and long periods of follow-up. Generally such an approach would require a large staff and a considerable budget. However, in a prospective approach it is sometimes possible to reduce time into manageable units by using predocumented data on potential causative characteristics. A few such studies have been funded and more may be financed in the near future.

References

1. Amkraut, A. A.; and Solomon, G. F.: From the symbolic stimulus to the pathophysiologic response: Immune mechanisms. *International Journal of Psychiatry in Medicine* 5:541–563, 1975.
2. Amkraut, A. A.; Solomon, G. F.; Kasper, P.; and Purdue, A.: Stress and hormonal intervention in the graft-versus-host response. In *Micro-environmental Aspects of Immunity*, eds. B. D. Jankovic and K. Isakovic, pp. 667–674. New York: Plenum Press, 1973.
3. Axtell, I. M.; Cutler, S. J.; and Myers, M. H., eds.: End Results in Cancer. Report no. 4. DHEW Pub. no. (NIH) 73–272, 1972.
4. Bach, F. H.; and van Rood, J. J.: The majority histocompatibility complex—genetics and biology (third part). *New England Journal of Medicine* 295:927–936, 1976.
5. Bacon, C. L.; Renneker, R.; and Cutler, M.: A psychosomatic survey of cancer of the breast. *Psychosomatic Medicine* 14:453–460, 1952.
6. Bahnson, C. B.: Psychophysiological complementarity in malignancies: past work and future vistas. *Annals of the New York Academy of Sciences* 164:458–461, 1969.
7. Bahnson, C. B.: Emotional and personality characteristics of cancer patients. In *Oncologic Medicine Clinical Topics and Practical Management*, eds. A. I. Sutnick, and P. F. Engstrom, pp. 357–378. Baltimore: University Park Press, 1976.
8. Bahnson, C. B.; and Bahnson, M. B.: Role of the ego defenses: Denial and repression in the etiology of malignant neoplasm. *Annals of the New York Academy of Sciences*, 125:827–845, 1966.
9. Bahnson, M. B.; and Bahnson, C. B.: Ego defenses in cancer patients. *Annals of the New York Academy of Sciences*, 164:346–359, 1969.

10. Baker, D. G.: The influence of a chronic environmental stress on radiation carcinogenesis. *Radiation Research,* 68:449–458, 1976.
11. Baker, D. G.: Influence of a chronic environmental stress on the incidence of methylcholanthrene-induced tumors. *Cancer Research* 37:3939–3944, 1977.
12. Beck, D.; Konig, U.; Blaser, P.; Meyer, R.; Styk, J.; and Ryhiner, O.: Zur Psychosomatik des Mamma-Carcinoms. (The psychosomatics of breast carcinoma.) *Zeitschrift für Psychosomatische Medizin und Psychoanalyse,* 21:101–117, 1975.
13. Blumberg, E. M.: Results of psychological testing of cancer patients. In *Psychological Variables in Human Cancer,* eds. J. A. Gengerelli and F. J. Kirkner, pp. 30–61. Berkeley: University of California Press, 1954.
14. Booth, G.: General and organ-specific object relationships in cancer. *Annals of the New York Academy of Sciences,* 164:568–577, 1969.
15. Bradford Hill, A.: *Principles of Medical Statistics.* New York: Oxford University Press, 1971.
16. Brown, J. H.; Varsamis, J.; Toews, J.; and Shane, M.: Psychiatry and oncology: A review. *Canadian Psychiatric Association Journal,* 19:219–222, 1974.
17. Bross, I. D. J.: Statistical criticism. *Cancer,* 13:393–400, 1960.
18. Burnet, F. M.: *Immunological Surveillance.* Oxford: Pergamon Press, 1970.
19. Buell, P. E.: The importance of tumor size in prognosis for resected bronchogenic carcinoma. *Journal of Surgical Oncology,* 3:539–551, 1971.
20. Cameron, A.; and Hinton, J.: Delay in seeking treatment for mammary tumors. *Cancer* 21:1121–1126, 1968.
21. Castro, J. R.; Mages, N. L.; Fobair, P.; Mendelsohn, G.; and Wolfson, A.: Exploratory studies for cancer patient rehabilitation. Unpublished report. 1979
22. Clayson, D. B.: Overview, fact, myth and speculation. In *Hazards from Toxic Chemicals,* eds. M. A. Mehlman, R. E. Shapiro, M. F. Cranmer, and M. J. Norvell, pp. 1–8. Park Forest South: Pathotox, 1978.
23. Cooley, B.; Henry, J. P.; and Stephens, P. M.: Enhancing effects of psychosocial stimulation on experimental mammary tumors. *Third International Symposium on Detection and Prevention of Cancer* 1976. Meeting abstract.
24. Corson, S. A.: Neuroendocrine and behavioral response patterns to psychologic stress and the problem of the target tissue in cerebrovisceral pathology. *Annals of the New York Academy of Sciences* 125:890–918, 1966.
25. Crisp, A. H.: Some psychosomatic aspects of neoplasia. *Journal of Medical Psychology* 43:313–331, 1970.
26. Dilman, V. M.: Metabolic immunodepression which increases the risk of cancer. *Lancet* 2:1207–1209, 1977.
27. Engel, G. L.: Psychologic factors in instantaneous cardiac death. *New England Journal of Medicine* 294:664–665, 1976.
28. Fasal, E.: Survey of cytology laboratories. California, April–August, 1974. Unpublished data.
29. Feder, S. L.: Psychological considerations in the care of patients with cancer. *Annals of the New York Academy of Sciences* 125:1020–1027, 1966.
30. Fidler, I. J.: Mechanisms of cancer invasion and metastasis. In *Cancer,* ed. F. E. Becker, vol. 4, pp. 101–131. New York: Plenum Press, 1975.
31. Foulds, L.: *Neoplastic Development,* vol. 2. New York: Academic Press, 1975.
32. Fox, B. H.: Premorbid psychological factors as related to cancer incidence. *Journal of Behavioral Medicine* 1:45–133, 1978.
33. Friedman, S. B.; Glasgow, L. A.; Ader, R.: Psychosocial factors modifying host resistance to experimental infections. *Annals of the New York Academy of Sciences* 164:381–392, 1969.

34. Gardner, B.: Breast cancer revisited. *Journal of American Medical Association* 232:742–743, 1975.
35. Garrett, W. J.: On the reduction of cancer mortality: Graham Crawford's experiment, 1949–1969. *Medical Journal of Australia* 1:1239–1243, 1970.
36. Gilby, E. D.: Diseases of the respiratory system: neoplasms of the lung. *British Medical Journal* 1:1331–1333, 1978.
37. Good, R. A.; Fernandes, G.; Yunis, E. J.; Cooper, W. C.; Jose, D. C.; Kramer T. R.; and Hansen, M. A.: Nutritional deficiency, immunologic function, and disease. *American Journal of Pathology*, 84:599–614, 1976.
38. Graham, S.; and Snell, L.: Social trauma as related to cancer of the breast. *British Journal of Cancer* 25:721–734, 1972.
39. Graham, S.; Snell, I. M.; Graham, J. B.; and Ford, L.: Social trauma in the epidemiology of cancer of the cervix. *Journal of Chronic Diseases* 24:711–725, 1971.
40. Green, T. H., Jr.: *Gynecology: Essentials of Clinical Practice.* Boston: Little, Brown & Co., 1971.
41. Greene, W. A.: The psychosocial setting of the development of leukemia and lymphoma. *Annals of the New York Academy of Sciences* 125:794–801, 1966.
42. Greene, W. A.; and Swisher, S. N.: Psychological and somatic variables associated with the development and course of monozygotic twins discordant for leukemia. *Annals of the New York Academy of Sciences* 164:394–408, 1969.
43. Greenwald, P.; Masca, P. C.; Lawrence, C. E., Horton, J.; McGarrah, R. P.; Gabriele, T.; and Carlton, K.: Effect of breast self-examination and routine physician examinations on breast cancer mortality. *New England Journal of Medicine*, 299:271–273, 1978.
44. Greer, S.; and Morris, T.: Psychological attributes of women who develop breast cancer: a controlled study. *Journal of Psychosomatic Research* 19:147–153, 1975.
45. Greer, G.; and Morris, T.: The study of psychological factors in breast cancer: problems of method. *Social Science and Medicine* 12:129–134, 1978.
46. Hagnell, O.: The premorbid personality of persons who develop cancer in a total population investigated in 1947 and 1957. *Annals of the New York Academy of Sciences* 125:846–855, 1966.
47. Haney, C. A.: Illness behavior and psychosocial correlates of cancer. *Social Science & Medicine* 11:223–228, 1977.
48. Henderson, J. G.: Denial and repression as factors in the delay of patients with cancer presenting themselves to the physician. *Annals of the New York Academy of Sciences,* 125:856–864, 1966.
49. Henry, J. P.; Stephens, P. M.; and Watson, F. M. C.: Force breeding, social disorder and mammary tumor formation in CBA/USC mouse colonies: a pilot study. *Psychosomatic Medicine* 37:277–283, 1975.
50. Herberman, R. B.; and Holden, H. T.: Natural cell mediated immunity. *Advances in Cancer Research,* 27:305–377, 1978.
51. Hewitt, H. B.; Blake, E. R.; Walder, A. S. : A critique of the evidence from active host defence against cancer, based on personal studies of 27 murine tumors of spontaneous origin. *British Journal of Cancer* 33:241–259, 1976.
52. Holmes, T. H.; and Masuda, M.: Life change and illness susceptibility. In *Stressful Life Events: Their Nature and Effects,* eds. B. S. Dohrenwend and B. P. Dohrenwend, pp. 45–72. New York: John Wiley & Sons, 1974.
53. Kaliss, N.; and Fuller, J. L.: Incidence of lymphatic leukemia and methylcholanthrene-induced cancer in laboratory mice subject to stress. *Journal of the National Cancer Institute* 41:967–983, 1968.
54. Katz, J.; Ackerman, P.; Rothwax, R.; Sachar, E. J.; Weiner, H.; Hellman, L.; and Gallagher, T. F.: Psychoendocrine aspects of cancer of the breast. *Psychosomatic Medicine* 32:1–18, 1970.

55. Katz, J. L.; Weiner, H.; Gallagher, T. F.; and Hellman, L.: Stress, distress, and ego defenses. *Archives General Psychiatry* 23:131-142, 1970.
56. Kissen, D. M.: The value of a psychosomatic approach to cancer. *Annals of the New York Academy of Sciences* 125:777-779, 1966*a*.
57. Kissen, D. M.: The significance of personality in lung cancer in men. *Annals of The New York Academy of Sciences* 125:820-826, 1966*b*.
58. Kissen, D. M.: Psychosocial factors, personality and lung cancer in men aged 55-64. *British Journal of Medical Psychology* 40:29-43, 1967.
59. Kissen, D. M.; Brown, R. I. F.; and Kissen, M.: A further report on personality and psychosocial factors in lung cancer. *Annals of the New York Academy of Sciences* 164:535-545, 1969.
60. Kissen, D. M.; and Rao, L. G. S.: Steroid excretion patterns and personality in lung cancer. *Annals of the New York Academy of Sciences* 164:476-482, 1969.
61. Klein, L. A.: Prostatic carcinoma. *New England Journal of Medicine* 300:824-833, 1979.
62. Klopfer, B.: Psychological variables in human cancer. *Journal of Projective Techniques* 21:221-40, 1957.
63. Kolata, G. B.: Frederick Mosteller and applied statistics. *Science* 204:397-398, 1979.
64. Kraus, A. S.; and Lilienfeld, A. M.: Some epidemiologic aspects of the high mortality rate in the young widowed group. *Journal of Chronic Diseases* 10:207-217, 1959.
65. Kripke, M. L.; and Borsos, T.: Immune surveillance revisited. *Journal of the National Cancer Institute* 52:1393-1395, 1974.
66. La Barba, R. C.: Experiential factors in cancer. A review of research with animals. *Psychosomatic Medicine* 32:259-275, 1970.
67. Lazarus, R. S.: Psychological stress and coping in adaptation and illness. *International Journal of Psychiatry in Medicine*, 8:321-333, 1974.
68. Lazarus, R. S.: *Patterns of Adjustment*. 3rd. ed. McGraw-Hill, 1976.
69. LeShan, L.: Some methodological problems in the study of the psychosomatic aspects of cancer. *Journal of General Psychology* 63:309-317, 1960.
70. LeShan, L.: An emotional life-history pattern associated with neoplastic disease. *Annals of The New York Academy of Sciences* 125:780-793, 1966.
71. LeShan, L.; and Worthington, R. E.: Loss of cathexes as a common psychodynamic characteristic of cancer patients. An attempt at statistical validation of a clinical hypothesis. *Psychological Reports* 2:183-193, 1956.
72. Levendel, L.; Mezei, A.; Erdely, E.; and Litvai, G.: Study of the personality characteristics of lung-cancer patients. *Zeitschrift für Psychosomatische Medizin und Psychoanalse*, 21:270-283, 1975.
73. Marx, J. L.: Tumor promoters: carcinogenesis gets more complicated. *Science* 201:515-518, 1978.
74. Mason, J. W.: Specificity in the organization of neuroendocrine response profiles. In *Frontiers in Neurology and Neuroscience Research*. First International Symposium of the Neuroscience Institute, eds. P. Seeman, G. M. Brown, pp. 68-80. University of Toronto: 1974.
75. Mason, J. W.: A historical view of the stress field. Part 1. *Journal of Human Stress* 1:6-12, 1975.
76. Mastrovito, R. C.; Deguire, K.; Clarkin, J.; Lewis, J. L.; Cooper, E.: Personality characteristics of women with gynecological cancer (meeting abstract). Third International Symposium on Detection and Prevention of Cancer, pp. 41-42. 1976.
77. McIntosh, J.: Processes of communication, information seeking and control associated with cancer: a selective review of the literature. *Social Science & Medicine* 8:167-187, 1974.
78. McIntosh, J.: Communication and awareness in a cancer ward. NY, *Prodist, 1977.*

79. Medical News. Change of home can help psychosocial dwarfs. *Journal of the American Medical Association* 232:898–899, 1975.
80. Miller, R. G., Jr.: *Simultaneous statistical inference.* New York: McGraw-Hill, 1966.
81. Molomut, N.; Lazere, F.; and Smith, L. W.: Effect of audiogenic stress upon methycholanthrene-induced carcinogenesis in mice. *Cancer Research* 23:1097–1101, 1963.
82. Moses, R.; and Cividali, N.: Differential levels of awareness of illness; their relation to some salient features in cancer patients. *Annals of the New York Academy of Sciences* 125:984–994, 1966.
83. Muslin, H. L.; Gyarfas, K.; Pieper, W. J.: Separation experience and cancer of the breast. *Annals of The New York Academy of Sciences* 125:802–806, 1966.
84. Nandi, S.: Hormonal carcinogenesis: a novel hypothesis for the role of hormones. In *Hazards from Toxic Chemicals,* eds. M. A. Mehlman, R. E. Shapiro, M. F. Cranmer, and M. H. Norvell, pp. 13–20. Park Forest South: Pathotox 1978.
85. National Center for Health Statistics: National ambulatory-medical care survey, 1977. Unpublished data.
86. Newberry, B. H.: Inhibitory effect of stress on experimental mammary tumors (meeting abstract). Third International Symposium on Detection and Prevention of Cancer, pp. 39–40. 1976.
87. Newberry, B. H.; Frankie, G.; Beatty, P. A.; et al.: Shock, stress and DMBA-induced mammary tumors. *Psychosomatic Medicine* 34:295–303, 1972.
88. Paloucek, F. P.; and Graham, J. B.: The influence of psycho-social factors on the prognosis in cancer of the cervix. *Annals of the New York Academy of Sciences* 125:814–816, 1966.
89. Papaioannou, A. N.: *The etiology of human breast cancer.* New York: Springer-Verlag, 1974.
90. Parkes, C. M.; Benjamin, B.; and Fitzgerald, R. G.: Broken heart: a statistical study of increased mortality among widowers. *British Medical Journal* 4:13–16, 1967.
91. Pauli, H. K.; and Schmid, V.: Psychosomatische Aspekte bei der klinischen Manifestationen von Mamma-Carcinomen—Eine psychosomatische Untersuchung. (Psychosomatic aspects in the clinical manifestation of mastocarcinoma: a psychosomatic investigation). *Zeitschrift für Psychotherapie und Medizinisch Psychologie,* 22:76–80, 1972.
92. Pradhan, S. N.; and Ray, P.: Effects of stress on growth of transplanted and 7, 12-dimethylbenzanthracene-induced tumors and their modification by psychotropic drugs. *Journal of the National Cancer Institute* 53:1242–1245, 1974.
93. Prehn, R. T.: The relationship of immunology to carcinogenesis. *Annals of the New York Academy of Sciences* 164:449–453, 1969.
94. Prehn, R. T.: Tumor progression and homeostasis. *Advances in Cancer Research* 23:203–235, 1976.
95. Rasmussen, A. F., Jr.: Emotions and immunity. *Annals of the New York Academy of Sciences* 164:458–461, 1969.
96. Ray, P.; and Pradhan, S. N.: Growth of transplanted and induced tumors in rats under a schedule of punished behavior. *Journal of the National Cancer Institute* 52:575–577, 1974.
97. Rees, W. D.; and Lutkins, S. G.: Mortality of bereavement. *British Medical Journal* 4:13–16, 1967.
98. Renneker, R.; and Cutler, M.: Psychological problems of adjustment to cancer of the breast. *Journal of the American Medical Association* 148:833–838, 1952.
99. Riley, V.; Mouse mammary tumors: alteration of incidence as apparent function of stress. *Science* 189:465–467, 1975.

100. Sakakibara, T.: Effects of brightness or darkness on carcinogenesis. *Journal of Nagoya City University Medical Association* 19:525-557, 1968.
101. Sartwell, P. E., ed.: *Maxcy-Rosenau Preventive Medicine and Public Health.* New York: Appleton-Century-Crofts, 1973.
102. Schmale, A.; and Iker, H.: The psychological setting of uterine cervical cancer. *Annals of the New York Academy of Sciences* 125:807-813, 1966.
103. Schwartz, R. S.: Another look at immunological surveillance. *New England Journal of Medicine* 293:181-184, 1975.
104. Seifter, E.: Modification by vitamin A of adrenal and thymus responses in skin-grafted, tumor-bearing, or otherwise stressed mice. *Proceedings of the American Association for Cancer Research,* 17:98, 1976.
105. Sell, S.: *Immunology, Immunopathology and Immunity.* Hagerstown: Harper & Row, 1975.
106. Silverberg, E.: Cancer statistics, 1979. *Ca-A Cancer Journal for Clinicians,* 29:6-21, 1979.
107. Simonton, O. C.: The role of the mind in cancer therapy. Presented at Dimensions of Healing Symposium, San Francisco, California, October 7, 1973.
108. Simonton, O. C.; and Simonton, S. M.: Belief systems and management of the emotional aspects of malignancy. *Journal of Transpersonal Psychology* 7:29-47, 1974.
109. Somogyi, S.; and Kovacs, K.: Effect of stress on the adrenocorticolytic and carcinogenic action of 7, 12-dimethylbenz(a)anthracene. *Zeitschrift für Krebsforschung,* 75:288-295, 1971.
110. Steel, G. G.: *Growth Kinetics of Tumors.* Oxford: Clarendon Press, 1977.
111. Sturdevant, R. A. L.: Epidemiology of peptic ulcer. *American Journal of Epidemiology* 104:9-14, 1976.
112. Suzuki S.: Effect of rotary motion on carcinogenesis. *Journal of Nagoya University Medical Association,* 19:1517-1558, 1969.
113. Syme, S. L.: Implications and future prospects. In *Social Stress and Cardiovascular Disease,* eds. S. L. Syme and L. G. Reeder, *Milbank Memorial Fund Quarterly* 45:175-180, 1967.
114. Thomas, C. B.: Precursors of premature disease and death: the predictive potential of habits and family attitudes. *Annals of Internal Medicine* 85:653-658, 1976.
115. Thomas, C. B.: Habits of Nervous Tension: Clues to the Human Condition. *The Precursors Study.* Johns Hopkins University School of Medicine, Baltimore, 1977.
116. Thomas, C. B.; and Duszynski, K. R.: Closeness to parents and the family constellation in a prospective study of five disease states: suicide, mental illness, malignant tumor, hypertension and coronary heart disease. *Johns Hopkins Medical Journal* 134:251-270, 1974.
117. Turbiner, S.; Shklar, G.; and Cataldo, E.: The effect of cold stress on chemical carcinogenesis of rat salivary glands. *Oral Surgery Oral Medicine Oral Pathology* 29:130-137, 1970.
118. Vaisrub, S.: Cancer staging (editorial). *Journal of the American Medical Association* 240:2570, 1978.
119. Weisman, A. D.: Early diagnosis of vulnerability in cancer patients. *American Journal of Medical Science* 271:187-196, 1976.
120. Winawer, S. J.: Colorectal neoplasia: current techniques for early diagnosis. *NY State Journal of Medicine* 78:1892-1894, 1978.
121. Wixen, J. S.: Cancer and the mind. *Modern Maturity,* 46-48, 1978-1979.
122. Wolff, C. T.; Friedman, S. B.; Hofer, M. A.; and Mason, J. W.: Relationship between psychological defenses and mean urinary 17-hydroxycorticosteroid excretion rates. *Psychosomatic Medicine,* 26:576-591, 1964.

123. Wood, R. A.: If I had Hodgkin's disease. *British Medical Journal* 1:1329–1331, 1978.
124. Worden, J. W.; and Weisman, A. D.: Psychosocial components of lagtime in cancer diagnosis. *Journal of Psychomatic Research* 19:69–79, 1975.
125. Young, M.; Benjamin, B.; and Wallis, C.: The mortality of widowers. *Lancet* 2:454–456, 1963.

Behavioral Influences on Immune Responses[1]

ROBERT ADER

We have recently initiated a program of research dealing with the modification of immune responses by conditioning procedures. Our initial efforts have been reasonably successful. We have observed small but reproducible effects of conditioning in suppressing immunologic reactivity, and these observations [5, 6] have been independently replicated in other laboratories [55, 70]. It would seem that studies of conditioned suppression or enhancement of immune responses may, indeed, provide a means for studying the role of the central nervous system in regulating immune processes in the intact, behaving organism. It may not be premature, then, to include a discussion of such observations in relation to cancer in a book devoted to behavioral factors in medicine.

Immune processes have been linked to cancer. Therefore, an understanding of the potential influence of behavioral factors on immune function would provide a link to understanding the role of psychological factors in cancer. It is not my purpose, however, to prove the point. Our studies were not initiated to establish a direct relationship between behavioral processes and the development of or response to cancer. Coming from a background of concern for developing an experimental foundation for and analysis of psychosomatic phenomena, we were struck by the possibility and potential importance of understanding how behavior and central nervous system function might influence the immune system—a system of immense complexity and of central importance as a mechanism of defense against disease

[1] Preparation of this chapter and related research of the author were supported by a Research Scientist Award (K5–MH–06318) and a research grant (NS–15071) from the United States Public Health Service.

in general and, perhaps, against cancer in particular. The immune system represents a relatively unexplored mechanism through which behavioral factors could exert an influence on susceptibility to disease as it develops in the real world, and, as such, it represents a promising area for interdisciplinary study in psychosomatic or behavioral medicine.

Despite the emergence and convergence of data from different disciplines and from studies at different biobehavioral levels of organization, it is not a universally accepted premise that there is central nervous system regulation of immune processes. For example, Spector [65] cites the opening statement of a recent textbook on immunology, "In all types of immune or allergic reactions an individual acquires specific information (learns) from contact with an antigen without the mediation of the nervous system [57]." Other authors [16] have also rejected the possibility of central nervous system involvement in specific immune phenomena, and even modern textbooks in immunology devote little or no attention to the central nervous system or to factors in the environment that, processed through the nervous system, could be operating to influence immune function. Most generously, we can perhaps attribute this limited vision to the complexity of the immune system itself and to the difficulties one encounters in studying and defining the nature of a field that is at an early stage of development but is growing rapidly. In some respects the strategy of immunologic research is reminiscent of the eminently successful approach adopted by Koch, Pasteur, and the following generation of investigators who designed and implemented their studies in such a way as to eliminate with care the effects of factors that might influence the phenomena being examined and, conversely, carefully chose conditions that would unconditionally elicit the phenomenon under study. As Dubos [18] has so eloquently argued, however, such an approach decreases or eliminates the myriad factors which do, in fact, contribute to the way in which the behaving individual adapts and maintains homeostasis in the real world. It is our own intellectual limitations that have led to the proliferation of arbitrary disciplinary boundaries which have no necessary relationship to a full understanding of natural phenomena. In statistical terms, the real world is not made up of simple "main effects," but of complex interactions. Such complex interactions (Figure 1) must be incorporated into our studies, even if it means crossing disciplinary boundaries. Like other interdependent physiologic systems, immune processes will not be completely understood until immunologic research considers the even more complex host within which such processes take place.

That host factors are of critical and, perhaps, primary importance in determining physiologic responsivity, disease susceptibility or, if you will, the maintenance of homeostasis is almost intuitively evident. There are,

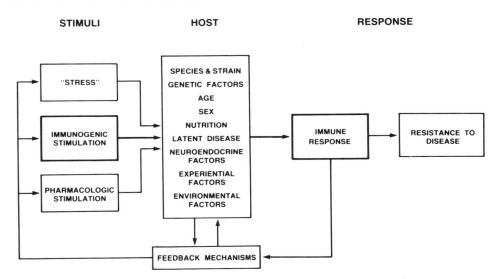

FIGURE 1. *This diagram shows role of host factors in the mediation of the organism's response to immunogenic stimulation.*

however, data that may be brought to bear on the issue. Immunologic research has, of course, attended to some characteristics of the host. For the most part these have included the species and strain of animals chosen for particular studies, genetic factors that make certain animals especially appropriate for study or that define the phenomena under investigation, and variables such as the age, sex, and nutritional status of the organism. Most frequently, though, these variables have been considered for methodological reasons rather than as an acknowledgment of the host factors that might modify immune processes. It is also possible that, whereas the potential role of central nervous system processes is acknowledged, such processes are purposely ignored in order to conduct relatively straightforward experiments or to avoid further complicating an already complex phenomenon. This approach is perhaps a pragmatic strategy at this stage in the development of our understanding of the immune system; but it is inadequate for a complete understanding of immune processes as adaptive mechanisms operating in concert with other adaptive mechanisms to maintain the integrity of the whole organism.

Let me turn now to the data that bear more or less directly on the potential relationship between behavioral and immune processes and illustrate some of the influences depicted in Figure 1. There are several quite disparate lines of evidence which support the proposition that CNS processes influence immunologic reactivity. There is, first and most generally, research documenting the effects of "stress" on susceptibility to diseases that involve immunologic mediation. Furthermore, there are studies that describe the effects of "stress" on various parameters of immunologic competence. I will discuss this literature only briefly, emphasizing the behavioral and psychosocial factors. More extensive reviews of data derived from studies in man and in animals have been prepared [8, 18, 22, 38, 54, 62], and new detailed and critical reviews are in preparation [4].

Another line of evidence consists of studies now being undertaken on conditioning. As extensions of the literature on the learning of visceral responses, these studies suggest that conditioning processes may modify immunologic responses. In fact, such studies were initiated in the Soviet Union 50 years ago and have been referred to in the American literature by as notable a source as Clark Hull [32]. A separate review of this latter material is also being prepared [4]. I will concentrate here on an overview of our own studies on conditioned immune responses.

Additional evidence for central nervous system involvement in immune processes may be derived from the parallel ontogenetic development of neuroendocrine and immune function [47], the effects of hormonal changes on immune processes [7, 12, 73], and the effects of pharmacologic agents [49], including psychomimetic drugs such as marijuana [44] on immune responses. Finally, there are the several reports on the effects of lesioning or stimulation of specific areas within the hypothalamus on immune mediated responses and on specific parameters of immunologic responsivity. These data have been reviewed by Jankovic and Isakovic [34] and Stein, Schiavi, and Camerino [66].

Disease Susceptibility

Studies of the effects of "stress" on neoplastic processes constitute one source of data with respect to experimentally induced disease processes that may involve immunologic mechanisms. Without going into detail, I would simply note that a variety of experimental conditions, including the manipulation of early life experiences, change in the psychosocial environment of laboratory animals, and a variety of presumably stressful stimulus conditions induce changes within the organism which, in interaction with the changes induced by the superimposed pathogen, result in alterations in susceptibility to mammary tumors, transplanted tumors, and experimentally induced as well as spontaneously occurring forms of leukemia. La Barba [38] has reviewed much of this research and Dr. Riley will be discussing more recent work in this field in his papers in this volume.

Viral disease represents another example. In general, it would appear that "stress" increases susceptibility to a variety of infectious agents, but, as is the case with the stimulus conditions used to influence neoplastic processes, it is not entirely clear that all the behavioral manipulations imposed can be subsumed under the single rubric of "stress," the results are not uniform or simple, and the effects are frequently small or equivocal. Rasmussen, Marsh, and Brill [52], for example, subjected mice to 6 hr of avoidance conditioning daily. Mortality to herpes simplex virus inoculation increased from 44% in controls to 56% in mice stimulated for 14 days, and to 74% in mice stimulated for 28 days before virus inoculation. Six hours per day of restraint plus food and water deprivation yielded the same results. Johnson, Lavender, and Marsh [37] used the same avoidance conditioning situation for a period of 4–5 weeks and then inoculated mice with Coxsackie B virus. The "stressed" animals showed significantly more weight loss than controls. Furthermore, all the animals that died came from the "stressed" group, and these animals also showed the greater amounts of virus present in various organs.

Similar results were obtained in a study in which an attempt was made to control for the direct physical effects of the electric shock used in avoidance conditioning paradigms [20]. Adult mice were individually housed in experimental chambers and subjected to a periodic schedule of a light followed by electric shock. Control groups experienced either the light or the shock stimulus alone, on the same periodic schedule, or remained unmanipulated. Stimulation was introduced 3 days before inoculation with Coxsackie B virus and continued for 4 days after inoculation. Additional groups of mice experienced the same environmental conditions but were not inoculated with virus. Under these conditions, neither the "stressful" stimulation nor the inoculum alone was sufficient to cause any weight change. Mice inoculated with Coxsackie virus *and* subjected to the periodic presentation of light–shock stimulation, however, showed a significant reduction in body weight. Moreover, all the animals that died came from this light–shock group.

Rasmussen, Hildemann, and Sellers [51] inoculated mice with polyoma virus at birth. Some time after weaning, the animals were subjected to an avoidance-conditioning paradigm plus high-intensity sound stimulation. In this instance, the stressful stimulation did not influence disease susceptibility. The negative results were attributed to the delay between virus inoculation and the initiation of "stress." When the environmental stimulation was introduced immediately after inoculation with virus (2–3 weeks of age), the stimulated mice were more susceptible than controls [14].

Further evidence of the critical nature of the temporal relationship between "stress" and susceptibility to viral infection comes from the study by Jensen and Rasmussen [35]. Mice were subjected to intense auditory stimulation for 3 hr per day and inoculated intranasally with vesicular stomatitis virus at different times in relation to the "stress" period. Initially, susceptibility was increased whether the animals were inoculated immediately before or after the stressful stimulation. In animals that were not inoculated with virus until the second "stress" day, a biphasic response was observed; mice inoculated before the period of auditory stimulation showed an increased mortality, whereas mice inoculated after the "stress" period were more resistant to the virus than controls. The biphasic character of host resistance was seen in all animals after the second day of stimulation. Adrenalectomized animals tested on the second "stress" day responded like intact animals tested on the first day; there was an increased susceptibility independent of the time of inoculation. In a subsequent experiment [74], mice were subjected to avoidance conditioning for 6 hr daily and the vesicular stomatitis virus was introduced intramuscularly. There were no observable effects when virus was introduced on the second day of avoidance conditioning. When animals were inoculated after 15 days of "stress," however, the rate of disappearance of virus was significantly retarded in the "stressed" animals, and the same effect was observed in adrenalectomized animals.

Susceptibility to parasitic infection may also be increased in animals subjected to stressful environmental circumstances. Weinmann and Rothman [71] observed a depressed resistance to *Hymenolepsis nana*, a tape worm, when intense fighting occurred among male mice. Hamilton [30] also observed an increased susceptibility to *H. nana* reflected by the rate of reinfection, which increased in proportion to the frequency with which immunized mice were subjected to "predator-induced stress" (i.e., were exposed to a cat).

Despite the apparent uniformity in the data just cited, stressful environmental stimulation does not always result in an increased susceptibility to infectious disease. In some instances no differences in susceptibility have been observed, whereas in other instances "stress" decreased susceptibility. Exposing mice to light and/or electric shock stimulation had no effect on the response to encephalomyocarditis virus, but increased resistance to *Plasmodium berghei*, a rodent malaria [21]. Monkeys exposed to stressful stimulation (avoidance conditioning) have been shown to have an increased resistance to poliomyelitis [41], and the physical restraint of rats (but not immersion in a cold bath) suppresses development of experimental allergic encephalomyelitis [39].

An especially compelling illustration of the multiple effects of "stress" on responses to infectious disease processes is provided by studies in which the social interactions among animals are altered or by studies on differential housing (i.e., the effects of housing animals in groups or individually).[2] To summarize these data, group housing or manipulations that effectively increase or alter the social interactions among animals have been found to increase resistance to encephalomyocarditis virus [23] and *Escherichia coli* [27] while increasing susceptibility to trichinosis [15], malaria [50], and rabies virus [60]. Comparable data could be cited in the case of neoplastic and other pathophysicologic processes. One related example is that Amkraut *et al.* [10] report that the "stress" of crowding increases susceptibility to adjuvant-induced arthritis in the rat, while Rogers *et al.* [56] observed an increased resistance to a collagen-induced arthritis in rats "stressed" by exposure to a cat.

These are some of the data which, in documenting the effects of environmental manipulations on susceptibility to infectious disease, suggest that environmental influences and behavioral responses may have an effect on the immune system. While these studies tell us little about the mechanisms that may be involved, they do contain something of a lesson with respect to the concepts and strategies that may have to be adopted if one is to pursue this line of research. Methodologically, a more detailed review of this literature indicates that the effects of "stress" on susceptibility to infectious disease (as is the case for other pathophysiologic processes) depends upon several factors, including, for example, the age, sex, and species of animal as well as the (experientially determined) psychophysiological state of the organism upon which potentially pathogenic stimulation is superimposed; that is, it is determined by a variety of factors interacting within the host. Susceptibility will also be determined by the nature and intensity (chronicity) of the stressful stimulation and by the nature and intensity (concentration) of the challenge to the host. It is clear that the various forms of stimulation used and referred to in most studies as being stressful do not necessarily have equivalent effects. Therefore, to refer to responses to electric shock, avoidance conditioning, restraint, "overcrowding," etc. as responses to stressors will contribute little to our understanding of the mechanisms that may mediate the altered susceptibility to disease, and, as I have argued before [1], such a generalization may even impede progress in this field by its implicit assumption of an equivalence of stimuli, fostering the search for simple, single-cause explanations. It is also clear that whatever stimulation is imposed and however it may be interpreted by the experimenter, the effects of such

---

[2] Differential housing is often referred to in terms of the effects of "crowding" or "isolation," terminology which, among other faults, bears a predictive relationship to the results obtained.

stimulation are not likely to be either uniformly detrimental or uniformly beneficial to the organism. Whether such experimentally imposed stimulation acts to increase or decrease susceptibility to disease depends upon the nature of the disease process under study. That is, the adaptive significance of the psychophysiological response to some alteration in environmental circumstances depends upon the pathogenic stimulus to which the organism may be exposed. Therefore, until such time as we can define which of the myriad physiologic (including, presumably, immunologic) changes that accompany the response and adaptation to environmental stimuli are relevant in mediating the effects of potentially pathogenic stimuli, we will be unable to predict (or control) the effects of behavioral factors on disease susceptibility. If behavioral scientists are going to contribute to an understanding of issues in health and disease and if these contributions are to be acknowledged and accepted in the instigation of research, we cannot afford to compound the complexities of the relationship between behavior and disease by premature generalizations. It would be much simpler to accept the statement that stress will increase susceptibility to disease; but it would be more consistent with a multifactorial approach to psychosomatic phenomena (and the available data) to ask what kind of psychosocial or environmental changes influence the response to which pathogenic stimuli in which individual(s).

Immunologic Reactivity

The second source of data with respect to the relation between behavior and immune function consists of studies in which the effects of "stress" have been detected within the immune system. The rapid technological advances that are being made in immunology now permit relatively sensitive *in vitro* assays that are just beginning to be applied to the analysis of psychoimmunologic phenomena. Gisler *et al.* [24], for example, found that spleen cell suspensions obtained 6–24 hr after mice were exposed to acceleration in a centrifuge or to ether anesthesia resulted in a suppression of *in vitro* immunologic reactivity. The onset and degree of suppression varied among the several mouse strains tested and the procedures used. Data obtained in a subsequent study [25] suggest that such "stress" effects can be reproduced by injection of ACTH. Soloman, however, reports in a personal communication that neither he nor Gisler have been able to suppress *in vivo* responses by such hormone administration. Although Solomon also reports that the "crowding" of rats (to an extent or for a duration sufficient to increase adrenocortical steroid levels) did not influence *in vitro* reactivity, Joasoo and McKenzie [36] did observe a decrease in the response to human thyroglobulin of splenic lymphocytes obtained from rats subjected to "crowding" for a period of 5 weeks before the introduction of antigen.

Increases as well as decreases in lymphocyte response have been observed in "stressed" animals [19, 43]. In the study by Monjan and Collector, mice were subjected to loud noise for periods of 1 or 3 hr daily. Initially, *in vitro* lymphocyte cytotoxicity and the response of splenic lymphocytes to mitogenic stimulation were depressed. After approximately one month of daily stimulation, however, there was an increase in reactivity. The description of a biphasic response to environmental stimulation confirms the critical effect of the time at which samples are obtained in attempting to characterize immunologic responses.

Changes in cellular immunity have also been observed *in vivo*. Using electric shock stimulation, Guy [28] and Mettrop and Visser [42] observed an increased reactivity in guinea pigs in response to a topically applied chemical irritant. A less severe delayed hypersensitivity reaction, however, was observed among mice subjected to high temperature [46]. Reduced responsivity was also reported by Wistar and Hildemann [72], who subjected mice to an avoidance-conditioning regimen and observed prolonged survival of a skin allograft. Amkraut *et al.* [9] observed changes in a graft-versus-host response in mice placed on a limited feeding schedule. Limited feeding introduced before and continuing after induction of the graft-versus-host response suppressed the response, whereas limited feeding confined to the period before the injection of donor cells was without effect. Further experiments in adrenalectomized or ACTH-treated hosts indicated that the effects of restricted feeding could not be attributed to changes in corticosteroid levels.

Adrenal changes do seem to be involved in resistance to anaphylactic shock. Rasmussen *et al.* [53] and Treadwell and Rasmussen [67] found that mice subjected to daily avoidance conditioning showed a less severe shock reaction and a lower mortality than unstimulated controls. A "stress"-induced resistance to anaphylaxis was not observed in adrenalectomized animals but was restored in adrenalectomized mice treated with hydrocortisone. That adrenalectomy can increase resistance to analphylactic shock is not at issue. That adrenal function can therefore account for the effects of acute and/or chronic environmental stimulation on resistance to analphylaxis, however, is not quite clear. Because of the literature indicating that "crowded" mice have higher levels of adrenocortical activity, Treadwell and Rasmussen [67] also examined the anaphylactic response in group-housed and individually housed animals. Under the smaller of two challenge doses, the "incidental stress of isolation" resulted in increased resistance to anaphylaxis.

Several studies have now documented the effects of a variety of experiential manipulations on the production of antibody in response to immunogenic stimulation, although the effects are frequently small and by no means uniform. Yamada *et al.* [74], for example, were able to demonstrate the effects of an avoidance conditioning regimen on the response to inoculation with vesicular stomatitis virus but were unable to detect differences in antibody response. Hill *et al.* [31] immunized monkeys with bovine serum albumin, exposed them to a variety of stimuli (noise, light, loss of support), and were able to observe a smaller and slower rise in antibody titer in the stimulated animals. Vessey [69] observed less precipitating antibody in response to beef serum in mice moved from individual to group housing conditions. In contrast, Glenn and Becker [26] observed that in mice previously immunized with bovine serum albumin, group-caged mice had higher levels of precipitating antibody in response to a booster injection of antigen than individually caged animals.

Solomon [61] noted a reduced primary and secondary response to flagellin, a bacterial antigen, when group housing was introduced before and maintained after immunization. Of the four "stressors" applied, though, group housing was the only one that influenced antibody responses. In reviewing some of their unpublished work, Solomon *et al.* [63] point out that while "stress" may be immunosuppressive when imposed before and immediately after inoculation with flagellin, "stress" imposed several days after inoculation is ineffective. Moreover, "stress" effects are observed only in response to relatively small doses of antigen; large doses of flagellin or sheep erythrocytes, for example, are evidently insensitive to the effects of environmental manipulations.

One final example of the effects of experientially induced host factors on humoral immunity is the observation that the immunologic reactivity of the adult may be influenced by early life experiences [64]. Rats handled daily during the period from birth through weaning were subsequently found to have a more pronounced primary and secondary antibody response to inoculation with flagellin than unstimulated controls.

Experiential factors appear to be capable of modifying immune responses. Like the previously cited data on disease susceptibility, the effects seem to depend upon the quality and quantity of the environmental stimulation, the immunogenic stimulus, a variety of host factors, and the parameters of immunologic reactivity that are measured [29]. Also, the effects of experiential factors on immunologic reactivity are generally small and at least superficially inconsistent, but this reflects upon our incomplete understanding of the mechanisms involved rather than upon the phenomenon itself.

Conditioning Effects

The most recent research implicating the central nervous system in the regulation of immune processes comes from our own studies of conditioning. The hypothesis that conditioning procedures could be used to suppress immunologic reactivity derived from the serendipitous observation of mortality among animals being tested in a taste aversion learning situation. Briefly, a single trial on which a novel, distinctively flavored drinking solution is paired with an injection of a toxin that elicits noxious gastrointestinal effects will result in an aversion to that drinking solution when it is subsequently presented. In one study, we were comparing the effects of different volumes of a saccharin solution, the conditioned stimulus (CS), paired with a constant dose of cyclophosphamide, the unconditioned stimulus (US). The magnitude of the initial aversion to saccharin and resistance to extinction varied directly with the volume of saccharin consumed on the single conditioning trial. During the course of extinction, however, some of the animals died, and mortality rate tended to vary directly with the volume of saccharin originally consumed. As it happens, the US in this study, cyclophosphamide, is a potent cytotoxic drug which suppresses immunologic responses [40, 68]. Therefore, in an attempt to account for this observation, it was hypothesized that pairing a neutral stimulus with an immunosuppressive agent could result in the conditioning of immunosuppression. If conditioned animals were repeatedly reexposed to such a CS and were thus immunologically impaired, they might have become susceptible to the superimposition of latent pathogens that were present in the environment.

These speculations were translated into a study designed to examine conditioned immunosuppression [5]. The general protocol is outlined in Table 1. Details of the initial experiment were as follows:

Individually caged rats were gradually adapted to a single 15-min drinking period at the same time each day, a regimen that was then maintained throughout the period of observation. On the day of conditioning, conditioned animals received a 0.1% saccharin chloride solution of tap water during their 15-min drinking period, followed by an intraperitoneal (ip) injection of cyclophosphamide (CY) in a dose of 50 mg/kg. Nonconditioned animals were, as usual, provided with plain tap water and similarly injected with CY. A placebo group received plain water and an injection of an equal volume of vehicle. Three days after conditioning, all animals were injected ip with sheep erythrocytes (SRBC). Thirty minutes later, one group of conditioned animals (Group CS) received a single drinking bottle containing the saccharin solution and was thereafter injected with saline.

TABLE 1
Experimental Treatments

Group	Adaptation	Conditioning Day 0 Drinking solution	Conditioning Day 0 Injection	Subgroup	Days after conditioning Day 3[a] Drinking solution	Day 3[a] Injection	Day 6 Drinking solution	Day 6 Injection
Conditioned	H_2O	SAC	CY	CS	SAC	saline	SAC	saline
				CS_0	H_2O	saline	H_2O	saline
				US	H_2O	CY	H_2O	saline
Nonconditioned	H_2O	H_2O	CY	NC	SAC	saline	SAC	saline
Placebo	H_2O	H_2O	saline	P	H_2O	—	H_2O	—

[a]Day of antigen treatment

To control for the effects of conditioning, per se, a second group of conditioned animals (Group CS_0) received plain water (i.e., no reexposure to the CS) and was injected with saline. To define the unconditioned immunosuppressive effects of CY, a third conditioned group (Group US) received plain water followed by an injection of CY. Following treatment with antigen, nonconditioned animals (Group NC) were, like Group CS, provided with the saccharin solution and injected with saline, while placebo-treated animals (Group P) received plain water and remained unmanipulated. In some experiments, these several groups were treated in the same way on a second occasion following the injection of antigen. In this initial experiment, independent groups were treated when they received antigen (Day 0), 3 days after antigen, or on Day 0 and Day 3. On intervening days, animals were provided with plain water during their scheduled drinking period. Six days after antigen, all animals were killed, and blood samples were obtained for titrating hemagglutinating antibody.

Data from our initial experiment are shown in Figure 2. Conditioned animals reexposed to saccharin on the day they received antigen or 3 days after antigen did not differ and were collapsed into a single group that

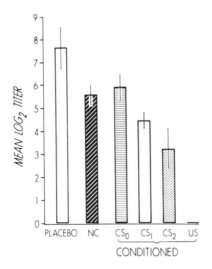

FIGURE 2.   *Hemagglutination titers (mean ± SE) were obtained 6 days after a ip injection of SRBC in placebo-treated animals (P), nonconditioned animals (NC), and in conditioned animals that received no reexposure to the conditioned stimulus (CS_0), those that received the immunosuppressive drugs (US), and those that received one (CS_1) or two (CS_2) reexposures to the conditioned stimulus following treatment with antigen. (Reprinted with permission of Elsevier North-Holland, Inc. from Ader and Cohen,* Psychosomatic Medicine, *1975, 37, p. 336.)*

received one CS presentation (Group CS_1). The comparable control groups did not differ either and were similarly combined. The relationship among the several groups were precisely as predicted. Placebo-treated animals showed the highest antibody titers and CY treatment at the time of antigenic stimulation suppressed the immune response. Nonconditioned animals exposed to saccharin and the subgroup of conditioned animals that were not reexposed to saccharin (Group CS_0) did not differ, but had lower titers than Group P. This, presumably, reflects the residual effects of the drug administered on the day of conditioning. It is, then, the NC and CS_0 groups that represent the appropriate control conditions against which to assess the effects of conditioning. The critical experimental groups, conditioned animals reexposed to the CS on either one or two occasions following inoculation with SRBC, showed an attenuated antibody response which was significantly below the titers seen in both the NC and the CS_0 groups. Our initial results, then, support the notion that the pairing of saccharin, a neutral stimulus, with an immunosuppressive drug enabled saccharin to elicit a conditioned immunosuppressive response.

These basic results on conditioned suppression of the antibody response to SRBC have been independently replicated by Rogers *et al.* [55] and Wayner *et al.* [70]. Moreover, the absolute values and degree of attenuation effected by conditioning are remarkably similar in these three studies.

Several additional experiments have been conducted in an effort to eliminate some of the variables we have come to recognize as potential sources of interference with the conditioning effect, to increase the magnitude of what is essentially a small effect, and to define the parameters of the conditioning paradigm that may be optimal for demonstrating conditioning effects. We have, for example, eliminated ip injections of saline for the several control groups, since there are abundant data to indicate that an ip injection itself can serve as a CS [17, 33, 45, 58]. This means that our control groups were being reexposed to a part of the original complex of stimuli that constituted the CS. Having shown that the mere presence of a saccharin solution in the colony room of animals in which a taste aversion has been conditioned to saccharin is sufficient to reduce the *water* consumption of conditioned animals [3], we now house the several different groups in separate colony rooms. We have defined for ourselves the dose-related residual effects of CY and, accordingly, increased the interval between conditioning and antigenic stimulation. We have changed the CS solution and the immunosuppressive drug and have varied the concentration of the US and the concentration of antigen. In all such instances we have observed a conditioned attenuation of the antibody response. However, there have been instances in which the conditioned animals reexposed to the CS have differed significantly from both the NC and CS_0

animals, instances in which group CS has differed significantly from only one of the two control groups, and instances in which the titers in Group CS were insignificantly lower than those in the control groups. Thus far, we have not been successful in increasing the magnitude of the conditioned response; it has remained on the order of approximately 25%. Thus, the compelling aspect of the conditioning data has been the consistency rather than the magnitude of the effect.

In addition to using a T-cell dependent antigen, SRBC, Wayner *et al.* [70] conducted a second experiment with *Brucella abortus*, a T-cell independent antigen and, in this instance, did not observe significant effects. These must be viewed as preliminary data since they are based on a single dose of antigen and a single sample obtained following antigen. Moreover, we have data to indicate the effects of conditioning can be generalized to a T-cell independent system [13]. Conditioned mice reexposed to the CS at the time of treatment with trinitrophenyllipopolysaccharide showed a significant attenuation of the antibody response.

There is no readily available explanation for the effects of conditioning. Antibody titer, as a reflection of immunologic responsivity, is determined by a complex chain of events that, at any of several points, might be influenced by neuroendocrine changes effected by conditioning. Since high levels of adrenocortical steroids may be immunosuppressive, it could be hypothesized that the attenuated antibody response seen in conditioned animals is a direct reflection of the nonspecific "stress" induced by the conditioning procedures or a conditioned elevation in steroid level [2]. This, however, does not seem to be the case. In one study, designed to control for the effects of reduced fluid consumption in conditioned animals that avoid consumption of saccharin on the day that antigen is introduced, a preference or two-bottle test procedure was used. Under these conditions, there is still a reduction in saccharin intake, but there is no reduction in the total volume of fluid consumed. Under these conditions there also appears to be no rise in corticosteroids [59]. Yet, we still observed a conditioned suppression of antibody titer. In the report by Ader and Cohen [5], there was a study in which LiCl was used instead of CY as the US in the conditioning paradigm. Lithium chloride, like CY, has noxious gastrointestinal effects sufficient to induce a taste aversion, and it is an effective stimulus for inducing and conditioning an elevation in steroid level [2]. However, LiCl is not immunosuppressive and did not produce a conditioned suppression of antibody titer.

It was still possible, however, that there could be some synergistic relation between an elevated steroid level and the residual immunosuppressive effects of CY. To examine this possibility, two additional experiments were conducted [6] in which an additional group of conditioned animals was injected with LiCl or with corticosterone, instead of being reexposed to the CS solution on the day that antigen was introduced. Reexposure to the CS caused a significant attenuation of antibody titer, but neither LiCl nor corticosterone was effective in suppressing the immune response. These results, then, provide no support for the hypothesis that the attenuation in antibody titer seen in conditioned animals is mediated simply by an elevation in corticosteroid level.

We are at the very earliest stages in studies of the conditioning of immune responses, although studies on the conditioning of immunobiological responses were initiated in the Soviet Union 50 years ago. I have had much of this literature translated and will be preparing a review, not because this literature represents sophisticated research or definitive findings, but both for historical interest and for the ideas it may generate. Like our own studies, the results are compelling because of the consistency rather than the magnitude of the effects observed. Surely, we are in a better position to undertake such studies today than we were several years ago and the effort would appear to be justified. The limited data that are already available reinforce the notion that there is, indeed, an intimate and virtually unexplored relationship between the CNS and immunologic processes, and that behavioral techniques are available for studying this relationship in the intact organism. To confirm and establish the impact of conditioning in the suppression or augmentation of immune responses would raise innumerable issues regarding the normal operation and modifiability of the immune system and the mediation of individual differences in the body's natural armamentarium for adaptation and survival under conditions that exist in the real world. As such, conditioning processes may represent a mechanism involved in the complex pathogenesis of psychosomatic disease, including the psychobiological factors that contribute to the etiology and pathogenesis of cancer.

Summary

One of the links between behavioral factors and susceptibility to cancer may involve the immune system. There are now several lines of evidence which implicate behavioral factors and the central nervous system in the regulation of immune processes. Of these, a brief review is provided of the effects of psychobiological factors ("stress") on susceptibility to disease processes that involve immunologic mediation, the effects of such factors on parameters of immunologic reactivity, and the author's current research on the application of conditioning procedures in modifying immune responses in animal subjects. The available data indicate that a variety of host factors play a role in determining immunologic reactivity and, although the mechanisms for the central nervous system regulation of immune processes have not been elaborated, the study of immune processes as an integrated part of the organism's psychobiological adaptation to its environment represents a fruitful area for interdisciplinary research.

References

1. Ader, R.: The effects of early life experiences on developmental processes and susceptibility to disease in animals. In *Minnesota Symposia on Child Psychology*, ed. J. P. Hill, pp. 3–35 Minneapolis: Univ. Minnesota Press, 1970.
2. Ader, R.: Conditioned adrenocortical steroid elevations in the rat. *Journal of Comparative and Physiological Psychology* 90:1156–1163, 1976.
3. Ader, R.: A note on the role of olfaction in taste aversion learning. *Bulletin of the Psychonomic Society* 10:402–404, 1977.
4. Ader, R., ed.: *Psychoneuroimmunology.* New York: Academic Press, 1981. In press.
5. Ader, R.; and Cohen, N.: Behaviorally conditioned immunosuppression. *Psychosomatic Medicine* 37:333–340, 1975.
6. Ader, R.; Cohen, N.; and Grota, L. J.: Adrenal involvement in conditioned immunosuppression. *International Journal of Immunopharmacology* 1:141–145, 1979.
7. Ahlqvist, J.: Endocrine influences on lymphatic organs, immune responses, inflammation and autoimmunity. *Acta Endocrinology* 83, Suppl. 206, 1976.
8. Amkraut, A.; and Solomon, G. F.: From the symbolic stimulus to the pathophysiologic response: Immune mechanisms. *International Journal of Psychiatry in Medicine* 5:541–563, 1974.
9. Amkraut, A. A.; Solomon, G. F.; Kasper, P.; and Purdue, P.: Stress and hormonal intervention in the graft-versus-host response. In *Microenvironmental Aspects of Immunity*, eds. B. D. Jankovic and K. Isakovic, pp. 667–674. New York: Plenum, 1973.
10. Amkraut, A. A.; Solomon, G. F.; and Kraemer, H. C.: Stress, early experience and adjuvant-induced arthritis in the rat. *Psychosomatic Medicine* 33:203–214, 1971.
11. Bahnson, C. B., ed: Second conference on psychophysiological aspects of cancer. *Annals of the New York Academy of Science* 164:307–634, 1969.
12. Besedovsky, H.; and Sorkin, E.: Network of immunoendocrine interactions. *Clinical and Experimental Immunology* 27:1–12, 1977.
13. Bovbjerg, D.; Cohen, N.; and Ader, R.: Conditioned immunosuppression: Response to a T-cell independent antigen. Paper presented at the meetings of the American Psychosomatic Society, Dallas, Texas, 1979.
14. Chang, S.; and Rasmussen, A. F., Jr.: Stress-induced suppression of interferon production in virus-infected mice. *Nature* 205:623–624, 1965.
15. Davis, D. E.; and Read, C. P.: Effect of behavior on development of resistance in trichinosis. *Proceedings of the Society for Experimental Biology and Medicine* 99:269–272, 1958.
16. DeWeck, A. L.; and Frey, J. R.: *Immunotolerance to Simple Chemicals.* Basel: S. Karger, 1966.
17. Dolin, A. O.; Krylov, V. N.; Luk'ianenko, V. I.; and Flerov, B. A.: New experimental data on the conditioned reflex production and suppression of immune and allergic reactions. *Zhurnal Vysshei Nervonoi Deiatel'nosti* 10:832–841, 1960.
18. Dubos, R.: *Mirage of Health.* New York: Harper, 1959.

19. Folch, H.; and Waksman, B. H.: The splenic suppressor cell: Activity of thymus dependent adherent cells: Changes with age and stress. *Journal of Immunology* 113:127–139, 1974.
20. Friedman, S. B.; Ader, R.; and Glasgow, L. A.: Effects of psychological stress in adult mice inoculated with Coxsakie B viruses. *Psychosomatic Medicine* 27, 361–368, 1965.
21. Friedman, S. B.; Ader, R.; and Grota, L. J.: Protective effect of noxious stimulation in mice infected with rodent malaria. *Psychosomatic Medicine* 35, 535–537, 1973.
22. Friedman, S. B. and Glasgow, L. A.: Psychologic factors and resistance to infectious disease. *Prediatric Clinics of North America* 13:315–335, 1966.
23. Friedman, S. B.; Glasgow, L. A.; and Ader, R.: Psychosocial factors modifying host resistance to experimental infections. *Annals of the New York Academy of Science* 164:381–392, 1969.
24. Gisler, R. H.; Bussard, A. E.; Mazie, J. C.; and Hess, R.: Hormonal regulation of the immune response: I. Induction of an immune response *in vitro* with lymphoid cells from mice exposed to acute systemic stress. *Cellular Immunology* 2:634–645, 1971.
25. Gisler, R. H.; and Schenkel-Hulliger, L.: Hormonal regulation of the immune response: II. Influence of pituitary and adrenal activity on immune responsiveness *in vitro*. *Cellular Immunology* 2:646–657, 1971.
26. Glenn, W. G. and Becker, R. E.: Individual versus group housing in mice: Immunological response to time-phased injections. *Physiological Zoology* 42:411–416, 1969.
27. Gross, W. B.; and Siegel, H. S.: The effect of social stress on resistance to infection with *Escherichia coli* or *Mycoplasma gallisepticum*. *Poultry Science* 44:98–1001, 1965.
28. Guy, W. B.: Neurogenic factors in contact dermatitis. *Archives of Dermatology and Syphilology* 66:1–8, 1952.
29. Hadden, J. W.: Immunopharmacology of mice and men. *International Journal of Immunopharmacology*, 1, 5–8, 1979.
30. Hamilton, D. R.: Immunosuppressive effects of predator induced stress in mice with acquired immunity to *Hymenolepsis nana*., *Journal of Psychosomatic Research*, 18:143–153, 1974.
31. Hill, C. W.; Greer, W. E.; and Felsenfeld, O.: Psychological stress, early response to foreign protein, and blood cortisol in vervets. *Psychosomatic Medicine* 29:279–283, 1967.
32. Hull, C. L.: Learning: II. The factor of the conditioned reflex. In *A Handbook of General Experimental Psychology*, ed. C. Murchison, pp. 382–455, Worcester: Clark Univ. Press, 1934.
33. Hutton, R. A.; Woods, S. C.; and Makous, W. L.: Conditioned hyperglycemia: pseudoconditioning controls. *Journal of Comparative and Physiological Psychology* 71:198–201, 1970.
34. Jankovic, B. D.; and Isakovic, K.: Neuroendocrine correlates of immune response: I. Effects of brain lesions on antibody production, arthus reactivity and delayed hypersensitivity in the rat. *International Archives of Allergy*, 45:360–372, 1973.
35. Jensen, M. M.; and Rasmussen, A. F., Jr.: Stress and susceptibility to viral infections: II. Sound stress and susceptibility to vesicular stomatitis virus. *Journal of Immunology* 90:21–23, 1963.
36. Joasoo, A.; and McKenzie, J. M.: Stress and the immune response in rats. *International Archives of Allergy* 50:659–663, 1976.
37. Johnson, T.; Lavender, J. F.; and Marsh, J. T.: The influence of avoidance learning stress on resistance to Coxsackie virus in mice. *Federation Proceedings* 18:575, 1959.
38. LaBarba, R. C.: Experiential and environmental factors in cancer. *Psychosomatic Medicine* 32:259–276, 1970.

39. Levine, S.; Strebel, R.; Wenk, E. J.; and Harman, P. J.: Suppression of experimental allergic encephalomyelitis by stress. *Proceedings of the Society for Experimental Biology and Medicine*, 109, 294–298, 1962.

40. Makinodan, T.; Santos, G. W.; and Quinn, R. P. Immunosuppressive drugs. *Pharmacological Reviews* 22:198–247, 1970.

41. Marsh, J. T.; Lavender, J. F.; Chang, S.; and Rasmussen, A. F., Jr.: Poliomyelitis in monkeys: Decreased susceptibility after avoidance stress. *Science* 140:1415–1416, 1963.

42. Mettrop, P. J. G.; and Visser, P.: Exteroceptive stimulation as a contingent factor in the induction and elicitation of delayed-type hypersensitivity reactions to 1-chloro-2-4, dinitrobenzene in guinea pigs. *Psychophysiology* 5:385–388, 1969.

43. Monjan, A. A. and Collector, M. I.: Stress-induced modulation of the immune response. *Science* 196:307–308, 1977.

44. Munson, A. E.; Levy, J. A.; Harris, L. S.; and Dewey, W. L.: Effects of Δ^9-tetrahydrocannabinol on the immune system. In *The Pharmacology of Marihuana*, eds. M. C. Braude and S. Szara, pp. 187–197. New York: Raven, 1976.

45. Pavlov, I. P.: *Lectures on Conditioned Reflexes*. New York: Liveright, 1928.

46. Pitkin, D. H.: Effect of physiological stress on the delayed hypersensitivity reaction. *Proceedings of the Society for Experimental Biology and Medicine* 120:350–351, 1965.

47. Pierpaoli, W.; Fabris, N.; and Sorkin, E. Developmental hormones and immunological maturation. In *Hormones and the Immune Response*, eds. G. E. Wolstenholme and J. Knight, pp. 126–143. London: Churchill, 1970.

48. Pierpaoli, W.; Kopp, H. G.; Muller, J.; and Keller, M.: Interdependence between neuroendocrine programming and the generation of immune recognition in ontogeny. *Cellular Immunology* 29:16–27, 1977.

49. Pierpaoli, W. and Maestroni, G. J. M.: Pharmacological control of the immune response by blockade of the early hormonal changes following antigen injection. *Cellular Immunology* 31:355–363, 1977.

50. Plaut, S. M.; Ader, R.; Friedman, S. B.; and Ritterson, A. L.: Social factors and resistance to malaria in the mouse: Effects of group vs. individual housing on resistance to *Plasmodium berghei* infection. *Psychosomatic Medicine*, 31:536–552, 1969.

51. Rasmussen, A. F., Jr.; Hildemann, W. H.; and Sellers, M.: Malignancy of polyoma virus infection in mice in relation to stress. *Journal of the National Cancer Institute*, 30:101–112, 1963.

52. Rasmussen, A. F., Jr.; Marsh, J. T.; and Brill, N. Q.: Increased susceptibility to herpes simplex in mice subjected to avoidance-learning stress or restraint. *Proceedings of the Society for Experimental Biology and Medicine* 96:183–189, 1957.

53. Rasmussen, A. F., Jr.: Spencer, E. S.; and Marsh, J. T.: Decrease in susceptibility of mice to passive anaphylaxis following avoidance-learning stress. *Proceedings of the Society for Experimental Biology and Medicine* 100:878–879, 1959.

54. Rogers, M. P.; Dubey, D.; and Reich, P.: The influence of the psyche and the brain on immunity and disease susceptibility. *Psychosomatic Medicine* 41:147–164, 1979.

55. Rogers, M. P.; Reich, P.; Strom, T. B.; and Carpenter, C. B.: Behaviorally conditioned immunosuppression: Replication of a recent study. *Psychosomatic Medicine* 38:447–451, 1976.

56. Rogers, M. P.; Trentham, D.; McCune, J.; Ginsberg, B.; Reich, P.; and David, J.: Abrogation of Type II collagen-induced arthritis in rats by psychological stress. *Clinical Research*, 27:513A, 1979.

57. Sell, G.: *Immunology, Immunopathology and Immunity*. Hagerstown, Maryland: Harper, 1972.

58. Siegel, S.: Conditioned insulin effects. *Journal of Comparative and Physiological Psychology*, 89:189–199, 1975.
59. Smotherman, W. P., Hennessy, J. W.; and Levine, S.: Plasma corticosterone levels during recovery from LiCl produced taste aversion. *Behavioral Biology* 16:401–412, 1976.
60. Soave, O. A.: Reactivation of rabies virus infection in the guinea pig due to the stress of crowding. *American Journal of Veterinary Research* 25:268–269, 1964.
61. Solomon, G. F.: Stress and antibody response in rats. *International Archives of Allergy* 35:97–104, 1969.
62. Solomon, G. F.: Pathophysiological aspects of rheumatoid arthritis and auto-immune disease. In *Modern Trends in Psychosomatic Medicine—2*, ed. O. W. Hill, pp. 189–216. London: Butterworths, 1970.
63. Solomon, G. F.; Amkraut, A. A.; and Kasper, P.: Immunity, emotions and stress. *Annals of Clinical Research* 6:313–322, 1974.
64. Solomon, G. F.; Levine, S.; and Kraft, J. K.: Early experience and immunity. *Nature* 220:821–822, 1968.
65. Spector, N. H.: The hypothalamus in health and disease: Old and new concepts. In *Handbook of the hypothalamus*, eds. P. J. Morgane and J. Panksepp. New York: Marcel Dekker, 1980.in press.
66. Stein, M.; Schiavi, R. C.; and Camerino, M.: Influence of brain and behavior on the immune system. *Science* 191:435–440, 1976.
67. Treadwell, P. E.; and Rasmussen, A. F., Jr.: Role of the adrenals in stress-induced resistance to anaphylactic shock. *Journal of Immunology* 87:492–497, 1961.
68. Vancil, M. E.: Workshop on immunosuppressive properties of cyclophosphamide. Mead-Johnson Co., Evansville, Ind., 1971.
69. Vessey, S. H.: Effects of grouping on levels of circulating antibodies in mice. *Proceedings of the Society for Experimental Biology and Medicine* 115:252–255, 1964.
70. Wayner, E. A.; Flannery, G. R.; and Singer, G.: Effects of taste aversion conditioning on the primary antibody response to sheep red blood cells and *Brucella abortus* in the albino rat. *Physiology and Behavior* 21:995–1000, 1978.
71. Weinmann, C. J.; and Rothman, A. H.: Effects of stress upon acquired immunity to the dwarf tapeworm *Hymenolepis nana*. *Experimental Parasitology* 21:61–67, 1967.
72. Wistar, R., Jr.; and Hildemann, W. H.: Effect of stress on skin transplantation immunity in mice. *Science* 131:159–160, 1960.
73. Wolstenholme, G. E.; and Knight, J., eds. *Hormones and the immune response*. London: Churchill, 1970.
74. Yamada, A.; Jensen, M. M.; and Rasmussen, A. F., Jr.: Stress and susceptibility to viral infections: III. Antibody response and viral retention during avoidance learning stress. *Proceedings of the Society for Experimental Biology and Medicine*, 116:677–680, 1964.

Biobehavioral Factors in Animal Work on Tumorigenesis

VERNON RILEY

Introduction

It has been shown that stress, stemming from a variety of sources, induces a series of biochemical events that are mediated through the neuroendocrine system. These biochemical responses lead to disruptive effects on specific cells involved in immunological defense. Thus, under stress, the organism is rendered less capable of defending itself against cancer cells, infectious agents, and many disease processes. It is possible that both humoral and cellular immunologic elements may be affected by stress; however, the clearest evidence appears to implicate hormonal mechanisms that lead to the destruction of circulating T-cell lymphocytes and involves those organs and tissues concerned with the production, maturation, and storage of T-cells, such as the blood, thymus, spleen, and lymph nodes.

Many careful investigators have examined the intriguing relationships between stress and disease. Interpretation of some of these studies, however, has been complicated by the formidable difficulties of establishing and maintaining authentic quiescent baseline conditions for experimental animals. In some cases, there was a conspicuous lack of access to biochemical and cellular measurements which are necessary to determine the quantitative manifestations of stress objectively, prior to its enhancement or inhibition of specific disease processes.

Irrespective of possible causes, the extensive literature describing the influence of "stress" on neoplastic and other diseases has generated contradictive but provocative data. There are, however, reasonable explanations for the inconsistencies of the findings, which are discussed in this review.

In addition to the experimental difficulties and pitfalls inherent in the ob-

183

jective measurement of stress and its varied pathological consequences, it seems likely that many of the experiments that were designed to demonstrate an influence of stress on disease were demanding more than could be provided by the limited sensitivities of the methods used, especially in view of the relatively weak forces that can be directed against neoplastic diseases through the immunological mechanisms of the host.

With the newer insight into the action of the glucocorticoids on elements of the immunological and surveillance apparatus, it is now feasible to design quantitative experiments capable of testing the influence of controlled stress on those specific types and stages of disease that respond to the chain of hormonal and cellular events induced by appropriate stressful stimuli. Also, rapid developments in the past few years delineating and characterizing many new facets of immunology and endocrinology provide a more effective base for reexamining and determining both the limitations and the potentialities of the effects of physiological stress on disease processes. Thus logical steps can now be devised to exploit the new information prophylactically or therapeutically.

It is not feasible in a limited review to provide an analytical examination of each of the many papers that have been published on stress that may relate directly or indirectly to cancer. Thus, the intent of this modest overview is to provide a perspective of this important area of research, with some emphasis on the puzzling contradictions and inconsistencies found in the published reports. The failure to obtain consistent results among investigators and between laboratories has undermined confidence in the reliability of research in this difficult field, and as a consequence, support has become difficult to obtain. As a step toward remedying this, a critique outlining some of the experimental difficulties that are inherent in stress research is presented, which may apply to some of the discrepancies in the reports.

Titles of additional relevant reports, although not reviewed here, will be listed in the bibliography (see Table 1).

Selected Studies on Stress and Cancer

Cage Crowding and Isolation

Dechambre and Gosse [26, 27] studied the influence of population density on the survival time of mice bearing two varieties of transplanted tumors. Virgin female C57BL/6 mice, bearing subcutaneous implantations of B-16 melanoma, were employed. When such mice were individually caged, their average survival time was 33 days, compared with 21 days

TABLE 1
References Dealing with Specific Experimental Topics Involving
Stress, Immunology, and Cancer

Topic number	Experimental subject	Reference numbers
1	Personality, emotional attributes, and cancer	49,50,51,63,77,79,81,88, 89,90,91,92,101,105,120, 126,169,170,185.
2	Central nervous system and cancer	68,70,71,74,121,129,165, 171,192,195.
3	Hypothalamus, stress, and cancer	30,70,71,72,75,80,109, 183,184.
4	Early experience and susceptibility to cancer	84,85,86,94,115,116,119.
5	Isolation and population density stress	46,93,107,108,194.
6	Nutritional restriction and cancer	59,182,191,191a,194a.
7	Effect of exercise on cancer	61,149.
8	Immunosurveillance and cancer	73,78,122,199.
9	Antibodies and stress	8,26,27,30,122,146,159.
10	Effect of stress on leucocytes	66
11	Temperature, stress, and cancer	38,84,87,104,113,196, 197,202.
12	Audiogenic stress and cancer	58,189,67.
13	Stress and mammary cancer	131,135,138,143,193.
14	Chemically induced tumors and stress effects	111.
15	Electric shock stress	96,97,111,117,119,131, 172.
16	Virus response to stress	36,60,52,64,118,124,67, 127,128,201.
17	Interferon and stress	22,65,174.
18	Stress reviews	81,83,91,99,100,120.

when the mice were caged in groups of 10. Similar tests were also made using Krebs-2 ascites carcinoma; in this experiment, the mice that were caged singly survived 27 days, whereas those in groups of 10 survived only 17 days. The authors concluded that the results of these experiments were statistically significant and that the observed reduction in survival time of the mice caged in groups of 10 probably resulted from endocrine disturbances caused by the stress of crowding, although this parameter was not measured.

Andervont [8] and Muhlbock [107, 108] investigated the influence of cage crowding on spontaneous mammary tumor latent periods. Mice reared in isolation were compared with those raised in groups. In contrast to the above findings, the isolation-reared mice developed mammary tumors earlier than did analogous mice raised in social groups. In view of other studies, this might be interpreted as a demonstration that under these experimental circumstances, prolonged isolation-rearing is a stressful experience, which modifies the immunological capacity of the mouse to cope with either the mammary tumor virus (MTV) or the malignant cells transformed by MTV. However, there is an apparent contradiction between these results and those of Dechambre and Gosse [26, 27].

In a related inquiry, Glenn and Becker [42] studied the influence of varying the housing congestion on immune competence in Swiss Webster female mice. They found that animals that were housed singly showed a significantly less vigorous humoral immune response to challenge by 0.1 % BSA than did similar mice that were housed in larger groups. This suggests that the immune capabilities of the mice housed singly were less than in those mice living in a more "normal" crowded social situation. These observations may be interpreted as being consistent with the studies of Santisteben et al. [151–158], who found that isolation-rearing handicaps mice in coping with stressful situations imposed later in life. Such observations would seem also to be consistent with those of Andervont [8] and Muhlbock [107, 108], but they do not conform with the findings of Dechambre and Gosse [26, 27] in respect to the stress-immune impairment concept.

Light Effects

Sakakibara [150], studied the effects of bright light, compared with total darkness or normal laboratory light, on chemical carcinogenesis. A 20-week course of dimethylbenzanthracene (DMBA), through the diet, was given to mice that were 11 weeks old at the initiation of the study. The experiment consisted of four groups: One group was exposed to flashing lights at 1000 lux, with the light being switched on and off 30 times per minute for 8 hr per day. In these mice, liver tumors developed, with an average latent period of 15 weeks and a tumor incidence of 79%. In mice exposed to steady fluorescent light of the same intensity and for the same time period, the tumors developed in 16 weeks, and the incidence was 64%. Similar mice kept in darkness developed tumors in an average of 18 weeks with an incidence of 24%. Mice which were termed "controls" were kept under natural room light, and in this case tumors developed in 18 weeks with an incidence of 36%. The authors attribute the shortened latent period and the increased incidence of liver tumors in the mice exposed to flashing or continuous light as resulting from a stress response.

Temperature Influences

Young [202] studied the effect of temperature on the production of dimethylbenzanthracene (DMBA)-induced mammary tumors, employing noninbred, specific pathogen-free rats. One group was maintained at a "warm" temperature of 32°C (90°F), while the other group was maintained at a "low" temperature of 5°C (40°F). All animals were on a standard diet and exposed to equal periods of light and darkness. A single dose of DMBA (30 mg, orally in corn oil) was administered to the rats at 50 days of age. The earliest mammary tumors occurred in the "warm" temperature group and appeared 5.5 weeks after DMBA administration. Those rats maintained at the "low" temperature developed tumors 2 weeks later. The total mammary tumor incidence at 120 days following DMBA administration was 26 out of 39 animals (67%) in the "warm" temperature group, as compared to only 16 out of 39 rats (41%) in the "low" temperature group. These differences were reported to be statistically significant. The higher tumor incidence and shortened latent period could be ascribed to the stress induced by the higher temperatures. However, since exposure to cold is also considered to be stressful, other mechanisms may have to be considered in order to account for the more rapid development of tumors in the "warm" environment, or it might be that both temperature extremes are stressful.

Wallace *et al.* [197] also examined the influence of environmental temperature on the incidence and course of spontaneous mammary tumors in C3H mice carrying the Bittner virus (MTV). Contrary to the findings of Young [202] with rats, the virgin mice that were employed in these experiments exhibited an increase in tumor incidence in "cool" environments of 68°F (20°C) as compared with "hot" environments of 91°F (33°C); although once the tumors appeared, they killed the hosts residing in the higher temperatures more quickly. Multiple tumors in the C3H mice were four times more frequent among the cool room mice than among those kept at 91°F. Again, the findings appear to be contradictory in these two studies; however, it is appropriate to bear in mind that both the carcinogen and animal species were different.

The same authors [196] did analogous experiments but employed subcutaneous injections of methycholanthrene (MCA) to induce sarcomas in C3H mice under two environmental conditions: specifically, "warm-humid" compared with normal temperatures. Tumors arose earlier in the mice held in the warm environment of 92°F (33°C), as compared with their littermates which were kept at 65°F (18°C). The average sarcoma latency period was 10 weeks in the "warm" room as compared with 12 weeks in the "cool" room. Thus, opposite effects were observed between viral (MTV) and chemical (MCA) tumor induction in the same laboratory following exposure of C3H mice to either "warm" or "cool" temperatures. It may be significant, however, that the Wallace MCA experiment in mice [196] gave results similar to the DMBA rat experiments of Young [202].

In a separate experiment by Wallace et al., one of the MCA-induced tumors was transplanted into C3H mice and maintained in the two thermal environments. When the tumor was implanted subcutaneously, the sarcomas grew rapidly in the "warm" room but grew slowly or regressed in the "cool" room. When injected intramuscularly, the sarcomas grew equally well in both environments.

Fuller et al. [38] also studied the effect of various environmental temperatures on spontaneous tumors in mice. Various groups of virgin female DBA mice were kept under conditions of moist warmth at 90–91°F (32–33°C), and in a cooler, more "stimulating" temperature of 65°F. They reported that the tumors which appeared under the moist–warm conditions grew more slowly and took over twice as long to kill their hosts as did tumors in animals kept at cooler temperatures. The tumor incidence found at 70–75°F was practically the same as at 65°F, but the tumors grew more slowly at the higher temperatures. The average of the periods between the appearance of the tumors and the death of the animals were 28 days at 65°F, 47 days at 70–75°F, and 60 days at 90–91°F.

If "stress" is invoked to explain these results, then low and normal temperatures would appear to be more "stressful" than high temperatures. However, the authors felt that the lower tumor incidence observed in warm environments represented a tumor suppression rather than merely a delay in tumor appearance. They compared their findings with the reported epidemiological rate of human cancer deaths by age groups in northern states compared with southern states, and pointed out that cancer rates in the north rise much more rapidly with advance in age than cancer rates in the south.

Of possible relevance, Newell and Waggoner [113] carried out epidemiological investigations on cancer mortality and environmental temperature in the United States. The authors suggested that the geographical differences in cancer mortality could be associated with both artifacts and indirect causative factors, rather than reflecting a direct environmental effect of temperature on cancer risk, and concluded that the statistical differences observed require careful interpretation.

Electric Shock, Stress, and Neoplasia

Marsh et al. [96] studied the effect of repeated brief exposures to "stress" on the growth of the Ehrlich carcinoma in a series of experiments in which mice that had been injected subcutaneously with Ehrlich tumor transplants were subjected to "stress," either by an electric shock shuttle box technique or by immobilization. In five out of the eight experiments, significantly smaller tumors were found in the "stressed" animals than in the controls. Two of the remaining three experiments yielded nonsignificant results, but in the same direction, and one experiment showed a significant increase in the size of the tumors in the "stressed" mice. The authors concluded that "stress," in the form of exposure to shuttle box electric shocks, or immobilization, represented an important variable to be considered in cancer research, and that studies on stress offer an additional context for the exploration of tumor–host relationships.

In later studies, Marsh and Rasmussen [97] observed typical stress syndromes consisting of adrenal hypertrophy, thymus involution, leukocytopenia, and a decrease in spleen weight, all following daily exposure to emotional stress, using shuttle box electric shock or stressful immobilization. These adverse effects on immunological elements are consistent with more recent observations of Riley et al. [141, 145, 148] but appear to conflict with the earlier report of Marsh et al. showing a stress-associated inhibition of Ehrlich tumor growth [96]. This is based upon the premise that stress which causes an impairment in elements of the immunological system should enhance tumor development.

Resnikoff and Martin [131] also studied the influence of electric shock on "spontaneous" mouse mammary cancer. They examined the incidence of spontaneous mammary tumors and the influence of "stress" on C3H mice that carried the mammary tumor virus (MTV), as compared with similar mice in which the virus was absent. Half of the animals in each of the two groups were stressed by daily intermittent electric shock for periods ranging from about 6 months to over a year. The authors reported that mice without a predisposition to mammary cancer as a result of the absence of MTV did not in any instance develop tumors, even when exposed to stress; whereas more than 75% of the "stressed" animals with MTV, and a comparable percentage of nonstressed MTV-infected controls, developed mammary tumors. The tumors tended to appear earlier, however, in the "stressed" group of MTV-infected mice. These findings were discussed by the authors with the caution that they were preliminary and require confirmation. The results are, however, consistent with the recent reports by Riley [137, 141, 148] indicating that protective animal housing significantly reduced mammary tumor incidence when compared with conventional facilities that are known to be stressful.

Solomon and Amkraut [172] explored the various effects of both sex-segregated housing and electric shock on the behavior of a tumor induced by a murine sarcoma virus in BALB/c mice. Larger tumors developed both in a "fighting" group of female mice, and also when electric shock was administered at various times following injection of the murine sarcoma virus. Tumor size was also increased in sex-segregated mice. In addition, these workers observed that stress induced a suppression of circulating antibody, and that IgG was more stress-responsive than IgM.

Newberry et al. [111, 112] have demonstrated that both electric shock and forced restraint, which they employed as forms of stress, have the capacity to reduce the number of tumors developing in rats injected with DMBA. These findings are of interest since they represent an opposite effect to that produced by stress on some other neoplastic processes. These and related studies suggest that there may be at least two influential components in the varieties of stress that have been employed; or, as an alternative, that the influence of stress on chemically induced tumors, as opposed to other malignancies, may be expressed differently. It may also be relevant, from the standpoint of stress and immune competence, that Newberry reported that there was little indication that the restraint manipulation produced a prolonged stress response. In all experiments, stress failed to influence the average size of the tumors which appeared. The duration of the shock period was influential. When severe shock stress was applied for either 40 or 85 consecutive days the tumor incidence was reduced; however, 25 days of the same stress did not significantly influence the number of tumors compared with untreated controls.

In view of the conflicting reports in the literature, Nieburgs et al. [117] undertook studies to examine the role of various types of stress on tumorigenesis at the cellular level. They examined the microscopic effects of changes occurring in the thyroid, thymus, lung, liver, stomach, adrenals, and testes following a variety of stress stimuli. These included electric shock, cold swim, handling, and transportation. Marked differences, associated with stress, were observed in the mitosis of liver cells harvested from stressed rats. Some changes were seen in animals that had received electric shock for a 2-hr period, but curiously enough, were absent in animals that had been under the same stress for 24 hours. However, other changes were more prominent in rats at 24 hours following electric shock, as well as at various periods following discontinuation of the stress.

It was reported that stress led to a reduction in blood lymphocytes, with a decrease in the percentage of small lymphocytes in contrast to a relative increase in large lymphocytes. The abnormal cellular changes which occurred as a result of transportation, handling, and cold-swim stress persisted longer than those produced by electric shock. In their studies on tumors, enhancement of DMBA-induced mammary tumors was observed following stress by handling and cold-swim. The cold-swim stress induced the greatest enhancement of tumor growth, which was seen at 90 days following oral administration of 40 mg of DMBA. Electric shock stress failed to enhance DMBA mammary tumorigenesis and appeared to exert some inhibitory effects. The latter findings are consistent with those reported by Newberry [111, 112].

Early Experience of Experimental Animals

Ader and Friedman [1–3] found that the handling of infant rats during their first week of life delayed transplanted tumor development, but increased the mortality when the rats were inoculated with the Walker 256 tumor on day 60.

Newton [114–116] carried out similar experiments and reported that tactile and visual experience, such as handling in the first few days of life, exposure to light, and closeness to the mother, lead to significant alterations in the animals' response to stress challenges. The parameters which these authors examined were emotional reactivity, weight gain, and learning behavior. They suggested that influences on the developmental process are more subtle than has heretofore been realized and that a historical record of each experimental subject would be relevant.

Otis and Scholler [119] attempted to confirm the findings of other investigators, namely, that repeated electric shocks given to infantile mice and rats result in a subsequent lowered resistance to cancer-producing agents and a decrease in the latent period of spontaneous tumors. These authors "stressed" mice and rats for short periods daily by electric shock (0.5 mA for 5 sec per day), either to the body surface or by convulsive shock to the brain. The stress treatments were given over a short period between birth and 24 days of age. This was followed either by implantation of transplantable tumors or tumor induction by chemical or viral agents. The experimental results failed to support the findings of other investigators, namely, that stress applied to infant or young adult subjects alters their future susceptibility to cancer. There are a number of possible reasons for such negative results, which are discussed in another section.

A series of related papers by Levine [93, 94], Ader [1–4], Friedman [35–37], Solomon [173], and LaBarba [83–86] have also examined the influence of "early experience" on the subsequent ability of the host to handle stress. Handling or manipulation was frequently used as a stressor in young rats and mice by these investigators. However, the effects of early weaning, electric shock, and other factors such as restraint, were also examined. A great deal of inconsistency and experimental contradictions appeared in these copious data; it is presumed that the many experimental variables among the various laboratories may be an explanation for some of the discrepancies in their data.

Santisteban and Henry [156] and Henry et al. [55, 56] have found that "early experience" has a profound effect upon the subsequent ability of mice or rats to cope with psychosocial stress. As an example, mice that were reared in isolation between 4 and 12 weeks of age, and then placed in a competitive population cage where they were subjected to the stress of frequent confrontation and social integration, developed hypertension, cardiovascular diseases, heart enlargement, and other pathologies more rapidly than mice that were raised in a competitive environment where the cage contained five to ten mice [55, 56]. Similar exposure of isolation-reared mice to subsequent psychosocial stress also enhanced mammary tumor production [57].

Cancer, Immunology, and the Central Nervous System

Of special relevance to this review on cancer and stress are the various studies undertaken on the relationships between immunological competence and cancer. A series of investigations by Khayetsky [75], Koneva, and Khai [80], Muhlbock [109], and Stein [183, 184], and others have examined the immunological consequences of producing lesions in the anterior hypothalamic area of experimental animals. In general, a lower antibody production was found in such animals as compared with those that had posterior hypothalamic lesions, or with no lesions at all. As a result of these experiments, it was suggested that psychosocial phenomena may modify the immune processes through the central nervous system. The Russian investigators Korneva and Khai [80] also found that in rabbits with lesions of the hypothalamus there was a suppression of antibodies and a prolonged retention of antigen in the blood. The implications of this work have been extended by Kavetsky et al. [70–72] through an examination of the relationships between alterations in the central nervous system and subsequent malignancies. They also reported that it is possible to alter the course of hormone-dependent tumors by procedures that act upon the hypothalamus. Not all authors have observed a direct relationship between the host immunological status and cancer. It has been reported, for example, that the immunological state of the host did not seem to affect the development of either the primary tumor or metastases in mice inoculated with the Lewis lung carcinoma.

Virus Behavior and Stress

A change in host resistance to infection brought about by psychosocial factors has been noted by several groups. Rasmussen, Friedman, Grundberg, Hirsch, Jensen, and others have shown that the stress induced by avoidance learning procedures (electric shock, etc.) increased susceptibility to herpes simplex virus [128], Coxsackie B virus [36, 52], and polyoma virus infection [127]. Physical restraint was also reported to enhance the herpes simplex infection [128].

Immune Responses and Stress

The physiological and immunobiological mechanisms that mediate the effects of psychosocial stresses on host resistance are complex and in need of further clarification. There seems little doubt, however, that many of the types of stresses that have been shown to modify susceptibility to infections and neoplasia also lead to a compromise or impairment of the host immune system, particularly the cell-mediated (T-cell) system [179, 181]. However, some investigators have also implicated humoral antibodies and thus B-cells [40, 172]. Marsh and Rasmussen [97] found that stress associated with avoidance learning (shuttle box) or confinement was accompanied by adrenal hypertrophy, lymphocytopenia, and a slow involution of the thymus and spleen. Gisler et al. [40] measured the immune response of spleen antibody-forming cells (Jerne plaque-forming cells) to injected sheep red blood cells as a measure of immune reactivity. They found that immune response was decreased in spleen cells harvested from donor mice that had been stressed by ether anesthesia or centrifugation prior to the removal of the spleen. A subsequent study showed that the degree of immunosuppression was correlated with an increase in plasma corticosterone [41]. The fluorimetric method used for their plasma corticosterone determinations gave values of about 120 ng/ml for both adrenalectomized mice and normal, "unstressed" animals. Although it may not invalidate the conclusions of the studies, their "normal" corticosterone values were two to three times above what are now known to be normal quiescent values, indicating that their controls were subject to stress.

Prolactin, Stress, and Mammary Tumors

Galla and Leginsky [39] reported finding a correlation between serum prolactin levels and the incidence of mammary tumors induced by DMBA in the rat. The authors used ether anesthesia as a means for inducing stress in these studies, and compared the incidence of mammary carcinomas in DMBA-treated Sprague–Dawley rats with that of similar rats which had received the same carcinogen followed by deep ether anesthesia. The average latent period of the stressed animals was 93 days, whereas control rats that had received the same dose of DMBA without ether anesthesia had a latent period of only 79 days. These differences were statistically significant at the .05 level of probability. Spontaneous tumor regression was 40% for the "stressed" experimental animals and 13% for the controls. The authors reported that serum prolactin levels were significantly higher in animals that did not develop tumors, or whose tumors had regressed, or whose tumors were static and did not grow progressively. The authors concluded that their data indicated that animals with a capacity to secrete high levels of prolactin, which was presumed to be stimulated by the ether stress, did not develop mammary tumors. The authors questioned whether this is a mechanism related specifically to prolactin increases or whether it involves the simultaneous elevation of other hormones that were not measured.

Work by Slaga et al. [167, 168] has shown that various exogenous corticoids such as dexamethasone are capable of preventing the carcinogenic action of DMBA and related substances applied to the skin. Hypothetically, if a similar mechanism were functioning systemically in the above experiments, any increase in endogenous corticosterone induced by the imposed stress could theoretically have prevented either the neoplastic initiation function of the carcinogens or their promotion.

Considerations Relevant to Experimental Design in Stress Studies

Caloric Restriction

The induction of stress by techniques that alter feeding schedules, deprive the animals of food and water or alter their nutritional status in any way generates a special experimental interpretation problem, since it has been shown that caloric restriction has an influence upon disease processes and can alter tumor incidence or growth rates [182, 191, 191a]. Riley and Spackman observed a significant reduction in the white blood count count and in the weight of the thymus, spleen, and lymph nodes following either food or water deprivation for 48 hr. Plasma corticosterone was also elevated, indicating that an acute food shortage may also induce the stress syndrome [145, 142]. Thus, inadvertent alteration of food intake can introduce complicating factors that may make it difficult to sort out experimental effects that were due to the imposed stress from the unintended influences of nutritional modification.

Restraint of the Animal as a Means of Inducing Stress

While this simple procedure undoubtedly causes anxiety and stress in the animal, the physically imposed immobilization in itself probably alters a number of physiological parameters that it would be preferable not to disturb. If immobilization is prolonged, the nutritional or metabolic status of the animal may be compromised in some respects, as well as alterations in breathing, blood flow, and catecholamine production. In any case, however, its metabolism would be altered in comparison with the free-ranging experimental animal. This is thus another stressor technique that should ordinarily be avoided in experiments designed to measure the effects of simple stress, unless it offers some unique possibilities not otherwise available.

Stress on Top of Stress

Studies by Riley *et al.* [137, 138, 141, 148] have shown that mice held in conventional animal storage facilities undergo chronic or intermittent stress, which may be inapparent to the unsuspecting researcher. When examined closely, these "control" animals show an increase in circulating corticosterone, a lymphocytopenia, thymus involution, and other physiological manifestations of stress, when compared with mice maintained in protective housing. If such conventionally maintained chronically stressed animals are used for "stress" experiments and are thus subjected to additional stress factors, the potential experimental difficulties are obvious. It is therefore essential that studies on stress employ originally nonstressed experimental animals, as well as permanently nonstressed controls, with both groups maintained in environmental circumstances that will assure quiescent baseline levels of the various stress-related biological components to be compared in the experimental and control animals.

Induction of Stress: Overstimulating Experimental Animals

Some of the earlier experiments on stress and its influences on the disease process employed rather harsh stimuli, including repeated surgical trauma, electric shock, exhaustion, starvation, chilling, heating, ether anesthesia, and other physical insults to the experimental subjects. Recent studies by Riley and Spackman have established that such harsh means for inducing psychosocial or physiological stress are not necessary and may actually defeat the aims of the experiment [141, 145, 148]. When the "stress-induction" process exceeds certain physiological thresholds, causing injury, shock, or metabolic exhaustion, many physiological parameters other than those affected by simple stress may be either stimulated or suppressed. The observed biological consequences may thus have only a limited bearing upon a specific, stress-induced train of events. For example, such experimental animals may exhibit alterations in respiration rate, blood flow and pressure, body temperature, and other factors that influence host metabolism, and thus induce complicating physiological effects which are unrelated to and superimposed upon the sensitive stress-associated pathways. In order to avoid these complications, it seems desirable to induce controlled stress carefully by the mildest procedures that will produce elevated circulating adrenal corticoids, and thus bring about a significant decrease in the thymus, lymphocytes, and other elements of the immunological and surveillance systems.

The Timing of Stress and the Onset of Malignancy

Certain influences on very young animals may constitute an "early experience" whose modifying effects upon the animal may be projected for long periods into the future. On the other hand, some imposed stressful stimuli may have a strictly limited time effect. In such cases, if a disease or neoplasm was initiated at a period considerably beyond the effective functional period of the original stress, no correlation of stress and disease development would logically be expected. It is therefore essential to know the duration of the effects of stress and to properly time the imposition of these in the disease process under test. Some of the negative correlations between stress and cancer in the data reviewed here may be explained by improper timing [119].

Segregating Stress Effects from Metabolic Changes

Inasmuch as the glucocorticoids affect protein and carbohydrate metabolism as well as directly influencing various elements of the immunological apparatus, it is pertinent to distinguish between these two actions by appropriate measurements, and to design experiments in such a way that the separate effects can be segregated in the ultimate analysis of the data.

Psychological versus Biochemical Techniques

In addition to Selye's basic studies [161–163], much of the pioneer experimentation on stress and disease was done by psychologists utilizing behavioral and related techniques. Use of the shuttle box with electric shock stimulation, and in some cases related to flashing warning lights for conditioning, are typical psychological techniques which have served valuable purposes. However, these techniques may not yield quantitative responses that are optimal for correlating emotional responses to stress with their biochemical and cellular effects, and ultimately with their potential influence on disease processes. The biochemical and immunological techniques that are now available for the study of stress-altered parameters provide more quantitative and more easily evaluated experimental results, which will serve psychologists as well as biologists as a basis for further research.

Strain and Personality of the Experimental Animal

In the case of mice, the DBA strain is a highly nervous animal, as is obvious by its general behavior. This can be demonstrated more specifically by its tendency to go into audiogenic seizure when stimulated by a loud noise. It seems obvious that stress studies using this sensitive animal might give somewhat different results from experiments carried out with a more phlegmatic strain such as the C3H mouse. Thus, selection of appropriate experimental animals for stress–cancer studies deserves special consideration.

Selection of Experimental Disease

Where measurements of the incidence and growth rate of a solid tumor are employed as a device to study the effects of stress on immunocompetence, selection of the type of tumor is important. A tumor that is perfectly syngeneic with its host behaves differently in the detection of subtle or weak immunological effects as compared with a tumor in which there are histoincompatibility factors. For example, the Gardner lymphosarcoma, when implanted subcutaneously in unstressed C3H mice, gives approximately 50% spontaneous regressions. This tumor thus provides an experimental equipoise in which the biological balance can be tipped one way or the other by either augmenting or compromising the host's immunological competence or surveillance process [144]. Such a tumor might thus detect the relatively subtle immunological influences resulting from stress, whereas a syngeneic tumor that invariably produces 100% "takes" and 100% deaths may never permit the detection of the moderate influences of stress. Such differences in tumor–host compatibility and sensitivities may explain some of the discrepancies reported in the literature.

Handling and "Gentling" Mice and Rats

Our studies show that the conventional handling of adult animals is highly stressful to them. However, it has also been reported that the daily handling of rats, starting at an early age, predisposes them to stress-adaptation in their immunological behavior later in life. Since such handling procedures can thus have apparently opposite effects, it is important to know and to distinguish between the consequences of occasional handling with its accompanying stress, and those of a systematic intentional "gentling" process which takes place over a substantial period of time and has future conditioning potential.

Age of Experimental Animals

Generally speaking, the thymus is larger in young animals, and tends to atrophy in older animals. Thus, experiments that are related to factors involving thymus involution and T-cell lymphocytopenia may be done most effectively in young adult mice. The studies of Teller *et al.* [190] have demonstrated differences in the transplantation response of nonsyngeneic tumors as a function of the age of the implanted animals. They have reported that old mice are more receptive to heterotransplantation, which may be an expression of change in the immunological capacity of the animal as a function of age. Thus, such factors are relevant in designing stress experiments, unless specific age differences are being studied. However, insofar as tumor behavior is concerned, certain age differences may be insignificant in mice between 6 and 30 weeks of age [139].

Circadian Rhythms and Diurnal Patterns

All living organisms exhibit circadian rhythms in certain of their biological and biochemical control systems. Rodents, for example, exhibit moderate circadian fluctuations in their plasma corticosteroid levels. The changing circadian concentrations of corticosterone in mice amount to a three- to fivefold increase from the early morning low levels to evening highs [141]. The human, by comparison, shows a high in plasma cortisol levels between 6 a.m. and noon, and a low late in the evening. It may be relevant that rodents are nocturnal creatures. Thus the time of day at which such stress-associated hormone levels are determined is of importance. Also, the phase of the diurnal cycle during which experimental stressful stimuli are initiated may be pertinent in respect to subsequent influences of such stress on the biochemical or the cellular events being studied. Again, the time of day at which stress-associated events are initiated should be controlled and recorded. Special attention directed to these rhythmic phenomena may provide additional insight into the relationships between stress, viruses, and neoplastic diseases. The time of day that therapeutic drugs are administered may also relate to their efficacy [141].

Discussion

Experimental Contradictions

It is apparent from an examination of the contradictory and inconsistent results obtained by various investigators that the complexities associated with stress–cancer research have heretofore exceeded our knowledge and ability to provide all of the necessary experimental controls, or to evaluate the relative potency of the independent variables employed in experimental efforts to demonstrate an influence of stress upon various neoplastic processes. It appears that these difficulties have arisen from a variety of inconspicuous experimental problems.

Animal Sensitivity

One troublesome aspect has been a failure to appreciate the extreme sensitivity of experimental animals in responding to uncontrolled environmental stress. Most rodents housed in conventional animal facilities are experiencing chronic stress. This may also be the case if they are handled without consideration for the extremely rapid increase in plasma corticoids that follows the mildest manipulative procedures. For example, when starting with a completely quiescent animal, physiological stress is generated by the simple act of transporting the animals from their holding facilities to the bench or to the working laboratory; or by the routine process of capturing animals for injection, bleeding, cage transfer, or other routine experimental procedures. Unless these operations are carried out within a three minute period following removal of the animal from its protective facilities, psychosocial stress will be manifested by initiation of the physiological stress syndrome resulting in elevated plasma corticosterone levels. As shown by Riley *et al.* [141, 145, 148] and others, critical phases of the stress syndrome are initiated within a few minutes following the slightest disturbance of the animals. The consequences of this stress may continue for hours or days, depending upon the nature and duration of the stimulus. Thus, when experimental stress is applied to animals that are already being stressed, the biological consequences are difficult to assess in terms of the independent variables being examined.

Tumor Differences

Other experimental factors that have produced discrepancies between experiments that were designed along similar lines are the use of different transplantable tumors by the various investigators, and the use of oncogenic viruses in one instance and chemical carcinogens in another. Accumulative data suggest that chemically induced tumors may behave differently in respect to stress response than tumors produced by oncogenic viruses such as the mouse mammary carcinomas.

Stress Hypothesis

An extension of the problem of differences in tumor behavior is found in the general case of rapidly growing malignancies that do not respond to the effects of stress. The question arises as to why there should be a striking differential response among tumors that are subjected to identical stress. A useful working hypothesis that relates to this problem is the concept that physiological stress is only capable of exerting an influence on a neoplastic process that is being partially restrained by the natural immunological forces of the host. Thus, if a malignancy is not held in check by the immunological apparatus of the host, impairment of that apparatus by the consequences of stress will not alter the behavior of such an independent neoplasm. A further extension of this hypothesis would contend that the enhancing effects of stress are only observable in any disease process when the unstressed host is able to exert some form of control over the disease. Thus, where the primary role of stress is associated with an impairment of the immunological process, it is expressed by the enhancement of a partially restrained malignancy or infection. The potential extent of such enhancement would presumably be proportional to the degree of restraint that the normal nonimpaired immunological apparatus was capable of exercising in controlling the affliction.

Multiple Responses to "Stress"

Since it must be assumed that stress phenomena are not as simple as implied by experimental protocols, it is prudent to be aware of the possibility that there may be several successive layers of physiological responses that can occur during an experiment employing "stress," depending on the nature of the stressor or the intensity of the stressing procedure. Since we know that mild anxiety is capable of activating the adrenal cortex, with the production of a significant (at least tenfold) elevation in circulating corticoids, the question occurs as to what additional physiological events may take place if the stressing procedure also generates fear or anger, or interferes with the nutritional state or the metabolism of the host. It has been shown by Tannenbaum [191, 191a] and others [149a, 194a] that reduced caloric intake has an inhibitory effect on a variety of tumors. Thus, where stressing procedures are severe, such as repeated electric shock, swimming, or other imposed exercises, or restraints that occupy a substantial portion of the day, there may be an interference with the food intake, and/or alterations in the metabolism of the host which, in turn, may have tangible influences on the various parameters that are being measured. Under such circumstances, it may be erroneous to assume that the alterations in the host or its tumor are due entirely to stress. Data obtained by Jose and Good suggest that deprivation of certain amino acids in the diet will impair the formation of antibodies and otherwise interfere with immunological competence. Thus, in stress studies, it would be helpful to know the various biological consequences of the application of severe "stress" that substantially exceeds the mild anxiety and readily activates the adrenal cortex.

Therapy for Stress Effects?

Since the adverse effects of the stress syndrome are a scientific reality despite the many contradictions in the published experimental data, it is relevant to consider what therapeutic possibilities may exist for blocking the undesirable physiological effects of either acute or chronic stress. If we accept the attractive hypothesis that the host response to stressful stimuli results in adrenal cortical hypersecretion, which produces lympholytic activity resulting in a depression of cell-mediated and possibly humoral immune reactions, and that such immune depression is responsible for an escape or encouragement of tumor activity in stressed animals, then it is obvious that it would be both desirable and possible to block the adverse biochemical effects of stress.

Seifter et al. [160, 160a] and others [131a] have tested this hypothesis directly and have demonstrated that metyrapone, a chemical that inhibits corticosterone production, prevented the typical stress syndrome and increased the resistance of stressed mice to a murine sarcoma virus. Since this compound directly inhibits glucocorticoid synthesis, its administration may have some undesirable hormone depletion effects. However, there may be other more suitable substances which can accomplish the desired therapy by competing for the receptor sites of target tissues, and thus block the destructive effects of elevated levels of corticoids without depleting important hormones below normal physiological levels. Steroids such as deoxycorticosterone, for example, have such competitive capacities for tissue receptor sites and may thus be beneficial. It has also been suggested that vitamin A may have such a capacity [131a]. Other natural substances such as progesterone may have a competitive capacity to prevent the adverse effects of cortisol or corticosterone. An expansion of these and related studies would seem to be justified, and might reduce the hazards of stress without at the same time altering the beneficial functions of the adrenal corticoids and other hormones associated with the stress syndrome. Irrespective of the ultimate consequences of these specific leads, the relationships between stress-associated modulations of pathological processes and the effects of stress on the thymus and on circulating T-and B-cells deserve serious concern by investigators.

Stress and the Immune Response

The most persuasive explanation for the tangible effects of stress upon disease processes, including cancer, appears to be the stress-associated modifications of various elements that make up the immunological apparatus of the animal organism. There are several obvious targets which, if adversely affected by the physiological consequences of stress, would in turn, permit certain latent diseases, incipient cancers, or subdued virus infections to escape immunological surveillance. There is evidence that all three of the basic cellular elements that make up the immunological system: macrophages, T-cells, and B-cells, are subject to modification, impairment, or destruction by elevated concentrations of specific hormones. While it is quite possible that all three of these cellular elements may be involved in the stress process, the most conspicuous differences are seen in the changes that occur in the thymus following a wide variety of stress-inducing circumstances. This includes the effect of some viruses, as well as psychosocial and other stimuli. The associated lymphocytopenia undoubtedly includes destruction or disappearance of T-cells and probably some B-cells.

The influence of stress on antibody response has been examined by Solomon, who has reported that cage crowding stress significantly reduced both primary and secondary antibody response to flagellin, a potent antigen of bacterial origin. When electric shock stress was administered 3 days prior to the inoculation of an oncogenic virus, both the tumor incidence and size of the resulting tumors were reduced, whereas in contrast, the same electric shock administered three days following inoculation of the virus seemed to increase tumor size.

Although there has been controversy over the reality of immune surveillance in controlling cancer and other diseases, there is a ponderance of opinion, based upon accumulated data, that this protective monitoring is a reality. George Klein [78] has suggested that immune surveillance may function most effectively where tumor-associated antigen systems are present that have been regularly encountered by the species during evolutionary processes. Some indirect evidence that is cited to support this hypothesis is the effective performance of immune systems in dealing with neoplastic transformants that have been induced by ubiquitous oncogenic viruses that presumably have been in the environment during the evolutionary development of the immunological apparatus. This protective performance is in contrast to its lessened ability to cope with tumors that are induced by chemical carcinogens that were presumably nonexistent in nature during evolutionary processes, having been introduced by the relatively recent events of industrialization.

Consequences of T-cell Deficiency

It has been shown, utilizing viruses such as polyoma and SV40, that many tumors arise in such virus-injected animals following thymectomy or treatment with antilymphocytic serum. In contrast, if the ablated T-cell system is replaced by thymus grafting, or by the inoculation of syngeneic lymphocyte suspensions containing mature T-cell populations, most of the tumors are then suppressed [78]. This indicates that the increased tumor incidence of the immunologically impaired animals was specifically related to a T-cell deficiency.

The inadvertent experiments with prolonged immunosuppression in man have indicated that patients maintained under long-term immunosuppression following kidney grafts have an increase in tumor incidence of about 200-fold or higher. Supporting evidence for the adverse effects of genetically determined immunodeficiency also shows an increased tumor incidence in patients with the Wiskott–Aldrich syndrome, or ataxia-telangiectasia. Both of these genetic diseases are known to affect the T-cell system adversely. It thus seems that the accumulative data indicate that a primary consequence of stress is a compromise of immunological status, and this in turn may permit what appear to be enhancing influences upon certain neoplastic processes.

Stress-Associated Inhibition of Neoplasia

Inhibition of tumor induction or growth by stress obviously does not fit logically into this immune impairment concept. Such observed inhibitory effects must thus be explained by other mechanisms. The most conspicuous inhibitory effects have been reported where the tumors have been chemically induced by DMBA or MCA, and the "stress" has been produced by electric shock or by long-term restraint.

This poses the interesting question as to whether there is something unique about the response of chemically induced tumors, or if the unexpected findings are due to the nature of the stressor systems. The solution of this problem obviously deserves some priority.

Summary

This overview of research on stress and cancer includes an examination of representative papers. These published studies demonstrate the widespread contradictions in the experimental results obtained by various investigators. Such discordant findings testify to the complexity of the relationships between stress and disease processes. In an effort to better understand the reasons for these puzzling experimental differences, a number of experimental factors that may relate to these problems are discussed. Notwithstanding the experimental difficulties and conflicting results, the accumulative data demonstrate that stress is capable of influencing various disease processes, including some neoplastic diseases. The importance of the problem deserves a more intensive research effort, with a magnitude of support that will permit experimental activities to proceed on an appropriately broad front, and in sufficient depth that the multiple factors responsible for the apparent contradictions can be resolved. It is conceivable that out of such studies a biochemical means for controlling the adverse consequences of physiological stress may result.

Bibliography

1. Ader, R.; and Friedman, S. B.: Social factors affecting emotionality and resistance to disease in animals: IV. Differential housing, emotionality, and Walker 256 carcinosarcoma in the rat. *Psychological Reviews* 15:535–541, 1964.
2. Ader, R.; and Friedman, S. B.: Differential early experiences and susceptibilities to transplanted tumors in the rat. *Journal of Comparative and Physiological Psychology* 59:361–364, 1965.
3. Ader, R.; and Friedman, S. B.: Social factors affecting emotionality and resistance to disease in animals: V. early separation from the mother and response to a transplanted tumor in the rat. *Psychosomatic Medicine* 27:119–122, 1965.
4. Ader, R.; and Grota, L. J.: Effects of early experience on adrenocortical reactivity. *Physiology and Behavior* 4:303–305, 1969.
5. Agosin, M.; *et al.*: Cortisone-induced mestastases of adenocarcinoma in mice. *Proceedings of the Society for Experimental Biology and Medicine* 80:128–131, 1952.
6. Amkraut, A.; and Solomon, G. F.: Stress and murine sarcoma virus (Moloney)-induced tumors. *Cancer Research* 32:1428–1433, 1972.
7. Amkraut, A.; and Solomon, G. F.: Effects of stress and of hormonal intervention on the graft-versus-host response. *Proceedings of the Fourth International Conference on Lymph Tissue Germ Centers and Immune Reactions* P:667, 1973.
8. Andervont, H. B.: The influence of environment on mammary cancer in mice. *Journal of the National Cancer Institute* 4:579–581, 1944.
9. Archer, O.; and Pierce, J. C.: Role of thymus in development of the immune response. *Federation Proceedings* 20:26, 1961.
10. Bacon, C. L.; Renneker, R.; and Cutler, M.: A psychosomatic survey of the breast. *Psychosomatic Medicine* 14:453–460, 1952.

11. Bahnson, C. B.: Psychophysiological complementarity in malignancies: Past work and future vistas. *Annals of the New York Academy of Science* 164:319–334, 1969.
12. Bahnson, C. B.: Emotional and personality characteristics of cancer patients. In *Recent Developments in Medical Oncology*, ed. Alton Sutnick. Baltimore: University Park Press, 1976.
13. Bahnson, M. B.; and Bahnson, C. B.: Development of a psychosocial screening questionnaire for cancer. *Abstracts, Third International Symposium on Detection and Prevention of Cancer.* New York: Marcel Dekker, 1976.
14. Bahnson, C. B.; and Kissen, D. M.: Psychophysiological aspects of cancer. *Annals of the New York Academy of Science* 125:773–1055, 1966.
15. Baker, D. G.; Jahn, A.; and Hollander, C. F.: The influence of a chronic environmental stress on radiation carcinogenesis. *Proceedings of the American Association for Cancer Research* 16:55, 1975.
16. Baltrusch, H. J. F.: Psychosocial stress and cancer. *Abstracts, Third International Symposium on Detection and Prevention of Cancer.* New York: Marcel Dekker, 1976.
17. Bard, M.: Effect of auditory stress on rats implanted with human tumors. *Journal of Nervous and Mental Diseases* 125:513–517, 1957.
18. Bennette, J. G.: Immunological mechanisms in possible mediators of psychosomatic competence in relation to chemical, viral, and physical carcinogenic changes. Presented at the Fourth International Conference on Psychosomatic Aspects of Neoplastic Disease, Turin, Italy, 1965.
19. Blumber, E. M.; West, P. M.; and Ellis, F. W.: Possible relationship between psychological factors and human cancer. *Psychosomatic Medicine* 16:277–286, 1954.
20. Booth, G.: Cancer and humanism: Psychosomatic aspects of evolution. In *Psychosomatic Aspects of Neoplastic Disease* Eds. D. M. Kissen and L. L. LeShan, pp. 159–169. London: Pitman, 1964.
21. Cannon, B.: *Bodily Changes in Pain, Hunger, Fear and Rage.* 2nd edition. New York: Appleton, 1929.
22. Chang, S. S.; and Rasmussen, A. F., Jr.: Stress-induced suppression of interferon production in virus-infected mice. *Nature* 205:623, 1965.
23. Cooley, B.; Henry, J. P.; and Stephens, P. M.: Enhancing effects of psychosocial stimulation on experimental mammary tumors. *Abstracts, Third International Symposium on Detection and Prevention of Cancer.* New York: Marcel Dekker, 1976.
24. Crispens, C. G., Jr.: Apparent inhibitory influence of stress on SJL/JDg neoplasia. *Psychology and Psychiatry* 4:169, 1976.
25. Cutler, M.: Behavioral characteristics of 40 women with cancer of the breast. In *The psychological variables in human cancer*, eds. J. A. Gengerelli and F. I. Kirkner. Berkley: University of California Press, 1954.
26. Dechambre, R. P.; and Gosse, C.: Influence of an isolation stress on the development of transplanted ascites tumors in mice. Role of the adrenals. *Comptes Rendus Hebdomadaires des Seances de l'Academie des Sciences. D: Sciences Naturalles (Paris)* 272:2720–2722, 1971.
27. Dechambre, R. P.; and Gosse, C.: Influence of population density on mortality in mice bearing transplanted tumors. *Comptes Rendus Hebdomadaires des Seances de l'Academie des Sciences. D. Sciences Naturalles (Paris)* 267:2200–2202, 1968.
28. Engel, F. L.; and Fredericks, J.: Contribution to understanding of the mechanism of permissive action of corticoids. *Proceedings of the Society for Experimental Biology and Medicine* 94:593–596, 1957.
29. Evans, E.: A psychological study of cancer. New York: Dodd, Mead, 1926.
30. Fessel, W. J.: Mental stress, blood proteins, hypothalamus: experimental results showing

effect of mental stress upon 4S and 19s proteins: Speculation that functional behavior disturbances may be expressions of general metabolic disorder. *Archives of General Psychiatry* 7:427, 1962.

31. Fitzmaurice, M. A.; Riley, V.; and Santisteban, G. A.: Biological synergism between the LDH-virus and *Eperythrozoon coccoides:* Studies on the mechanism. *Pathologie-Biologie* 20:743–750, 1972.

32. Fogue, E.: Le problem du cancer dans ses aspects psychiques. *Gaz. Hop.,* 104:827–833, 1931.

33. Fortier, C.: Sensitivity of the plasma free corticosteroid response to environmental change in the rat. *Archives Internationales de Physiologie et de Biochimie* (Liege) 66:672, 1958.

34. Fox, B. H.; and Howell, M. A.: Cancer risk among psychiatric patients: A hypothesis. *International Journal of Epidemiology* 3:207–208, 1974.

35. Friedman, S. B.; and Ader, R.: Parameters relevant to the experimental production of "stress" in the mouse. *Psychosomatic Medicine* 27:27–30, 1965.

36. Friedman, S. B.; Ader, R.; and Glasgow, L. A.: Effects of psychological stress in adult mice inoculated with Coxsackie B viruses. *Psychosomatic Medicine* 27:361–368, 1965.

37. Friedman, S. B.; Glasgow, L. A.; and Ader, R.: Psychosocial factors modifying host resistance to experimental infections. *Annals of the New York Academy of Science* 164:381–393, 1969.

38. Fuller, R. H.; Brown, E.; and Mills, C. A.: Environmental temperatures and spontaneous tumors in mice. *Cancer Research* 1:130–133, 1941.

39. Gala, R.; and Leginsky, S. J.: Correlation between serum prolactin levels and incidence of mammary tumors induced by 7, 12-Dimethylbenz(a)anthracene in the rat. *Journal of the National Cancer Institute* 51:593–597, 1973.

40. Gisler, R. H.; Bussar, A. E.; Mazie, J. C.; and Hess, R.: Hormonal regulation of the immune response. I. Induction of an immune response in vitro with lymphoid cells from mice exposed to acute systematic stress. *Cell Immunology* 2:634, 1971.

41. Gisler, R. H.; and Schenkel-Hullinger, L.: Hormonal regulation of the immune response. II. Influence of pituitary and adrenal activity on immune responsiveness *in vitro. Cell Immunology* 2:646, 1971.

42. Glenn, W. G.; and Becker, R. E.: Individual versus group housing in mice: Immunological response to time and phase injections. *Physiological Zoology* 42:411–416, 1969.

43. Glick, D.; Von Redlick, D.; and Levine, S.: Fluorometric determination of corticosterone and cortisol in 0.02–0.05 milliliters of plasma or submilligram samples of adrenal tissue. *Endocrinology* 74:653–655, 1964.

44. Gotlieb-Stematsky, T.; Karbi, S.; and Allison, A. C.: Increased tumor formation by polyoma virus in the presence of non-oncogenic viruses. *Nature* 212:421–422, 1966.

45. Gottfried, B.; and Molomut, N.: Effects of surgical trauma and other environmental stressors on tumor growth and wound healing. *Proceedings of the Eighth International Cancer Congress* 3:1617, 1963.

46. Green, S.; Diefenbach, K.; and Santisteban, G. A.: Comparison of the adrenocortical responses to the stressing effects of crowding and life in a complex environment in CBA mice. *Anatomical Record* 157:2, 1967.

47. Greene, W. A.: Psychological factors and reticuloendothelial disease. I. Preliminary observations of a group of males with lymphomas and leukemias. *Psychosomatic Medicine* 16:220–230, 1954.

48. Greene, W. A.: The psychosocial setting of the development of leukemia and lymphoma. *Annals of the New York Academy of Science* 125:794–801, 1966.

49. Greene, W.; Young, L. E.; and Swisher, S. N.: Psychological factors and reticuloendothelial disease. II. Observations on a group of women with lymphomas and leukemias. *Psychosomatic Medicine* 18:284–303, 1956.
50. Greer, S.; and Morris, T.: Psychological attributes of women who develop breast cancer: A controlled study. *Journal of Psychosomatic Research* 19:147–153, 1975.
51. Greer, S.: Psychological attributes of women who develop breast cancer. *Abstracts, Third International Symposium on Detection and Prevention of Cancer.* New York: Marcel Dekker, 1976.
52. Grundberg, E.; and Prince, H. N.: Lethal infection of adult mice with Coxsackie B-1 virus. *Proceedings of the Society for Experimental Biology and Medicine,* 114:494–496, 1963.
53. Habel, K.: Immunologic aspects of oncogenesis by polyoma virus. In *Conceptual advances in immunology and oncology.* New York: Hoeber, 1963.
54. Harlow, C. M.; and Selye, H.: The blood picture in the alarm reaction. Proceedings of the Society for Experimental Biology and Medicine 36:141–144, 1937.
55. Henry, J. P.: and Santisteban, G. A.: The induction of arteriosclerosis by psycho-social factors in CBA mice: Observations on the heart, aorta, and kidneys. *Arteriosclerosis* 14:203–218, 1971.
56. Henry, J. P.; Ely, D. L.; and Stephens, P. M.: Mental factors and cardiovascular disease. *Psychiatric Annals* 2(7):25–71, 1972.
57. Henry, J. P.; Stephens, P. M.; and Watson, F. M. C.: Force breeding, social disorder and mammary tumor formation in CBA/USC mouse colonies. A pilot study. *Psychosomatic Medicine* 37:277–283, 1975.
58. Henry, K. R.: Audiogenic seizure susceptibility induced in C57BL/6J mice by prior auditory exposure. *Science* 158:938–940, 1967.
59. Herbst, A. L.; Yates, F. E.; Glenister, D. W.; and Urquhart, J.: Variations in hepatic inactivation of corticosterone with changes in food intake: An explanation of impaired corticosterone metabolism following noxious stimuli. *Endocrinology* 67:222, 1960.
60. Hirsch, M. S.: Immunological activation of oncogenic viruses: Interrelationship of immunostimulation and immunosuppression. *Johns Hopkins Medical Journal* (Supplement) 3:177–185, 1974.
61. Hoffman, S. A.; Paschkir, K. E.; DeBias, D. A.; Cantarow, A.; and Williams, T. I.: The influence of exercise on the growth of transplanted rat tumors. *Cancer Research* 22:597–599, 1962.
62. Howard, R. J.; Notkins, A. L.; and Mergenhagen, S. E.: Inhibition of cellular immune reactions in mice infected with lactate dehydrogenase virus. *Nature* 221:873–874, 1969.
63. Hughes, C. H.: The relations of nervous depression to the development of cancer. *Surgery (St. Louis)* May, 1969.
64. Jensen, M. M.: The influence of stress on murine leukemia virus infection. *Proceedings of the Society for Experimental Biology and Medicine* 127:610, 1968.
65. Jensen, M. M.: Transitory impairment of interferon production on stressed mice. *Proceedings of the Society for Experimental Biology and Medicine* 128:174, 1968.
66. Jensen, M. M.: Changes in leukocyte counts associated with various stressors. *Journal of the Reticuloendothelial Society* 6:457–465, 1969.
67. Jensen, M. M.; and Rasmussen, A. F., Jr.: Stress and susceptibility to viral infection. II. Sound stress and susceptibility to vesicular stomatitis virus. *Journal of Immunology* 90:21, 1963.
68. Jonas, A. D.: Theoretical considerations concerning the influences of the central nervous system on cancerous growth. *Annals of the New York Academy of Sciences* 125:856–864, 1966.

68a.Jose, D. G.; and Good, R. A.: Quantitative effects of nutritionally essential amino acid deficiency upon immune response to tumors in mice. *Journal of Experimental Medicine* 137:1–9, 1973.

69. Katz, J.; Gallagher, T.; Hellman, L.; Sachar, E.; and Weiner, H.: Psycho-endocrine considerations in cancer of the breast. *Annals of the New York Academy of Sciences* 164:509–516, 1969.

70. Kavetsky, R. E.: *Tumors and the Nervous System.* Gos. Meditsinskoe Izd. Kiev, USSR (In Russian), 1958.

71. Kavetsky, R. E.; Turkevich, N. M.; Avimeva, R. M.; and Khayetsky, I. K.: Induced cancerogenesis under various influences on the hypothalamus. *Annals of the New York Academy of Sciences* 164(3):517–519, 1969.

72. Kavetsky, R. E.; Turkevich, N. M.; and Balitsky, K. P.: On the psychophysiological mechanisms of the organism's resistance to tumor growth. *Annals of the New York Academy of Sciences* 125:933–945, 1969.

73. Keast, D.: Immunosurveillance and cancer. *Lancet* 1:710–712, 1970.

74. Khalestkaia, F. M.: The influence of excessiveness of activity of the nervous system in the development of individual tumors in mice. *Zhurnal Vysshei Deiatel'mosti Imini* 4:869–876 1954.

75. Khayetsky, I. K.: The influence of hypothalamo-pituitary disturbances produced by continuous light on development of induced mammary tumours in rats. *Voprosy Oncologii* 1:87–94, 1965.

76. Kissen, D. M.; and LeShan, L. L., eds.: *Psychosomatic aspects of neoplastic Disease.* London: Pittman, 1964.

77. Kissen, D. M.: Psychosocial factors, personality and lung cancer in men aged 55–64. *British Journal of Medical Psychology* 40:29–43, 1967.

78. Klein, G.: Immunological surveillance against neoplasia. *Harvey Lectures* 69:71–102, 1975.

79. Klopfer, B.: Psychological variables in human cancer. *Journal of Projective Techniques* 21:331, 1957.

80. Korneva, E. A.; and Khai, L. M.: Effect of destruction of hypothalamic areas on immunogenesis. *Fiziologicheskii Zhurnal SSSR Imeni I. M. Sechenova* 49:42 (Leningrad) 1963.

81. Kowal, S. J.: Emotions as a cause of cancer: Eighteenth and nineteenth century contributions. *Psychoanalytic Review* 42:217–227, 1955.

82. Kruger, S.; Standeffer, W. C.; and Schueler, F. W.: Some effects of reserpine on normal and leukemic mice. *Archives Internationales de Pharmacodynamie et de Therapie* 129:395–400, 1960.

83. LaBarba, R. C.: Experimental and environmental factors in cancer. A review of research with animals. *Psychosomatic Medicine* 32:259–275, 1970.

84. LaBarba, R. C.; Klein, M.; White, J. L.; and Lazar, L.: The effects of early cold stress and handling on the growth of Ehrlich carcinoma in the BALB/c mice. *Developmental Psychology* 2:312, 1970.

85. LaBarba, R. C.; Martini, J.; and White, J.: The effect of maternal separation on the growth of Ehrlich carcinoma in the BALB/c mice. *Psychosomatic Medicine* 31:129–133, 1967.

86. LaBarba, R.; White, J. L.; Lazar, J.; and Klein, M.: Early maternal separation and the response to Ehrlich carcinoma in BALB/c mice. *Developmental Psychology* 3:78–80, 1970.

86a.Lazarus, L.; Georgy, E. P.; and Stuart, M.: Effect of varying doses of methopyrapone

(Metopirone) on the secretion rate of cortisol. *Journal of Clinical Endocrinology and Metabolism* 23:773-775, 1963.

87. Lea, A. J.: Environmental temperature and death-rate of women from breast neoplasms. *Lancet* 2:1040, 1968.

88. LeShan, L. L.; and Worthington, R. E.: Some psychologic correlates of neoplastic disease: A preliminary report. *Journal of Clinical and Experimental Psychopathology* 16:281, 1955.

89. LeShan, L. L.; and Worthington, R. E.: Personality as a factor in pathogenesis of cancer: Review of the literature. *British Journal of Medical Psychology* 29:49, 1956.

90. LeShan, L. L.; and Worthington, R. E.: Some recurrent life history patterns observed in patients with malignant disease. *Journal of Nervous and Mental Disease* 124:460-465, 1956.

91. LeShan, L. L.: Psychological states as factors in the development of malignant disease: A critical review. *Journal of the National Cancer Institute* 22:1-18, 1959.

92. LeShan, L. L.: An emotional life-history pattern associated with neoplastic disease. *Annals of the New York Academy of Sciences* 125:780-793, 1966.

93. Levine, S.: Maternal and environmental influences on the adrenocortical response to stress in weaning rats. *Science* 156:258-260, 1967.

94. Levine, S.; and Cohen, C.: Differential survival to leukemia as a function of infantile stimulation in DBA/2 mice. *Proceedings of the Society for Experimental Biology and Medicine* 102:53-54, 1959.

95. Marmorston, J.; Crowley, L. G.; Myers, S. M.; Stern, R.; and Hopkins, C. E.: Urinary excretion of neutral 17-ketosteroids and pregnanediol by patients with breast cancer and benign breast disease. *American Journal of Obstetrics and Gynecology* 92:447-459, 1965.

96. Marsh, J. T.; Miller, B. E.; and Lamson, B. G.: Effect of repeated brief stress on the growth of Ehrlich carcinoma in the mouse. *Journal of the National Cancer Institute* 22:961, 1959.

97. Marsh, J. T.; and Rasmussen, A. F., Jr.: Response of adrenals, thymus, spleen, and leucocytes to shuttle box and confinement stress. *Proceedings of the Society for Experimental Biology and Medicine* 104:180-183, 1960.

98. Mason, J. W.; Harwood, T.; and Rosenthal, N. R.: Influence of some environmental factors on plasma and urinary 17-hydroxycorticosteroid levels in the rhesus monkey. *American Journal of Physiology* 190:429, 1957.

99. Mason, J. W.: A historical view of the stress field, part I. *Journal of Human Stress*, pp. 6-11, March, 1975.

100. Mason, J. W.: A historical view of the stress field, Part II. *Journal of Human Stress*, pp. 22-36, June, 1975.

101. Mastrovito, R. C.; Deguire, K.; Clarkin, J.; Lewis, J. L.; and Cooper, E.: Personality characteristics of women with gynecological cancer. *Abstracts, Third International Symposium on Detection and Prevention of Cancer.* New York: Marcel Dekker, 1976.

102. Matthes, T. H.: Experimental contribution to the question of emotional reactions on the growth of tumors in animals. *Proceedings of the Eighth International Cancer Congress* 3:1608, 1963.

103. Matthes, T. H.: Experimental data on the effect of emotional stress on tumor growth in aminals. *Proceedings of the Eighth International Cancer Congress* 3:1608, 1963.

104. McVay, J. R.: Environmental temperature and death-rate from intestinal neoplasms. *Lancet* 2:1393, 1968.

105. Miller, F. R.; and Jones, H. W.: The possibility of precipitating the leukemic state by emotional factors. *Blood* 3:880-884, 1948.

106. Moore, D. H.; and Charney, J.: Breast cancer: Etiology and possible prevention. *American Scientist* 63:160–168, 1975.

107. Muhlbock, O.: Effect of environment on development of cancer: studies on mammary cancer in mice. *Nederlands Tijdschrift voor Geneeskunde* 94:3747–3752, 1950.

108. Muhlbock, O.: Influence of environment on the incidence of mammary tumors in mice. *Acta International Union against Cancer* 7:351, 1951.

109. Muhlbock, O.; and Bott, L. M.: Induction of mammary cancer in mice without the mammary tumor agent by isography of hypophyses. *Cancer Research* 19:402–412, 1959.

110. Nandi, S.: Interactions among hormonal, viral and genetic factors in mouse mammary tumorigenesis. In *Proceedings of the Sixth Canadian Cancer Conference*, pp. 69–81. New York: Pergamon Press, 1964.

111. Newberry, B. H.; Frankie, G.; Beatty, P. A.; Maloney, B.; and Gilchrist, J.: Shock stress and DMBA-induced mammary tumors. *Psychosomatic Medicine* 34:295–303, 1972.

112. Newberry, B. H.: Inhibitory effects of stress on experimental mammary tumors. *Cancer Detection and Prevention* 2:225–234, 1979.

113. Newall, G. R.; and Waggoner, D. E.: Cancer mortality and environmental temperature in the United States. *Lancet* 1:766–768, 1970.

114. Newton G.: Early experiences and resistance to tumor growth. In *Psychosomatic Aspects of Neoplastic Disease*, eds. D. M. Kissen and L. L. LeShan, p. 71. Philadelphia: Lippencott, 1964.

115. Newton, G.: Tumor susceptibility in rats: Role of infantile manipulation and later exercise. *Psychological Reports* 16:127–132, 1965.

116. Newton, G.; Bly, C. G.; and McCrary, C.: Effects of early experience on the response to transplanted tumor. *Journal of Nervous and Mental Disease* 134:522–527, 1962.

117. Nieburgs, H. E.; Weiss, J.; Navarrete, M.; Grillione, G.; and Siedlecki, B.: Inhibitory and enhancing effects of various stresses on experimental mammary tumorigenesis. *Abstracts, Third International Symposium on Detection and Prevention of Cancer*, New York: Marcel Dekker, 1976.

118. Notkins, A.: Enzymatic and immunological alterations in mice infected with lactic dehydrogenase virus. *American Journal of Pathology* 64:733–746, 1971.

119. Otis, L. S.; and Scholler, J.: Effects of stress during infancy on tumor development and tumor growth. *Psychological Reports* 20:167–173, 1967.

120. Perrin, G. M.; and Pierce, L. R.: Psychosomatic aspects of cancer: A review. *Psychosomatic Medicine* 5:397–421, 1959.

121. Petrova, M. K.: The role of a functionally weakened cerebral cortex in the onset of various pathologic processes in the organism. *Medgiz.* Moscow, U.S.S.R. (in Russian), 1955.

122. Prehn, R. T.: Role of immune mechanisms in biology of chemically and physically induced tumors. In: *Conceptual Advances in Immunology and Oncology.* New York: Hoeber, 1963.

123. Prehn, R. T.: The relationship of immunology to carcinogenesis. *Annals of the New York Academy of Sciences* 164:449–457, 1969.

124. Profitt, M. R.; and Congdon, C. C.: Effect of a large dose of LDH-virus on mouse lymphatic tissue. *Federation Proceedings* 29:559, 1970.

125. Rashkis, H. A.: Systematic stress as an inhibitor of experimental tumors in Swiss mice. *Science* 116:169–171, 1952.

126. Rasmussen, A. F., Jr.: Emotions and immunity. *Annals of the New York Academy of Sciences* 164:458–462, 1969.

127. Rasmussen, A. F., Jr.; Hildemann, W. H.; and Sellers, M.: Malignancy of Polyoma virus infection in mice in relation to stress. *Journal of the National Cancer Institute* 30:101, 1963.

128. Rasmussen, A. F., Jr.; Spencer, E. S.; and Marsh, J. T.: Increased susceptibility to Herpes simplex in mice subjected to avoidance-learning stress or restraint. *Proceedings of the Society for Experimental Biology and Medicine* 96:183, 1957.

129. Raushenbakh, M. O.; Zhorova, E. M.; and Khokhlova, M. P.: The influence of overstraining of the central nervous system in mice on the development of experimental leukocytosis *Arkhiv Patologie* (Moscow) 14:23–31, 1952.

130. Ray, P.; and Pradhan, S. N.: Growth of transplanted and induced tumors in rats under a schedule of punished behavior. *Journal of the National Cancer Institute* 52:575–577, 1974.

131. Reznikoff, M.; and Martin, D. E.: The influence of stress on mammary cancer. *Journal of Psychosomatic Research* 2:56, 1957.

131a. Reitura, G.; Seifter, J.; Zisblatt, M.; *et al.*: Metyrapone-inhibited oncogenesis in mice inoculated with a murine sarcoma virus. *Journal of the National Cancer Institute* 51:1983–1985, 1973.

132. Riley, V.: Adaption of orbital bleeding technique to rapid serial blood series. *Proceedings of the Society for Experimental Biology and Medicine* 104:751–754, 1960.

133. Riley, V.: Biological contaminants and scientific misinterpretations. *Cancer Research* 34:1752–1754, 1974.

134. Riley, V.: Erroneous interpretation of valid experimental observations through interference by the LDH-virus. *Journal of the National Cancer Institute* 52:1673–1677, 1974.

135. Riley, V.: Mouse mammary tumors: Alteration of incidence as an apparent function of stress. *Science* 189:465–467, 1975.

136. Riley, V.: Persistence and other characteristics of the lactate dehydrogenase-elevating virus (LDH-Virus). In *Progress in Medicine Virology: Slow Virus Diseases* 18:198–213. eds.: J. L. Melnick and J. Hotchin. Basel: S. Karger, 1973.

137. Riley, V.: Protective ventilated shelves for experimental animal storage, *Proceedings of the American Association for Laboratory Animal Sciences* 23rd Annual Session, #22A. St. Louis, 1972.

138. Riley, V.: Spontaneous mammary tumors: Decrease of incidence in mice infected with an enzyme-elevating virus. *Science* 153:1657–1658, 1966.

139. Riley, V.: Unpublished data.

140. Riley, V.; Fitzmaurice, M. A.; and Loveless, J. D.: Decrease in "spontaneous" mammary tumor incidence. *Proceedings of the American Association for Cancer Research* 7:59, 1966.

141. Riley, V.; and Spackman, D.: Modifying effects of a benign virus on the malignant process and the role of physiological stress on tumor incidence. Fogarty International Cancer Proceedings, No. 28, pp. 319–336. Washington: U.S. Government Printing Office, 1976.

142. Riley, V.; and Spackman, D. Unpublished data.

143. Riley, V.; Spackman, D.; and Santisteban, G.: The role of physiological stress on breast tumor incidence in mice. *Proceedings of the American Association for Cancer Research* 16:152, 1975.

144. Riley, V.; and Spackman, D.: Melanoma enhancement by viral-induced stress. In *The Pigment Cell Melanomas: Basic Properties and Clinical Behavior*. Vol. 2, pp. 163–173. ed. V. Riley. Basel: S. Karger, 1976.

145. Riley, V.; Spackman, D.; McClanahan, H.; and Santisteban, G.: The role of stress in malignancy. *Proceedings of the Third International Symposium on Detection and Prevention of Cancer*. New York: Marcel Dekker, 1976.

146. Riley, V.; Braun, W.; Ishizuka, M.; and Spackman, D.: Antibody-producing cells: Virus-induced alteration of response to antigen. *Proceedings of the National Academy of Sciences* 73:1707–1711, 1976.

147. Riley, V.; Spackman, D.; Fitzmaurice, M. A.; Santisteban, G.; McClanahan, H.; Louthan, S.; Dennis, M.; and Bloom, J.: Enhancement and inhibition of lymphosarcoma by fluocinolone acetonide. *Proceedings of the American Association for Cancer Research* 17:161, 1976.

148. Riley, V.; Spackman, D.; McClanahan, H.; and Santisteban, G.A.: The role of stress in malignancy. *Cancer Detection and Prevention* 2:235-255, 1979.

149. Rusch, H. P.; and Kline; B. E.: The Effect of exercise on the growth of a mouse tumor. *Cancer Research* 4:116, 1944.

149a.Rusch, H. P.: Extrinsic factors that influence carcinogenesis. *Physiological Reviews* 24:177-204, 1944.

150. Sakakibera,T.: Effects of brightness or darkness on carcinogenesis. *Minoya Shiritsj Baiga-U Igakkai Sasshi* 19:525-557, 1966.

151. Santisteban, G. A.: Comparison of the influences of various forms of stress stimuli upon the adrenocortico-thymico-lymphatic system in CBA mice. *Anatomical Record* 133:331, 1959.

152. Santisteban, G. A.: Studies of the development of adrenal cortical function. *Proceedings of the IX International Congress of the Anatomists*, Leningrad, 1970.

153. Santisteban, G. A.: Studies on the relationships of the acute involution of lymphatic organs to the severity of stress stimuli. *Anatomical Record* 130:2, 1958.

154. Santisteban, G. A.; and Dougherty, T. F.: Comparison of the influences of adrenocortical hormones on the growth and involution of lymphatic organs. *Endocrinology* 54:130-146, 1954.

155. Santisteban, G. A.; Guslander, C.; and Willhight, K.: Studies on the maturation of the adrenal cortical-lymphatic tissue interrelationships. *Anatomical Record* 163:2, 1969.

156. Santisteban, G. A., and Henry, J.P.: The induction of arteriosclerosis by psychosocial factors in CBA mice: Observations on the heart, aorta, and kidneys. *Anatomical Record* 169:2, 1971.

157. Santisteban, G. A.; and Riley, V.: Thymo-lymphatic organ response to the LDH-virus. *Proceedings of the American Association for Cancer Research* 14:112, 1973.

158. Santisteban, G. A.; Riley, V.; and Fitzmaurice, M.: Thymolytic and adrenal cortical responses to the LDH-elevating virus. *Proceeding of the Society for Experimental Biology and Medicine* 139:202-206, 1972.

159. Schwartz, R. S.: Defective immune responses and malignancy. *Johns Hopkins Medical Journal* (Supplement) 3:173-176, 1974.

160. Seifter, E.; Rettura, G.; Zisblatt, M.; *et al.:* Enhancement of tumor development in physically-stressed mice inoculated with an oncogenic virus. *Experimentia* 29:1379-1382, 1973.

160a.Seifter, E.; Zisblatt, M.; Levine, N.; *et al.*: Inhibitory action of vitamin A on a murine sarcoma. *Life Sciences* 13:945-952, 1973.

160b.Seifter, E.; Cohen, M. H.; and Riley, V.: Of stress, vitamin A, and tumors. *Science* 193:74-75, 1976.

161. Selye, H.: A syndrome produced by diverse nocuous agents. *Nature* 138:32, London, 1936.

162. Selye, H.: The general adaptation syndrome and the diseases of adaptation. *Journal of Clinical Endocrinology* 6:117-230, 1946.

163. Selye, H.: *The Story of the Adaptation Syndrome.* Montreal: Acta Incorporated, Medical Publishers, 1952.

164. Selye, H.: Confusion and controversy in the stress field. *Journal of Human Stress*, pp. 37-44, June, 1975.

165. Schevchenko, I. T.: The characteristics of the clinical course of neoplastic disease in rela-

tion to the condition of higher nervous activity. *Proceedings, Scientific Session on the Problem: The Nervous System in the Neoplastic Process.* pp. 74–79. Kiev, USSR, 1955.

166. Sjogren, H. O.: Effects of tumor growth in vivo by manipulation of the tumor immune response. *Johns Hopkins Medical Journal* 3:51–61, 1974.

167. Slaga, T. J.; Thompson, S.; and Smuckler, E. A.: Prolonged inhibition of mouse epidermal DNA synthesis by dexamethasome. *Journal of the National Cancer Institute* 54:931–936, 1975.

168. Slaga, T. J.; Thompson, S.; and Schwarz, J. A.: Mechanism of action of steroidal anti-inflammatory agents that inhibit skin carcinogenesis. *Proceedings of the American Association for Cancer Research* 16:37, 1975.

169. Schmale, A. H., Jr.; and Iker, H. P.: The affect of hopelessness in the development of cancer. I. The prediction of uterine cervical cancer in women with atypical cytology. *Psychosomatic Medicine* 26:634–635, 1964.

170. Schmale, A. H., Jr.; and Iker, H. P.: The psychological setting of uterine cervical cancer. *Annals of the New York Academy of Science* 125:807–813, 1966.

171. Solomon, G.: Emotions, stress, the CNS, and immunological function. *Annals of the New York Academy of Science* 164:335–343, 1969.

172. Solomon, G. F.; and Amkraut, A. A.: Emotions, stress, and immunity. In *Frontiers of Radiation Therapy and Oncology.* Vol. 7, pp. 84–96, ed. J. M. Vaeth. Baltimore: University Park Press, 1972.

173. Solomon, G. F.; Amkraut, A. A.; and Kasper, P.: Immunity, emotions, and stress. *Annals of Clinical Research* 6:313–322, 1974.

174. Solomon, G. F.; Merigan, T.; and Levine, S.: Variation in adrenal cortical hormones within physiological ranges; stress and interferon production in mice. *Proceedings of the Society for Experimental Biology and Medicine* 126:74, 1967.

175. Solomon, G. F.; and Moos, R. H.: Emotions, immunity and disease. *Archives of General Psychiatry* 2:657–674, 1964.

176. Southam, C. M.: Discussion. Emotions, immunity, and cancer: how might the psyche influence neoplasia? *Annals of the New York Academy of Sciences* 164:473–475, 1969.

177. Spackman, D.; and Riley, V.: Increased corticosterone, a factor in LDH-virus induced alterations of immunological responses in mice. *Proceedings of the American Association for Cancer Research* 15:143, 1974.

178. Spackman, D.; and Riley, V.: Stress effects of the LDH-virus in altering the Gardner tumor in mice. *Proceedings of the American Association for Cancer Research* 16:170, 1975.

179. Spackman, D.; and Riley, V.: The modification of cancer by stress: effects of plasma corticosterone elevations on immunological system components in mice. *Federation Proceedings* 35:1693, 1976.

180. Spackman, D.; and Riley, V.: Unpublished data.

181. Spackman, D.; Riley, V.; Santisteban, G. A.; Kirk, W.; and Bredberg, L.: The role of stress in producing elevated corticosterone levels and thymus involution in mice. *Abstracts, XIth International Cancer Congress* 3:382–383, 1974.

182. Sprunt, D. H.; and Flanigan, C. C.: The effect of malnutrition on the susceptibility of the host to viral infection. *Journal of Experimental Medicine* 104:687–706, 1956.

183. Stein, M.; Schiari, R. C.; and Luparello, T. J.: The hypothalamus and immune processes. *Annals of the New York Academy of Science* 164:463–472, 1969.

184. Stein, M.; Schiari, R. C.; and Camerino, M.: Influence of brain and behavior on the immune system. *Science* 191:435–440, 1976.

185. Stephenson, H.; and Grace, W. J.: Life stress and cancer of the cervix. *Psychosomatic Medicine* 16:287, 1954.

186. Stern, E.; Mickey, M.; and Gorski, R.: Neuroendocrine factors in experimental carcinogenesis. *Annals of the New York Academy of Sciences* 164:494–508, 1969.
187. Stern, K.: The Reticuloendothelial system and neoplasia. In *Reticuloendothelial Structure and Function*, pp. 233–258, ed. J. H. Heller. New York: Ronald Press, 1960.
188. Stern, K.; and Joyce, C. A.: Reticuloendothelial phagocytosis in mice with spontaneous tumors. *Proceedings of the American Association for Cancer Research* 5:61, 1964.
189. Sze, P.: Neurochemical factors in auditory stimulation and development of susceptibility to audiogenic seizures. In *Physiological Effects of Audible Sound*, eds. B. Welch and A. Welch. New York: Plenum Press, 1970.
190. Teller, M. N.; Stohr, G.; Curlett, W.; Kubisek, M. L.; and Curtis, D.: Ageing and cancerigenesis. I. Immunity to tumor and skin graft. *Journal of the National Cancer Institute* 33:649–656, 1964.
191. Tannenbaum, A.: The initiation and growth of tumors. I. The effects of underfeeding. *American Journal of Cancer* 38:335–350, 1940.
191a. Tannenbaum, A.; and Silverstone, H.: Nutrition in relation to cancer. *Advances in Cancer Research* 1:451–501, 1953.
192. Turkevich, N. M.: The significance of the typological characteristics of the nervous system in the onset and development of cancer of the mammary gland in mice. *Voprosy Oncologii* 1:64–70, 1965.
193. Turkevich, N. M.; Kunitsa, L. K.; and Matveichuk, J. D.: Effect of reserpine on development of induced tumor of the mammaries in rats. *Voprosy Oncologii* 1:94–102, 1965.
194. Vessey, S. H.: Effects of grouping on levels of circulating antibodies in mice. *Proceedings of the Society for Experimental Biology and Medicine* 115:252, 1964.
194a. Visscher, B.; Ball, Z.; Barnes, R. H.; and Silvertsen, I.: The influence of caloric restriction upon the incidence of spontaneous mammary carcinoma in mice. *Surgery* 11:48–55, 1942.
195. Voskresenskaia, A. K.: An attempt to obtain experimental cancer in dogs and the role of the nervous system in the origin of the neoplastic process. In *Publications from the I. P. Pavlov Physiological Laboratories*, Vol. 14, 1948.
196. Wallace, E. W.; Wallace, H. M.; and Mills, C. A.: Effect of climatic environment upon the genesis of subcutaneous tumors induced by methylcholanthrene and upon the growth of a transplantable sarcoma in C3H mice. *Journal of the National Cancer Institute* 3:99–110, 1942.
197. Wallace, E. W.; Wallace, H. M.; and Mills, C. A.: Influence of environmental temperature upon the incidence and course of spontaneous tumors in C3H mice. *Cancer Research* 4:279–281, 1944.
198. Weiss, D. W.: Immunological Parameters of the host-parasite relationship in neoplasia. *Annals of the New York Academy of Science* 164:431–448, 1969.
199. Weston, B. J.: The thymus and immune surveillance. In *Contemporary Topics in Immunobiology*, Vol. 2, pp. 237–263, eds. A. J. S. Davies, and R. L. Carter. New York: Plenum Press, 1973.
200. Wister, R. T.; and Hildemann, W. H.: Effect of stress on skin transplantation immunity in mice. *Science* 131:159, 1960.
201. Yamada, A.; Jensen, M. M.; and Rasmussen, A. F., Jr.: Stress and susceptibility to viral infections: III. antibody response and viral retention during avoidance-learning stress. *Proceedings of the Society for Experimental Biology and Medicine* 116:677, 1964.
202. Young, S. Effect of temperature on the production of induced rat mammary tumors. *Nature* 219:1254–1255, 1958.

Biobehavioral Approaches to Cancer Prevention and Detection[1]

LAWRENCE W. GREEN
BARBARA RIMER
THOMAS W. ELWOOD

Biobehavioral approaches to prevention and detection for cancer control refer to interventions that relate to a biological or health outcome and require some form of educational input. We shall refer to them generally as cancer education. The purpose of this paper is to describe a process that would have applicability in arriving at the most appropriate educational interventions for various community settings. This chapter, therefore, lays out a model for combining epidemiological, behavioral and educational diagnosis, planning, and evaluation, applicable to various cancer sites and community settings. The approaches designed for different sites and settings can be integrated by linkages that create a community cancer education program.

In considering the different types of programs for cancer education that might be required in different settings, we have tried to maintain a community perspective, one that maintains a view of each setting as a part of the community and attempts to treat the process of educational development in different settings as part of the community-wide cancer control planning process and to identify ways in which cancer education in one setting can support and reinforce education occurring in other settings.

Public education protocols should be related to various problems of cancer control identified through various sources of data and opinion, including community-wide surveys and special surveys in schools, clinical settings, and work sites. The priorities that are placed on the problems

[1] Preparation of this paper was supported, in part, by NIH Grants 1R18 HL22934–01, 2R18-CA-17448–04, and 5R18-CA-10322–02. A revised version of this paper is to appear as Chapter 70 in David Shottenfeld and Joseph Fraumeni (eds.) *Cancer Epidemiology and Prevention.* Philadelphia: W. B. Saunders Company, 1981.

identified in these various epidemiological and behavioral surveys are determined by a critical process of educational diagnosis, planning, and evaluation [40].

A Model for Educational Diagnosis and Planning

Organized cancer education attempts to intervene in the process of development and change in such a way as to maintain positive health behavior, or to interrupt a behavioral pattern which is linked to increased risks for cancer. The behavior usually is that of the people whose health is in question, but it often includes the behavior of others who control resources or rewards for behavior, such as community leaders, parents, employers, peers, teachers, and health professionals. Whether it is at the primary, secondary, or tertiary stage of prevention, a cancer education program may be seen accurately as an intervention, the purpose of which is to prevent disability, illness, or death, or to enhance quality of life through voluntary change of cancer-related behavior.

The model described in Figure 1 applies broadly to health education in a variety of situations; it has served as a successful model in a number of rigorously evaluated "real world" clinical trials [15, 35, 56, 63]; as a useful guide to the development of local health department programs, adopted by state health departments [57]; as a guide to the review of maternal and child health projects [38]; as an analytical tool for policy analysis for health education on a national and international scale [17, 32, 39, 74]; and as an organizing framework for curriculum development in health education for physicians [75], nurses [1], pharmacists [26], and allied health professionals [6].

Cancer education programs often tend to initiate the planning process first by considering or even designing the actual intervention to be employed. In cancer control, this tendency is based on highly oversimplified assumptions concerning cause–effect relationships between educational activities and medical outcomes.

INPUTS   ?   OUTCOMES
(Education) ————————————————————————▶ (Cancer   Control)

The "inputs" on the left represent a health education intervention or process and the "outcomes" to the right denote the anticipated results of the intervention in terms of changes in medical or vital conditions. Decreases in incidence of cancer reflect definitive health changes, whereas shifts in absenteeism from work and improvements in work performance are manifestations of social or quality-of-life changes. Health practitioners, because

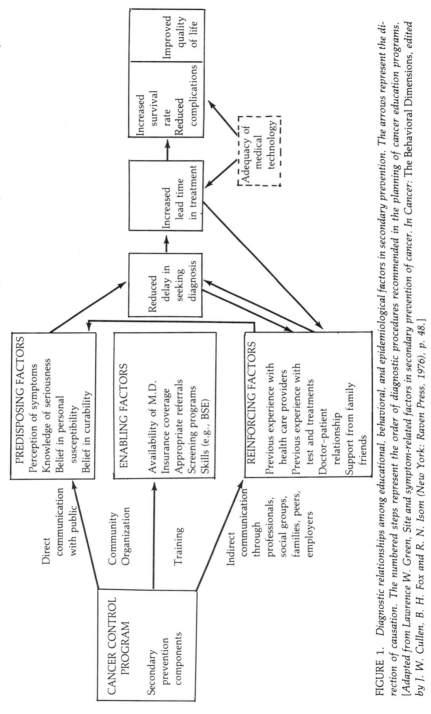

FIGURE 1. *Diagnostic relationships among educational, behavioral, and epidemiological factors in secondary prevention. The arrows represent the direction of causation. The numbered steps represent the order of diagnostic procedures recommended in the planning of cancer education programs. [Adapted from Lawrence W. Green, B. H. Fox and R. N. Isom (New York: Raven Press, 1976), p. 48.]* Site and symptom-related factors in secondary prevention of cancer. In Cancer: The Behavioral Dimensions, edited by J. W. Cullen,

of their service orientation, have an understandable tendency to begin at the left. After a quick glance at the general problem at hand, they immediately begin to design and implement the health education intervention and then assume the outcome will occur automatically.

The diagnostic model directs initial attention to ultimate rather than immediate concerns, forcing the planner to begin the health education process from the "outcome" end. It encourages one to ask the "why" questions before asking the "how" questions. It proceeds from an utlimate outcome and asks what must precede that outcome. Interventions based on guesswork concerning the important factors causing the outcomes can lead to misdirected and ineffective educational efforts in cancer control.

The Diagnostic Steps in Cancer Education

The planner must think in a diagnostic way, starting with the ultimate damage and working back to the original cause. There are five basic steps in the procedure:

Step 1: Social Diagnosis

Ideally, the planning process begins with a consideration of "quality of life" by assessing some of the general problems of concern to the people in a given population of patients, students, workers, or consumers. Social problems are good barometers of the quality of life of a given community. Such problems may be ascertained by several methods which are discussed in some detail elsewhere [40].

Step 2: Epidemiological Diagnosis

The second task is to identify those specific health problems which appear to be contributing to the social problem(s) noted in phase one. Available data and some generated by original investigation, together with epidemiological and medical knowledge, can be used to rank the several cancer problems by priority. Using epidemiological methods, it is possible to select the specific cancer problems most deserving of scarce educational resources.

Step 3: Behavioral Diagnosis

This step should identify those specific behaviors believed to be linked to the cancer problems chosen in step two. Because it will be those behaviors that educational intervention will be tailored to affect, it is essential that one apply great specificity in selecting and arranging them in priority fashion.

Step 4: Educational Diagnosis

On the basis of the cumulative research on health behavior, the diagnostic model identifies three "classes" of factors which have potential influence on cancer behavior: predisposing factors, enabling factors, and reinforcing factors. *Predisposing factors* facilitate or hinder personal motivation for change. They include attitudes, beliefs, and values. *Enabling factors* may be characterized as barriers created mainly by societal forces or systems. Limited facilities, inadequate personal or community resources, lack of income or health insurance, and even restrictive laws and statutes are examples of enabling factors [3]. Enabling factors also include skills and knowledge required for a desired behavior to occur. *Reinforcing factors* are those related to the feedback the learner receives from others, the result of which may either encourage or discourage behavioral change. The fourth step then would be to sort out and categorize, according to the three "classes" just cited, those forces which seem to have direct impact on the behavior selected. Once the several antecedents to health behavior have been classified under one of the three categories, the planner once again sets priorities and narrows the list for greater specificity as to whether all, a part, or a combination of the three factors should be the focus of the eventual intervention, based on their relative importance and the resources available to influence them.

Step 5: Administrative Diagnosis

The pertinent and systematically organized diagnostic information leads to the actual development and implementation of a cancer education program. Resources, time constraints, and abilities are assessed in Step 5. The appropriate educational interventions will be almost self-evident from the diagnosis of predisposing, enabling, and reinforcing factors. All that remains is an assessment of administrative problems and resources and the design or selection of the right combination of interventions.

Multiple Causation and Interdisciplinary Participation

The foundations of the diagnostic model for cancer education are shaped by four disciplines: epidemiology, social and behavioral sciences, administration and education. Although the four are necessarily integrated throughout, each stands as a primary support to a specific diagnostic phase. Activities necessary for the successful completion of steps one and two rely heavily on epidemiological methods and information. To work effectively through Steps 3 and 4, familiarity with social and behavioral theory and concepts is essential. To handle the complex task of designing and implementing a health education protocol, educational and administrative theory and experience are needed.

Two basic propositions are emphasized:

1. Cancer and health behavior are caused by multiple factors.
2. Because cancer and health behavior are determined by multiple factors, health education efforts to affect behavior must be multidimensional and multidisciplinary.

It is the multidimensional nature of the cancer education process that demands interdisciplinary participation in the preparation of protocols that integrate epidemiology, behavioral science, administration, and education. This model offers a framework for such a synthesis for cancer education.

The Literature of Cancer Education

In 1928, T. S. Cullen, a surgeon, was using the vehicle of women's magazines to encourage women with suspected cervical cancer to see their doctors early. In 1937, the American Cancer Society (ACS) launched the first truly national public education program—on uterine cancer. The program was directed at motivating women to seek cytotests, changing negative attitudes of physicians, reducing delay, improving access, and reaching out to lower socioeconomic status (SES) women. In the years since then, health education has played a significant role in applying educational principles to the quest for prevention and early detection of cancer. As Breslow [9] noted, "We have the means to take the first steps toward cancer prevention; the means include a wide variety of methods for imparting knowledge and influencing behavior regarding cigarettes and other known cancer causing agents [p. 686]."

Some of the important developmental work concerning preventive behaviors was conducted by Rosenstock [61], Kegeles [52] and others at the Public Health Service, and Beryl Roberts [60] at the University of California at Berkeley. Rosenstock's model included health motive or threat, beliefs regarding the utility of various courses of action in reducing the health threat, and the conflict among motives and potential courses of action. The individual must believe that the preventive measure is available and effective, that the threat is real, and the potential consequences of not taking action are serious. When this model was applied to screening, the most important belief was that one could have the disease, even if asymptomatic. Other beliefs predictive of whether people obtained screening were that the tests can detect asymptomatic problems and that early detection will improve prognosis. A 1948 public opinion poll indicated that 29% of the public believed in susceptibility to cancer, 80% believed in its seriousness, and 80% believed that they could have it and still be asymptomatic.

Obviously, each of these points involves an educational corollary. Different health education programs have focused on different beliefs. An important observation made by Rosenstock [61] and others was that the intensity of a motive to take action may be diminished if delay occurs between the point of decision and the earliest time at which action may be taken. This should be considered by oncologists active in counseling patients or developing community programs. Haefner et al. [43] reported on a national survey of preventive actions in dental disease, tuberculosis, and cancer. Respondents were asked, additionally, why they had been examined or tested for cancer. The authors found consistency within the survey groups over time. Those who took one preventive action were most likely to take others. Higher SES groups took more preventive actions. Older persons took fewer preventive actions. Interestingly, the majority of tests were either compulsory or medically dictated. Although 30% of respondents mentioned that they had cancer tests, only 3.4% obtained such tests voluntarily.

Also based on the national study of health beliefs, Kirscht et al. [54] found that major belief variables included perceived negative consequences of disease, perceived vulnerability to disease, and benefits of action. Data were collected through personal interviews about tuberculosis, cancer, and tooth decay. Cancer was regarded as serious and likely to occur, and 31% of the respondents selected the most extreme category of worry for cancer. For each condition however, most respondents reported that others are more likely to contract the disease than themselves.

According to the health belief model, belief in susceptibility, severity and benefits are interrelated parts of an individual's total perception of a disease. While nearly one-fifth of the respondents held all three beliefs about cancer, a nearly equal number lacked a belief in susceptibility and benefits. While cancer was seen as a universal threat, belief in the efficacy of preventive and diagnostic measures was positively associated with education and income and negatively associated with age [54].

Kegeles [52] found that women who believed in the benefits of early detection were more likely to have had a pap test.

Samora [64] determined the level of medical information about 10 common diseases in a group of clinic patients through interviews with 118 patients. He found wide regional differences but overall, actual knowledge about cancer was low.

Gochman [28] examined two psychological correlates of preventive encounters—health motivation and perceived vulnerability. Preventive encounters are conceptually defined as a class of actions undertaken to ward off potential health problems. Health motive is defined as a general preference for a relatively disease free state, and perceived vulnerability as the sense of being susceptible to a variety of health problems.

Roberts [60] contributed early thinking about factors influencing decision making related to health behavior. She examined the variety of influences which determine whether, for example, a woman will seek a cytotest. There are factors which relate to the woman herself, her family, the health system, and health professionals. Any of these can increase or decrease her likelihood of seeking tests or taking preventive actions. Her work strongly asserted the need to examine the multitude of forces that define a given health problem and the target group identified for intervention.

Bunton [12] analyzed different kinds of cancer risks and suggested educational strategies for each. First is the case when the individual at risk has little or no control over the hazard (e.g., occupational carcinogens). This requires good education and planning, feedback, and evaluation with involvement of those at risk. Second is when individuals and communities share responsibility (e.g., environmental health education, which should be addressed through education for collective action). Third is when those at risk are responsible for their own protection (e.g., smoking). Here health education can increase public awareness and support people who want to change behavior.

Physicians and other health professionals have two distinct though occasionally merging roles in public education. One is to assist in the large scale campaign to acquaint the public with those forms of cancer that are responsive to early detection and treatment, and those risk factors which can be avoided or kept under calm medical surveillance. The second role has to do with their more personal relationship with patients and their families.

A recent study of Americans' beliefs and attitudes toward cancer revealed that a majority (63%) underestimate the incidence of cancer (especially of colon and rectum) and chances for survival. Seventy-five percent of women polled were unaware that only 20% of all breast lumps are malignant; only 71% were aware that breast cancer, detected early, has an 85% chance of cure. While 67% of women in the sample reported doing breast self-examination, nearly 50% said that it took them less than 2 min.

Experts say at least 5 min are necessary. Forty-five percent of women do not realize that an endometrial suction test is available to detect early uterine cancer. Thirty-six percent of the public now have regular cancer checkups compared to only 26% 12 years ago [13[.

Estimates from the 1978 Health Interview Survey indicate that 33% of the U.S. population 17 years of age and older smoke. It has been estimated that 95% of the 29 million smokers who have quit since 1964 have done so on their own. Survey data show that only one-third or less of smokers motivated to quit are interested in formal programs and only a small minority of those actually attend programs when offered [14]. Objective data are lacking on most of the smokers who have attended formal programs, and controlled research has yet to produce a clearly superior intervention strategy [33].

Young people might resist beginning the cigarette habit, or could more easily stop it, if figures of authority and influence such as teachers and physicians set better examples and urged them not to smoke. Of the young nonsmokers surveyed in 1969, 72% said physicians were the one group that could persuade them not to start smoking; of the smokers, 42% said that advice from a physician would influence them to stop [69].

The U.S. Senate [72] Subcommitee on Health and Scientific Research conducted hearings on a measure aimed at establishing a Comprehensive Disease Prevention and Health Promotion Program in the United States. Sections 7 and 8 of Senate bill S.3118 provided for the establishment of a "health protection tax." These provisions would, in effect, amend the tax codes to create a varying tax on cigarettes ranging from 5 to 50 cents a pack, based on "toxic units" which are derived from the milligrams of tar and nicotine contained in each brand of cigarettes. The proceeds from such a tax would be used to support payments to the states in the form of formula grants to assist them in meeting the costs of preventive health services.

It is uncertain what the effects of such legislation would be if the measure were to pass. A lowering of Federal taxes on low-yield cigarettes might encourage more smoking by young people. Imposing high taxes on the highest yield cigarettes, however, might have no effect on confirmed smokers.

Fear

Considerable research has been conducted on the relationship between fear arousing information and preventive health behavior. This literature is of particular interest to health professionals planning cancer education programs.

Leventhal [55] conducted some of the most extensive research into the relationship between fear level and the acceptance of preventive health practices, identifying two ways to introduce drive and reward: (1) arouse approach or positive drives about the value of a health behavior, or (2) arouse avoidance or aversive drives. In a study at the 1961 New York Health Exposition, the investigator made two recommendations to visitors: that they take an X ray immediately after the health communication and that they stop smoking. There were three conditions: high fear, mild fear, and a control condition. The fear level of a film and pamphlet were adjusted accordingly. Leventhal discovered that subjects in the control group expressed a stronger intention to give up smoking. There were no significant differences between the groups with regard to X rays, but a greater proportion of X rays were taken by subjects exposed to films than control. Leventhal's analyses suggested a positive relationship between the intensity of fear reported after a communication and the desire to take either of the two preventive actions. However, there was no overall superiority for the high fear group. The implication now, as in the earlier research, seems to be that high fear arousal can be effective if the person can be provided immediately with the recommended health action and if it is relatively easy to undertake. It appears to be an unwise strategy where resources do not approach demand, and people must be placed on waiting lists or must maintain the behavior over a long period of time. Under these latter circumstances, the fear will tend to be rationalized away and the person will be even more resistant to the next fear-arousing message about cancer.

Bishop [8] examined more recently the impact of frightening cancer information materials. Especially concerned with the impact of anxiety on learning, he conducted a study to test the interaction of anxiety, threat, and reassurance in a natural context. Of 123 students between the ages of 18 and 23 in a college journalism class, one-half were given a frightening message and one-half a hopeful message. Students with initial high anxiety tended to read more of the stories with reassuring headlines, although the reverse did not hold true for persons with low anxiety. In general, there was more retention of the low anxiety articles.

Detection

An extensive literature describes the role of health education in cancer detection programs. Detection is an aspect of cancer control that is particularly important in high-risk populations. In 1947, the American College of Surgeons issued guidelines for detection centers. These stressed the importance of public education as an essential aspect of detection and screening services [18].

A series of Gallup surveys has catalogued changing American attitudes and practices regarding cancer detection tests. In 1966, 43% of respondents believed that doctors encourage checkups, and 43% did not know how doctors felt. Only 6% said they would not have checkups even if their doctor recommended them. Women had more checkups than men, as did better educated and higher income groups. If a person has ever gone for a complete checkup, there is a good likelihood that he or she will continue to go. The first checkup, then, becomes a critical opportunity to reinforce a positive health behavior.

While there was wide recognition that cancer may strike anyone, in general respondents underestimated the likelihood of getting cancer. This tendency has been verified in comparative studies of risk assessment [66].

TABLE 1
Increases in Public Use of Cancer Detection Tests as Measured in Three National Surveys, by Sex

| | Percentage who had test | | | | | |
| | 1961 | | 1963 | | 1966 | |
	Men	Women	Men	Women	Men	Women
Chest X-ray	52	48	57	54	68	58
Skin exam	13	10	14	12	21	17
Digital	—	—	—	—	27	28
Procto	3	14	15	15	15	14
Breast	—	38	—	43	—	63
Pap	—	30	—	48	—	67

A more recent survey was conducted for the ACS in 1976 [27,48]. Findings showed that 46% of respondents had a complete checkup in that year. Awareness of the pap test was now almost universal—93% of women had heard of it, 80% had the test, 72% of women had it annually, and 86% got the pap test from their private doctors. By contrast, only 38% of respondents said they had heard of the hemoccult test for colorectal cancer, and 17% had actually undergone the test. Awareness of proctoscopy as a means of cancer detection had declined from 61% of respondents in 1974 to 56% in 1976. Whereas 59% of respondents had heard of oral cancer tests, only 28% had ever had one. Awareness of clinical breast exams as a means of detecting breast cancer is increasing among women; 91% of respondents had heard of the clinical breast exam, and 75% of the respondents had such an exam. Awareness of the breast self-examination (BSE) is almost universal; 95% of women have heard of it, 75% have done BSE at some time, 70% in the last year, and 24% do it once a month. Interestingly, 25% of respondents claim they do not know how to do the BSE, and of those 37% are interested in learning. More women than men, more older persons and those with some college education had heard of the tests.

These statistics point out some of the areas where public education is needed. They indicate that most women are aware now of the pap test; efforts should be directed at young women becoming of age for the tests, at the socioeconomically disadvantaged, and at providing reinforcement for the periodicity required for effective screening. Awareness of X ray for lung cancer is at 90%. This probably cannot go much higher without costs disproportionate to the payoff. Awareness of proctoscopy increased from 35% in 1961 to 61% in 1974, then declined to 56% in 1976; this appears to be a test which will require constant effort because of the inherent unacceptability of the test. Awareness and practice of breast exams has increased markedly over the years. Efforts could well be directed toward increasing the 24% of women who practice BSE monthly. Education about what people can do for themselves, as with BSE, and how often they need to see their physicians or other health professionals, are the kind of educational programs that community health professionals should maintain with all populations on a regular basis. Evidence indicates that mobile detection, industrial detection programs, and other "one shot" detection programs can induce people to seek screening once, but they do not inculcate in these same people the "screening habit," which is a critical aspect of cancer detection behavior. For example, detection programs in the industrial setting can induce a woman to have one pap test but cannot seem to generate repeat behavior, and such programs are most successful in attracting lower income women [10]. Allen [2] conducted cervical screening and education at the work site but was disappointed with the turnout.

Van den Heuvel [73] compared participants and nonparticipants in a mammographic mass screening program. He concluded that the effectiveness of mass screening depends on (a) incidence and history of the disease, (b) diagnostic sensitivity, (c) existence of a therapy which results in high long-term survival, (d) information and health education programs to motivate women to participate, and (e) costs as a result of the previous four factors. Factors that differentiated participants and nonparticipants included knowledge of breast cancer, knowledge of symptoms, patterns of seeking medical care, age, sense of powerlessness, independency, other participants in neighborhood, whether they had read promotional material. Participants were younger and of higher socioeconomic status than nonparticipants.

A series of prospective studies was undertaken by Hulka [50] to evaluate different techniques to increase attendance of low-income women at a clinic for cancer screening. Methods used included mail with phone followup versus a personal contact. The design was confounded by an overwhelming response, which forced the investigators to place many of those women on a waiting list. Thirty-one percent of the women to whom they were sent returned the mail cards; of those, 50% attended the clinic. The cards had been sent out with welfare checks. If three mailed appointment notices were ignored, a telephone call was made, but even a skilled interviewer had limited success; only 10% of calls resulted in clinic visits. Two-thirds of the women contacted in person made an appointment but only one-third kept them. The difference in percentages of contacts that resulted in examinations was not pronounced; 22% after personal referral and 16% after mailing. The home visits obviously were more costly in both time and dollars. Home visiting of nonrespondents was superior to telephoning in one important respect—the most financially deprived women did not have phones. Health department nurses were found to be most successful in recruiting women to be examined. Nurses and caseworker referrals brought a greater percentage of women contacted to examination than a notice with the welfare checks.

Another article by Hulka [51] discussed successful and unsuccessful methods for stimulating women to accept cervical screening. Through a community-wide cervical screening program, clinics were established in 12 low-income neighborhoods. Different locations and methods were tested for their success in bringing low income women for screening. Great care was taken to assure the accuracy of the referral source. Hulka claimed that "the problem of motivating women to accept a health service can be avoided by screening captive groups, which provide the highest yield of abnormal smears for effort expended [p. 238]." She concluded that methods which require women to request an appointment themselves result in a greater number of kept appointments. Also, women should be contacted in a health-oriented environment. For example, it did not work well for women to be approached about cervical screening when they came to pick up their welfare checks. Patient referrals were the most outstanding form of personal contact, and the most significant method of gaining community support among potential recipients. Mass media were not effective in inducing women to seek screening. One screening experience did not necessarily make women amenable to repeating the experience. Volunteers were effective in recruiting women, but they had to be carefully trained and supervised. Finally, referrals from physicians resulted in a high percentage of patient acceptance, and word of mouth from one friend to another was also relatively effective in referring women to screening.

Brown [11], in a Southern Appalachian community, found that 77% of

women sampled had had a pap test. However, 40% of them could not identify a test for cervical cancer. Again, we see evidence of the need to educate
women about the reason for the test; otherwise, subsequent and regular
screening becomes unlikely. Single women were least likely to have had a
pap test. Sibary et al. [65] found that widowed and divorced women were
least likely to get cervical screening.

Stillman asked nurses about their health beliefs regarding breast cancer
and BSE. She administered a questionnaire to 122 nurses, 48% of whom
practiced BSE monthly. Another 20% held high beliefs but were nonprac-
ticers. Less than 50% of the women had learned about BSE from their doctors. Again, the data indicated the educational responsibility which must
be shouldered by the private practitioner. Esson [21] emphasized that
physicians have a responsibility to educate patients and that they should
consider how best to communicate, bearing in mind the special needs and
requirements of individual patients.

In a collaborative study, Elwood et al. [23] used five approaches to
motivate retired people to seek colorectal cancer screening. These included
(a) total mail out, (b) selective mail out, where recipients had to request the
hemoccult slides, (c) come-in method, where recipients were sent literature
which described the test, but they had to pick up the slides at a specific
location, (d) group meeting approach, where an ACS representative attended an American Association of Retired Persons meeting to explain the
hemoccult, and (e) an at-home method which used home visits. In order of
success, groups were most successful, followed by home visits, total mail
out, selective mail out, and the come-in approaches. Home visits and group
sessions were found to be the most cost effective. Including postage had a
positive effect on response rates, whereas asking people to adhere to a
meat-free diet had a slightly negative effect. Sponsorship was found not important in influencing screening behavior.

Delay

Greenwald et al. [42] evaluated screening programs to determine why
some people failed to comply with a directive to seek prompt medical attention when informed of suspicious indications resulting from screening.

Clients who listed a family physician on the intake forms did not delay as
long in contacting a physician as those who listed none. Respondents who
reported relatively recent visits to a physician also tended to delay
followup less than others. Those respondents who were referred to the
detection facility by health care providers tended to avoid delay, as did
those who cited a periodic routine to maintain good health as an important

reason for seeking screening, those with several relatives who had had cancer, and those with relatively high occupational status.

Clients who never followed up their visits to the detection facility or did so after 16 weeks explained their noncompliance in terms of difficulties in obtaining medical care. Maintaining a list of physicians may be one way of addressing this issue.

Interviews with clients suggested that mistrust of the health-care system may have been a deterrent. Many noncompliers expressed highly critical attitudes in response to a question about the merits of physicians in America today. Dread of cancer may also have contributed to their inaction.

The quality of communication between physician and patient appeared quite important in promoting or discouraging followup. The physician often played an important though inadvertent part in facilitating the clients' process of denial. A large proportion of noncompliers reported that the physician told them of a finding, but either stated or implied that it was not serious. Thus, physicians' words influence the patient's future followup behavior. Doctors must decide when to calm anxieties and when to stimulate concern.

Earlier literature on delay is reviewed by Antonovsky and Hartman [4] and Green and Roberts [34].

Informed Consent in Cancer Epidemiology and Prevention

In the last few years, health education has devoted increasing attention to the issue of informed consent. This interest has spanned the spectrum from a broad analysis of ethics in health education [25] to the development of health education interventions intended to enhance the informed consent process [24].

The doctrine of informed consent is related to health education in cancer epidemiology and prevention at several levels. The process of informed consent is essentially an educational exchange. At a minimum, most health education and cancer research must be conducted in accordance with Department of Health and Human Services (DHHS) guidelines; this usually requires the informed consent of intended participants, whether it be a smoking cessation program, a community cervical screening program, an intervention designed to test the efficacy of alternative BSE teaching strategies or the clinical trial of a new chemotherapeutic agent. But more than that, health education offers tools to ensure that the informed consent process is more than merely a formality with which investigators must comply.

These tools can be used to design interventions, based on the model described at the beginning of this chapter, to utilize the informed consent process to increase a person's comprehension of his or her disease or preventive regimen, increase patient satisfaction with information conveyed, enhance the quality of the decision-making process, reduce anxiety, and possibly to improve compliance with recommended behaviors [20].

A national study by Gray *et al.* [30] indicates that the current informed consent practices may not be all they should be. He found that most informed consent forms tend to be written in scientific or academic language that would be difficult for the layperson to understand. Only 7% of the informed consent forms sampled were written in language as simple as *Time* magazine. In addition, over 30% (and on some of the information items, as high as 70%) of the forms failed to mention risks, benefits, and/or purpose of the research, and 60% failed to mention that the procedure was experimental. Besch [7] argued that it is relatively easy to obtain the signature of research subjects on a consent form. "A more vital concern in the consent procedures is informing patients adequately and ensuring that they are cognizant of the information you have given them [7, p. 32]." Consent without comprehension cannot be considered informed, but documentation of comprehension is not required by most legal standards, despite abundant commentary in favor of such an obligation [37].

Informed consent has special application to occupational health and safety. People who will be subjected daily to carcinogenic exposures need to be informed of the risks, benefits, and alternatives, just as they are in medical experimentation. In addition, the worker must be taught appropriate methods of protection from these hazards. Tabershaw [68, p. 676] has observed that, "In the case of the private practitioner, he generally feels that he has no responsibility to look at the work environment and usually acquiesces with his patient's evaluation of the hazards of his job." Health professionals can play a role in which they actively seek to inform workers of both the consequences of employment and methods of protection.

Summary and Conclusions

This paper has offered a model and a review of literature on the behavioral aspects of cancer prevention and control that can be influenced through education of the public. Emphasis has been laid on those procedures and concepts currently useful to physicians and other health workers who must cooperate in community-wide efforts to achieve more comprehensive solutions to cancer prevention, detection, and delay. Further research is needed on the natural determinants of protective behavior, risk-taking behavior, and denial of symptoms. Evaluative research is needed to establish the relative cost-effectiveness of various educational methods in facilitating voluntary adaptations of these behaviors in relation to specific sites and symptoms of cancer, specific demographic categories of the public, and specific settings in which education will occur.

Acknowledgments

The assistance of faculty and staff of the Johns Hopkins Oncology Center and Health Services Research and Development Center are gratefully acknowledged.

References

1. Ackerman, A.; and Kalmer, H.: *Health Education and A Baccalaureate Nursing Curriculum - Myth or Reality*. Presented at the 105th Annual Meeting, American Public Health Association, Washington, D.C., Nov. 1, 1977.
2. Allen. W. A.; MacFalls, D. E.; and Mattucci, L.P.: Getting the cancer message to the community. *International Journal of Health Education* 16:61, 1973.
3. Andersen, R.: *A behavioral model of families' use of health services*. University of Chicago Center for Health Administration Studies, Research Series No. 25, 1968.
4. Antonovsky, A.; and Hartman, H.: Delay in the detection of cancer: A review of the literature. *Health Education Monographs* 2:98, 1974.
5. Becker, M. H., ed.: The health belief model and personal health behavior. *Health Education Monographs* 2:324, 1974.
6. Bennett, B. I.: A model for teaching health education skills to primary care practitioners. *International Journal of Health Education* 20:232, 1977.
7. Besch, L.: Informed consent: A patient's right. *Nursing Outlook* 27:32, 1979.
8. Bishop, R. L.: Anxiety and readership of health information. *Journalism Quarterly* 51:40, 1974.
9. Breslow, L.: Cancer control: Implication from its history. *Journal of the National Cancer Institute* 59:supplement, pp. 671–686, 1977.
10. Brindle, G.; Higham, E.; Roberts, D.; Wakefield, J.; and Yule, R.: Public education about cancer. In *Public Education about Cancer, Recent Research and Current Programmes*, J. Wakefield, ed., pp. 56–62, UICC, Geneva, 1978.
11. Brown, A.: Awarness and use of cervical cancer tests in a southern Appalachian community. *Public Health Reports* 1:236, 1976.
12. Bunton, J.: The role of education in cancer prevention. *International Journal of Health Education* 7:68, 1968.
13. *Cancer News*, (American Cancer Society) Public awareness and attitudes. 33:16, 1979.
14. Center for Disease Control: *Morbidity and Mortality Weekly Report* 28:1, 1979.
15. Chwalow, A. J.: *Contact vs. Content: The Effect of the Multiplicity of Health Education Encounters on Compliance and Blood Pressure Control*. Unpublished doctoral dissertation, Baltimore, Johns Hopkins University School of Hygiene and Public Health, 1978.
16. Cullen, J. S.: How cancer education of the public got started. *Bulletin of the American College of Surgeons* 48:87, 1963.

17. Danforth, N.; and Swaboda, B.: *Agency for International Development Health Education Study.* Washington, D.C.: Westinghouse Health Systems, March 17, 1978.

18. Day, E.: Cancer screening and detection: Medical aspects. *Journal of Chronic Disease* 16:397, 1963.

19. Delany, T. G.: Editorial in *Public Education About Cancer, Recent Research and Current Programmes,* J. Wakefield, ed., p. 1, UICC, Geneva, 1978.

20. Denny, M. K.: Informed consent—emotional responses. *Postgraduate Medicine* 60:205, 1975.

21. Easson, E. C.: The Role of the Doctor in Public Education, *UICC Technical Report Series* 10, 1974.

22. Elkind, A. K.: Can it really be cured? What people ask nurses about cancer. *Public Education About Cancer, Recent Research and Current Programmes,* J. Wakefield, ed., UICC, Geneva, 1978.

23. Elwood, T.; Erickson, A.; and Lieberman, S.: Comparative Educational Approaches to Screening for Colo-Rectal Cancer. In *Public Education About Cancer, Recent Research and Current Programmes,* J. Wakefield, ed., pp. 26–34, UICC, Geneva, 1978.

24. Faden, R.: Disclosure and informed consent: Does it matter how we tell it? *Health Education Monographs* 5:198, 1977.

25. Faden, R.; and Faden, A.: The ethics of health education as public health policy. *Health Education Monographs* 6:180, 1978.

26. Fedder, D.; and Beardsley, R.: *Training Pharmacists to become Patient Educators.* Presented to the section of Teachers of Pharmacy Administration of the annual meeting of the American Association of Colleges of Pharmacy, Orlando, Florida, July 18, 1978.

27. Gallup, G.: A Survey Concerning Cigarette Smoking, Health Check-Ups, Cancer Detection Tests. Princeton Gallup Org., Conducted for American Cancer Society, January, 1977.

28. Gochman, D.: Preventive encounters and their psychological correlates. *American Journal of Public Health* 64:1096, 1974.

29. Golden, R. K.: Patient delay in seeking cancer diagnosis: Behavioral aspects. *Journal of Chronic Disease* 16:427, 1963.

30. Gray, B.; Cooke, R.; and Tannenbaum, A.: Research involving human subjects. *Science* 201:22, 1978.

31. Green, L. W.: Should health education abandon attitude change strategies? Perspectives from recent research. *Health Education Monographs* 1:25, 1970.

32. Green, L. W.: Toward cost–benefit evaluation of health education: Some concepts, methods and examples. *Health Education Monographs* 2 (suppl.):24, 1974.

33. Green, L. W.; Rimer, B.; and Bertera, B.: How cost-effective are smoking cessation strategies? *World Smoking and Health* 3:33, 1978.

34. Green, L.W.; and Roberts, B. J.: The research literature on why women delay in seeking medical care for breast symptoms. *Health Education Monographs* 2:129, 1974.

35. Green, L. W.; Levine, D. M.; and Deeds, S.G.: Clinical trials of health education for hypertensive outpatient : Design and baseline data. *Preventive Medicine* 4:417, 1975.

36. Green, L. W.: Site and Symptom-Related Factors in Secondary Prevention of Cancer. In *The Behavioral Dimensions,* eds., J. W. Cullen, B. H. Fox, and R. N. Isom, New York, Raven Press, 1976.

37. Green, L.W.; and Faden, R.: The potential impact on patients (of patient package inserts.) *Drug Information Journal* 2 (suppl.): pp. 64–70, 1978.

38. Green, L. W.; Wang, V. L.; Deeds, S. G.; Fisher, A. A.; and Bennett, A.: Guidelines for health education in maternal and child health. *International Journal of Health Education* 21 (Suppl.):3, 1978.

39. Green, L. W.: Determining the impact and effectiveness of health education as it relates to federal policy. *Health Education Monographs* 6 (Suppl. 1):28, 1978.
40. Green, L. W.; Kreuter, M.; Partridge, K.; and Deeds, S. G.: *Health Education Planning: A Diagnostic Approach.* Palo Alto: Mayfield Publishing Co., 1980.
41. Green, L. W.: Educational strategies to improve compliance with therapeutic and preventive regimens: The recent evidence. In *Compliance in Health Care*, eds., R. B. Haynes, D. M. Sackett, and W. Taylor, Baltimore: Johns Hopkins University Press, 1979.
42. Greenwald, H. P.; Becker, S.; Nevitt, M.: Delay and noncompliance in cancer detection. *Milbank Memorial Fund Quarterly/Health and Society* 56:212, 1978.
43. Haefner, D.; Kegeles, S.; Kirscht, J.; and Rosenstock, I. M.: Preventive actions in dental disease, TB and cancer. *Public Health Reports* 82:May, 1967.
44. Health Education in Cancer Control. *Proceedings of the Seminar on Health Education in Uterine Cancer Programs.* University of Michigan, May, 1967.
45. Hermann, W. E.: Cancer education and detection programs at the plant level. *Journal of Occupational Health* 7:431, 1965.
46. Hill, D.: Community Education About Cancer. In *Public Education About Cancer, Recent Research and Current Programmes*, ed., J. Wakefield, pp. 63–74, UICC, Geneva, 1978.
47. Hobbs, P.; Eardley, A.; and Wakefield, J.: Motivation and education in breast cancer screening. In *Public Education About Cancer, Recent Research and Current Programmes*, ed., J. Wakefield, pp. 75–80, UICC, Geneva, 1978.
48. Holleb, A.: Public awareness of cancer detection tests: Results of a recent Gallup poll. In *Public Education About Cancer, Recent Research and Current Programmes*, ed., J. Wakefield, pp. 53–55, UICC, Geneva, 1978.
49. Horn, D.: Public attitudes and beliefs relative to cancer prevention, cancer health care services and access thereto. *Health Education Monographs* 36:11, 1973.
50. Hulka, B.: Motivation techniques in a cancer detection program: Contact by mail and person. *Public Health Reports* 81:1009, 1966.
51. Hulka, B.: Motivation technics in a cancer detection program: Utilization of community resources. *American Journal of Public Health* 57:229, 1967.
52. Kegeles, S.: Attitudes and behavior of public regarding cervical cytology. *Journal of Chronic Diseases*, 28:911, 1967.
53. Kegeles, S. S.: A field experimental attempt to change beliefs and behavior of women in an urban ghetto. *Journal of Health and Social Behavior* 10:115, 1969.
54. Kirscht, J. P.; Haefner, D. P.; Kegeles, S. S.; and Rosenstock, I. M.: A national study of health beliefs. *Journal of Health and Human Behavior* 7:248, 1966.
55. Leventhal, H.: Fear communications in the acceptance of preventive health practices. *Bulletin of the New York Academy of Medicine* 41:1144, 1965.
56. Maiman, L.; Green, L. W.; and Gibson, G.: Education for self-treatment by adult asthmatics. *Journal of the American Medical Association* 241:1919, 1979.
57. Maryland Health Education Center: *Strategies for Health Education in Local Health Departments.* Baltimore: Maryland State Department of Health and Mental Hygiene, 1977.
58. Palko, M.; and Harrison, C.: Television as a tool of health education. In *Public Education About Cancer, Recent Research and Current Programmes*, ed., J. Wakefield, UICC, Geneva, 1978.
59. Pomerleau, O.: Role of behavior modification in preventive Medicine. *New England Journal of Medicine* 292:1277, 1975.
60. Roberts, B. J.: Factors and Forces Influencing Decision-Making Related to Health

Behavior. *Health Education and Cancer Control,* Ann Arbor: School of Public Health, University of Michigan, 1967.

61. Rosenstock, I. M.: Public response to cancer screening and detection programs. Determinants of health behavior. *Journal of Chronic Disease* 16:407, 1963.

62. Rosenstock, I. M.: Why people use health services. *Milbank Memorial Fund Quarterly* 44:94, 1966.

63. Roter, D. L.: Patient participation in the patient–provider interaction: The effects of patient question-asking on the quality of interaction, satisfaction and compliance. *Health Education Monographs* 5:281, 1977.

64. Samora, J.; Saunders, L.; and Larson, R. F.: Knowledge about specific diseases in four selected samples. *Journal of Health and Human Behavior* 3:176, 1962.

65. Sibary, K.; Davis, F.; Wakefield, J.; and Yule, R.: Women with cervical cancer detected through population screening: Implications for health education. In *Public Education About Cancer, Recent Research and Current Programmes,* ed., J. Wakefield, pp. 88–96, UICC, Geneva, 1978.

66. Slovic, P.: The psychology of protective behavior. *Journal of Safety Research* 10:58, 1978.

67. Stillman, M.: Women's Health Beliefs About Breast Cancer and BSE. *Nursing Research* 26:121, 1977.

68. Tabershaw, I.: How is the acceptability of risks to the health of the workers to be determined? *Journal of Occupational Medicine* 18:10, 1976.

69. Teenage smoking, new American Cancer Society study shows young people's beliefs and behavior. *Cancer News* 23:3, 1969.

70. Turnbull, E.: Effect of basic preventive health practices and mass media on practice of BSE. *Nursing Research* 27:98, 1978.

71. Turns, D.; and Stevenson, J.: Health Education and Work Mistrust in A Cancer Prevention Project. In *Public Education About Cancer, Recent Research and Current Programmes,* ed., J. Wakefield, pp. 47–52, UICC, Geneva, 1978.

72. U.S. Senate, Disease Prevention and Health Promotion Act of 1978, Hearings before the Subcommittee on Health and Scientific Research of the Committee on Human Resources, May 25; June 7 and 9, 1978.

73. Van de Heuvel, W. J. A.: Participants and nonparticipants in a mammographic mass screening: Who is who. In *Public Education About Cancer, Recent Research and Current Programmes,* J. Wakefield, ed., UICC, Geneva, 1978.

74. Wang, V. L.: Application of social science theories to family planning: Health education in the People's Republic of China. *American Journal of Public Health* 66:440, 1976.

75. Wang, V. L.; Terry, P.; Flynn, B. S.; Williamson, J. W.; Green, L. W.; and Faden, R.: Evaluation of continuing medical education for chronic obstructive pulmonary diseases. *Journal of Medical Education* 54:803, 1979.

Psychiatric, Psychosocial, and Behavioral Interventions in the Treatment of Cancer: An Historical Review

JIMMIE C. HOLLAND
JULIA H. ROWLAND

Introduction

The recent increased interest in the psychosocial aspects of cancer stems from three major developments. First, growing numbers of patients are being cured of cancer, and others have longer disease-free intervals. As a result, those working in oncology have been given the comparative luxury of taking a greater interest in the patient's "quality of life" both during and after treatment [24]. Second, the field of psychiatry itself has become far more interested in the psychological problems of the medically ill, developing a subspecialty of general hospital psychiatry that focuses on the psychologic and social stress imposed by physical illness, as well as problems which attend the health-care environment—a complex social system in itself [22,75].

Because of these two positive forces, one arising from oncology, the other from psychiatry, psychiatrists in greater numbers have become consultants to oncology departments and have brought psychiatric expertise to bear on multidisciplinary collaborative cancer research. With participation of psychiatrists in clinical and research areas, it has become possible not only to identify psychological problems of patients but to design psychologic, social, and behavioral interventions, and test them in research protocols.

Coinciding with these two developments, more favorable and sensitive attitudes from the public at large have also grown apace. This combination of positive medical, psychiatric, and social forces has created a new emotional climate for cancer patients, in which far more effort and concern is exerted to assure a positive quality of life.

The current psychosocial and behavioral interventions in cancer are perhaps best understood in historical perspective.

Early Interface of Psychiatry with Oncology

With rare exceptions [4], early psychiatric studies in oncology occurred largely in isolation from the cancer treatment setting. Most were anecdotal studies of cancer patients which attempted to deduce the contribution of premorbid personality to cancer risk. The search for a cancer-prone personality paralleled developments in psychosomatic medicine in general, which in the 1950s sought to isolate personality constellations associated with major diseases, for which the etiology was poorly understood and thought to be multifactorial. A smaller number of papers described psychotherapy with advanced cancer patients [41,52]. Together, these research efforts generated a psychological description of the cancer patient at the beginning and end points of his or her disease, but few took their findings to the next logical step—planning and application of appropriate therapeutic interventions.

The single clinical issue which brought psychiatrists and cancer treatment staffs together was whether or not to tell the patient that he or she had cancer. Until 15 years ago, most cancer physicians, who were surgeons and radiotherapists, did *not* disclose the painful diagnosis. Death was usually certain and available treatments uncertain. Often, the patient, his or her family, and society at large willingly participated in a conspiracy of silence about the diagnosis of cancer [70]. To avoid mentioning the word cancer seemed to diminish the stigma of "uncleanness," guilt, and shame associated with the disease. Despite the recommendation of social scientists for more candor in the discussion of cancer and death, it was not until the 1960s that the attitudes of many physicians in this country began to change. As compared to 90% who did *not* tell in 1961, a survey in Rochester, New York in 1979 found that 97% of physicians favored telling cancer patients their diagnosis [53].

Along with these changes, the disciplines which were involved in the treatment of cancer patients increased to broaden the focus of care more toward the total patient, rather than a narrower focus on the cancer therapy alone. In addition, the public became more concerned with the rights of patients to participate in the decisions made about their own care, which also provided a degree of outside pressure to hasten these ongoing internal reforms.

Recent Interface of Psychiatry with Oncology

As psychiatry broadened its participation in the general hospital, psychiatrists have increasingly consulted on oncology units, leading, predictably, to a heightened awareness of psychological issues in patient care and management [75]. Initially, the psychiatrist offered consultation on specific patients whose behavior was abnormal or difficult, and assisted in devising appropriate treatment plans. The consultative function quickly expanded on many oncology units to include the use of multidisciplinary rounds which focused on the psychological and behavioral problems in patient management [62,64,74]. In addition to aiding communication, the rounds also became a forum to discuss, and often diminish, conflicts among groups, especially between patients and nursing staff [77]. Progress has also occurred toward achieving a better understanding of the difficulties physicians experience in dealing with severely ill patients [2,31]. There has been increasingly more open discussion of ethical dilemmas around the selective discontinuance of life-support systems.

Both inter- and intradisciplinary groups have provided a setting in which emotional stresses upon staff are more openly admitted and more efficacious ways of dealing with them pursued. Though no formal evaluation has been made of these psychiatric consultation programs, most oncology staff acknowledge the usefulness of a weekly clinical meeting on the psychological management of patients in addition to available consultation and management of the patient with psychological problems. This work, in turn, has led to important contributions to liaison psychiatry.

Work with respect to the psychological problems of patients has proceeded more systematically. The psychiatrist's ability to work as a member of the team caring for cancer patients has led not only to descriptions of common psychological problems in adaptation to illness, but also to the identification and delineation of treatment plans for the most frequent psychiatric syndromes encountered in cancer [42,44]. The four most common reasons for psychiatric referral in cancer are (a) presence of significant anxiety, depression, or suicidal ideation; (b) central nervous system dysfunction associated with the disease or its treatment; (c) serious emotional disturbance in response to illness, medical management, or concurrent family problems; and (d) preexisting psychiatric illness or personality disorder exacerbated by physical illness. Psychotherapeutic and psychopharmacologic interventions for these syndromes have been reviewed in the literature [19,25].

During the first year of the full-time Psychiatric Service at Memorial Hospital, the most frequent consultation was for reactive depression [44]. Though in most cases the severity of the depression was mild to moderate, the significantly depressed tended to be older patients with more advanced stages of disease. Central nervous system dysfunction associated with significant behavioral, affective, or psychotic manifestations was the second most frequent diagnosis.

The following sections review in detail the evolution of the three principal approaches which psychiatrists have applied to the treatment of cancer patients: (a) the psychotherapeutic approach, (b) the psychophar-macologic approach, and (c) the behavioral approach.

Psychotherapeutic Approach

Psychotherapy and Counseling

Psychotherapeutic approaches in cancer have developed broadly in the past 10 years, by and large using a crisis intervention model based on the tenets of brief psychotherapy. Patients experiencing an acute emotional stress with transient psychological decompensation, will often be substan-tially improved over one to six visits. Antidepressant or antianxiety medication may be used concomitantly, then tapered and stopped when the illness-related stress diminishes. More problematic is the smaller number of patients who enter lengthy psychotherapy during cancer illness; both pa-tient and therapist must deal with life-task problems within the context of uncertainty about the future imposed by the diagnosis of cancer.

The crisis intervention model is also widely used by social workers, nurses, and mental health professionals working with cancer patients. The resulting overlap of counseling skills among these health professionals re-quires special attention to ensure that treatment is in fact being given by the appropriate person. By the same token, oncologic physicians must under-stand how to assess patients' psychological status in order to make ap-propriate referrals for counseling. Many times, the primary consultation by a psychiatrist is preferable because of the need to rule out central nervous system dysfunction, since it is such a frequent complication of the disease and its treatment. As patients live longer with cancer, the incidence of in-tracranial metastases and neurologic complications is increasing [60]. A high level of clinical acuity is needed to monitor for the presence of an organic basis underlying emotional distress [25].

Counseling by clergy trained in pastoral psychology frequently meets the emotional needs of patients in the context of meeting their spiritual needs. The clergy represent a critical component of support, especially for those patients who have relied upon religion in the past when facing stressful situations. Most hospital chaplains give a considerable part of their time to oncology units. Their full participation, especially in multidisciplinary meetings, promotes their best integration with the staff and also results in optimal use of their skills.

Finally, emotional support for the family after the patient's death is an important task and function of bereavement counseling, regrettably one that is often not fulfilled. A Palliative Care Unit created by Krant, offered such continuous, prolonged support to its patients and families [36]. The use of preventive psychiatric interventions among bereaved children and spouses of cancer patients is an important and underdeveloped area. The treatment, to be most effective, must begin prior to the patient's death.

GROUP COUNSELING

The newest model of psychological support to be introduced in cancer psychotherapy is group counseling. Two general types can be recognized: (a) psychotherapeutic groups, run by professionals for patients and/or families, and (b) self-help or mutual support groups. While generally independent of the medical care system, the latter groups frequently provide a unique link between patients sharing the same disease, their families, and their physician, in addition to making available more opportunities for patient-to-patient counseling.

PSYCHOTHERAPEUTIC GROUPS

Initially there was considerable caution about the use of therapy groups in cancer. A major reservation revolved around concerns for the potentially harmful effect the death of a member might have upon other participants in the group. The caution was ill-founded. Not only has participation not appeared harmful, but patients have found groups to be *helpful* in dealing with anxiety about their own possible death. In a sense, personal death was "detoxified" by dealing with the death of others. Yalom and associates have had the most extensive experience in this area, gleaned from work with a group for patients with advanced cancer, which has met 90 min a week over several years [73,82]. In their experience, the optimal number of persons in the group proved to be seven, new patients being allowed to join the group as places were available. A philosophy of living to the maximal extent, even though within the context of dying, appeared to be uniquely accomplished by their group. Feelings of alienation were lessened by talking with others "in the same boat"; belonging to the group resulted in identification with others who were successfully coping with similar problems. The sense of personal psychological growth countered the uncomfortable feelings of being victimized and powerless. Participants felt less sad, lonely, and isolated. They also experienced a heightened self-esteem and better communication with their physician and family.

Contrary to early fears about its harmful potential, the outcome suggested by Yalom's group is that patients had less need to deny cancer, and experienced more depth and meaning to life as a consequence of their group experiences. These findings are supported by Kennedy and co-workers. In a randomized controlled study of group therapy in cancer patients, they found that those selected for group participation appeared to gain a greater sense of well-being and stability than those who did not have access to the group sessions [35].

Similar results have been achieved by others when patients in the group share a common disease site or treatment. Groups at Memorial Hospital currently include special sessions for outpatients with Hodgkin's disease, for women in the early postmastectomy period, and for women receiving adjuvant chemotherapy for breast cancer. Working with the psychological problems which arise in adapting to illness in the course of daily living is particularly amenable to group discussion. Group work with laryngectomy patients in the immediate postoperative period and with patients who have had recent head and neck surgery for cancer is being explored as a means to encourage early socialization and easier confrontation with the common feelings of self-consciousness faced by these individuals after surgery.

The benefits gained by participation in such groups is not restricted to patients alone; family members also experience their benefit. Parents of children with cancer have observed that a greater feeling of emotional support during crises, and a greater sense of understanding of their own and their children's responses, was gained by sharing and identifying with other parents through group meetings. Most pediatric oncology units now have regular meetings for parents which vary from a purely educational to a group therapy model [1,23].

The use of groups for hospitalized inpatients has proved more difficult, in part due to the nature and severity of illness in hospitalized patients. They have been found most useful, however, when organized as discussion groups coordinated usually by a social worker, a nurse, or psychiatrist. The groups may be structured for patients alone, patients and their families, or families alone [21]. At Memorial Hospital, social workers, often with nurses, lead weekly meetings on each floor dealing with the psychological problems of relatives who have patients in the hospital.

Patients with tumors of a specific site will require that sessions be devised to meet their specific needs. A daily group meeting, started 7 years ago at Memorial Hospital, is held on the surgical floor for women following mastectomy [16]. Patients are taught physiotherapy exercises from a physical therapist to facilitate early arm mobility and to prevent complications, such as lymphedema of the arm. They ask questions of the nurse about medical problems, and they participate in discussions led by the social worker about the impact of mastectomy. A Reach-to-Recovery volunteer representing the "veteran patient" who has been through it, and is recognized to appreciate the feelings as no one on the staff could do, attends once each week. The increasing interest in breast reconstruction has led to the inclusion of two additional optional sessions conducted by a woman plastic surgeon, who answers questions about postsurgical reconstruction as an option for some women. In radiotherapy clinics, an orientation to the clinic, its routines, equipment, and technicians has helped new patients prepare themselves emotionally and has helped diminish the anxiety often associated with the onset of new and sometimes frightening treatments [30].

SELF-HELP AND MUTUAL SUPPORT GROUPS

The long and successful history of Alcoholics Anonymous and Parents without Partners has served as a model to demonstrate the value of groups that form to deal with a specific shared problem [33]. These groups, independent of the medical system, offer concrete ongoing advice and support to those persons who share the same problem, and often one—like mental illness or cancer—that carries special social stigma. The open discussion of the problem, which must usually be kept secret, increases the person's sense of personal worth. Helping others with the same problems also increases both a sense of mastery and self-esteem through altruistic participation.

These self-help efforts often combine group support with two other self-help concepts: counseling by the "veteran" patient and the "fellow" patient. While we consider self-help groups as a new movement in cancer, actually the first, the Cured Cancer Club, was established in 1956, by a woman who was successfully treated for colon cancer and who saw a need for better emotional help for patients during and after treatment for cancer [80]. Chapters were developed in several cities to offer advice, personal help, and at times, financial support.

The development of Reach-to-Recovery was started in a similar fashion by Terese Lasser in the early 1950s and grew out of the recognition of her own problems following mastectomy, at a time when breast cancer and mastectomy were still unmentionable. The program has become so successful that it has been taken over by the American Cancer Society and is now international in its scope. At the request of her surgeon, Reach-to-Recovery sponsors a postoperative visit to a woman immediately after mastectomy, while she is still in the hospital. A volunteer who has had a mastectomy makes the visit, provides the patient with a temporary bra and materials to use for exercises, and discusses problems and answers questions, particularly about prostheses. The volunteers are trained to capitalize on their healthy, attractive appearance, self-assurance, and the fact that, as a "veteran" of the same procedure, they have "made it." The positive identification with the volunteer, seen as an individual who has been through the same crisis and mastered it, is helpful to the new patient. Most surgeons now accept that a woman who has had a mastectomy and who chooses to help others in this way can provide a special understanding of the woman who has just lost a breast. The opportunity to the "veteran" patient to help others in this manner often helps to consolidate her own sense of mastery [79].

A variant of the veteran patient model is the "veteran parent"—the mother or father who has lost a child to cancer. The participation on the pediatric oncology treatment team by a parent has been described by Lansky. Inclusion of a mature and perceptive mother who is emotionally stable has been found of special value in providing a sounding board for feelings and offering a kind of support to parents which cannot be given by medical staff [40]. "Veteran" counseling, also called "peer counseling," [20] is especially useful as a means of diminishing anxiety of new patients and their families in the acute stages of illness or in anticipation of a new treatment.

Some of the groups organized around a particular patient population may be able to make the special concerns of that group known at a national level. The Candlelighters is a powerful group supported by parents who have had a child with cancer. They have demonstrated the ability to help other parents and their children and also to provide public and political visibility for the needs of their constituency.

Success of the "self-help" concept has worked best in cancer when the mutual support relates to cancer of a special site [55]. Laryngectomees have an active organization to help new patients learn esophageal speech; Ostomy Clubs are available for those who have had a colostomy; both have international chapters. These groups also use the "veteran" patient to help the preoperative patient who is confronted with the decision to accept the loss of such a major body function as speaking or normal bowel control. The postoperative period is likewise a time for their visits with the practical, concrete advice sometimes privy only to someone who has had the same experience.

Most recently developed is the "fellow" patient support group, organized to allow patients currently ill with cancer to help others with the same stage of disease. Make Today Count, started by Orville Kelly, was organized to provide a socially supportive group for patients with a limited life span. Its chapters have proliferated perhaps in part because of their attempt to address emotional needs not being met by the medical community. The success of Make Today Count and its brother and sister organizations may also reflect a social climate in which altruism, participation, and greater concern for the humanistic side of the patient experience are more highly valued. Living with Cancer, CanCervive, Can-Do, and Project Living are all groups which combine mutual support and personal visits by a person who has or has had a similar experience with cancer. An outstandingly successful project is Cansurmount in Denver. Started by Hamilton, an oncologist, and Lynn Ringer, a patient volunteer, Cansurmount members now visit all patients with cancer in several Denver hospitals, providing support to patients and their families. Both this unit and a similar one in Westchester County, New York, are supported by the American Cancer Society and are becoming models for like units across the country.

At Memorial Hospital, informal patient-to-patient counseling has been provided by a particularly intuitive man, Bob Fisher, who has chronic myelocytic leukemia. He works closely with physicians who respect the unique support he can give to new leukemia patients and their families. The "fellow" patient support system in this institution has been expanded to include patients with tumors of various sites who counsel other patients with a similar illness.

Oncology has been cautious in accepting the "fellow" patient concept of employing contemporary patients in the cancer treatment process to help one another; the caution, however, is diminishing. This is particularly true as oncologists recognize the unique nature of fellow-patient support, which goes beyond that available in the medical setting and is of mutual benefit to those who receive and provide it. These social and mutual patient help efforts are being increasingly accepted by the medical community and reflect the current trend toward greater willingness to utilize psychological and social interventions.

Terminal State Interventions

The concern for helping patients living with cancer has been paralleled by developments in patient care aimed toward maximum humanistic goals in the care of those dying of cancer.

HOSPICE PHILOSOPHY

For centuries, care of the dying has been accepted as a responsibility by religious groups. Calvary Hospital in New York, started by Dominican nuns in the late 1800s, is a notable example of a specialized facility for care of terminally ill patients, primarily with cancer. Twenty years ago, the plight of patients dying with cancer was made more visible by Cicely Saunders, when she founded St. Christopher's Hospice for patients who were being sent home to die from London hospitals. This was the beginning of the hospice movement, which has since spread to the United States.

The care of terminally ill patients is planned to improve comfort care in two ways: by supporting efforts to keep patients at home as long as feasible and by developing units geographically separate from acute care centers which, when home care is no longer possible, provide a hospital-like environment that offers optimal control of pain in a setting that maintains maximal interaction with the family [68]. The need for better care for the incurably ill is apparent, but the direction of the hospice movement in this country is still unclear. It has been plagued by early requirements generated by insurance and licensing agencies to define services and levels of care. Modification of the hospice concept to its best "fit" in the American culture is still needed. This is especially true if fragmentation of medical care is to be prevented at a time in the cancer patient's experience when continuity is critical. Maintaining the tie to the family or primary physician during hospice care may be an important means of assuring continuity.

HOME CARE

Adoption of the basic premise of the hospice concept, the facilitation of maximum time spent at home by dying patients, has fostered in many sectors across the country a return to the former common custom of allowing a patient to die at home. Ultimately, the death of a family member, just as illness, becomes a family matter. The effectiveness of interventions which enable the patient to remain at home, however, is clearly tied to the qualities of back-up services the medical system can provide. Martinson *et al.* have demonstrated the efficacy of a home-care model in the care and management of dying children and their families [43]. They developed a pilot program combining home visits by a primary care nurse with adjunct hospital services available as needed through the time of the child's death. While the authors add that "home care" may not be the best option for every child dying of cancer, in their experience, it proved to be an effective and desirable option for over 80% of the participant families. A program in rural Vermont that provided support to patients dying at home and their families proved highly satisfactory. Families and patients received regular visits from a team including a nurse practitioner, physician, social worker, and nutritionist [83]. Pain control was effectively managed by the nurses, and the ability to maintain patients at home was enhanced. Moreover, in both these projects the cost of home care was impressively *lower* than comparable care for patients dying in the hospital.

Comprehensive Rehabilitation

Psychotherapeutic interventions are not restricted to patients with limited life expectancy nor to those in acute distress. Cancer specialists are becoming more aware of the need to address the social and emotional as well as physical impact of cancer and its treatment for patients at *all* stages of illness. One consequence is a growing emphasis on "total care," which integrates all aspects of a patient's care. As defined by Cherkasky and Oppenheim, comprehensive rehabilitation includes giving (*a*) the best scientific and medical treatment; (b) attention to the patient as a social being whose relationships to family and society may be disrupted by illness; and (c) attention to the multiple needs through provisions of a health care team [8]. A Home Care Unit in Israel provides one model of a health care team which provided total care of the patient, combining optimal medical care with full recognition of the social and family needs that were often disrupted by illness [32]. A system of quantified clinical judgments, made at the time of each patient's clinical visit, was used to evaluate patients over a time and to provide a clear clinical basis for both medical and psychological interventions. This type of comprehensive approach in the ambulatory setting should be further studied in this country.

Psychopharmacologic Approach

The introduction of psychotropic drugs has been useful in the management of patients with cancer. An early application among cancer patients of this class of drugs was in the control of nausea and vomiting. More recently, researchers have been exploring the use of psychotropic drugs as a means to potentiate the effect of morphine and its derivatives for control of pain. Their use as appetite stimulants in the control of anorexia has been less successful. Finally, in addition to these unique usages, more traditional requests for psychotropic medication to control symptoms of anxiety, depression, and confusional states are seen in the oncology setting.

Nausea and Vomiting

Two classes of drugs have proven partially effective in the control of emetic side effects of chemotherapy: anticholinergic–antihistamines and the major tranquilizers. Among the former, promethazine (Phenergan), trimethobenzamide (Tigan), and diphenhydramine (Benadryl) are used with some success. Of the major tranquilizers, chlorpromazine (Thorazine), prochlorperazine (Compazine), haloperidol (Haldol), and triethylperazine (Torecan) are used. These agents should be given 8 to 12 hr before coming to the hospital, with a preloading dose to diminish anticipatory anxiety.

Following anecdotal reports of its use among chemotherapy patients, marijuana, containing the active substance delta-9-tetrahydrocannabinol (THC) has been shown to possess antiemetic and appetite-stimulating effects [61]. THC has proved superior to placebos in several clinical trials [67]. Comparison against the standard antiemetic, prochlorperazine (Compazine), however, has led to mixed reports of efficacy [17]. The level of dosage required to produce antiemetic effects often produces unpleasant side effects, particularly in older persons, varying from drowsy, lightheaded feelings to depersonalization, feelings of unreality, and hallucinations. Efforts to remove the "high" while retaining the antiemetic qualities have been unsuccessful; nabilone, one such new derivative, is no longer under study, due to observed neurotoxic effects of long-term use in dogs.

PAIN

Morphine and derivatives, including methadone, are the standard analgesics for cancer-related pain. They are often potentiated in their effectiveness by the addition of phenothiazines. Control of pain by the usual analgesics often is improved by the addition of drugs that diminish associated emotional distress of anxiety or depression and are felt, by this indirect route, to contribute to control of pain. The antianxiety drugs, major tranquilizers, and antidepressants have been thought to act this way.

The question is being increasingly posed as to whether the psychotropic drugs, in particular antidepressants, may themselves have a direct analgesic effect. Phenothiazines, for example, have been extensively used for pain in Europe. In experimental pain models, some have been effective and others have not [48]. Antidepressants, alone or in combination with phenothiazines, have also been effective in pain control. Of considerable interest is the fact that amitriptyline has been effective in relieving pain associated with herpes zoster and migraine without having an effect upon the concomitant depression [10]. This suggests that tricyclic compounds may have a direct effect on pain, which is not mediated through effect upon mood. Pasternak speculates that an enkephalin-related analgesic system exists within the brain, which could explain the interaction of the various transmitters [56].

Brompton's Mixture is a liquid composed of heroin, cocaine, chloroform water, ethyl alcohol, flavoring, and a phenothiazine first used in England to keep terminally ill patients comfortable yet alert. The combination used in this country substitutes morphine—and in some cases, methadone—for heroin and appears to be as effective as its parent combination in England. The fact that use of this liquid allows control of dose amount and frequency by the patient may account in part for their reports of increased satisfaction when it is used. Orders for a drug to be given by a nurse only on the patient's request (p.r.n.), rather than in scheduled dosage, often increases anxiety. The increasing exploration of patient's control over his or her own pain medication has failed to reveal patterns of abuse and indicates that self-medication seems to provide a sense of security and control that permits the patient actually to use less, not more. Controlled studies should be instituted in this area.

Anorexia

One of the most troublesome symptoms to treat in cancer is anorexia. Transient anorexia occurs with anxiety, and as a side effect of chemotherapy and radiotherapy. The mechanism producing the profound ano-rexia of advanced cancer associated with cachexia, however, is still unknown. In a study of these patients, no correlation of anorexia with significant depression was found, suggesting that a functional origin is unlikely and a central hypothalamic mechanism should be explored [30].

Several drugs have been tried which act as appetite stimulants: mari-juana, steroids, insulin, and recently, with some success, cyproheptadine (Periactin). No appetite stimulants have been outstandingly successful thus far. Dietary supplements and hyperalimentation are still more effective than appetite stimulants.

Depression

Many persons with cancer experience the sadness of anticipatory griev-ing for loss of health and threat of death. Beyond normal grief, however, some patients have significant depressive symptoms. Care must be taken in singling out these patients to focus on their psychologic state and dysphoric mood, since vegetative signs of depression may be present related to the ef-fects of cancer itself [59]. Antidepressants are of value with these patients, even though the depression is assumed to be reactive to medical illness. The sedating effect of amitriptyline is also useful to replace other hypnotics at bedtime. Although the action is not understood, empirical evidence in our experience suggests that antidepressants should be tried in reactively depressed cancer patients.

Anxiety

Antianxiety drugs as a group have been useful in managing patients' anx-iety prior to procedures and when anxiety about illness requires daily con-trol by a hypnotic. They have proven to be much superior to the earlier use of barbiturates which were often too sedating when given in sufficient quantity to reduce anxiety. The benzodiazepines have provided highly ef-fective control of anxiety. Of these, diazepam (Valium) has been the most widely used along with flurazepam (Dalmane) for bedtime sedation; both are safer in overdose, produce fewer side effects, and are nonaddicting. Valium 5 mg three times a day will control most anxiety in ambulatory pa-tients, with a change to an as-needed basis when acute anxiety abates.

Behavioral Approaches

The most recent of the interventions to be applied in cancer are behavioral. Proper use of these approaches is still being explored in cancer. Briefly reviewed here are hypnosis, suggestion, meditation, biofeedback, and relaxation techniques, which represent interventions that may poten-tially have effective application for highly specific situations.

Hypnosis

By no means a novel technique [66], the use of hypnosis in cancer patients has recently received new attention. The rekindling of interest in its application reflects its usefulness in controlling and managing problem areas in patient care that have been resistant to more strictly conventional therapeutic approaches. Specifically, these included control of pain, improvement of appetite, and, generally, enhancement of a sense of well-being.

USE IN PAIN

The treatment of pain related to cancer has been found to respond to hypnosis and posthypnotic suggestion in patients who are hypnotizable and motivated [37]. Mastrovito has noted that hypnosis is more effective in pain associated with cancer which has an organic basis; it is less effective in pain with a strong psychogenic component [45]. The technique is already being explored in children to reduce anxiety before painful procedures and in group sessions, to promote a sense of well-being and optimism that can improve appetite and mood [39,54]. Its potential utility as an adjunct to traditional treatment suggests that hypnosis should be tried earlier rather than as a last resort.

SUGGESTION AND RELAXATION

The increasing interest in a holistic approach to cancer therapy has led to approaches which combine meditation, self-hypnosis, and positive suggestion through the use of visual imagery. The goal of such approaches is to achieve improved physical status through positive mental health. The assumption is made that by positive suggestion, the body's immune defenses against the cancer will be enhanced [3,38]. Simonton, drawing upon early psychosomatic theories of vulnerability to cancer, has developed a technique combining these three elements [71]. Patients participate in group sessions in which they are encouraged to assume personal responsibility for the cancer's original growth by mental means. Positive suggestion is enhanced by the request to visualize the "white cells acting on the disease"; this is then reinforced by listening to taped relaxation sessions at home. The temporarily enhanced sense of mastery and increased control of a situation in which the patient feels powerless against his or her cancer is, no doubt, useful. The sense of well-being, however, may be dispelled by advancing disease. Most patients who turn to these techniques have advanced cancer and are highly likely to experience progressive disease. When the tumor progresses, an increased sense of failure has been seen, accompanied by severe depression. There is also significant risk of intensifying the burden of guilt for the patient with cancer who may already feel that he has contributed in some way to having cancer, even if only by having delayed in seeing a physician. Simonton also suggests that those patients who use the mental exercises survive longer, though no carefully controlled studies have been done. Regrettably, claims for longer survival using the Simonton technique have reached the public, although risks and problems associated with its use have not been widely publicized. It is unfortunate that a clinical trial within the scientific community has not been done.

There is some question now as to whether such a trial will take place given the recent questioning of the premises of the immunosurveillance theory per se and our growing understanding of the complexity of functional components within the immune system. Calabresi summarizes the current situation by noting that there has been a decline in the popularity of the immune surveillance theory for several reasons. First, the development of T-cell immunity and neoplasia are not linked in evolution. Second, the patients who are immune deficient, by virtue of disease or treatment, are not universally more susceptible to cancer, but to neoplasia of the cells of the immune system. Third, experimental data derived from neonatal thymectomy appears to demonstrate increased risk of DNA-virus-induced tumors, not spontaneous ones or those arising from carcinogens, suggesting a diminished antiviral, not antitumor state. Also, the athymic or "nude" mouse has no higher incidence of tumor development. Due to the presence of both immune effectors and blocking immune components in the immune system, it is not clear how the immune system influences development or growth of cancer [7]. Lewis Thomas, with his rich knowledge of immunology, and wisdon, has wryly commented that he would fear, at present, suggesting that a particular cell group attack cancer cells since, from an immunologic point of view, it is unclear which cell groups to encourage to stronger action [76].

Behavior Modification

One means of altering behavior is to change the way a patient thinks about a given procedure or sensation, the hypothesis being that by modulating a person's feelings, for example through hypnosis, about what is happening to him or her, the actual physical perception of that event will indirectly be affected. A more direct intervention is to change the behavior or response itself, either by altering the manner in which the individual responds or by altering the way in which the stimulus is presented, or some combination of the two. Behavior modification techniques are only just beginning to be employed as tools to combat two of the most debilitating side effects of cancer and its treatment: nausea and vomiting, and anorexia.

NAUSEA AND VOMITING

Nausea and vomiting are near-limiting side effects of several important chemotherapy regimens: cyclophosphamide, CCNU derivatives, MOPP, platinum, and adriamycin. These drugs are hypothesized to exert their emetic effect by activating the chemoreceptor trigger zones (CTZ) around the fourth ventricle. The repeated occurrence of vomiting following treatment can result in a conditioned response in some patients. The person develops nausea and vomiting in anticipation of treatment, sometimes up to 2 to 3 days in advance of administration of a drug. Desensitizing techniques have been tried in some patients to control the conditioned distress. Some explanation of whether these are persons who are particularly anxious or who develop aversions easily is needed.

ANOREXIA

Efforts to use behavior modification with regard to eating, similar to those used in the treatment of anorexia nervosa, have been tried but have not met with success in cancer. Attention to behavioral modes of increasing food intake by altering meal patterns and setting should be pursued [30]. A hypothesis that learned food aversion during radio- and chemotherapy treatment is a mechanism producing anorexia suggests that it might be amenable to a desensitization approach similar to anticipatory vomiting. For example, it is now known that many patients undergoing radiation therapy, particularly to the head and neck region, experience a physiological alteration in their taste thresholds [14,49a]. Sensitivity to bitter tastes (urea) is heightened (lower threshold), whereas that to sweet (sucrose) tastes is diminished (higher threshold). The consequence is that those foods with a high acid content (e.g., beef, coffee, certain amino acid elemental diets) are no longer tolerated by patients. If patients could be encouraged to increase low acid (e.g., fish, chicken) foods in their diet for the duration of the treatments, perhaps the early pattern of weight loss and poor food intake could be short-circuited.

Possible New Directions for Interventions

Several provocative observations are pointed out which suggest new areas for development of psychologic and behavioral interventions. Each is included because of new findings as yet preliminary, but worthy of further study. A common theme throughout is that improved knowledge of the discrete psychosocial problems of cancer is clearly needed to allow the rational planning of interventions. The major thrust in clarifying this has been in the investigation and development of techniques to evaluate and promote optimal ways for patients to deal with their illness.

Acceptance and Adherance to a Treatment Regimen

At a concrete level, optimal adjustment to illness may involve a patient's willingness to participate in and ability to comply with an often rigorous treatment regimen. Patients who are able to adhere to a treatment regimen in cancer despite adverse side effects have been shown to survive longer. Data from a national clinical trials group Cancer and Leukemia Group B (CALGB) protocol for treatment of osteogenic sarcoma found that the patients whose treatment was not altered from the original plan survived longer [9]. A current study by the Psychosocial Collaborative Oncology Group (PSYCOG), a national collaborative research group, is assessing patients' (a) acceptance of an investigational chemotherapy drug protocol; (b) their recall and perception of the interview and their informed consent form describing treatment; (c) the effect of the doctor-patient interaction upon their acceptance (or rejection) of treatment; and (d) the factors which promoted their staying in treatment [28]. The positive and negative interactions between oncology and clinic staff and chemotherapy patients may reveal new interventions to improve compliance, and for some, survival. These issues of presentation of diagnosis and treatment become crucial in improved survival when it is clear that *compliance* alters outcome.

Techniques to improve understanding of the diagnosis and plan for treatment are clearly needed. These need not necessarily be complex. For example, one oncologist makes an audio tape of his discussions of diagnosis and treatment with the patient and gives it to him or her to carry home to review at home with family members [65]. In addition to reducing confusion about medical facts, diagnosis, and treatment, he found taped discussions led to increased communication and confidence between physician and patient. Even when the written informed consent paper is taken home overnight, the increased time to think about and digest the information helps the patient to make a more knowledgeable decision [49]. Certainly, compliance and adherence to effective cancer therapy requires further study.

Teaching Adaptive Coping Strategies

Just as in issues of compliance, a patient's characteristic manner of dealing with problems and decisions may affect his or her well-being. Investigators have been identifying the nature and type of adaptive responses of individuals to cancer as they relate both to tumor site and to stage of disease. These responses are best described as the coping strategies or behaviors with which the person faces the stress of cancer. Penman has suggested that an active, tackling, and confronting style of coping characterized those who coped better with breast cancer, whereas women who used more passive, avoiding, and capitulating strategies later had more psychopathological symptoms and experienced greater dysphoria [57]. Whether mood and coping are concurrent phenomena, whether better coping leads to better mood or whether positive mood and adaptive qualities lead to the use of active coping strategies is not clear, but further study is suggested. The Project Omega group at Massachusetts General Hospital has suggested that teaching adaptive coping strategies might be possible in cancer, suggesting a cognitive approach based in part on the work of Meichenbaum [46,78]. If coping styles are subject to change by learning approaches, then this is a challenging new concept to be pursued.

Dysphoric State and Survival

The potential importance of being able to monitor response states is highlighted by a recent study by Derogatis and Abeloff of women who had been studied psychologically at the beginning of chemotherapy treatment for advanced breast cancer. Preliminary findings revealed that the women could later be separated into groups, those who survived less than one year (short) and those who survived more than one year (long), based upon the level of their emotional expressiveness, particularly of anger [13]. Women who survived longer all exhibited elevated ratings on Hostility, Anxiety, and Psychoticism scales of a symptom checklist along with higher negative mood states than their shorter-lived peers. While these data were obtained from a small group of women and the survival times are close in length, the findings are provocative and would appear to suggest that a coping style that externalizes negative, angry emotions may be associated with a better prognosis. Since suppression of anger has been found to correlate in breast cancer patients with elevation of serum IgA, the need for further study with attention to the possible interplay of endocrine and immunologic parameters of emotion is suggested [58].

A paradigm for such a study is seen in the work by Gorzynski and colleagues. Their project evaluated the women who could be located whom Katz and co-workers had studied with psychoendocrine measures prior to breast biopsy and mastectomy 10 years earlier [18, 34]. Both psychological defenses and cortisol levels were found to be constant at the two points in time, prior to breast biopsy, and later, at 10 years, suggesting that these are abiding qualities, largely biologically tuned. The long surviving women, in comparison to those who had died in the interim, showed an interesting trend toward greater expression of emotional distress, lower weight, and slightly higher cortisol levels.

While these data obtained in humans suggest on the one hand that expression of emotional distress, and in particular anger, might be associated with longer survival, it is clear that the relationship between stress and cancer remains unclear and complex. Riley's work with mice has shown *increased* incidence of mammary tumors in stressed mice [63]. Work of others, particularly Monjan and Collector, has shown that chronic stress causes immunosuppression followed by a rebound-enhanced effect [47]. The role, if any, of emotions on immune state is far from clear, yet it is an area of great interest precisely because of the possible neurohormonal link [6].

Social Support

Increasing evidence also suggests that the response of an individual to stress is modulated not only by coping style but also by social support [33]. Murawski, Penman, and Schmitt have recently reviewed the concept of social support and its measurement in cancer [50]. The stress-buffering role of the individual's support network likely exerts an important effect upon adaptation to the stress of cancer. Any model that attempts to identify psychosocial factors in cancer must include the present or available level of social support. The potential for planned interventions in this area is challenging.

Weight Control and Breast Cancer

Gorzynski and colleagues' previously mentioned study of women who had survived 10 years after surgery for breast cancer, showed this group had lower body weights at the time of original breast biopsy than the women who died [18]. Recent epidemiologic evidence has noted that obesity is a factor both in risk of cancer and shorter survival [15]. Helping women to control or reduce their weight may play a role in both prevention and survival for women, and in particular those already at high risk of breast cancer by virtue of genetic predisposition. Women who have had a mastectomy for breast cancer often are very fearful of recurrence and overeat out of fear that weight loss means return of the cancer. Counseling to retain normal weight would not only enhance self-esteem, but could also play a role in risk of recurrence.

Research Approaches to the Search for New Interventions

Medical research in cancer has focused primarily upon survival in the past. Research protocols have carefully monitored progression of disease, side effects of treatment, and physical function in relation to investigational treatments designed and studied in controlled clinical trials. Notable by it absence, however, has been any systematic monitoring of the patient's "quality of life" during a given treatment. Observations have been impeded by both the lack of psychological instruments readily available for use in the medically ill and fact that previously, psychiatric input into collaborative clinical cancer research did not exist.

The first attempt to monitor psychosocial function of patients being treated on national investigational protocols began in 1976 in the NCI-supported CALGB Clinical Trials Group. Quantifiable, serial observations are now being recorded of the patients' behavioral and mood changes associated with different treatment arms, providing a basis for the assessment of psychologic "toxicity" and central nervous system dysfunction. By using standardized tests, the psychologic response of patients to cancer of different sites and varying treatments can be made by comparing data obtained across treatment arms and protocols. Currently, 11 treatment protocols for adult patients under treatment for cancer of various sites are accruing sociodemographic and psychosocial data. The first of the two components of the data is an observer (usually a research nurse) assessment of global psychosocial function and evaluation of five discrete areas of social functioning. The other component is the patient's report of sociodemographic data and response to a mood scale, the Profile of Mood States (POMS). Exploration of similar data collection for children with cancer is currently under way. These and like observations will eventually provide a way to test the effectiveness of interventions in altering measured levels of emotional distress in the course of cancer of specific sites and treatment regimens [27]. The opportunity to study patients who are stratified for stage of disease and who are receiving uniform treatment is unique in the clinical trials group, providing a prospective study of psychologic response as it relates to treatment, morbidity, and survival.

More recently, Barofsky has studied patients' responses to randomized treatment with chemotherapy alone or in combination with limb amputation in an intergroup surgical study of soft tissue sarcomas [5]. He used a social change model to assess quality of life. Assessment of patients' perceptions of the medical alternatives would, he felt, provide information to the surgeons about ways to modify the process of caring for the patient. The development of a quality of life assessment having as its goal the collection of clinically relevant information for change constitutes an important approach to this area.

Another active group exploring psychologic issues in cancer is the Psychosocial Collaborative Oncology Group [69]. Schmale and coinvestigators have placed a priority on research in instrument development to identify, modify, adapt, and test psychologic assessment instruments for use in cancer patients. Two studies involving videotaped interviews with cancer patients have explored the applicability of several brief instruments for use by oncology staff to assess changes in patients' emotional adjustment. Development of reliable single instruments will allow psychological interventions to be tested in an appropriate research design. Such studies, like other clinical trials, will have to be prospectively planned to be tested in a stratified patient population who have a defined level of distress and in whom a uniform intervention can be randomly used. Tests of psychotropic drugs and counseling constitute areas of priority for such studies [26]. These studies should eventually more clearly define the appropriate intervention for a specific patient, and clarify at what stage of the cancer illness it should be applied.

Summary

A chronological review of psychotherapeutic, psychopharmacologic, and behavioral approaches in the management of the cancer patient reveals a considerable growth in interest in all three areas over the past 20 years. General psychotherapeutic approaches have developed out of the application of consultation–liaison concepts to the field of oncology, psychotherapeutic counseling in individual and group modes, improved psychosocial care of terminally ill patients, and comprehensive concepts of rehabilitation that incorporate psychological parameters. More specific interventions have developed as they may apply to cancer though most have only quite recently come under study. Since the social sciences, particularly liaison psychiatry, are now represented in multidisciplinary cancer research, the opportunities to test new psychological, social, and behavioral approaches is now possible. The stage has been set for a new era of research in the psychosocial and behavioral areas of oncology, which should be highly productive in the next decade.

One note of caution about the risks of premature application of new psychological interventions needs to be interjected. The current interest of our society in holistic health has created a climate in which psychologic interventions are particularly attractive in cancer. Sontag has called ours a "psychologizing" society [72]. Norman Cousins has noted that we are in a "holistic health explosion" in which the alternatives to traditional medicine represent a spectrum from valid procedures to those that are not only unscientific but potentially dangerous [11]. Psychological and behavioral approaches in cancer are particularly vulnerable to exploitation in a society that no longer relies as heavily on spiritual values and which has unrealistic expectations of psychology.

The cancer patient who senses traditional medicine has nothing more to offer sometimes begins a search for unorthodox or unproven remedies. The unproven cancer remedies fall primarily into four areas: diet, drugs, immunologic, and psychological [81]. The psychological remedies which offer a "naturalistic" approach are in vogue.

The current situation, in which provocative and challenging research data in psychological risk factors in cancer is being presented to the public as having established effects upon survival, threatens the whole movement of legitimate inquiry into those psychological factors which may indeed be active in etiology or survival. The research methodology and collaborative opportunities are available now to test both clinical observations and hypotheses. It is important that therapeutic zeal to apply speculative approaches to the clinical setting does not proceed ahead of sound research.

Bibliography

1. Adams, M. A.: Helping the parents of children with malignancy. *Journal of Pediatrics* 93:734-738, 1978.
2. Artiss, L. K.; and Levine, H. S.: Doctor-patient relation in severe illness: a seminar for oncology fellows. *New England Journal of Medicine* 388:1210-1214, 1973.
3. Balon, J. S.: Meditation-psychotherapy in the treatment of cancer. *Psychiatry* 6:19-22, 1974.
4. Bard, M.; and Sutherland, A. M.: Psychological impact of cancer and its treatment. IV. Adaptation to radical mastectomy. *Cancer* 8:656-672, 1955.
5. Barofsky, I.; and Sugarbaker, P. H.: Quality of Life Assessment, Cancer Treatment and Clinical Trials. Unpublished paper presented at American Psychological Association Annual Meeting, Toronto, Ontario, Canada, August 28, 1978.
6. Bartrop, R. W.; Lazarus, L.; Luckhurst, E.; Kiloh, L. G.; and Penny, R.: Depressed lymphocyte function after bereavement. *Lancet* 1:834-836, 1977.
7. Calabresi, P.: General principles of antineoplastic therapy. In *Cecil textbook of Medicine*, eds. P. B. Beeson, W. McDermott, and J. B. Wyngaarden, 15th edition, part XIX, pp. 1922-1927. Philadelphia: W. B. Saunders Co., 1979.
8. Cherasky, M.; and Oppenheim, A.: Organization of a program for home-care of the cancer patient. In *Treatment of Cancer and Allied Disease*, eds. G. T. Pack and I. M. Ariel, pp. 47-51. New York: Paul B. Hoeber, Inc., 1958.
9. Cortes, E. P.; Holland, J. F.; and Glidewell, O.: Amputation and adriamycin in primary osteosarcoma: A five-year report. *Cancer Treatment Reports* 62:271-277, 1978.
10. Couch, J. R.; Siegler, D. K.; and Hassamein, R.: Amitriptyline in the prophylaxis of migraine. *Neurology* 26:121-127, 1976.
11. Cousins, N.: The holistic health explosion. *Saturday Review*, pp. 17-21, March 31, 1979.
12. Derogatis, L.: Psychological assessment of the cancer patient: A strategy of approach. 1978. Unpublished manuscript.
13. Derogatis, L. R.; Abeloff, M. D.; and Melisaratos, N.: Psychological coping mechanisms and survival time in metastatic breast cancer. *Journal of the American Medical Association* 242:1504-1508, 1979.

14. DeWys, W. D.: Abnormalities of taste as a remote effect of a neoplasm. *Annals of the New York Academy of Sciences* 230:427–434, 1974.
15. Donegan, W.; Harts, A.; and Rimm, A.: The association of body weight with recurrent cancer of the breast. *Cancer* 41:1590–1594, 1978.
16. Euster, S.: Rehabilitation after mastectomy: the group process. *Social Work in Health Care* 4:251–263, 1979.
17. Frytak, S.; Moertel, C. G.; and O'Fallon, J. R.: A comparison of delta-9-tetrahydrocannabinol (THC), prochlorperazine (PCP) and placebo as antiemetics for cancer chemotherapy. *Proceedings of the American Society of Clinical Oncology* 20:391, 1979.
18. Gorzynski, J. G.; Holland, J.; Katz, J. L.; Weiner, H.; Zumoff, B.; Fukushima, D.; and Levin, J.: Stability of ego defenses and endocrine responses in women prior to breast biopsy and ten years later. *Psychosomatic Medicine* 42:323–328, 1980.
19. Greenblatt, D. J.; and Shader, R. I.: Psychotropic drugs in the general hospital. In *Manual of Psychiatric Therapeutics*, ed. R. I. Shader, pp. 1–27. Boston: Little, Brown, 1975.
20. Guggenheim, F.; and O'Hara, S.: Peer counseling in a general hospital. *American Journal of Psychiatry* 133:1197–1199, 1976.
21. Gustafson, J.; and Whitman, H.: Toward a balanced social environment on the oncology service: the cancer patients' group. *Social Psychology* 13:147–152, 1978.
22. Hackett, T.; and Cassem, N., eds.: *Massachusetts General Hospital Psychiatry Handbook*. Saint Louis: The C. V. Mosby Co., 1973.
23. Heffron, W. A.; Bommelaere, K.; and Masters, R.: Group discussions with parents of leukemic children. *Pediatrics* 52:831–840, 1973.
24. Holland, J. C.: Psychologic aspects of cancer. In *Cancer Medicine*, eds. J. F. Holland and E. Frei, pp. 991–1022. Philadelphia: Lea and Febiger, 1973.
25. Holland, J. C.: Psychological aspects of oncology. *Medical Clinics of North America* 61:737–748, 1977.
26. Holland, J. C.: Psychosocial intervention area. In Summary Progress Report of the Psychosocial Collaborative Oncology Group (PSYCOG) to the Division of Cancer Control and Rehabilitation, NCI, Grant #CA-19681, 1978.
27. Holland, J. C.; and Bahna, G.: Guidelines for psychosocial data collection. Cancer and Leukemia Group B. (CALGB) Psychiatry Division, New York, 1978. Available upon request from author.
28. Holland, J. C.; Penman, D.; Bahna, G.; Morrow, G.; Morse, I.; Schmale, A.; and Derogatis, L.; Patient's perception of giving informed consent for investigational chemotherapy. *Proceedings of the American Association of Cancer Research* 21:188, 1980.
29. Holland, J. C.; Rowland, J.; Lebovits, A.; and Rusalem, R.: Reactions to cancer treatment: assessment of emotional response to adjuvant radiotherapy as a guide to planned intervention. *Psychiatric Clinics of North America* 2:347–358, 1979.
30. Holland, J. C.; Rowland, J.; and Plumb, M.: Psychological aspects of anorexia in cancer patients. *Cancer Research* 37:2425–2428, 1977.
31. Holland, J. C. B.; and Rowland, J.: Psychological consequences of long-term/adjuvant treatment of cancer: a developmental model for teaching life threatening illness. Paper presented at the American Society of Clinical Oncology, Education Workshop #5, Washington, D.C., April 3, 1978.
32. Izak, R.; Engel, J.; and Medalie, J.: Comprehensive rehabilitation of the patient with cancer. Five-year experience of a home care unit. *Journal of Chronic Disease* 24:363–374, 1973.
33. Kaplan, G.; and Killilea, M.: *Support Systems and Mental Health*. New York: Grune & Stratton, Inc., 1976.
34. Katz, J. L.; Ackman, P.; Rothwax, Y.; Sachar, E.; Weiner, H.; Hellman, L.; and Gal-

lagher, T.: Psychoendocrine aspects of cancer of the breast. *Psychosomatic Medicine* 32:1–18, 1970.

35. Kennedy, B. J.; Goldman, A.; and Ferlic, M.: Group counseling in adult patients with cancer. *Proceedings of the American Society of Clinical Oncology* 19:375, 1978.

36. Krant, M. J.; Beiser, M.; Adler, G.; and Johnston, L.: The role of a hospital-based psychosocial unit in terminal cancer illness and bereavement. *Journal of Chronic Disease* 29:115–127, 1976.

37. Kroger, W. S.: *Clinical and Experimental Hypnosis.* Philadelphia: J. B. Lippincott, 1979.

38. Kroger, W. S.; and Fezler, W. D.: *Hypnosis and Behavior Modification: Imagery Conditioning.* Philadelphia: J. B. Lippincott, 1976.

39. LaBaw, W.; Holton, C.; Tewell, K.; and Eccles, D.: The use of self-hypnosis by children with cancer. *Hypnosis* 17:233–238, 1975.

40. Lansky, S. B.: Childhood leukemia: the child psychiatrist as a member of the oncology team. *Journal of the American Academy of Child Psychiatry* 13:499–508, 1974.

41. LeShan, L. L.; and Gassmann, M. L.: Some observations on psychotherapy with patients suffering from neoplastic disease. *American Journal of Psychotherapy* 12:723–734, 1958.

42. Levine, P. M.; Silberfarb, P. M.; and Lipowski, Z. J.: Mental disorders in cancer patients, a study of 100 psychiatric referrals. *Cancer* 42:1385–1391, 1978.

43. Martinson, I. M.; Armstrong, G. D.; Geis, D. P.; Anglim, M. A.; Gronseth, E. C.; MacInnis, H.; Nesbit, M. E.; and Kersey, J. H.; Facilitating home care for children dying of cancer. *Cancer Nursing* 1:41–45, 1978.

44. Massie, M. J.; Gorzynski, G.; Mastrovito, R.; Theis, D.; and Holland, J.: The diagnosis of depression in hospitalized patients with cancer. *Proceedings of the American Society of Clinical Oncology* 20:432, 1979.

45. Mastrovito, R.: Personal Communication.

46. Meichenbaum, D.; Turk, D.; and Burstein, S.: The nature of coping with stress. In *Stress and Anxiety,* vol. 2, eds. I. G. Sarason and C. D. Spielberger, pp. 337–360. New York, John Wiley and Sons, 1975.

47. Monjan, A.; and Collector, M.: Stress-induced modulation of immune function. *Science* 196:307–308, 1977.

48. Moore, J.; and Dundee, J.: Alterations to somatic pain associated with anesthesia. VII. The effects of phenothiazine derivatives. *British Journal of Anesthesia* 33:422–431, 1961.

49. Morrow, G.; Gootnick, J.; and Schmale, A.: A simple technique for increasing patients' informed consent to treatment. *Cancer* 42:793–799, 1978.

49a. Mossman, K. L.; and Henkin, R. I.: Radiation-induced changes in taste acuity in cancer patients. *International Journal of Radiation Oncology Biology and Physiology* 4:663–670, 1978.

50. Murawski, B. J.; Penman, D.; and Schmitt, M.: Social support in health and illness: the concept and its measurement. *Cancer Nursing* 1:365–371, 1978.

51. Myers, W. L. P.: Internist's approach to the cancer patient. In *Cecil Textbook of Medicine,* eds. P. B. Beeson, W. McDermott and J. B. Wyngaarden, 15th edition, part XIX, pp. 1898–1901. Philadelphia: W. B. Saunders Co., 1979.

52. Norton, J.: Treatment of a dying patient. *Psychoanalytic Study of the Child* 18:541–560, 1963.

53. Novack, D. H.; Plumer, R.; Smith, R. L.; Ochitill, H.; Morrow, G. R.; and Bennett, J.: Changes in physicians' attitudes toward telling the cancer patient. *Journal of the American Medical Association* 241:897–900, 1979.

54. Olness, K.; and Gardner, G. G.: Some guidelines for use of hypnotherapy in pediatrics. *Pediatrics* 62:228–233, 1978.
55. Parsell, S.; and Lagliareni, E.: Cancer patients help each other. *American Journal of Neurology* 74:650–651, 1974.
56. Pasternak, G.: Psychotropic Drugs and Chronic Pain. 1979. Unpublished manuscript.
57. Penman, D.: Coping Strategies in Adaptation to Mastectomy. Unpublished doctoral dissertation, Yeshiva University, New York, 1979.
58. Pettingale, K. W.; Greer, S.; and Tee, D. H.: Serum IgA and emotional expression in breast cancer patients. *Journal of Psychosomatic Research* 21:395–399, 1977.
59. Plumb, M. M.; and Holland, J.: Comparative studies of psychological function in patients with advanced cancer—I. Self-reported depressive symptoms. *Psychosomatic Medicine* 39:264–276, 1977.
60. Posner, J.: Neurologic complications of systemic cancer. *Disease-A-Month* 25:1–60, 1978.
61. Regelson, W.; Butler, J. R.; Schulz, J.; Kirk, T.; Peek, L.; Green, M. L.; and Zalis, M. O.: △-9-Tetrahydrocannabinol as an effective antidepressant and appetite-stimulating agent in advanced cancer patients. In *The Pharmacology of Marijuana*, eds. M. C. Braude and S. Szara, pp. 763–776. New York; Raven Press, 1975.
62. Richards, A. I.; and Schmale, A. H.: Psychosocial conferences in medical oncology: role in a training program. *Annals of Internal Medicine* 80: 541–545, 1974.
63. Riley, V.: Mouse mammary tumors: alteration of incidence as apparent function of stress. *Science* 189:465–467, 1975.
64. Rosenbaum, C.; Abramson, R.; Hardy, D.; and Hogan, L.: Psychosocial oncology rounds. *Proceedings of the American Society of Clinical Oncology* 19:375, 1978.
65. Rosenbaum, E. H.; and Rosenbaum, I.: Improved communication technique for consultative interviews. *Proceedings of the American Society of Clinical Oncology* 18:316, 1977.
66. Sacerdote, P.: Hypnosis in cancer patients. *American Journal of Clinical Hypnosis* 9:100–108, 1966.
67. Sallan, S.; Zinberg, N.; and Frei, E., III: Antiemetic effect of delta-9-tetrahydrocannabinol in patients receiving cancer chemotherapy. *New England Journal of Medicine* 293:795–797, 1975.
68. Saunders, C.: The last stages of life. *American Journal of Nursing.* 65:70–75, 1965.
69. Schmale, A. H.: Psychosocial Collaborative Oncology Group (PSYCOG), Renewal Grant #CA-19681. Submitted to the Division of Cancer Control and Rehabilitation, NCI, 1978.
70. Shands, H. C.; Finesinger, J. E.; Cobb, S.; and Abrams, R. D.: Psychological mechanisms in patients with cancer. *Cancer* 4:1159–1170, 1951.
71. Simonton, O. C.; and Simonton, S. S.: Belief systems and management of the emotional aspects of malignancy. *Journal of Transpersonal Psychology* 7:29–47, 1975.
72. Sontag, S.: *Illness as Metaphor*. New York: Farrar, Straus and Giroux, 1977.
73. Spiegel, D.; and Yalom, I.: A support group for dying patients. *International Journal of Group Psychotherapy* 28:233–245, 1978.
74. Spikes, J.; and Holland, J.: The physician's response to the dying patient. In *Psychological Care of the Medically Ill*, eds. J. Strain and S. Grossman, pp. 138–148. New York: Appleton, 1975.
75. Strain, J.; and Grossman, S., eds.: *Psychological Care of the Medically Ill.* New York: Appleton, 1975.
76. Thomas, L.: *The Medusa and the Snail.* New York: Viking, 1979.
77. Vachon, M. L.; Lyall, W.; and Freeman, S. J.: Measurement and management of stress

in health professionals working with advanced cancer patients. *Death Education* 1:365–375, 1978.

78. Weisman, A. D.; and Sobel, H. J.: Coping with cancer through self-instruction: a hypothesis. *Journal of Human Stress* 5:3–8, 1974.

79. Wieder, S.; Schwartzfeld, J.; Fromewick, J.; and Holland, J.: Psychosocial support program for patients with breast cancer at Montefiore Hospital: team effort. *Quality Review Bulletin* 4:10–13, 1978.

80. Wolfe, N.: The Cured Cancer Club. *Todays Health*, pp. 33–35, January issue, 1956.

81. Wood, C.: American Cancer Society, personal communication.

82. Yalom, I.; and Greaves, C.: Group therapy with the terminally ill. *American Journal of Psychiatry* 134:396–400, 1977.

83. Yates, J.; and Haines, C. R.: A rural alternative to the hospice. *Proceedings of the American Society of Clinical Oncology* 20:395, 1979.

In light of former HEW Secretary Califano's announcement of a national antismoking campaign with a focus on prevention, the creation of the Office of Smoking and Health within HEW, and the 1979 Surgeon General's Report on Smoking and Health, the attention of the behavioral sciences to all aspects of the smoking problem should greatly accelerate. In order to provide some direction for such future research programs, it would appear to be valuable to examine some current research efforts and programs concerned with control of smoking behavior. This paper will not be exhaustive, but will critically review selected reports reflecting behavioral, social, and educational approaches to smoking control. However, before we examine these reports, we will present some current trends of smoking in the U.S. that appear to support the need for more carefully conceptualized and evaluated programs.

Current Smoking Trends

Despite the fact that smokers are a declining minority, more than 50 million Americans, or about one-third of the adult population, continue to smoke [66]. Surveys reveal that in the past 10 years, although the percentage of adult smokers in the United States has significantly declined, the percentage of teenage smokers has slightly increased [61]. Changes in the patterns of smoking behavior over this period are quite different for adults and teenagers as well as for males and females. The rate of smoking is decreasing among adult males, adult females, and male teenagers, with the only increase, a notable one, occurring among females in their teens and early twenties [61]. Furthermore, the onset of smoking, specifically "experimental smoking," is occurring at earlier ages over this same period of time. Additional data reveal a trend among smokers to use a "safer" cigarette as reflected in the increased purchase of longer, filter-tipped cigarettes with lowered tar and nicotine content. However, the consumption of cigarettes is increasing among the individuals who continue to smoke [32], which appears to support Schachter's contention [78] that nicotine addicts will simply smoke more low-nicotine cigarettes to compensate for the loss of nicotine. Jarvik and his associates [43] raise some questions concerning the term "addiction" with respect to nicotine. They contend that since virtually no stimulants are addictive, and since nicotine is a stimulant, it might be better to refer to an individual who habitually smokes as being nicotine-dependent. Furthermore, they contend that as a nonaddictive drug, the individual may not "seek" a certain nicotine level by smoking more low-nicotine cigarettes. One fact that virtually all investigations in this area report is that smokers and nonsmokers alike really believe that smoking is potentially dangerous to one's health [32]. Obviously, this fear does not appear to be enough to deter the onset of smoking or to be sufficiently successful in motivating smokers to stop [29].

Format of the Review

The present paper will critically review selected programs and research concerned with controlling smoking behavior. It will attempt to demonstrate the need for major changes in the smoking control area at both the conceptual and programmatic levels. Rather than attempting an exhaustive, superficial review of all the available literature, this paper will consider more intensively a representative sample of the current literature presented within a framework of certain broad categories. The categories will include information campaigns, specific in-school educational programs, legislative action, direct cessation programs, and longitudinal comprehensive programs.

Within the framework of these categories a central focus will be to assess the validity of the evaluations employed in the reports. In this regard, a surprising number of reports include no objective evaluations at all, just anecdotal communications. Another group of reports only includes post hoc evaluations (based on both systematic and spontaneous observations). A third and smallest group of reports can be truly described as research projects involving preplanned evaluations of programmed treatments.

The bulk of behavioral research concerned with smoking and health involves efforts to control the smoking of habitual or addicted smokers.

Unfortunately, many of the studies possess serious methodological limitations. Schwartz [81, p. 14] states,

> Despite much experimentation, behavioral investigators have not been able to design effective methods of attracting and involving the general public . . .If methods are to be replicated, clearer descriptions of the procedures used will have to be provided. Weak methodological design in most smoking control efforts, particularly poor data collection, lack of controls, incomplete follow-ups, and reliance on reduction rather than cessation as a measure of success, has made it difficult to analyze and interpret results. Also needed are careful evaluations of results based on comparisons and long-term follow-ups.

Public Information Campaigns

The effectiveness of antismoking campaigns is relevant to the general issue of whether or not health information can alter behavior presumed to be deleterious to health. In most of the reports examined for this review, insufficient evaluative data are reported. The criterion for success of a campaign should involve evaluating the validity of the measures administered and the appropriateness of the analysis procedures employed. Warner [90, p. 649] measures the impact of the overall antismoking campaign, which he defines as the "collective, mostly uncoordinated, activities of various organizations from 1964 to the present," on the consumption of cigarettes. By fitting cigarette demand functions to precampaign data, projected "ahead" as if the campaign had not occurred, he compares these predictions with realized consumption. According to Warner, the analysis

> suggests that major "events" in the campaign (e.g., the Surgeon General's Report) caused immediate though transitory decreases of four to five percent in annual per capita consumption. However, the cumulative effect of persistent publicity, supported by other public policies, has been substantial: In the absence of the campaign, per capita consumption likely would have exceeded its actual 1975 value by 20 to 30 percent. This is a conservative indication of the effectiveness of the campaign, for it ignores other potentially important and desirable behavior changes, such as the shift to low "tar" and nicotine cigarettes.

As Warner indicates, other studies measure success in terms of shifts in consumption from cigarettes high in tar and nicotine to cigarettes low in tar and nicotine or the amount of each cigarette smoked, whereas other studies measure self-reported smoking behavior and changes in attitudes toward smoking [49]. This application of different criteria to evaluate success or failure of a campaign can make the same campaign yield both positive and negative results. Also, the use of different measures makes it difficult to compare results across studies.

A quite different approach to analyzing the effects of information campaigns is reflected in Dubren's [24] study evaluating a televised "stop smoking clinic" program in New York City in August, 1975. A step-by-step quitting plan consisting of 30 90-second segments was broadcasted each weekday evening for four weeks. A sample of 310 viewers, out of 4800 who registered by postcard to participate in the program, was followed up at the end of the program and one month later. In general, the respondents were similar to the hard-core smokers (average 30 cigarettes a day, smoked for 20–30 years, and average 48 years of age) that usually attend stop smoking clinics. The results indicate that 10% reported having stopped smoking by the end of the program, although the quitting rate for men was twice as high as for women. Dubren (p. 84) concludes that, "use of the mass media may be an effective way to reach the large number of smokers who would not attend organized clinics but who may be able to stop smoking on their own with minimal support and guidance." One major difficulty in evaluating the study is that the participants were asked to fill out and mail back to the investigator a questionnaire which included only a self-report of smoking behavior. Self-reports such as these may be suspect.

Another difficulty encountered with many information campaigns pertains to the problem inherent in coordinating and evaluating complex field studies. For example, a 3-year longitudinal field study at Stanford University [16] consists of mass communications coupled with interpersonal communications. Three different communication conditions were set up in three different California communities: mass media only, mass media plus interpersonal communications, and a control community. Results from the second year show a continuum of effects on smoking across the communities, with the control community showing a slight reduction in smoking, the media only group showing a greater reduction in smoking, and the media–interpersonal communications group showing the greatest reduction in smoking. This study is among the most innovative efforts truly to evaluate the effectiveness of a public information campaign attempting to reduce smoking on a large scale. Unfortunately, despite the imagination and research design sophistication exhibited by these investigators, analyzing the effects on smoking as only one component of a program which addresses itself to several other risk factors in cardiovascular disease makes it very difficult to ferret out interaction effects. But most limiting in this investigation is the difficulty of controlling for other types of influences on smoking behavior when three entire communities are involved in this type of information campaign over such a long period of time.

On the other hand, many of the public information campaigns are very narrow in scope and even when they are targeted to only a specific population they encounter similar problems. Auger et al. [4] report that no significant differences were found in the number of cigarettes smoked by college students or staff members of a state mental health treatment center when antismoking mobiles and posters were displayed throughout the facility. In this instance, it is even difficult to generalize from negative results, because of the difficulties in controlling for competing influences in the field setting. Another problem in both massive and limited public information campaigns such as the ones just described is that the investigations fail to specify the characteristics of the content of the messages used in their communications. For example, it is well known in social psychology that fear-arousal communications may have different effects from nonfear arousal communications [27]. Furthermore, investigations such as one conducted by Evans *et al.* [29] ideally present an empirical rationale for the content and design of the message which they finally select. Although the Evans *et al.* study is an in-school program rather than a public information campaign, and therefore will be discussed later in this review, it illustrates how an empirical rationale for communication messages can be developed.

One other problem often encountered in trying to evaluate the effects of public information campaigns is the frequency with which unsubstantiated generalizations are used in support of an impact of a program rather than more systematically, objectively generated evidence. A statement in a recent editorial [38, p. 303] is a good example: "Cigarette smoking declined during the period 1967–1971 as a result of broadcasted antismoking information. The messages were discontinued following the ban on cigarette advertising. Shortly thereafter, consumption began to rise again." Many such statements about smoking and health are often made without reference to sources. Misconceptions or confusing information are thus often disseminated. A recent Task Force Report on Respiratory Diseases [89, p. 24] best summarizes the present situation involving the effectiveness of public information campaigns by stating, "Mass media have been used extensively in antismoking efforts, but exactly how they influence behavior is unclear."

In-School Educational Programs

As has been dealt with elsewhere by the present authors [28,29] there is a systematic effort to document and evaluate formal preventive programs in the schools. The experiences with direct smoking cessation programs, however, appear to be only imperfectly documented. Interpreting from our discussions with school educators, direct-cessation programs for students are usually voluntary and allied with some ongoing program of a local volunteer health agency. Such efforts are very difficult to evaluate in terms of their effectiveness in actually modifying the smoking behavior of school children.

An alarming proportion of the school population must be categorized as regular, habituated smokers. A survey published by the Department of Health, Education and Welfare [88] indicates that 15.3% of females and 15.8% of males between the ages of 12 and 18 smoke cigarettes on a regular basis and consider themselves to be regular smokers. If school health programs are to follow the current trend of linking educational objectives to behavioral change [2] then a realistic approach should involve data-based action programs designed in such a way that evaluations of their effectiveness can be made available to school health professionals at the intervention level.

The more traditional disciplinary approach to the control of smoking in the school setting has not been systematically explored, but appears at best to be ineffective [36] and may even contribute to the continuance of cigarette-smoking behavior in those students who are not offered viable alternative behaviors [63]. Studies which rigorously assess the effectiveness of current cessation programs of in-school cessation programs specifically designed for students may offer hypotheses concerning promising smoking control programs [3, 36, 92]. Since such programs will involve a population of established smokers within the framework of a multiple experimental–control group research design, a variety of cessation approaches can be evaluated. Even the development and incorporation of smoking cessation programs into a school health curriculum might offer at least useful retrospective data related to the initiation and maintenance of cigarette smoking behavior in those school children who are not exposed to primary prevention programs.

Legislative Action

Investigations delineating the relationship between legislative action and the elimination or reduction of smoking are almost nonexistent. This situation most likely exists because few laws or policies have been enacted primarily to modify smoking behavior. The majority of existing laws and regulations restricting smoking were instituted for such public safety concerns as fire prevention [76]. With an increasing demand for stricter prohibitions on smoking in public places, there would appear to be increasing opportunities to design research to evaluate the impact of such prohibitions, although no extensive behavioral studies of such control techniques appear to have been undertaken so far.

One regulation instituted by the Federal Trade Commission in 1970 in direct response to the health dangers of smoking is the ban on television and radio advertisements of cigarettes. Despite the potential significance of this ban, very little research concerned with its effects on smoking initiation or cessation has been conducted. At best it appears that only indirect data such as sales figures have been examined in this regard.

One reported observation is that for the past fifteen years tobacco taxes have steadily increased without any apparent effect on smoking behavior [15]. Yet, when Joyce *et al.* [44] in a recent study asked college students what effect an increase in cigarette taxes would have on smoking, a majority of smokers indicated that a 50% increase in cigarette taxes would cause them to reduce or stop their smoking. Nonsmoking subjects in this study indicated that high cigarette taxes would decrease the likelihood that they would initiate smoking. It is evident that more systematic evaluations of the effects of increasing cigarette taxes on smoking are needed.

The impact of governmental regulations on smoking is not the only area of legislative action requiring evaluation. The regulations and policies initiated by private industry deserve the attention of researchers as well. In fact, more employers are being pressured to regulate smoking on work sites. Although this pressure mainly reflects concern for the rights of nonsmoking employees, it may inadvertently contribute to quit-smoking efforts on the part of smoking employees.

Most approaches to the regulation of smoking appear to involve prohibition, with little attention being given to alternative types of policies. One interesting and promising alternative to policies that focus on prohibitions is illustrated in a recent study conducted by Rosen and Lichtenstein [73]. In this study, an incentive program was introduced by an owner of an ambulance company. Employees who did not smoke on the job during any given month would receive a $5 bonus, with accumulated monthly bonuses being matched at Christmas-time by the company. Twenty-seven of 31 male employees (12 smokers and 15 nonsmokers) voluntarily participated in the project. After 2 months of this program, 7 of the 12 original smokers had quit smoking, with 4 of the 12 still abstaining from smoking after one year. An interesting result is that the four nonparticipant smokers also reported reduced smoking.

The typical research design problem that the ambulance company study illustrates is the lack of comparisons of such alternative approaches to policies of prohibition. Also, this study depends on self-reports instead of a more direct measure of smoking. This dearth of reported studies clearly suggests that more research must be undertaken to determine the effects on smoking of various government and private sector policies and regulations.

Direct Cessation Programs

One area of smoking research which is reflected in much of the theoretical and applied literature is that of cessation. Such endeavors employ various strategies in their attempts to help people stop smoking.

An area of investigation very common in the smoking literature deals with the application of behavior modification. Behavior modification attempts to modify smoking behavior by applying variations of positive or negative reinforcers. An excellent recent review of the literature of the various behavior modification techniques in smoking programs is found in Bernstein and McAlister [9].

Behavior modification is usually focused on (1) decreasing the smoking behavior, or (2) developing or increasing an alternative nonsmoking behavior. Most investigations report attempts to connect conditioned aversive responses to smoking. Aversive conditioning is widely used with various types of addictive behaviors such as the use of hard narcotics, alcohol consumption, and with various other clinical problems, such as sexual deviancy. There are various kinds of aversion techniques used with smokers. They essentially consist of the presentation to the subject of one stimulus (e.g., image of the individual smoking) repeatedly followed by some aversive stimulus (depiction of cancer ward, cancerous lung, coronary care unit, etc.).

The rationale for using such techniques in modifying smoking behavior is that learned avoidance of certain conditions resulting from smoking might alter the smoking behavior itself. However, aversive techniques are only of limited value in permanently controlling addictive behaviors, and smoking is no exception [9].

The use of the rapid smoking technique [52] currently appears to be one of the most seriously considered control strategies. This procedure involves subjecting the smoker to an unpleasant environment filled with warm, smokey air in association with inhaling cigarette smoke every few seconds while concentrating on the resulting negative effects. Aside from the ethical issue involved with this procedure, such aversive techniques would not be recommended for individuals who should be under the greatest pressure to quit smoking (e.g., patients at high risk for cardiovascular disease or postmyocardial infarction patients). Such patients may not physically be able to tolerate this aversive control technique. This concern is specifically expressed by some investigators [35]. Although at least one other researcher [22] suggests that rapid smoking is relatively more effective than other smoking control strategies, others [8] qualify such assessments by pointing out certain features limiting the power of this treatment technique. They state: "It appears that rapid smoking, when employed with proper safeguards and combined with strong therapist support and positive expectation (and when continued at least until subjects are abstinent) is one of the more powerful techniques available. In the absence of these features, it is not clearly superior to other approaches [p. 15]."

Another behavior modification approach, which reflects more directly the orientation of B. F. Skinner [26], is the use of the so-called operant conditioning paradigm. Today, the focus of operant conditioning is increasingly on self-management [53], as opposed to various types of external control of the individual's behavior. Techniques now being widely advocated by behavior modifiers working with the operant conditioning paradigm emphasize the individual "taking over" the management of his or her own behavior. In the case of smoking behavior, the control spectrum might be from (a) the smoker becoming more dependent on external control by the physician or therapist and his or her assistant taking charge of all of the patient's smoking control program (the so-called "medical model"); (b) the smoker becoming less dependent on external control through a "therapeutic alliance" between the patient and smoking control therapist to diminish the possibility of the excessive dependency fostered by the "medical model"; or (c) either systematically weaning the patient away from dependency on the smoking control therapist once the dependency exists, or beginning with the premise of self-management as part of a smoking control program, minimizing external control elements in the program from the very beginning.

These self-management approaches include self-monitoring of smoking behavior (e.g., recording of time, place, situation of smoking, lighting up, etc.), environmental planning by the smoker (control of the stimulus conditions which might affect smoking such as arranging places where few temptations to smoke exist or the placing of messages encouraging continued nonsmoking behavior), and behavioral programming (e.g., contingency contracts, token economies, self-rewards, and self-punishments) strategies. The results of these self-programming strategies are systematically evaluated in a few short-term studies [5, 58]. Various clinical practitioners, based on data generated from poorly controlled investigations, report promising results [57]. Unfortunately, such investigations often involve a biased sample of patients (those who want to participate in such a program), lack long-term follow-ups, and may reflect the interpersonal style of the smoking control therapist or receptivity of the patient rather than anything implicit in the technique itself. New behavioral maintenance strategies to overcome the effects of "back-sliding" may be the most important new direction for research programs in this area [8].

Probably more studies are reported on cessation clinics than any other kind of smoking control programs. Such clinics employ a variety of methods, most of which usually involve a combination of influences on the smoker to quit smoking. Bernstein and McAlister [9] identify such influences as health information, encouragement, group therapy, moral support, social pressure, and suggestions for resisting temptations to smoke.

Cure rates are often described as "outstanding" in clinical programs. However, these assessments are also usually the result of relatively unsophisticated evaluations of the effects of the programs.

A third type of program related to smoking cessation involves the use of various drugs. To date, drug therapy appears to be at best of only short-term value in its capability for decreasing smoking. In fact, though results are not yet conclusive, nicotine appears to be influential in the *maintenance* of smoking behavior [30, 41, 42, 78]. Lobeline sulphate has been widely tested both alone and in combination with stimulants and tranquilizers to mimic the effects of nicotine. On the other hand, nicotine itself may be useful in decreasing cigarette smoking. Very recently, nicotine-bearing substitutes have been employed as smoking control devices [14, 77, 80], but cannot be meaningfully assessed until long-term investigations in the context of the smoker's life style are undertaken. Nevertheless, these studies suggest that continued attention to the possibility of providing nicotine to smokers in a safe and palatable form, maximizing its metabolized efficiency and blocking its reinforcing properties, is indeed justified and may result in useful adjuncts to treatment techniques focusing on nonpharmacological programs to control smoking [8].

Yet another type of cessation endeavor, which has received little attention in the literature surveyed, is that of individual counseling. Clinics often provide smoking control counseling, but usually heavy case loads dictate that counseling be conducted with groups rather than individuals. When individual counseling is employed, it is extremely difficult to evaluate, since different techniques as well as different client and setting characteristics make each counseling session idiosyncratic. Furthermore, personal counseling can be quite expensive and often provides no more than the instructional material that can be more inexpensively disseminated through self-instruction booklets, pamphlets, etc.

Organized group methods may also be of limited value because of the negative reactions to organized efforts to control smoking. For example, a 1974 Gallup poll [33] indicates that only about one-third of smokers who wish to quit smoking are interested in participating in organized group activities.

Other investigators have documented the demand for self-help materials [83, 84]. The National Clearinghouse on Smoking and Health's *Smoker's Aid to Nonsmoking* and *Smoker's Self-Test Kit* are intended to meet these demands. Of course, difficulties in measuring the effects of such self-help programs are obvious since any sort of systematic follow-up measures are difficult to obtain.

Finally, a wide variety of blatantly commercial programs have been promoted to aid the smoker in his or her attempt to quit smoking. These programs include those of profit-making organizations which employ many of the techniques already discussed. For example, the Schick Corporation utilizes behavior modification (aversive control) techniques such as the use of electric shock and rapid smoking. The cost of this program to the client is between $400 and $500. Another widely publicized organization, Smokenders, uses group therapy. Group reinforcement during the treatment itself and during later reunions of the treatment groups are expected to aid the smoker in his or her efforts to quit smoking. The average cost for this program is $175. Other available commercial aids include the actual reduction of nicotine content through the use of filters. Water Pik's "One-Step-at-a-Time" is one example.

The impact of these programs is difficult to measure since avowedly commercial organizations, possibly because of self-interest, may be threatened by external evaluation efforts. In-house evaluation of these programs, even if they are carefully implemented, would be suspect in the eyes of many investigators.

Regardless of what kind of cessation program is under consideration, great variability in cure rates is reported. Often this variability may be due to the uneven quality of reported evaluation procedures. As mentioned earlier, one critical evaluation component neglected by many investigators is a long-term follow-up. Schwartz [81], for example, points out that many evaluated programs are limited to 3- to 6-month follow-ups. Longer follow-ups have usually yielded disapointing results, which have caused at least some investigators [39] to question seriously the effectiveness of most treatments reported to date, as they indicate:

> In any case, it is apparent that our programs for modifying smoking behavior need some modifying themselves. Considering the preliminary selection of subjects involved, since presumably only the motivated present themselves for treatment, and considering that a sizable number of these in turn drop out before the completion of the treatment, is it a notable achievement that two-thirds of those who do succeed in stopping smoking are back at it within the following three months and that only one-fourth of them seem able to remain nonsmokers for any considerable period of time? Obviously, our treatment techniques need beefing up [p. 108].

Raw [72] discusses the self-proclaimed-as-successful Maudsley smoking clinic in England. It primarily employs three smoking cessation treatments: aversion therapy (the smoker is required to associate unpleasantness with the formerly pleasant experience of smoking), satiation (the smoker is required to rapidly smoke many cigarettes within a limited time period), and relaxation (the smoker learns to confront tense situations with relaxation rather than dependence on cigarettes). While aversion therapy and satiation have been the most effective techniques, even these methods are of limited success, because they apparently tend to be short-lived in their impact. From those who complete the program, only one in four remains a nonsmoker beyond one year. Disappointing long-term results are also generated by several other studies as well [23, 34, 93].

Such disappointing long-term results are not limited to behavior modification programs. After evaluating reports of various smoking control clinics featuring group support, hypnosis, use of tobacco substitutes and drugs, and information on the harmful effects of smoking, Maurer and Schwartz [56] conclude that most success rates after one year are only in the 25–30% range. Considering the ineffectiveness of these external support treatments, McAlister [57] questions whether self-help treatments will be any more effective.

One important area of smoking research which has unfortunately been neglected involves a determination of the reasons for the high rate of recidivism. As suggested earlier, the majority of smokers who truly wish to quit smoking can apparently quit temporarily. The maintenance of abstinence from cigarette smoking appears to be the crucial problem. Of the investigations reviewed, in the few instances where recidivism is reported, no explanations are generally offered. When attempts at explanation are made, they are rarely grounded in systematic observation. McAlister [57] suggests from the personal experience of his own counseling clients that temporary lapses of self-discipline resulting from self-pity or self-destructive cognitions may at least partially explain recidivism. In the domain of individual counseling, McAlister cites evidence [7, 45, 46, 79] that suggests that the constant interpersonal contact with a counselor, rather than the individual assuming responsibility, increases the client's susceptibility to relapse, although at least one investigator (Bakewell, Note B) does not appear to agree with this conclusion. McAlister's conclusion lends support for the self-management programs discussed earlier.

But these findings are especially disturbing when one considers that those participating in cessation programs are self-selected volunteers. Hunt and Matarazzo [39] elaborate on this self-selection problem. They point out that individuals who are initially in the program are clearly not representative of smokers as a whole. This observation is supported by the Gallup survey [33] referred to earlier, which found that only one-third of the smokers are "interested" in joining organized cessation programs. From among these potential participants in programs, it would be logical to assume that even a smaller percentage of these actually join programs.

The attrition or dropout problem further biases this sample. Certainly an intense, demanding program will increase the attrition rate. One report [66] confirms that most reported success rates are based only on those people who complete the program rather than on the total number of people who join the program. So, in sampling terms, a serious biased–sampling error already present through a self-selection volunteer process is further confounded. Shewchuck [85] reports an American Health Foundation study of smokers attending group therapy sessions, which dramatically demonstrates the sample attrition problem. In that study, only 44% of the original sample of clients completed the five therapy sessions. If success rates are based only on those finishing the programs, then clearly, reported results are inflated. As Schwartz and Dubitzky [83] point out, the criterion for success of a program is not only its effectiveness, but also its "holding power" on its participants.

In our review of many reports, we observed how reported results may be misleading since the criteria of success among programs vary. Obviously, program evaluators should be encouraged to standardize their criteria of success. The importance of such standardization is stressed by other reviewers as well [7, 52, 91]. One reviewer [85] even goes so far as to propose possible evaluation criteria. He suggests:

> 1) all individuals attending even one session must be counted and every effort made to reach all persons who began the program; 2) those persons who cannot be reached within a reasonable time (say one month) or after several attempts (say six) should be counted as failures; 3) follow-up periods should extend to one year after treatment, with interim data-collection points a) within one month and b) within six months after treatment ends; 4) at least four basic status groups should be reported on a) those who quit by the end of treatment and maintain this status for the entire year (success group), 3) those who make no change by the end of the treatment and make no change in their smoking status for the entire year (failure group), c) those who quit by the end of treatment but fluctuate throughout the year (recidivist group), d) those who do not quit by the end of treatment but who experience temporary quit periods throughout the year (fluctuate group) [p. 97].

Programs often cannot be properly assessed because of inadequate evaluation designs. Such inadequate designs also make it virtually impossible to differentiate between the effects of the programmed treatment and the spontaneous smoking control efforts of the subject. Many reports [13, 31, 48, 75] conclude that any reduction in smoking behavior is necessarily the result of the programmed treatment when, in fact, there is no control for any spontaneous efforts on the part of the smoker to stop. In a well conducted experiment, Marston and McFall [54] find that merely urging smokers to quit through their personal initiative is apparently as effective as a variety of other more elaborate external control modification techniques. Furthermore, after 6 months, those who quit smoking on their own are evidently no more susceptible to a smoking relapse than are those who have received an externally controlled treatment. If there is no control for the spontaneous efforts of the smoker to quit on his or her own while being exposed to an external programmed treatment, any reported success rates of a program should be qualified accordingly.

Paul [68] suggests than an "unaided effort" control group be incorporated in evaluations of smoking control programs. However, finding matched control groups is often extremely difficult. Therefore, it is not surprising that such control groups are not employed in many of the reported studies. Yet the fact remains that in the absence of such groups, we would have to agree with Bernstein [6] when he states, "Claims for success notwithstanding, this type of clinic activity tells us little or nothing about smoking behavior or the means by which it can be reliably modified. Thus, except for the smokers who are helped, most clinic procedures reported to date represent a great deal of wasted time and effort [p. 431]."

Berstein and McAlister [9] refer to "nonspecific" treatment factors contained in treatment settings. Here, they are pointing to nonprogrammed effects on the client such as suggestion, placebo effects, and optimistic expectations of the client that can produce results comparable to those of the specified treatment itself. Sipich et al. [86] support the notion that nonspecific treatment factors in themselves can have an impact on the smoker. They find that "monitoring control" and "attention placebo" are as effective in reducing smoking behavior as a planned treatment of covert sensitization. McFall and Hammen [59] also provide support for the influence of nonspecific treatments. These investigators observe that the nonspecific factors of motivation, structured participation, and self-monitoring can yield outcomes comparable to those obtained with more elaborate and specifically programmed stop-smoking procedures. In fact, they suggest that nonspecific treatment factors may account for smoking behavior changes attributed to most specified treatment programs. Paul [68] suggests a possible solution to this problem. He believes that an "attention placebo" control condition could be utilized which would be subject to the nonspecific factors of the treatment setting but not the specified treatment itself. Again, despite the immense difficulty in effectively obtaining a matched control group for still another generally uncontrolled variable, nonspecific treatment factors must be considered if adequate evaluations of programs are to be offered.

Occasionally, a specific type of treatment would appear to lend itself to the application of adequate controls. An excellent example of this is Rosenburg's study [74] which reports an affirmative evaluation of the effectiveness of Tabmint, an antismoking chewing gum. When this gum is chewed as tobacco smoke is inhaled, an unpleasant taste results. An experimental group of 30 subjects chewed a placebo gum. By comparing the subsequent smoking behavior of the two groups, the effectiveness of the gum can be assessed. The placebo gum condition should help control for nonspecific effects such as participating in an experiment.

To date, as suggested earlier at several points, the evaluation designs of most smoking cessation programs are not sufficiently precise to truly judge their worth. But even within the constraints of inadequate evaluations, the results of cessation programs are disappointing. For the health professional who is asked to recommend or even judge a program, there is very little basis for favoring one program over another. In fact, it would be difficult to recommend any program at all with any degree of confidence.

Longitudinal Comprehensive Programs

One important trend with some promise involves preplanned longitudinal, comprehensive studies in school settings by a large institution with a strong commitment to evaluation. While it is expected that results from such projects will be forthcoming eventually, the pressure to produce immediate and specific effects on smoking is somewhat lessened because they are being carried out in the context of long-range evaluation. Thus the investigator has the opportunity to design conceptually sound projects based on sophisticated models. Such studies are also fruitful in producing spinoff studies that test specific hypotheses, pinpoint effects, and eliminate unworkable approaches. Stringent preplanned evaluation is an integral part of the best of these in-school programs. While such long range programs, implemented and evaluated over substantial periods of time, are both costly and difficult to manage scientifically and logistically, the data produced have important implications in developing systematic theoretical concepts and in generating new research that comes closer to isolating the complex social, physiological, and psychological factors that underlie the smoking phenomenon. Generally, such programs are carried out so that the community continues to benefit from the program after its completion, since it provides pretested and evaluated materials for incorporation into school curricula.

One of the best known of the longitudinal, comprehensive studies is the National Clearinghouse for Smoking and Health's School Health Curriculum Project (based on the so-called Berkeley model) that has been introduced into more than 200 school districts in 28 states. The curriculum is based on results of empirically tested concepts related to smoking and health, and is being implemented in programs from kindergarten through seventh grade at the present time. Preplanned evaluation components of the program are just now beginning to yield results, showing a substantial relationship between enrollment and non-enrollment in the program, and smoking knowledge and behavior [66]. Specific descriptions of the implementation of this program in school settings are given by Edson [25], Caramanica et al. [17] and Albino and Davis [1]. Important aspects of the School Health Curriculum Project include student participation, community involvement, and a multimedia, multimethod approach. The Berkeley project's major innovation is direct student involvement in class activities in which they learn about the body and potential threats to its well-being. Unfortunately, in the past, this project has lacked comparison control groups and measures of actual smoking behavior because of its primary emphasis on increasing knowledge and creating constructive attitudes toward health. At this time, however, in addition to comparing enrollees and non-enrollees in the program, the comparative effects of the Berkeley model, and more traditional health curricula, are being evaluated.

The University of Illinois Antismoking Education Study [20, 21] has been underway for more than a decade. It has produced several smoking measurement instruments that have been used in a number of smoking studies. These instruments incorporate informational, attitudinal, and self-report behavioral components but have not been validated against more objective measures of actual smoking.

The Illinois Antismoking Educational Study generated several kinds of studies which address themselves to evaluating various in-school approaches to control smoking. For example, in one study, Irwin et al. [40] examine the relative impact of the regular classroom teacher as a smoking information communicator, compared with teachers especially trained in health communication. Although he finds that the classroom teacher was at least as effective as the specially trained teacher, more recent studies [87] do not necessarily support this conclusion. An intention-to-smoke measure was also developed as a result of the Illinois study. Using this measure, Laoye et al. [47] find that a 2-year projection of smoking could be successfully demonstrated. Merki [60] explores smoking behavior of rural high school students and finds that student smoking is related to parental smoking habits, participation in school group activities, and lower educational aspirations. In a 9-month participant–observation study, Newman's [63–65] results suggest that both covert and overt smoking are low-status activities for ninth grade girls and overt smoking is a low-status activity for boys.

Matthews [55] reports another major longitudinal study of 1691 students ages 10–17 in Canadian schools, in which students themselves design smoking control materials for younger students. The study also compares smoking habits, attitudes, economic, religious, educational and social factors, family background, age, and sex ratios of smokers and nonsmokers. The study demonstrates a positive relationship between such factors as peer and parental smoking behavior, and a negative relationship between smoking and religious activity. The technique of using older students in presenting smoking control programs for younger students appears to be promising. Since its inception, continuing evaluations of the study are reported regularly in Canadian public health journals [69–71]. Despite the promising elements in this study, it still contains deficiencies, such as the dependence on student self-reports of smoking rather than more valid indicators of actual smoking.

In Houston, as mentioned earlier, a 3-year longitudinal study [28,29] designed to train junior high school students to resist the pressures to smoke from peers, the media, and models of smoking parents has been completed. Also involved in this study are interventions that monitor smoking and communicate immediate physiological effects of smoking. A major purpose of the study is an effort to build into school curricula programs which use "inoculations" against pressures to smoke in lieu of fear arousal, information-centered programs. Results indicate that such intervention strategies, which are based on feedback from students themselves, incorporated into films, can be effective in deterring the onset of addicted smoking in junior high school students. While the Houston 3-year longitudinal study was preceded by a 10-week pilot study [29], further replications are being undertaken.

Terry and Woodward [87] have developed a comprehensive statewide health education curriculum project in Maryland. This project involves an integrated health education program with a broad conceptual approach and specifically defined and stated behavioral objectives for kindergarten through twelfth grade. The curriculum draws on resources from a multidisciplinary group including psychologists, physicians, public health officials, and educators. A pilot study attempted to establish whether students exposed to the curriculum make greater improvement in health knowledge, self-concepts, and attitudes about health than do students who have not been exposed to the program, and whether there is any measurable change in behavior of students so exposed. The pilot study involved 11 complete school systems and approximately 2500 students. Only those components of the curriculum that appeared to be useful in meeting the objectives of increased knowledge, enhanced self-concepts, and more positive attitudes toward health, and also led to noticeably changed health behaviors, were selected for full implementation. Other important criteria for selection included generalizability to different school populations (e.g., urban, suburban, rural) and teaching methods (regular classroom instruction, integration with other school subjects, etc.). Although an ongoing evaluation is being carried out as the program is implemented on a statewide basis, the effectiveness of such an approach must await long-term evaluation.

No attempt has been made in this section of the review to be exhaustive; rather, studies have been selected that are representative of efforts by universities, public health agencies, state and federal agencies and school systems to address the problem of cigarette smoking in children through long-term, multiphasic programs that attempt at some level to incorporate controlled evaluation (see Table 1).

Factors That Influence Initiation of and Maintenance of Smoking

Factors that may influence, directly or indirectly, the initiation and maintenance of cigarette smoking in children have always been an important area of interest to researchers. While these factors range over a wide area, the current literature reflects the influence of peers, the role of parental and sibling smoking behavior, and smoking versus nonsmoking behavior by significant others perceived as role models or exemplars by children (e.g., teachers, physicians, nurses) [12, 19, 25, 28, 29, 37, 50, 55, 62, 63, 64, 67, 94].

The best efforts at present appear to be related to long-term, multiphasic studies attempting to establish good baseline data, develop and test specific hypotheses using carefully controlled methods of investigation and objective measures of smoking behavior to supplement self-reports, and include follow up efforts to evaluate the program through several years of implementation.

The ideal program would follow the example of Sweden [81], where a 25-year effort has begun whose objective is to make those born in 1975 a nonsmoking generation. The program began in 1974 with expectant parents and is presently concentrating on withdrawal clinics and other

TABLE 1
State Legislation for 1976 and 1977 Concerned with Cigarette Smoking

Type of legislation	1976		1977	
	Introduced	Passed	Introduced	Passed
Limitations on smoking	68	4	133	12
Commerce of tobacco products	125	16	219	29
Control of smoking in public schools	7	1	16	1
Advertising Cigarettes	3	0	7	0
Sales to minors	8	0	5	1
Other	8	2	12	1
Total	215	23	392	44

measures to develop a nonsmoking environment for those children born in 1974. Educational efforts for adults and children, increased governmental control on advertising and marketing of tobacco products, and an all-out effort is being made to create a nonsmoking generation in a nonsmoking environment, supported by both governmental efforts and the general public.

Some Concluding Remarks

After examining the many current trends in smoking research, it is increasingly evident that focusing primarily on programs to persuade already addicted smokers to stop smoking will be of only limited value. One of the reasons for this appears to be a regression effect. Study after study suggests that it is clearly possible to persuade smokers to stop for varying lengths of time over a period of several months. These same studies (where adequate evaluative data are presented) either directly or indirectly support the notion that most former smokers will not continue to abstain from smoking. The number of individuals who can be expected to stop smoking permanently, whether through their own volition or with the assistance of external control programs, may be "bottoming out." In other words, it is possible that at psychological and/or physiological levels, a certain percentage of hard-core addicted smokers are literally unable to stop smoking permanently, regardless of the control programs to which they are exposed. This might very well be due to a differing degree of susceptibility to nicotine addiction. Decreased intake of nicotine which results from the use of low tar and nicotine cigarettes for such individuals may lead only to smoking additional cigarettes so the nicotine level they may require will be reached. In fact, the statistical evidence of the continued high *total* sales of cigarettes (despite fewer smokers in general) supports Schachter's [78] suggestion that this is a definite possibility.

Consequently, it would appear only logical to deal with the problem of influencing preaddictive smokers to curtail the incidence of smoking before they become addicted or nicotine-dependent, or to focus on preventing individuals from beginning to smoke in the first place. This would, of course, necessitate the increased targeting of smoking prevention programs to nonsmokers or preaddicted smokers, beginning with preteenaged children and progressing to teenagers. As our review of the literature clearly suggests, strategies for intervention with this group must move away from depending solely on fear arousal and the mere dissemination of facts about smoking. Preteens and teenagers must be taught to cope "on the spot" with the pressures to smoke that they encounter. Some of the early reports of investigations which utilize such a strategy seemed sufficiently promising so that then Secretary of Health, Education, and Welfare Joseph Califano decided to focus on such prevention programs in the newly created Office of Smoking and Health.

Finally, it is hoped that regardless of the goals of smoking control programs much more attention will be given to highly sophisticated evaluation of the truly long-term effects of these programs. Otherwise, we will develop overly optimistic views of the effectiveness of these programs, which in turn will lead to inappropriate policy decisions in both government and private agencies concerned with the smoking problem. The authors of this report completed one of the chapters in the 1979 United States Surgeon General's Report on Smoking and Health, which amplifies suggestions for further prevention strategies.

Reference Notes

A. Axelrod, S.; Hall, R. V.; Weiss, L.; & Rohrer, S. Use of Self-imposed Contingencies to Reduce the Frequency of Smoking Behavior. Paper presented at the Fifth Annual Meeting of the Association for the Advancement of Behavior Therapy, Washington, D.C., 1971.

B. Bakewell, H. The Relevance of Goal Setting in a Smoking Reduction Program. Paper presented at a meeting of the Western Psychological Association, Portland, Oregon, 1972.

References

1. Albino, J. and Davis, R.: A health education program that works. *Phi Delta Kappan* 57:256–259, 1975.
2. American Association of Health, Physical Education, and Recreation. Smoking education: The school's responsibility (position statement). *Journal of School Health* 41:444–445, 1971.
3. App, H.: Suggested guidelines for a high school smoking intervention clinic. *Journal of School Health* 43:221–224, 1973.
4. Auger, T. J.; Wright, E.; and Simpson, R. H.: Posters as smoking deterrents. *Journal of Applied Psychology* 56:169–171, 1972.
5. Berecz, J.: Modification of smoking behavior through self-administered punishment of imagined behavior: A new approach to aversive therapy. *Journal of Consulting and Clinical Psychology* 38:244–250, 1972.
6. Bernstein, D. A.: Modification of smoking behavior: An evaluative review. *Psychological Bulletin* 71:418–440, 1969.
7. Bernstein, D. A.: Modification of smoking behaivor: A search for effective variables. *Behavior Research and Therapy* 8:133–146, 1970.
8. Bernstein, D. A. and Glasgow, R. E.: The modification of smoking behavior. In O. F. Pomerleau and J. P. Brady, eds.: *Behavioral medicine: Theory and practice.* Baltimore: Williams & Wilkins, 1978.
9. Bernstein, D. A. and McAlister, A.: The modification of smoking behavior: Progress and problems. *Addictive Behavior* 1:89–102, 1976.

10. Best, J. A.: Tailoring smoking withdrawal procedures to personality and motivational differences. *Journal of Consulting and Clinical Psychology* 43:1-8, 1975.
11. Best, J. A. and Steffy, R. A.: Smoking modification procedures tailored to subject characteristics. *Behavior Therapy* 2:177-191, 1971.
12. Borland, B. L. and Rudolph, J. P.: Relative effects of low socio-economic status, parental smoking and poor scholastic performance among high school students. *Social Science and Medicine* 9:27-30, 1975.
13. Bozetti, L. P.: Group psychotherapy with addicted smokers. *Psychotherapy Psychosomatic* 20:172-175, 1972.
14. Brantmark, B.; Ohlin, P.; and Westling, H.: Nicotine-containing chewing gum as an anti-smoking aid. *Psychopharmacologia,* 31:191-200, 1973.
15. Brecher, R. and Brecher, E.: *Smoking—The great dilemma.* New York: The Public Affairs Committee, 1964.
16. Butler, M. and Paisley, W.: The potential of mass communication and interpersonal communication for cancer control. In *Cancer: The behavioral dimensions,* ed., J. W. Cullen and B. H. Fox, New York: Raven Press, 205-229, 1976.
17. Caramanica, V. P.; Feiler, E. G.; & Olsen, L. L.: Evaluation of the effects of performance based teacher education on the health knowledge and attitudes of fifth grade students. *Journal of School Health* 44:449-454, 1974.
18. Chen, T. L. and Rakip, W.: Are teachers prepared to implement smoking education in the schools? *Journal of School Health* 44:438-441, 1974.
19. Chen, T. L. and Rakip, W. R.: The effect of the teachers' smoking behavior on their involvement in smoking education in the schools. *Journal of School Health* 45:455-461, 1975.
20. Creswell, W. H., Jr.; Huffman, W. J.; Stone, D. B.; Merki, D. J.; and Newman, I. M.: University of Illinois anti-smoking education study. *Illinois Journal of Education* 69:27-37, 1969.
21. Creswell, W. H., Jr.; Stone, D. B.; Huffman, W. J.; and Newman, I. M.: Anti-smoking education study at the University of Illinois. *Health Reports* 86:565-576, 1971.
22. Danaher, B. G.: Research on rapid smoking: Interim summary and recommendations. *Addictive Behaviors* 2:151-166, 1977.
23. Delarue, N. C.: A study in smoking withdrawal—The Toronto smoking withdrawal *study center—Description of activities. Canadian Journal of Public Health* 64:515-519, 1973.
24. Dubren, R.: Evaluation of a televised stop smoking clinic. *Public Health Reports* 92:81-84, 1977.
25. Edson, L.: Schools attacking the smoking problem. *American Education* 9:10-14, 1973.
26. Evans, R. I.: *The making of psychology: Discussions with creative contributors.* New York: Alfred A. Knopf, 1976a.
27. Evans, R. I.; Rozelle, R. M.; Lasater, T. M.; Dembroski, T. M.; and Allen, B. P.: Fear arousal, persuasion and actual versus implied behavior change: New perspective utilizing a real-life dental hygiene program. Journal of Personality and Social Psychology 16:220-227, 1970.
28. Evans, R. I.; Rozelle, R. M.; Maxwell, S. E.; Raines, B. E.; Dill, C. A.; Guthrie, T. J.; Henderson, A. H.; and Hill, P. C.: Social modeling films to deter smoking in adolescents: Results of a three-year field investigation. *Journal of Applied Psychology,* in press.
29. Evans, R. I.; Rozelle, R. M.; Mittelmark, M. B.; Hansen, W. B.; Bane, A. L.; and Havis, J.: Deterring the onset of smoking in children: Knowledge of immediate physiological effects and coping with peer pressure, media pressure and parent modeling. *Journal of Applied Social Psychology* 8:126-135, 1978.

30. Eysenck, H. J.: Personality and the maintenance of the smoking habit. In *Smoking behavior: Motives and incentives*, ed. W. L. Dunn, pp. 113–146, Washington D.C.: V. H. Winston & Sons, 1973.
31. Filbey, E. E.; Reed, K. E.; and Lloyd, F. T.: An inpatient smoking control service. *Hospital Management* 103:60–64, 1967.
32. Fishbein, M.: Consumer beliefs and behavior with respect to cigarette smoking: A critical analysis of the public literature. Report prepared for the staff of the Federal Trade Commission, 1977 (unpublished).
33. Gallup International, Inc.: *Gallup opinion index*, Report No. 108, 20–21, 1974.
34. Guilford, J.: Group treatment versus individual initiative in the cessation of smoking. *Journal of Applied Psychology* 56:162–167, 1972.
35. Hauser, R.: Rapid smoking as a technique of behavior modification: Caution in the selection of subjects. *Journal of Consulting and Clinical Psychology* 42:625–626, 1974.
36. Herzog, M.: Seminar and suspension? Education as punishment for teen-age smokers? *Clearing House* 45:146–149, 1970.
37. Hill, D.: Peer group conformity in adolescent smoking and its relationship to affiliation and autonomy needs. *Australian Journal of Psychology* 23:189–199, 1971.
38. Holleb, A.: Do you mind if I smoke? (Editorial). *Cancer Journal for Clinicians* 25:303–304, 1975.
39. Hunt, W. A. and Matarazzo, J. D.: Three years later: Recent developments in the experimental modification of smoking behavior. *Journal of Abnormal Psychology* 81:107–114, 1973.
40. Irwin, R. P.; Creswell, W. H.; and Stauffer, D. J.: The effect of the teacher and three different classroom approaches on seventh grade students' knowledge, attitudes and beliefs about smoking. *Journal of School Health* 40:355–359, 1970.
41. Jarvik, M. E.: The role of nicotine in the smoking habit. In *Learning mechanisms in smoking*, ed. A. Hunt, pp. 33–49, Chicago: Aldine, 1970.
42. Jarvik, M. E.: Further observations on nicotine as the reinforcing agent in smoking. In *Smoking behavior: Motives and incentives*, ed. W. L. Dunn, pp. 33–49. Washington, D.C.: V. H. Winston & Sons, 1973.
43. Jarvik, M. E.; Cullen, J. W.; Gritz, E. R.; Vogt, T. M.; and West, L. J., eds.: *Research on smoking behavior*. Washington: Public Health Service, 1977.
44. Joyce, A. M.; O'Rourke, T. W.; and O'Rourke, D. M.: Assessment of the perceived impact of taxation upon smoking behavior: Implications for health education. *Journal of Drug Education* 6:231–240, 1976.
45. Koenig, K. P. and Master, J.: Experimental treatment of habitual smoking. *Behavior Research and Therapy* 3:235–243, 1965.
46. Kopel, S. and Lichtenstein, E.: Effects of self-control, booster sessions, and cognitive factors on the maintenance of smoking reduction, (abstract #662). *1974 Directory of ongoing research in smoking and health*. Bethesda: National Clearinghouse on Smoking and Health, 1974.
47. Laoye, J.; Cresswell, W. H.; and Stone, D. B.: A cohort study of 1205 secondary school smokers. *Journal of School Health* 42:47–52, 1972.
48. Lawton, M. P.: Group methods in smoking withdrawal. *Archives of Environmental Health* 14:258–265, 1970.
49. Leventhal, H.: Experimental studies of anti-smoking communications. In *Smoking, health, and behavior*, eds, E. F. Borgatta and R. R. Evans, pp. 95–121. Chicago: Aldine Press, 1968.
50. Levitt, E. E. and Edwards, J. A.: A multivariate study of correlative factors in youthful cigarette smoking. *Developmental Psychology* 3:5–11, 1970.

51. Lichtenstein, E. and Glasgow, R. E.: Rapid smoking: Side effects and safeguards. *Journal of Consulting and Clinical Psychology* 45:815–821, 1977.
52. Lichtenstein, E.; Harris, D. E.; Birchler, G. R.; Whal, J. M.; and Schmahl, D. P.: Comparison of rapid smoking, warm smoky air, and attention placebo in the modification of smoking behavior. *Journal of Consulting and Clinical Psychology* 40:92–98, 1973.
53. Mahoney, M. J.: *Cognition and behavior modification.* Cambridge, Mass: Ballinger, 1974.
54. Marston, A. R. and McFall, R. M.: Comparison of behavior modification approaches to smoking reduction. *Journal of Consulting and Clinical Psychology* 36:153–162, 1971.
55. Matthews, V. L.: *The Saskatoon smoking study: Habits and beliefs of children in grades seven and eight about smoking.* Saskatoon: University of Saskatchewan, 1974.
56. Maurer, H. and Schwartz, J. L.: Do smokers' clinics really work? *Science Digest* 78:72–76, 1975.
57. McAlister, A.: Helping people quit smoking. In *Applying behavioral science to cardiovascular disease,* ed. A. Enelow. New York: American Heart Association, 1975.
58. McFall, R. M.: The effects of self-monitoring on normal smoking behavior. *Journal of Consulting and Clinical Psychology* 35:135–142, 1970.
59. McFall, R. M. and Hammen, C. L.: Motivation, structure, and self-monitoring: Role of nonspecific factors in smoking reduction. *Journal of Consulting and Clinical Psychology* 37:80–86, 1971.
60. Merki, D. J.: The effects of two educational methods and message themes on rural youth smoking behavior. *Journal of School Health* 38:448–454, 1968.
61. National Clearinghouse for Smoking and Health Publications: *Adult use of tobacco.* Washington, D.C.: U.S. Department of Health, Education, and Welfare, Public Health Services, 1966.
62. Newman, A.: How teachers see themselves in the exemplar role in smoking education as evidenced by their attitudes and practice. *Journal of School Health* 41:275–279, 1971.
63. Newman, I. M.: Adolescent cigarette smoking as compensatory behavior. *Journal of School Health* 40:316–321, 1970a.
64. Newman, I. M.: Peer pressure hypothesis for adolescent cigarette smoking. *School Health Review* 1:15–18, 1970b.
65. Newman, I. M.: Status configurations and cigarette smoking in a junior high school. *Journal of School Health* 1:15–18, 1970c.
66. Office of Cancer Communications: *The smoking digest: Progress report on a nation kicking the habit.* Bethesda: National Cancer Institute, 1977.
67. Palmer, A. B.: Some variables contributing to the onset of cigarette smoking among junior high school students. *Social Science and Medicine* 4:358–366, 1970.
68. Paul, G. L.: Behavior modification research: Design and tactics. In *Behavior Therapy: Appraisal and Status,* ed. C. M. Franks, pp. 29–62. New York: McGraw-Hill, 1969.
69. Piper, G. W.; Jones, J. A.; and Matthews, V. L.: The Saskatoon smoking project—The model. *Canadian Journal of Public Health* 61:503–508, 1970.
70. Piper, G. W.; Jones, J. A.; and Matthews, V. L.: The Saskatoon smoking study— Results of the first year. *Canadian Journal of Public Health* 62:432–440, 1971.
71. Piper, G. W.; Jones, J. A.; and Matthews, V. L.: The Saskatoon smoking study— Results of the second year. *Canadian Journal of Public Health* 65:127–129, 1974.
72. Raw, M.: The psychological treatment of smoking and current work at the Maudsley smoker's clinic. *Health* 12:23–26, 1976.
73. Rosen, G. M. and Lichtenstein, E.: Employee incentive program to reduce cigarette smoking. *Journal of Consulting and Clinical Psychology* 45:957–959, 1977.
74. Rosenburg, A.: An investigation into the effect on cigarette smoking of a new antismoking chewing gum. *Journal of International Medical Research* 5:68–70, 1977.

75. Ross, C. A.: Smoking withdrawal research clinics. *American Journal of Public Health* 57:677–681, 1967.
76. Rozovsky, L. E.: Smoking and the law. *Dimensions in Health Service* 52:58–60, 1975.
77. Russell, M. A. H.; Wilson, C.; Feyerabend, C.; and Cole, P. V.: Effect of nicotine chewing gum on smoking behavior and as an aid to cigarette withdrawal. *British Medical Journal* 2:391–393, 1976.
78. Schachter, S.: Pharmacological and psychological determinants of smoking. *Annals of Internal Medicine* 88:104–114, 1978.
79. Schmahl, D. P.; Lichtenstein, E.; and Harris, D. E.: Successful treatment of habitual smokers with warm, smoky air, and rapid smoking. *Journal of Consulting and Clinical Psychology* 38:105–111, 1972.
80. Schneider, N. G.; Popek, P.; Jarvik, M. E.; and Gritz, E. R.: The use of nicotine gum during cessation of smoking. *American Journal of Psychiatry* 134:439–440, 1977.
81. Schwartz, J. L.: Smoking cures: Ways to kick an unhealthy habit. In *Cancer: The behavioral dimensions*, eds. J. W. Cullen, B. H. Fox, and R. N. Isom. New York: Raven Press, 1976.
82. Schwartz, J. L.: Recent developments in smoking cessation methods. In *National Conference on Smoking and Health*, eds., National Interagency Council on Smoking and Health, pp. 101–113, 1970.
83. Schwartz, J. L. and Dubitzky, M.: *Psychosocial factors involved in cigarette smoking and cessation.* Berkeley: Institute for Health Research, 1968.
84. Schwartz, J. L. and Dubitzky, M.: Maximizing success in smoking cessation methods. *American Journal of Public Health* 59:1392–1399, 1969.
85. Shewchuck, L. A.: Problems of high-risk populations and high-risk nonresponders: Smoking behavior. In *Cancer: The behavioral dimensions*, eds. J. W. Cullen, B. H. Fox, and R. N. Isom, pp. 93–99. New York: Raven Press, 1976.
86. Sipich, J. F.; Russell, R. K.; Tobias, L.: A comparison of covert sensitization and "nonspecific" treatment in the modification of smoking behavior. *Journal of Behavior Therapy and Experimental Psychiatry* 5:201–203, 1974.
87. Terry, D. E. and Woodward, L. H.: A five-year plan for designing and implementing a statewide health education curriculum in Maryland. *Journal of School Health* 56:282–285, 1976.
88. U.S. Public Health Service: *Teenage smoking. National patterns of cigarette smoking, ages 12 through 18, in 1972 and 1974* DHEW publication no. (NIH) 76–931. U.S. Department of Health, Education & Welfare, Public Health Service, National Institute of Health, 1976. Washington, D.C.
89. U.S. Public Health Service. *Respiratory diseases: Task force report on prevention, control, and education* DHEW publication no. (NIH) 77–1248. U.S. Department of Health, Education & Welfare, Public Health Services, National Institute of Health, 1977. Washington, D.C.
90. Warner, K. E.: Effects of anti-smoking campaign on cigarette consumption. *American Journal of Public Health* 67:645–650, 1977.
91. Whitman, T. L.: Modification of chronic smoking behavior: A comparison of three approaches. *Behavior Research and Therapy* 7:257–263, 1969.
92. Winett, R.: *Parameters of deposit contracts in the modification of smoking.* Unpublished doctoral dissertation, State University of New York at Stony Brook, Stony Brook, N.Y., 1971.
93. Winston, S.: Easing the smoking dilemma for secondary schools (or) I'll take four hours after school. *Phi Delta Kappan* 52:181–182, 1970.
94. Wohlford, P.: Initiation of cigarette smoking: Is it related to parental behavior? *Journal of Consulting and Clinical Psychology* 34:148–151, 1970.

Working Groups

Life Events, Stress, and Social Milieu

GEORGE STONE [1]

Placing 10 persons purposefully chosen for heterogenous backgrounds in an unilluminated room for three hours with the assignment to appraise the state of our knowledge concerning stress creates a good deal of stress for the participants. In this case, we coped admirably with our situation, and even arrived at some agreements while keeping our physiological and affective responses in bounds.

In this brief summary, I make no attempt to convey the temporal sequence of ideas in our wide-ranging discussion. I have tried to capture the major themes that we addressed, to give some idea of the degree of engagement or concern they elicited, and some notion of the extent of agreement we reached about them. I refrain almost entirely from attributing statements, questions, and positions to individual participants, since they are unable to check the accuracy of my listening, distilling, and reporting.

Three types of concerns were apparent in our discussion: (1) theoretical issues about the nature of the variables and their relationships to each other; (2) methodological issues about how these variables could be measured, and their influences separated; and (3) practical issues regarding the consequences for human lives of our efforts to understand. Predictably, these issues were intertwined, and our discussion of them was mingled with the various substantive topics we discussed.

With regard to theory, we noted that there were several lines leading to our present state of knowledge (or confusion). Endocrinologists, epidemi-

---

[1] This working group was chaired by George Stone, who compiled this report with the assistance of Tom Garrity and Bert Kaplan. Others participating in the working group were F. Fitz, B. Fox, J. House, F. Morrison, J. Singer, G. Solomon, S. Taylor, and C. Wortman.

ologists, physiological psychologists, personality psychologists, and "literary psychologists" (or psychological novelists) have defined variables in very different ways, and have articulated questions in such a variety of ways that it is not simple to determine whether or not their conclusions agree. Our major recommendation, that the Academy provide an opportunity for spokespersons of these various approaches to confront one another, was much influenced by this recognition. We were not in full agreement among ourselves as to the desirability or the possibility of developing a single comprehensive theory at this time.

Several important methodological issues were addressed. We were all in agreement about the urgency of developing clearly defined, objective measures of all relevant variables and of seeing common measures adopted quite uniformly in order to permit comparison of results among various groups of investigators. It does *not* seem possible at this stage of our understanding to agree on a single set of instruments, but rather to seek a few that can be added on to the batteries of measures developed for specific studies in order to permit cross-comparisons. We did not reach agreement as to whether we would do better to select such standard instruments from among those presently available, with which considerable amounts of data have already been collected, or to design new and improved instruments at this time, making use of the information collected with instruments that are generally agreed to have important shortcomings.

Some participants urged that we place as little reliance as possible on variables measured by self-report. Others stressed the critical importance of variables such as affective state, attributions of blame, and meanings of environmental stressors that can *only* be tapped through verbal report.

Other methodological issues were at the level of experimental design. The need for new designs that would free us from dependence on cross-sectional, retrospective studies was stressed by some. Others emphasized the risks of turning too completely to *prospective* designs in view of the relatively low levels of relative risk associated with psychosocial factors, the complexities of their interaction, and the poor degree of specification we have thus far achieved in isolating the important variables.

A second design issue arises from the confounding of variables in our studies. When populations experience the stresses of social transition during development and urbanization, they also encounter the environmental pollutants that are associated with life in industrial societies. Sex differences in neuroendocrine responses to certain kinds of stress might be the result of physiological/genetic differences between the sexes, but equally well they might arise from different social meanings attributed to the "identical" stressor events by most members of the two sexes.

A related problem is the difficulty for research designs posed by feedback from one phase of the process being studied to earlier stages. For example, the very conditions that constitute the stressor (terminal illness, say) may alter the conditions of social support available to the patient under study during the period of the study, as the family turns away from the dying person. Or the impact of stress at one time may alter the individual's capacity to deal with later stressors. These problems call for research designs that can cope with a dynamic system.

There was some difference of opinion as to the relative merits of focusing sharply on relationships between variables that are thought to be closely linked by presumptive causal mechanisms, such as precisely defined stressor events and the pattern of physiological response to it, thereby gaining greater predictability or control over outcomes in the studies; seeking relationships that span the entire causal chain between potentially stressful events (life events) and outcomes measured in terms of disease processes. Those who practice the latter strategy might have to be content with very tenuous relationships, but they would avoid the risks of excluding important but previously unnoticed factors and also of concentrating on the elucidation of short-term effects of stress that turned out to be inconsequential in the development of disease. Issues of this kind will not be resolved on an either/or basis, of course, but in terms of allocation of resources between the two kinds of studies.

Substantive Issues

It is not surprising that in the course of three hours we were unable to develop a framework that was completely agreeable to all participants. The organization used to present these remarks is that of the recorder, and some of its aspects were challenged directly by the viewpoints of some participants. The issues are posed by three questions submitted to the work group by Bert Kaplan:

1. What is stress?
2. What is abnormal stress?
3. How is stress handled?

Dr. Kaplan later augmented these questions with four more:

4. How does stress lead to illness?
5. How does stress and the response to it vary at different points in the life cycle?
6. How can we intervene to modify stress?
7. What are the various psychobiological models of disease and how are they related?

In our discussion we noted, but also fell victim to the tendency, on occasion, to confuse stress as stimulus or input to the organism with the organism's response to it. Conceptually, we can identify (a) an external stressor; (b) the social and physical context in which the stress occurs; (c) the social, psychological, and biological characteristics of the stressed individual; (d) the immediate response of the individual to the stressor (as modulated by context and individual characteristics); and (e) the long-term changes, pathological or otherwise, that result from sustained or repeated occurrences of the stressor. In concept, research on stress and illness can investigate the relationships between any two, or more, of these sets of variables (those describing stressors, contexts, individuals, responses, and long-term outcomes), subject to the methodological difficulties already mentioned. A number of participants, however, took the position that it is impossible to define or measure stress independent of the situational and individual contexts in which it occurs. Life-events measures, which at least in their earlier forms attempted to do so, were looked upon with considerable disfavor by some of these critics. An alternative view, which we did not succeed in formulating very completely, held that it was desirable to *seek* independent descriptions of events, but to recognize that these descriptions could not accurately predict stress responses without taking account of the context variables.

In part out of these views of what was possible, there were those who felt that an empirical investigation of the links between life events and illness, without regard to the intervening steps, was the appropriate strategy. There were also participants who urged that attention be paid to illness as a stress, and to the ways in which individuals cope with the changes in life style that it imposes on them, and the ways in which social support operates in these situations.

In general agreement about the difficulties of defining and measuring stressful impacts on the individual, we nevertheless took note of several properties of such situations that were associated with the degree of the response. At the least, we can say with some assurance that physical intensity of stimuli, their duration, frequency, predictability, and controllability all tend to affect responses, although not in simple, unidimensional ways. It was also recognized that identical stimulus conditions may be sought out under certain social circumstances or by certain individuals and avoided in other cases.

Variables of social support and individual ways of handling or coping with stress were of central interest to a number of those present. Social support is perhaps best conceived as a contextual variable, while individual coping is a response. But the ability of the individual to cope is clearly influenced greatly—if not determined—by characteristics and circumstances of the individual at the time the stress occurs. Among the kinds of variables descriptive of individuals that were mentioned as having importance were (*a*) life-cycle stage of development at the time of stress; (*b*) life-style (for which it was agreed no satisfactory measures are now available); (*c*) prior experience with the present stress or with stress in general; (*d*) and competence and motivation for handling the stress. We noted that prior experience could either enhance or impair the individual's capacity to deal with stress, and the suggestion was made that the determination of which result would occur was based—in part, at least—on whether the individual had been successful or unsuccessful in mastering the stressor in earlier encounters, with consequent impact on both competence and motivation. Attributions of meaning and other cognitive mediators would also be greatly influenced by prior experience (both direct and vicarious).

In considering *response* to stress, it was noted that there are at least three broad categories: effects on work performance, on affective states, and on physiological and neuroendocrine systems. Influences on these three types of variables are by no means perfectly correlated, and there is already evidence to indicate that certain types of stressors have differential impact on the three areas of response. Recognition of this fact will undoubtedly pose value dilemmas for future interventionists, who will have to decide whether to design stress-management procedures in order to maximize work output or minimize affective distress or physiological arousal. With regard to value choices, it was also suggested by one participant that students of stress may be at risk of imposing their own values in developing interventions. They might, for example, have a belief that denial is not a good way to approach life, even if it does protect the body from certain physiological costs of the stress response. A spirited, if brief and inconclusive, discussion of terminal and instrumental values and of short term and long term costs ensued. The issue of positive stress, good stress, or *eustress*, to use Selye's term, came up here (and at some other points). It was acknowledged that just because people choose to do something, it is not necessarily adaptive. But there was a viewpoint that mastered stress could lead to growth of the individual, as well as possibly providing protection against future stress.

The processes by which experiential effects exerted their influence on bodily systems, and the ways in which short-term effects led to long-term effects were of primary interest to a few of our participants. A separation of variables was noted in the course of disease that resembled the separation of acute responses to stress: there may be independent variations in *progression* of the disease, in its *incapacitating* effect on the individual, and on the degree to which it responds to medical treatment. Exploration of the factors that affect these variables will be of importance.

In the time available to our work group we were not able to take inventory of what we know and what we do not know about the various questions implicit in this formulation of the area. We did observe that the different traditions of research and kinds of interests of investigators gave rise to different kinds of knowledge. We felt that there would be substantial value in providing an opportunity for representatives of the different models of stress and of coping with stress to confront jointly a series of questions about the area. To this end we adopted as a formal recommendation to the Academy that one of the sessions at the next meeting be devoted to defining the state of the art regarding models of stress, addressing at least the issues of the definition of normal and abnormal stress, successful and unsuccessful coping, the relation of stress to the development of disease, and methods of modifying stressful, noxious situations.

Physiological Concomitants of Behavioral Processes

JOHN I. LACEY[1]

All of us, I can safely say, were exceedingly pleased at the opportunity to get together. I cannot convey to you easily the vigor and collegiality of the discussion despite an almost inevitable terminologic confusion, and at-first-unverbalized hidden assumptions. The discussions proceeded so well and with such good feeling that the group formally recommends that it be made a permanent working group. The issues were so complex that we would like to continue talking to each other.

By universal agreement, we rapidly dropped the last part of the title of our workshop. We discussed physiological concomitants of behavior processes in general, not just in the context of neoplastic and cardiovascular disease. We considered the general problems inherent in the acquisition of data dealing with concomitant behavioral and physiological processes; and, more importantly, the problems that are raised in interpreting such data to further our understanding of what we conceived of as two separable phases: first, the *development* of a frank clinical disorder, and second, the *maintenance* of the disease process.

The problems we addressed were divisible into two groups, technological and theoretical. The theoretical verged on the philosophical and the logical. The basic problem seems to be this: A wide variety of possibly relevant, but many times irrelevant, physiological changes occur with a wide variety of behavioral processes and in a wide variety of stimulating conditions. The physiological variables can be rather more easily and logically

[1] This working group was chaired by John I. Lacey, who compiled this report. Others participating in the working group were T. Dembrowski, R. Eliot, B. Hamburg, B. Lacey, N. Miller, P. Obrist, H. Pardes, R. Rose, A. Shapiro, S. Weiss, and R. Williams.

293

categorized than the behavioral. Even the physiological variables, however, often are not easily understood in terms of a functional, integrative, organ-system approach, which seems to be necessary. Because "we don't know how to cut the pie," a central problem is: What shall we measure, and when, and under what stimulating conditions?

The discussion, unprogrammed and spontaneous as it was, did not proceed in a smooth linear way. But a recurrent theme emerged and finally was labeled. What is needed, we felt, was a *taxonomy* of environmental challenges.

"Stress" and "arousal" are tautological and circular concepts as presently employed. While most of us seem to acknowledge this (at least partially) when we use these words, we often hastily add that "of course, we all know what we mean." We do not. We need to characterize objectively and with a very high degree of specificity those behavioral circumstances which elicit quantifiable physiological changes relevant to disease processes. We need to characterize objectively and with a high degree of specificity (like the Type A–Type B specification) the processes by which the reacting organism appraises the meaning and significance, the saliency, for himself or herself, of the stimulating conditions; and, with equal specificity, the determinants, (ranging from the genetic to the sociocultural) of the ways in which the organism then responds. Our current knowledge and theory is inadequate to meet this need. Perhaps, as Dr. Eliot suggested in his paper, we really need to go directly to the clinical patients, to listen with sympathy and understanding to the patients' reports of what was the "straw that broke the camel's back."

It was the consensus of the group that large amounts of basic descriptive data were still needed, and that behavioral investigations should be expanded in at least two ways. First, it was noted that behavioral scientists have favorite ways of proceeding with experiments, but these ways may or may not be clinically relevant. In so far as possible, systematic investigations should attempt to elicit analogies to dose–response curves. Do increasing increments in magnitude and frequency of challenge result in systematic variations of response? This might be one criterion for tagging disease-relevant physiological processes. Second, in quantitating the responses of individuals in the stimulating conditions, we need to know whether we are dealing with a *state* variable—a momentary phasic reaction specifically or situationally produced, or a *trait* variable—a repeatedly emerging response pattern generalizable over a wide variety of circumstances.

A potentially stressful challenge, it seems clear, is in fact stressful only to the extent that it engages the complex motivational and need structure of the individual. We need, therefore, to elucidate techniques and provide interpretive models to judge the fit, the matching points between, the potential challenge and the challenged organism.

These are highly abstract considerations. They perhaps are no different from those that would have emerged in similar discussions 10, 20, or even 30 years ago. The difference is that today the emphases seem to be on the need for specificity and for detail in both the behavioral and physiological domains, on the concept of multiple risk factors rather than linear causation, and on the inclusion of sociocultural factors, in particular social support systems, as determinants of the ultimate clinical outcome. Finally, the processes by which repeated phasic acute responses become transformed into chronic disease states need to be elucidated.

So much for the abstract considerations. The technical problems are much more easily described. We all saw a need for an intensive effort in the development of reliable noninvasive measurement devices, miniaturized to the point of portability, so our observations need not be limited to fixed laboratory environments. We saw needs for standardization of measurement techniques, for selection of the relevant physiological variables, for consideration of circadian and ultradian cycle variations, and for the elucidation of principles to be followed in setting up control groups. None of these is an easy problem.

Animal Models in Research

J. ALAN HERD[1]

The participants in the workshop on use of animal models have a broad range of experience in biobehavioral research. Several of the participants have made important contributions to our understanding of physiological processes such as control of heart rate, blood pressure, and renal function under various behavioral conditions. Several have contributed to our knowledge of pathological processes such as tumor formation and production of peptic ulcer using behavioral procedures. Others have demonstrated important neurophysiological and endocrine mechanisms in production of pathological conditions in animals. All are experienced in use of behavioral and physiological techniques to induce pathophysiological processes in animals that are similar to those seen in human subjects with cardiovascular disease.

After a brief review of recent progress in biobehavioral research using animal models the participants settled upon three topics for more extensive discussion: (a) contributions from research in animal models to behavioral medicine; (b) study of intervening variables in behavioral processes influencing pathological conditions; and (c) recommendations for future directions in use of animal models for biobehavioral research. A brief abstract of our discussion is presented as the report from this workshop.

Three contributions from research in animal models were discussed extensively. The first concerned the determinants of behavior studied using classical and operant-conditioning procedures in animals. Results of studies

---

[1] This working group was chaired by J. Alan Herd, who compiled this report. Others participating in the working group were R. Ader, D. Anderson, B. Dworkin, B. Newberry, V. Riley, N. Scheiderman, and H. Weiner.

297

with animals have introduced much of our knowledge concerning conditional and unconditional responses, stimulus control, principles of reinforcement, extinction, and punishment. These principles of behavior form the foundation for behavior therapy and biofeedback procedures in human subjects. Here is an outstanding example of contributions from animal research to behavioral medicine.

The second contribution from animal models that was addressed concerned pathophysiology and treatment of arterial hypertension. Results of studies with animals have revealed neurophysiological, cardiac, renal, and endocrine mechanisms regulating blood pressure that are influenced by behavioral procedures. These physiological and behavioral processes studied in animal models form the foundation for behavioral treatment of arterial hypertension in human patients.

The third contribution that was addressed concerned the pathophysiology of atherosclerosis. Experiments with animals have provided information about the basic process of atherosclerosis through studies of nutrition, lipid biochemistry, and pathology of aorta, coronary arteries, and carotid arteries. Studies of arterial pathology under the influence of neurogenic and humoral factors form the foundation for our understanding of intervening variables linking behavioral processes and atherosclerosis.

An important contribution of animal models to biobehavioral research is the opportunity to study intervening variables. Many studies of physiological, biochemical, and pathological processes require control conditions and invasive procedures that are unacceptable for human subjects. Measurements of blood pressure and regional blood flow frequently require restraint or implantation of instruments. Measurements of metabolic activity and organ function frequently require extensive removal of tissues. Gross and microscopic studies of tissue structure also require removal of tissues. In addition, precise control of independent variables frequently requires highly standardized conditions. Genetic characteristics often must be controlled, and environmental conditions such as diet, physical activity, temperature, and social structure also influence physiological variables. Behavioral experiments, in particular, often demand precise control of environmental conditions and involve complex schedules of reinforcement. Specific examples of animal models used for biobehavioral research were discussed, and many applications for future research were suggested during the workshop.

Future directions in the use of animal models for biobehavioral research appear to depend upon the application of existing models to new areas of research. Many behavioral scientists have extensive experience with animal models in study of behavior but little experience with physiological and biochemical techniques. Similarly, many biomedical scientists are unfamiliar with behavioral techniques. It was the opinion of participants in the workshop that new applications of animal models to biobehavioral research will require professional training of personnel at all levels. New opportunities for interdisciplinary programs must be developed to familiarize career scientists, doctoral students, and laboratory technicians with modern techniques in biobehavioral research.

A more general statement about future directions concerns the relevance of animal models to human disease. The participants in the workshop perceived a need to determine critical characteristics of human function and human disease in development of animal models. We need to know the nature of dependent and independent variables that are clinically relevant in order to focus attention on pathophysiological processes linking environment, behavior, and human disease.

The workshop participants were unanimous in expressing optimism concerning prospects for obtaining useful information from animal models in biobehavioral research. Concrete examples from previous studies include information about tumor formation, peptic ulcer production, and atherosclerosis. Even more important has been the increase in our understanding of the physiological and biochemical links between behavior and normal function under controlled experimental conditions. This understanding provides a firm foundation for promoting research and clinical application in behavioral medicine.

Intervention Strategies

A. BARNEY ALEXANDER[1]

The discussion on intervention strategies provided the opportunity for an interchange that was both lively and intellectually stimulating. Following some early discussion, the group decided to focus on the problem of adherence. There was quick agreement that adherence is one of the most imposing problems that we face during clinical interventions. We conjectured that this difficulty has raised its ugly head in part because we now have behavioral treatments that work when they are in fact applied properly and adhered to by the patient; whereas, heretofore we did not really have many effective behavioral treatments in the area that was formally called psychosomatic medicine. Now that we have effective treatments, the second order problem of adherence is becoming an important one. There was a comment made that in problems like Raynaud's disease, adherence is possibly not a real difficulty. A quick analysis of this claim revealed that the difference between something like Raynaud's disease and, for example, hypertension is that the symptoms in Raynaud's are quite painful, and the relief to be derived from successful treatment is prompt and immediately obvious. By contrast, in hypertension neither the symptoms nor the effects of successful treatment are apparent to the patient. There resulted a suggestion that behavioral medicine experts ought to study primarily those kinds or problems in which, like Raynaud's, the most impact can be expected. However, the consensus of the group was that we should not be relieved of the responsibility of trying to deal with important problems, such as

---

[1] This working group was co-chaired by A. Stunkard and A. B. Alexander. This report was compiled by A. B. Alexander. Others participating in the working group were P. Bryant, J. Cullen, L. Green, S. Hulley, C. D. Jenkins, J. Johnson, N. Krasnegor, and R. Surwit.

hypertension, even though they be considerably more difficult to deal with. Certainly, the problem of adherence is one of the most difficult we face in working with hypertension.

There was also a good deal of discussion generated by the fact that currently most of the techniques we employ are behavior-modification methods that place only scant emphasis on what are broadly referred to as cognitive factors. This included, of course, factors such as beliefs and attitudes as well as, for example, how people react emotionally to the treatment situation and the treatment itself. These factors clearly affect adherence. There was a prediction made that belief and attitude change is probably going to represent one of the real waves of the future in behavioral medicine generally. It was suggested that many of the problems that we are trying to address right now will probably be successfully dealt with only by technologies designed to change attitudes and beliefs. A majority, but certainly not everybody, agreed with these claims. Strong minority disagreement issued from those with a commitment to studying events at a much more molecular level, particularly in the area of smoking behavior.

A considerable amount of time, effort, and money has been expended in studying the variables which control smoking behavior (e.g., the porosity of the paper and its relationship to nicotine content). This topic led to our most lively interchange, which had to do with the issue of where we should be putting our major emphasis in the area of smoking: Should we be putting most of our money into a very detailed analysis of the variables which control and maintain smoking behavior so that we can then presumably be in a better position from which to derive successful intervention strategies? Or should we be putting most of our eggs in the primary prevention basket? There was no doubt that the clear consensus of the group was that the major focus ought to be in primary prevention. It is fine to try to develop techniques designed to help people *stop* smoking, but certainly the most cost-effective, and ultimately the most impactful, strategy has got to be primary prevention. Discouraging people from beginning to smoke in the first place will require technologies which are, unfortunately, yet to be fully worked out. Attitude and belief variables may well become involved in the venture. Nevertheless, the nature and strength of the relationships between attitudes and beliefs and behavior, and, correspondingly, the relationships between attitude and belief-change and behavior-change, are still hazy. Within traditional social psychology, the pessimism which settled in regarding these relationships in the early 1970s, which itself followed the great optimism and research activity of the 1960s, has again turned to optimism, albeit guarded, with a commensurate increase in research endeavor. Should the current more positive appraisal of the attitude–behavior relationship prove warranted, we will have to invest more effort in the development of a useful applied technology of attitude change with which to ultimately change behavior. Within the broader context of primary prevention technology in general, we also find ourselves at the fledgling stage but on a distinctly upbeat note. The value of effective life skills in relation to disease prevention is being affirmed, and a technology of skills training is already well on its way. The application of the latter to healthy life styles is obvious and, hence, is already the object of applied research.

Also in regard to smoking, but in another vein, there was a point raised about the advisability of studying former smokers who have effectively quit smoking on their own, to find out how they did it and why they were successful in maintaining the elimination of the habit. No one in the group was aware of any existing research on such people, but there was certainly a good deal of agreement that this could be a fruitful area to pursue. Since substance abusers, broadly speaking, represent people who are in a sense very good "adherers," they may represent a good adherence model. Such people adhere exquisitely to their regimens of overeating, oversmoking, and overuse of other substances, and/or continual indulgence in unhealthy habits of one kind or another. In short, the study of the variables that effect the very adherence to these regimens of overindulgence might tell us a great deal about how to get others to adhere to regimens which are known to be more adaptive and appropriate.

A point was also made regarding a similarity between what is going on right now with the study of variables that relate to smoking behavior and what happened with psychotherapy research. In the 1960s, we abandoned in despair the study of psychotherapy outcome, which we always knew was the most important question, for two reasons: (1) it proved frustratingly difficult at the time to do valid outcome research, and (2) the data that we did have were already very discouraging. Thus, we turned to process research even while acknowledging that the study of process was only important if psychotherapy worked. It may be that we are doing somewhat the same thing in smoking research. The big questions are the effects of smoking (to which we feel confident we have the answer) and how to stop it (to which we have almost no answers). Process research in smoking may amount in large measure to ducking the big challenge (cessation and especially prevention), just as process research in psychotherapy had ducked the outcome question two decades earlier. This is not to say that process research in substance abuse is useless. On the contrary, it is important research and should provide some valuable information. Nevertheless, the question remains, simply, where do we put the lion's share of our resources? There was a strong consensus in the group that the major focus should be on remediation and prevention rather than study of process.

Finally, there was some discussion concerning the iatrogenic effects associated with the promulgation of risk factor information both in general and in individual cases. When we tell someone that they are at risk, we rarely bother to tell them just how remotely they are at risk in most instances. Indeed, they may be at increased risk in relation to the general population, but often the actual size of that increased risk is rather small. Yet, they are told little more than that they are at risk and that they ought to consider trying to reduce the risk by changing their behavior when this is possible. There was a good deal of concern expressed regarding whether in some cases we may not be doing more harm than good. For example, telling someone they are at risk for cervical cancer may influence the rest of their lives in unfortunate ways when there may be precious little the person can do about altering the risk. A related problem concerning overly hasty risk factor promulgation is the loss of credibility when new data change the picture. The public has seen us change our minds on presumably significant risk factors many times. Careless and/or premature dissemination on our part here may undermine future risk factor behavior-change programs in both related and unrelated areas. Caution seemed to be advisable, especially in those areas where the behavior change required to reduce a risk factor would necessitate change of highly cherished or difficult to alter behaviors in the absence of thoroughly convincing data.

Special Topics

Inhibitory Behavioral Stress Effects upon Blood Pressure Regulation

DAVID E. ANDERSON

The origins of essential hypertension have long remained one of the most important and baffling mysteries in biomedical science. This most common of cardiovascular disorders is characterized by a chronic elevation in arterial pressure mediated by an increased total peripheral resistance to blood flow [11, 35]. Individual expression of hypertension is clearly determined in part by genetic influences [18, 33], but environmental factors may also participate significantly in the pathogenetic process. Among the environmental variables most frequently mentioned in this regard are psychological stress and salt ingestion [41]. Experimental studies have shown that it is possible to induce chronic hypertension in laboratory rats by social stresses [20] or by increasing dietary salt intake [30]. With larger experimental animals, such as dogs and primates, however, it has proven more difficult to develop chronically hypertensive preparations, except via surgical or pharmacological interventions which compromise renal functions.

Progress toward understanding the role of environmental factors in long-term blood pressure regulation can be facilitated by studies of the effects of behavioral procedures upon physiological regulatory systems, such as the autonomic nervous system, the adrenal glands, and the kidney, which are important to long-term blood pressure control. It is important to note in this regard that some behavioral procedures that have dramatic short-term effects upon blood pressure, may not be relevant to long-term blood pressure control, whereas other behavioral procedures, whose acute blood pressure effects are more subtle, may be of critical significance for long-term blood pressure regulation. Large-magnitude increases in arterial pressure can be produced, for example, by experimental procedures that

307

evoke cardiac activation and increased cardiac output [6, 12]. These sympathetically mediated cardiovascular responses include vasodilation in skeletal muscle (and typically, decreases in total peripheral resistance) that facilitates emergency "fight or flight" behavior [1]. It has been suggested frequently that experimentally induced "defense" reflexes participate in the pathogenesis of essential hypertension, but empirical support for this hypothesis is limited.

Less dramatic elevations in blood pressure can also be observed under a variety of behavioral conditions that result from an increased total peripheral resistance and a decreased cardiac output. This hemodynamic response can occur over periods of seconds when an environmental stimulus causes an individual to hold his breath (see Figure 1), and over much longer intervals of time immediately *preceding* the occurrence of behaviorally significant environmental events. Studies with instrumented dogs have shown, for example, that progressive elevation in blood pressure and decrease in heart rate and cardiac output can occur over periods of at least as long as 16 hr immediately preceding performance on shock-avoidance tasks [4, 7, 24]. Figure 2 shows sections of a polygraph tracing from a 16-hr preavoidance period with one dog trained on the avoidance task (upper panel), and a 16-hr period of confinement of a second dog, not trained on the avoidance task (lower panel). The conditioned dog shows a gradual divergence of blood pressure and heart rate during the preavoidance period, whereas cardiovascular activity of the control subject remains relatively stable.

Performance of the avoidance task (not shown in Figure 2) is accompanied by a sustained elevation in arterial pressure, heart rate, and cardiac output [7, 24].

The preavoidance cardiovascular response pattern occurs only in well-trained dogs who have been exposed repeatedly to a standard procedure in which they are placed in the experimental environment for a fixed period of time immediately before each avoidance session, and who have learned to await quietly the stimulus that signals the onset of the avoidance contingency. These observations suggest that the cardiovascular response is part of a more general "orienting" reaction, which, because of the behavioral significance of the stimuli, does not habituate with repeated exposures. This preavoidance cardiovascular response has been observed to recur during more than 100 successive daily sessions in an individual subject, with day-to-day variations in the form of the response being primarily a function of levels of blood pressure and heart rate at the beginning of the session. By contrast, this cardiovascular response pattern was not observed in a group of dogs during an interval of time immediately preceding sessions in which the same operant response (panel pressing) was maintained

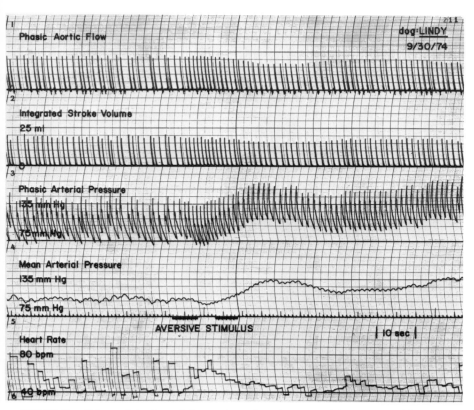

FIGURE 1.   *Polygraph tracings of changes in stroke volume, arterial pressure, and heart rate in response to a stimulus presented to a chronically instrumented dog. The rise in arterial pressure must be due to an increase in total peripheral resistance, since neither stroke volume nor heart rate increased.*

by positive reinforcement [3]. Thus, the aversiveness of the experimental conditions appears to be a critical component of the observed cardiovascular adaptation.

Components of this cardiovascular response pattern have been observed in laboratory animals and man in a number of other behavioral situations. For example, decreases in heart rate together with increases in blood pressure have been observed in studies of aversive stimulation of rabbits [44] and rats [42], which typically "freeze" under such conditions. Decreases in heart rate typically occur in human subjects under conditions of vigilant attention to the environment, such as during the preparatory period of a reaction time task [22, 32]. At least one study [31] has found that blood pressure remains stable under these conditions, suggesting that

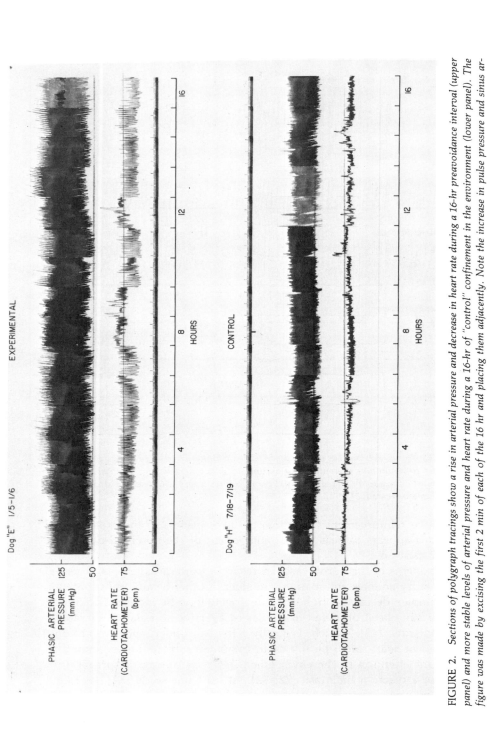

FIGURE 2. Sections of polygraph tracings show a rise in arterial pressure and decrease in heart rate during a 16-hr preavoidance interval (upper panel) and more stable levels of arterial pressure and heart rate during a 16-hr of "control" confinement in the environment (lower panel). The figure was made by excising the first 2 min of each of the 16 hr and placing them adjacently. Note the increase in pulse pressure and sinus arrhythmia in the preavoidance record.

there is a shift in the balance between cardiac output (decreased) and total peripheral resistance (increased) in the regulation of arterial pressure during attentional behavior. Williams *et al.* [43] have reported that performance of a complex perceptual task is associated with a significant increase in forearm vascular resistance. Lacey [23] has argued persuasively that decreases in heart rate occurring under such conditions have the effect of increasing sensitivity to environmental stimulation, a proposal which finds some support in research on the "orienting" reflex [38, 26].

Situations which elicit the attention of subjects tend not only to be associated with decreases in heart rate, but also respiration rate [32]. Decreases in respiration rate are also observed consistently in studies of preavoidance conditioning, frequently to levels well below those observed at rest. For example, some indication of respiratory activity can be inferred from the cardiotachometric record of heart rate in the upper panel of Figure 2. The cyclic oscillations observed on this channel reflect respiration rate, and can be seen to average 8–9 per minute during the final few hours of this particular preavoidance session. A physiological response pattern involving increases in total peripheral resistance and decreases in heart rate and cardiac output are also observed, more dramatically but over much shorter intervals, in the diving reflex [2, 39], during which respiratory activity ceases. Diving physiology has been studied extensively in a variety of species for more than a century, and this literature may provide clues to other effects of behavioral procedures which induce such cardiorespiratory changes over more prolonged intervals. It has been shown, for example, that the cessation of respiration during diving evokes a decrease in blood pH, resulting in a "leakage" of potassium ions from the intracellular to the extracellular fluid [2].

Recent studies have shown that preavoidance conditioning is also associated with significant increases in levels of plasma potassium [9]. In these experiments, two dogs were placed in an experimental chamber at 4 P.M., and after a 16-hr overnight preavoidance period, completed a 1-hr shock-avoidance session between 8 and 9 A.M. Two other dogs were placed in the chamber at 10 A.M., and after a 5-hr preavoidance period, completed a 30-min avoidance session from 3 to 3:30 P.M. The avoidance task required the dog to reset a recycling timer, which, if permitted to complete its cycle, delivered a brief electric shock. Training on this contingency resulted in stable rates of avoidance behavior (panel pressing responses), which effectively postponed virtually all shocks during the daily sessions. Each dog was run 5 days per week for at least 4 weeks, and then during the next five successive sessions, blood samples were obtained during the first and last hours of preavoidance periods, and analyzed for levels of plasma potassium and sodium by a flame photometer. Two other dogs served as "control" subjects, one run overnight between 4 P.M. and 8 A.M., and the other run from 10 A.M. to 3 P.M. Having dogs run on both schedules enabled interpretation of the results with less concern for effects of diurnal variations.

Figure 3 summarizes the changes during preavoidance, and shows that blood pressure increased by a mean of 9/4 mm Hg, whereas heart rate decreased by a mean of 18 bpm. Under these conditions, plasma potassium levels increased by mean of 11% from 3.41 to 3.81 mEq/liter. By contrast, no such changes in potassium levels were observed in the control group, which maintained relatively stable levels of blood pressure and heart rate during these sessions. In addition, preavoidance conditioning was associated with a small (1–2%) but marginally significant rise in plasma sodium levels, whereas no such effects were observed in the control group. These findings are the first known evidence supporting the view that ex-

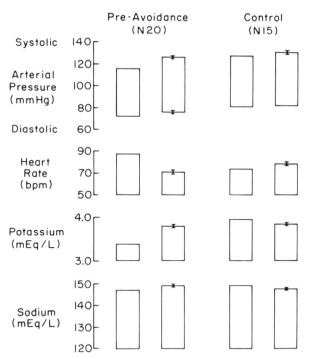

FIGURE 3. *The graph shows mean levels and standard errors of the difference scores of arterial pressure, heart rate, and plasma potassium and sodium levels during the first and last hours of preavoidance for the "experimental" group (N = 20) and the first and last hours for the "control" group (N = 15).*

perimental behavioral stress-conditioning procedures can induce significant and sustained increases in plasma electrolyte levels. Previously, it was reported that increases in urinary potassium/sodium ratios occurred in human patients during a postsurgical convalescent period [29] and in human subjects following exposure to moderate cold conditions for 2–6 days [25]. Similarly, exposure of rats to moderate cold for 3 hr resulted in significant increases in urinary potassium levels [10], although no such effects were observed in rats exposed for 22 days to an aversive conditioning procedure.

The significance of these behaviorally induced changes in potassium levels is related to the fact that small increases in plasma potassium can induce significant increases in secretion of aldosterone, the most potent of the salt-retaining hormones [21]. Although increases in aldosterone levels have not been reported in the context of diving behavior, several studies have found that urinary aldosterone levels are increased in subjects exposed to experimental or "real life" stresses. Mason [27] showed that aldosterone levels were increased in monkeys as a function of avoidance conditioning procedures, with some monkeys showing higher levels of aldosterone between sessions than during sessions. Increases in urinary levels of aldosterone have also been observed in humans under conditions of medical school examinations, military combat, and presentation of scientific papers [14]. In addition, urinary aldosterone levels were reported to be increased in highly emotional psychiatric patients, and subnormal in chronic schizophrenics [15]. These reports support the view that aldosterone metabolism is responsive to psychological influences.

Variations in aldosterone can be due to changes in levels of circulating ACTH and renin–angiotensin, both of which are known to be reactive to behavioral conditioning procedures. For example, a study with sheep [16] reported that the stress of cannulation was followed by correlated changes in levels of cortisol and aldosterone but not in potassium or renin. It was concluded that the primary determinant of aldosterone response to stress is ACTH. However, Oken [34] reported that aldosterone responses in human subjects under stress were frequently not correlated with changes in ACTH levels. Studies of electrolyte changes in preavoidance conditioning suggest that, at least under some conditions, stress-induced increases in circulating and urinary aldosterone levels may be mediated by a respiratory-potassium mechanism, which can continue to operate continuously over extended time intervals. Studies in progress in our laboratory with avoidance-trained dogs have shown that plasma aldosterone levels can increase during preavoidance periods by as much as 100% above initial values. One consequence of an increase in aldosterone secretion is an inhibition of release of renin by the kidney.

Another important effect of aldosterone is to decrease excretion of sodium and water by the kidney. A more direct effect upon renal functions of preavoidance conditioning may include a decrease in renal blood flow. Studies of the effects of diving [2] and automatic respiration of conscious dogs [37] have shown clearly that inhibition of respiration can be associated with a significant decrease in renal blood flow. Similarly, decreases in renal blood flow have been observed in human subjects exposed to moderate cold conditions, which also increased blood pressure and decreased heart rate [25]. Presumably, such decreases in renal blood flow would be mediated by increases in sympathetic nervous system activity.

The role of the sympathetic nervous system in the mediation of increases in total peripheral resistance and blood pressure during preavoidance periods remains problematic. It is clear that increases in blood pressure and decreases in heart rate can be evoked in anesthetized animals by electrical stimulation of a number of central nervous system sites [17, 36]. However, experimental studies with avoidance-trained dogs have shown that divergent changes in blood pressure and heart rate during preavoidance periods were *not* prevented by infusions of drugs which blocked alpha [8] and beta [5] adrenergic receptor activity. Moreover, similar cardiovascular responses elicited by electrical stimulation of the amygdala of anesthetized monkeys *were* prevented by concurrent oxygenation of the blood.

Ongoing experiments in our laboratory have shown, however, that plasma norepinephrine levels increase during preavoidance periods. In these experiments, two dogs were trained on a free-operant avoidance task, and run in daily 5-hr preavoidance intervals followed by 30-min avoidance sessions until stable behavioral and cardiovascular patterns emerged. In six subsequent experiments with these two subjects, blood samples were obtained remotely from indwelling catheters during the first and last preavoidance hour. Figure 4 summarizes levels of cardiovascular and catecholamine activity, averaged over the six sessions. Blood pressure increased by an average of 16/9 mm Hg, while heart rate levels did not change significantly. Plasma norepinephrine levels increased during all six preavoidance sessions by an average of 46%, whereas plasma epinephrine levels did not change significantly. Confirmation of these findings with additional experiments would support the view that the increases in total peripheral resistance and blood pressure during preavoidance periods are mediated by an increase in alpha adrenergic activity, though a minor contribution may also be made by the adrenal medulla.

Similar effects upon urinary catecholamines have been reported in previous studies of avoidance conditioning with rhesus monkeys [28]. It was observed that levels of norepinephrine tended to be higher between

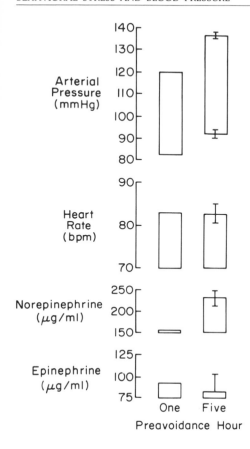

FIGURE 4. *The graph shows mean levels and standard errors of the difference scores of arterial pressure, heart rate, and plasma norepinephrine and epinephrine during the first and last hours of the preavoidance periods* (N = 6).

avoidance sessions than during them, whereas the reverse was true for levels of epinephrine.

Increases in blood pressure during preavoidance periods should stimulate the kidney to increase excretion of water and sodium, decreasing levels of blood volume which would return pressure to homeostatic levels. The work of Guyton and his colleagues [19] has shown the dominance of the kidney among all the autoregulatory mechanisms, due to its "infinite" capacity to adjust blood volume to maintain pressure at a precise "set point". They have suggested that the key to understanding the pathogenesis of hypertension will involve elucidation of the mechanisms by which the "set point" at which the kidney maintains pressure is modified. In their view, hypertension is a disorder of blood volume, in which very small increases in blood volume will have very great effects upon blood pressure levels.

Support for this view is obtained from the fact that most of the experimental procedures for inducing chronic hypertension in animals involve methods which reduce renal excretory functions. The severity of the hypertension is increased by increasing salt intake [13]. Behavioral procedures such as preavoidance conditioning may also result in a decrease in renal excretory ability by effects upon salt-retaining hormones or renal blood flow levels. The concurrent effect of increases in total peripheral resistance during such behavioral stresses suggest that an increase in salt and water retention will not be accommodated by the compliance vessels, but will result in tissue flows which are inappropriately high for metabolic needs. Ultimately, the systemic peripheral arterioles may undergo a "waterlogging" and thickening of their walls, as is observed in experimental and essential hypertension [40].

From consideration of the experimental and epidemiological literature on hypertension, a formulation is arrived at in which chronic elevation in blood pressure appears to represent an interaction between (a) environmental stresses that increase total peripheral resistance and decrease renal excretory capacity, and (b) ingestion of salt. Rate of increase in blood pressure over time is viewed as being a joint function of both variables. Under conditions of minimal stress, relatively large amounts of salt can be consumed with little effect on blood pressure. Conversely, on a sodium restricted diet, environmental stresses will not increase blood volume levels significantly, with little effect upon blood pressure. Only when both variables are present to some degree will significant elevations in long-term blood pressure be observed.

Cultural, vocational, and individual personality variables should all influence the extent to which sustained psychophysiological adaptations, characterized by increased resistance and decreased cardiac output, develop in man. It is of interest to observe that species such as the rat or rabbit, which are relatively more susceptible to the hypertensive effects of environmental influences, tend to respond to environmental threat with inhibition of behavioral activity and bradycardia. However, species such as the dog or monkey, which are relatively less susceptible to the hypertensive effects of environmental conditions, tend to respond to environmental challenges with behavioral activation and increased heart rate. It would be of interest to know whether rats bred to be either susceptible or resistant to the hypertensive effects of salt feeding differ in terms of their modal cardiovascular response to environmental stress.

Much remains to be done to validate this theory of the role of the environment in the pathogenesis of chronic hypertension. In any event, the accumulation of basic knowledge concerning the interacting effects of inhibitory behavioral stress conditioning upon behavioral and physiological functions should help to elucidate pathophysiological mechanisms involved in long-term blood pressure control. From this understanding will finally emerge the development of rational behavioral programs for prevention of this cardiovascular disorder.

Acknowledgments

This research was supported in part by grants HL 17970 and HL 22934 from the National Heart, Lung and Blood Institute. The author is grateful to Sandra L. Anderson for her assistance with the manuscript.

References

1. Abrahams, V. C.; Hilton, S. M.; and Zbrozyna, A. W.: The role of active muscle vasodilation in the alerting stage of the defense reaction. *Journal of Physiology* 171:189–202, 1964.
2. Andersen, H. T.: Physiological adaptations in diving vertebrates. *Physiological Reviews* 46:212–243, 1966.
3. Anderson, D. E. and Brady, J. V.: Differential preparatory cardiovascular responses to aversive and appetitive behavioral conditioning. *Conditional Reflex* 7:82–96, 1972.
4. Anderson, D. E. and Brady, J. V.: Prelonged preavoidance effects upon blood pressure and heart rate in the dog. *Psychosomatic Medicine* 35:4–12, 1973.
5. Anderson, D. E. and Brady, J. V.: Cardiovascular responses to avoidance conditioning: effects of beta adrenergic blockade. *Psychosomatic Medicine* 38:181–189, 1976.
6. Anderson, D. E. and Brady, J. V.: Experimental analysis of psychosomatic interactions: behavioral influences upon physiological regulation. In *Modification of Pathological Behavior*, ed. R. S. Davidson, pp. 189–231. New York: Gardner Press, 1979.
7. Anderson, D. E. and Tosheff, J. G.: Cardiac output and total peripheral resistance changes during preavoidance periods in the dog. *Applied Journal of Physiology* 35:650–654, 1973.
8. Anderson, D. E.; Yingling, J. E.; and Brady, J. V.: Cardiovascular responses to avoidance conditioning: effects of alpha adrenergic blockade. *Pavlovian Journal of Biological Science* 11:150–161, 1976.
9. Anderson, D. E.; Ray, R. L.; and Lease, S.: Plasma electrolyte effects of preavoidance conditioning in the dog. *Pavlovian Journal of Biological Science* 1980. In Press.
10. Beattie, D.: Physiological changes in rats exposed to cold/restraint stress. *Life Sciences* 23:2307–2314, 1978.
11. Brody, M. J. and Zimmerman, B. G.: Peripheral circulation in arterial hypertension. *Progress in Cardiovascular Diseases* 18:323–340, 1976.
12. Cohen, D. H. and Obrist, P. A.: Interactions between behavior and the cardiovascular system. *Circulation Research* 37:693–706, 1975.
13. Coleman, T. G. and Guyton, A. C.: Hypertension caused by salt loading in the dog. III. Onset transients of cardiac output and other circulatory variables. *Circulation Research* 25:153–160, 1969.

14. Elmadjian, F.: Aldosterone excretion in behavioral disorders. In *Ultrastructure and metabolism of the nervous system*, eds. S. R. Korey, A. Pope, and E. Robins, pp. 414–419. Ass Res. Nerv. Ment. Dis., 40, Baltimore: Williams & Wilkins, 1962.

15. Elmadjian, F.: Adrenaline and noradrenaline. In *Methods in Hormone Research*, ed. R. I. Dorfman, pp. 337–349. Vol. 1. New York: Academic Press, 1962.

16. Espiner, E. A.; Lun, S.; and Hart, D. S.: Role of ACTH, angiotensin and potassium in stress-induced aldosterone secretion. *Journal of Steroid Biochemistry* 9:109–113, 1978.

17. Feigl, E. and Folkow, B.: Cardiovascular responses in diving and during brain stimulation in ducks, *Acta Physiologica Scandinavia* 57:99–110, 1963.

18. Folkow, B. and Hallback, M.: Physiopathology of spontaneous hypertension in rats. In *Hypertension*, eds. J. Genest, E. Kiow, and O. Kuchel, pp. 507–528. New York: McGraw-Hill, 1977.

19. Guyton, A. C.: Personal views on mechanisms of hypertension. In *Hypertension*, eds. J. Genest, E. Kiow, and O. Kuchel, pp. 566–575. New York: McGraw-Hill, 1977.

20. Henry, J. P.; Ely, D. L.; and Stephens, P. M.: Blood pressure, catecholamines and social role in relation to the development of cardiovascular disease in mice. In *Neural and Psychological Mechanisms in Cardiovascular Disease*, ed. A. Zanchetti, pp. 211–228. Milan: Il Ponte, 1972.

21. Himathongkam, T. R.; Dluhy, R. G.; and Williams, G. H.: Potassium-aldosterone-renin relationships. *Journal of Clinical and Endocrinological Metabolism* 41:153–161, 1975.

22. Lacey, J. I.: Somatic response patterning and stress: some revisions of activation theory. In *Psychological Stress: Issues in Research*, eds. M. H. Appley, and R. Trumbull, pp. 14–42. New York: Appleton , 1967.

23. Lacey, J. I.: Some cardiovascular correlates of sensorimotor behavior: examples of visceral afferent feedback. In *Limbic System Mechanisms and Autonomic Function*, ed. C. H. Hockman, pp. 15–34. Springfield, Ill.: Charles C Thomas, 1970.

24. Lawler, J. E.; Obrist, P. A.; and Lawler, K. A.: Cardiovascular function during pre-avoidance, avoidance and postavoidance in dogs. *Psychophysiology* 12:4–11, 1975.

25. Lennquist, S.: Cold-induced diuresis. *Scandinavian Journal of Urology and Nephrology* Supplement 9, pp. 1–46, 1972.

26. Lynn, R.: *Attention, Arousal and the Orienting Reflex*. Oxford: Pergamon Press, 1966.

27. Mason, J. W.: Urinary aldosterone and urine volume responses to 72-hour avoidance sessions in the monkey. *Psychosomatic Medicine* 30:733–745, 1968.

28. Mason, J. W.: Urinary epinephrine and norepinephrine responses to 72-hour avoidance sessions in the monkey. *Psychosomatic Medicine* 30:654–665, 1968.

29. Moore, F. D.: Bodily changes in surgical convalescence: I. The normal sequence-observations and interpretations. *Annals of Surgery* 137:289–315, 1953.

30. Meneely, G. R.; Tucker, R. G.; Darby, W. J.; and Auerbach, S. H.: Chronic sodium chloride toxicity in the albino rat. II. Occurrence of hypertension and syndrome of edema and renal failure. *Journal of Experimental Medicine* 98:71–80, 1953.

31. Obrist, P. A.; Wood, D.; and Perez-Reyes, M.: Heart rate during conditioning in humans: Effects of UCS intensity, vagal blockade and adrenergic blockade of vasomotor activity. *Journal of Experimental Psychology* 70:32–42, 1965.

32. Obrist, P. A.; Webb, R. A.; Sutterer, J. R.; and Howard, J. L.: The cardiac–somatic relationships: some reformulations. *Psychophysiology* 6:569–587, 1970.

33. Okomoto, K. and Aoki, K.: Development of a strain of spontaneously hypertensive rats. *Japanese Circulation Journal* 27:282–293, 1963.

34. Oken, D.: The psychophysiology and psychoendocrinology of stress and emotion. In *Psychological Stress: Issues in Research*, eds. M. H. Appley and R. Trumbull, pp. 43–76. New York: Appleton-Century Crofts, 1967.

35. Page, I. H. and McCubbins, J. W.: The physiology of arterial hypertension. In *Handbook of Physiology: Circulation*, pp. 2163. III (2), Baltimore: Waverly Press, 1965.
36. Reis, D. J. and McHugh, P. R.: Hypoxia as a cause of bradycardia during amygdala stimulation in monkeys. *American Journal of Physiology* 214:601–610, 1968.
37. Rutherford, J. D. and Vatner, S. F.: Integrated carotid chemoreceptor and pulmonary inflation reflex control of peripheral vasoactivity in conscious dogs. *Circulation Research* 43:200–208, 1978.
38. Sokolov, E. N.: *Perception and the Conditioned Reflex*. Oxford: Pergamon Press, 1963.
39. Spencer, M. P. Systemic circulation. *Annual Review of Physiology*, 28:311–346, 1966.
40. Tobian, L.: A viewpoint concerning the state of arterial hypertension. In *Hypertension*, eds. J. Genest, E. Kiow, and O. Kuchel, pp. 606–612. New York: McGraw-Hill, 1977.
41. Weiner, H.: Personality factors and the importance of emotional stresses in hypertension. In *Hypertension*, eds. J. Genest, E. Kiow, and O. Kuchel, pp. 661–673. New York: McGraw-Hill, 1977.
42. Williams, R. B.; Bittker, T. E.; Buchsbaum, M. S.; and Wynne, L. C.: Cardiovascular and neurophysiological correlates of sensory intake and rejection. I. Effects of cognitive tasks. *Psychophysiology* 12:427–433, 1975.
43. Williams, R. B. and Euchelman, B.: Social setting: influence of the physiological response by electric shock in the rat. *Science* 174:613–614, 1971.
44. Yehle, A.; Dauth, G.; and Schneiderman, N.: Correlates of heart rate on classical conditioning in curarized rabbits. *Journal of Comparative and Physiological Psychology* 64:99–104, 1967.

Environmentally Induced Cardiovascular Response in Type A and B Individuals[1]

THEODORE M. DEMBROSKI

The Type A coronary-prone behavior pattern has been related to the prevalence and incidence of coronary heart disease (CHD) and severity of arteriographically documented atherosclerosis [1,2,3,10,18,20,35,46].[2] The most viable hypothesis advanced to explain how the behavior pattern is translated into CHD is the assumption that Type As, relative to Bs, are more prone to respond to the social, psychological, and physical challenges of everyday life with enhanced physiological response, and that such response, if chronic over a lifetime, has the potential to participate in atherogenesis and/or precipitate clinical events [9, 13, 19, 31, 39, 42]. To explore the first part of the above hypothesis, a number of researchers have been examining the physiological response of Type A and B subjects in laboratory settings.

Early on, Friedman, Rosenman, and associates recognized the importance of the environmental situation in evoking differential levels of physiological response in Type A and B subjects when they demonstrated higher levels of catecholamines in the former only during the working day [15]. Later they demonstrated that higher levels of norepinephrine were observed in Type A compared to Type B subjects in response to a challenging contest involving puzzle-solving skills, even though no difference between the types was observed during baseline conditions [14]. In another

[1] Research from our laboratory reported in this chapter was supported by research Grant HL-22809-01 awarded to the author by the National Heart, Lung, and Blood Institute of the National Institutes of Health.

[2] The Type A pattern is characterized by excessive displays of hostility, impatience, time urgency, and hard-driving competitiveness, which are readily evoked by a range of environmental circumstances.

early study, they also showed that viewing of an irritating film induced more motor and respiratory changes in Type As than in Type Bs [37].

Work in our laboratory has suggested that Type As are prone to respond significantly more than Type Bs to a variety of challenges involving cognitive, psychomotor, or physical abilities with elevated systolic blood pressure (SBP) and heart rate (HR). For example, we have found that challenging instructions to perform rapidly and accurately in a choice reaction-time task, a TV pong game, and an anagrams solution task resulted in higher SBP and HR changes in Type A relative to B subjects, despite the fact that baseline values were not significantly different between the Types [8]. Similarly, Glass has shown that working adult Type As, compared to Type Bs responded with greater HR, blood pressure, and serum epinephrine levels while playing a TV pong game under high challenge instructions [16]. In another study designed to investigate the role of environmental challenge in evoking such differences, we subjected male college students to a cold-pressor test and a reaction-time task under conditions that either maximized or minimized the challenging nature of the tasks [6]. Differences in SBP and HR responses between the types were highest under high challenge conditions, particularly for the cold-pressor task, which produced no significant physiological difference between the Types under low-challenge instructions.

Glass et al. [16] have demonstrated the importance of environmental challenge in evoking both cardiovascular and catecholamine response differences in Type A and B subjects. During a TV pong game with an experimental confederate, subjects were either allowed to play the game in silence (no harassment) or were criticized and berated by the confederate for poor performance (harassment). Under no harassment, Type As and Bs did not significantly differ in physiological response, but under harassment, Type As responded with significantly greater increases than Bs in SBP, HR, and plasma epinephrine.

In using the term "Type A" it is important to recognize that the concept is multidimensional and that epidemiologic research has suggested that some elements of the Type A pattern are more strongly associated with CHD than other components. For example, Matthews et al. showed that potential for hostility, vigorous voice stylistics, competitiveness, and impatience prospectively discriminated CHD patients from controls in the Western Collaborative Group Study whereas job involvement, past accomplishments, and speed of activity did not [30]. In addition, Williams et al. demonstrated that potential for hostility (MMPI defined) and the Type A pattern independently predicted severity of atherosclerosis [43]. Through component scoring of the interview [5], we have generally found that the attributes most closely related to CHD are also most predictive of challenge-induced physiological response in our subjects (i.e., vigorous voice stylistics and potential for hostility). In fact, in our research, potential for hostility has tended to correlate significantly with physiological response within Type A subjects alone [6, 7, 8]. Moreover, high-hostile Type As responded with equally high physiological elevations under *both* low- and high-challenge conditions in the study described above, whereas low-hostile Type As showed such reaction only under the high-challenge condition [6].

The importance of considering both environmental factors *and* person variables in predicting physiological response was again illustrated in study in our laboratory involving female subjects [27]. These subjects were subjected to the cold-pressor test and a reaction-time task under high challenge instructions which, in effect, replicated the condition of the experiment described earlier that involved only male subjects. Two major findings emerged. First, females tended to respond with lower physiological response than male subjects in the reaction-time task, but not in response to cold stress. Second, there was no difference in physiological response between Type A and B subjects in either task, except that Type As rated high in hostility responded with significantly greater SBP changes than those A and B subjects designated low in potential for hostility.

Since the Type A pattern is predictive of CHD in females [1, 18, 36, 43], we were puzzled by the failure to find a main effect for Type A. In reflecting on the problem, we realized that females may generally respond with less involvement to certain tasks than males. Some research suggests, for instance, that females may be more concerned with skills in interpersonal exchanges than psychomotor processes [23]. Following this lead, we recruited a new sample of female college students and subjected them to the standard Type A interview administered by a highly trained female interviewer who engaged in the appropriate verbal competiveness that is called for by the interview protocol. Following the interview, subjects were challenged to answer a number of questions on allegedly "well known events in American history." In addition, to determine whether we could replicate the results of the first study, following a second baseline, these females were subjected to a choice reaction-time task, again with high challenge instructions, but this time we also added a monetary incentive to further enhance the challenge of the situation.

The results revealed a highly significant difference between Type A and B females in SBP change during the interview and quiz. As in the first female study, however, during the reaction-time task there was no significant difference between the types in blood pressure response. Here, despite our efforts to increase the challenge, Type A females again showed virtually identical blood pressure response to their Type B counterparts, which was substantially less than that which they had just displayed during the interview and quiz. In fact, the SBP change values during reaction time for both Type A and B females were highly comparable to those displayed by female subjects in the first study. Such findings show that it is critical to examine carefully the nature of the environmental challenge if both female and male subjects are included in research study of A–B physiological differences.

To our knowledge, only three studies have examined physiological response characteristics of Type A and B subjects *and* coronary patients. Friedman and Rosenman found that coronary patients and symptom-free Type A subjects responded with significantly greater plasma norepinephrine levels during a challenging puzzle-solving contest than symptom-free Type B subjects [34]. In a similar approach, we exposed Type A and B coronary patients and matched controls to the Type A interview and a history quiz and found that Type As responded with greater SBP increases than Type Bs regardless of disease condition [7]. However, during the history quiz, coronary patients, but not patient controls, significantly increased their SBP over that displayed in the interview despite the fact that virtually all were taking beta-adrenergic blocking medication. In a very different and interesting study, Kahn *et al.* found that Type A scores were significantly related to SBP increases in *anesthetized* patients who were undergoing coronary bypass surgery [22]. These results raise the intriguing notion of possible differences in ANS functioning per se between Type A and B individuals, especially Type As who score high in potential for hostility [6, 43].

In this line of research, another variable that is absolutely essential to consider is the method of assessing Type A and B. All of the studies discussed thus far used the Structured Interview (SI) to assess subjects as Type A and B [33]. In our research program, we have consistently found the SI to be a better predictor of challenge-induced physiological response than the Jenkins Activity Survey (JAS) method of assessing Type A [21], as is the case for CHD [1, 3]. Nevertheless, the JAS does predict CHD (albeit not as strongly as the SI), and several studies have found that it also predicts physiologic response in laboratory settings.

As in the research with the SI, environmental setting appears critical in establishing physiological response differences between JAS defined As and Bs. For example, Manuck and his co-workers in three independent studies have reported that SBP change in JAS defined As differed from Bs during challenging cognitive tasks [28, 29]. However, they also found that under monetary incentive conditions, JAS scores were uncorrelated with any physiological response, whereas under the low-incentive condition, JAS scores were correlated with SBP and HR [29]. On the other hand, in a similar paradigm, Williams has reported greater change in forearm blood flow in JAS defined As relative to Bs only under a monetary incentive condition [44]. Using a different paradigm, Van Egeren subjected JAS defined As and Bs to a mixed motive game and in one study found higher HR reactions in As during the display of outcomes against a competitive co-player [40]. However, in a second study using the same paradigm he found significant preinteraction differences between the types in digital vasconstriction, but not during the task itself [41]. Similarly, Golband did not find differentially greater decreases in pulse transit time in JAS defined As relative to Bs under challenging or nonchallenging conditions [17]. In fact, under conditions of low challenge, Type A subjects showed markedly smaller decreases in PTT than Type B subjects. Other researchers have failed to report SBP and HR differences between JAS-defined As and Bs in a cold-pressor task [24], or differences in HR and spontaneous skin potentials during a series of cognitive tasks [32]. Along the same line, no HR or catecholamine secretion differences between JAS defined As and Bs (Swedish translation) were reported by Frankenhauser and her co-workers, who used the challenge of a choice reaction-time task [11]. However, in the same program of research, Lundberg and Forsman showed higher levels of cortisol in JAS-defined Type As than Bs during a vigilance task, but not during an information-processing task [25]. In a different approach, Frankenhauser *et al.* reported greater levels of cortisol and epinephrine secretion in JAS-defined As relative to Bs under circumstances of forced and prolonged *inactivity* [12]. Similarly, Zoleman *et al.* reported that JAS-defined As showed significantly less occipital alpha activity than Bs during a 10-min recording session [45].

In sum, although a number of studies have reported physiological differences between JAS defined As and Bs, both the magnitude and consistency of the results are less striking than those found in studies using the interview method of assessment. This should not be surprising, since the two methods correlate only modestly in designating subjects as A and B [14, 26]. However, at least one study has failed to report differential physiological reactions between both JAS defined and SI defined subjects until Type As were subdivided on an additional dimension said to be indicative of self-involvement [38]. All told, then, it appears clear that the Type A pattern is not invariably associated with excessive physiologic responses to environmental challenge, and in recognizing this it should be remembered that it is far from perfectly correlated with CHD. Nevertheless, in exploring A–B differences in physiological reactivity, it now seems essential that researchers should be aware of the complexity and importance of different kinds, levels, or aspects of (*a*) environmental challenge; (*b*) the Type A pattern itself; (*c*) individual difference variables not included in the Type A pattern; and (d) physiological endpoints. Moreover, in virtually all of the studies thus reviewed it is impossible to identify the precise mechanisms responsible for the observed physiological changes. Blood pressure can be influenced by both systemic resistance and cardiac output; heart rate increases can be induced by sympathetic activity and parasympathetic withdrawal. A high priority should be given to multidimensional exploration of the variables listed above and of the exact mechanisms responsible for individual differences in physiological reaction. Sophisticated research of this kind offers the potential of identifying environmental challenges that can be used to explore physiological reactivity as a direct predictor of disease endpoints and thereby eventually transcend the error inherent in purely behavioral assessment techniques [26].

References

1. Blumenthal, J. A.; Williams, R.; Kong, Y.; et al.: Type A behavior and angiographically documented coronary disease. *Circulation* 58:634–639, 1978.
2. Brand, R. J.: Coronary-prone behavior as an independent risk factor for coronary heart disease. In *Coronary-prone behavior*, eds. T. M. Dembroski, S. M. Weiss, J. L. Shields *et al.* New York: Springer-Verlag, 1978.
3. Brand, R. J.; Rosenman, R. H.; Jenkins, C. D.; et al. Comparison of coronary heart disease prediction in the Western Collaborative Group Study using the Structured Interview and the Jenkins Activity Survey assessments of the coronary-prone Type A behavior pattern. Submitted manuscript.
4. Chesney, M.; Black, G.; Feuerstein, M.; et al. *Coronary-prone behavior: Characteristics and therapeutic implications.* Paper presented at the annual meeting of the American Psychological Association, Toronto, August 1978.
5. Dembroski, T. M.: Reliability and validity of methods used to assess coronary-prone behavior. In *Coronary-prone behavior*, eds. T. M. Dembroski, S. M. Weiss, J. L. Shields *et al.* New York: Springer-Verlag, 1978.
6. Dembroski, T. M.; MacDougall, J. M.; Herd, J. A.; and Shields, J. L.: Effects of level of challenge on pressor and heart rate responses in Type A and B subjects. *Journal of Applied Social Psychology*, 9:209–228, 1979.
7. Dembroski, T. M.; MacDougall, J. M.; and Lushene, R.: Interpersonal interaction and cardiovascular response in Type A subjects and coronary patients. *Journal of Human Stress*, 5:28–36, 1979.
8. Dembroski, T. M.; MacDougall, J. M.; Shields, J. L., *et al.* Components of the Type A coronary-prone behavior pattern and cardiovascular responses to psychomotor performance challenge. *Journal of Behavioral Medicine* 1:159–176, 1978.
9. Eliot, R. S.: *Stress and the major cardiovascular disorders.* Mount Kisco, N. Y.: Futura, 1979.
10. Frank, K. A.; Heller, S. S.; Kornfeld, D. S.; et al. Type A behavior pattern and coronary angiographic findings. *Journal of the American Medical Association* 240:761–763, 1978.
11. Frankenhaeuser, M.; Lundberg, U.; and Forsman, L.: *Dissociation between sympathetic-adrenal and pituitary-adrenal responses to an achievement situation character-*

ized by high controllability: Comparison between Type A and Type B males and females. Report from the Department of Psychology, University of Stockholm, 1978a.

12. Frankenhaeuser, M.; Lundberg, U.; and Forsman, L.: *Note on arousing Type A persons by depriving them of work.* Report from the Department of Psychology, University of Stockholm, 1978b.

13. Friedman, M.: Type A behavior pattern: Some of its pathophysiological components. *Bulletin of the New York Academy of Medicine*, 53:593-604, 1977.

14. Friedman, M.; Byers, S. O.; Diamant, J.; and Rosenman, R. H.: Plasma catecholamine response of coronary-prone subjects (Type A) to a specific challenge. *Metabolism* 4:205-210, 1975.

15. Friedman, M.; St. George, S.; and Byers, S. O.: Excretion of catecholamines, 17-ketosteroids, 17-hydroxycorticoids, and 5-hydroxyindole in men exhibiting a particular behavior pattern (A) associated with high incidence of clinical coronary artery disease. *Journal of Clinical Investigation* 39:758-765, 1960.

16. Glass, C. D.; Krakoff, L. R.; Contrada, R.; *et al.*: Effect of harassment and competition upon cardiovascular and catecholaminic responses in Type A and Type B individuals. *Psychophysiology.* In press.

17. Goldband, S.: *Environmental specificity of physiological response to stress in coronary-prone subjects.* Unpublished doctoral dissertation, State University of New York at Buffalo, 1978.

18. Haynes, S. G.; Feinleib, M.; and Kannel, W. B.: Psychosocial factors and CHD incidence in Framingham: Results from an 8-year follow-up study. *American Journal of Epidemiology* 108:229, 1978.

19. Herd, J. A.: Physiological correlates of coronary prone behavior. In *Coronary-prone behavior.* eds. T. M. Dembroski, S. M. Weiss, and J. L. Shields, *et al.* New York: Springer-Verlag, 1978.

20. Jenkins, C. D.: Behavioral risk factors in coronary artery disease. *Annual Review of Medicine* 29:543-562, 1978.

21. Jenkins, C. D.; Rosenman, R. H.; and Friedman, M.: Development of an objective psychological test for the determination of the coronary-prone behavior pattern in employed men. *Journal of Chronic Diseases* 20:371-379, 1967.

22. Kahn, J. P.; Kornfeld, D. S.; Frank, K. A.; Heller, S. S.; and Hoar, P.: *Type A behavior and blood pressure response during coronary artery surgery.* Paper presented at the meeting of the American Psychosomatic Society, Dallas, 1979.

23. Lenney, E.: Women's self-confidence in achievement settings. *Psychological Bulletin* 84:1-13, 1977.

24. Lott, G. G.; and Gatchel, R. J.: A multi-response analysis of learned heart rate control. *Psychophysiology* 15:576-581, 1978.

25. Lundberg, U. and Forsman, L.: *Adrenal-medullary and adrenal-cortical responses to understimulation and overstimulation: Comparison between Type A and Type B persons.* Reports from the Department of Psychology, University of Stockholm, 1978.

26. MacDougall, J. M.; Dembroski, T. M.; and Musante, L.: The structured interview and questionnaire methods of assessing coronary-prone behavior in male and female college students. *Journal of Behavioral Medicine* 2:71-83, 1979.

27. MacDougall, J. M.; Dembroski, T. M.; and Krantz, D. S.: Effects of types of challenge on pressor and heart rate responses in Type A and B females. *Psychophysiology.* In press.

28. Manuck, S. B.; Craft, S. A.; and Gold, K. J.: Coronary-prone behavior pattern and cardiovascular response. *Psychophysiology* 15:403-411, 1978.

29. Manuck, S. B. and Garland, F. N.: Coronary-prone behavior pattern, task incentive and cardiovascular response. *Psychophysiology* 2:136-142, 1979.

30. Matthews, K. A.; Glass, D. C.; Rosenman, R. H.; and Bortner, R. W.: Competitive drive, Pattern A, and coronary heart disease: A further analysis of some data from the Western Collaborative Group Study. *Journal of Chronic Diseases* 30:489–498, 1977.

31. Obrist, P. A.: The cardiovascular–behavioral interaction—as it appears today. *Psychophysiology* 13:95–107, 1976.

32. Price, K. P. and Clarke, L. K.: Behavioral and psychophysiological correlates of the coronary-prone personality: New data and unanswered questions. *Journal of Psychosomatic Research* 40:478–486, 1978.

33. Rosenman, R. H.: The interview method of assessment of the coronary-prone behavior pattern. In *Coronary-prone behavior*. eds. T. M. Dembroski, S. M. Weiss, J. L. Shields, *et al.*, pp. 55–59. New York: Springer-Verlag, 1978.

34. Rosenman, R. H.: The role of the Type A behavior pattern in ischaemic heart disease: Modification of its effects by beta-blocking agents. *British Journal of Clinical Practice* 32 (Supplement 1):58–65, 1978.

35. Rosenman, R. H.; Brand, R. J.; Sholtz, R. I.; and Friedman, M.: Multivariate prediction of coronary heart disease during 8.5 year follow-up in the Western Collaborative Group Study. *American Journal of Cardiology* 37:903–910, 1976.

36. Rosenman, R. H. and Friedman, M.: Association of a specific overt behavior pattern in females with blood and cardiovascular findings. *Circulation* 24:1173–1184, 1961.

37. Rosenman, R. H.; Friedman, M.; Straus, R.; *et al.* A predictive study of coronary heart disease: The Western Collaborative Group Study. *Journal of the American Medical Association* 189:15–22, 1964.

38. Scherwitz, L.; Berton, K.; and Leventhal, H.: Type A behavior, self-involvement, and cardiovascular response. *Psychosomatic Medicine* 40:593–609, 1979.

39. Schneiderman, N.: Animal models relating behavioral stress and cardiovascular pathology. In *Coronary-prone behavior*, eds. T. M. Dembroski, S. M. Weiss, J. L. Shields, *et al.* pp. 155–182. New York: Springer-Verlag, 1978.

40. Van Egeren, L. F.: Cardiovascular changes during social competition in a mixed-motive game. *Journal of Personality and Social Psychology* 37:858–864, 1979.

41. Van Egeren, L. F.: Social interactions, communications, and the coronary-prone behavior pattern: A psychophysiological study. *Psychosomatic Medicine* 41:2–18, 1979.

42. Williams, R. B.: Psychophysiological processes, the coronary-prone behavior pattern, and coronary heart disease. In *Coronary-prone behavior*, eds. T. M. Dembroski, S. M. Weiss, J. M. Shields, pp. 141–146. New York: Springer-Verlag, 1978.

43. Williams, R. B.; Haney, T.; Gentry, W. D.; and Kong, Y.: Relation between hostility and arteriographically documented coronary atherosclerosis. *Psychosomatic Medicine* 40:88, 1978.

44. Williams, R. B.: Unpublished data presented at the first annual meeting of the Academy of Behavioral Medicine Research, Snow Bird, Utah, 1979.

45. Zoleman, T. M.; Thomas, G.; Olewine, P. A.; *et al.* Coronary-prone behavior patterns: Relationship to alpha and self-concept. *Personality and Social Psychology Bulletin* 36:350, 1978.

46. Zyzanski, S. J.: Coronary prone behavior pattern and coronary heart disease: Epidemiological evidence. In *Coronary-prone behavior*, eds. T. M. Dembroski, S. M. Weiss, and J. L. Shields, *et al.* pp. 25–40. New York: Springer-Verlag, 1978.

Effects of Presumably Stressful Stimulation (PSS) on the Development of Animal Tumors: Some Issues[1]

BENJAMIN H. NEWBERRY

As two excellent reviews of the literature in this area are already available (LaBarba [23] and Riley, this volume), this paper will focus on selected problems relating to psychological influences on cancer, with some examples illustrating why simple approaches to the "psychology of cancer" seem inappropriate and inadequate at present. The argument will be made, from our findings and others, that we know very little at present about psychological influences on animal tumors, and that, because of its importance and complexity, the area demands more attention from the biobehavioral research community than has been forthcoming to date.

These are hardly new ideas. A decade ago LaBarba [23] noted the confusion in this literature and called for more systematic research. Nearly every author since has referred to the situation. What is disappointing—though understandable—is that LaBarba's assessment is about as accurate today as it was in 1970. At neither the molar level of relationships between type of stimulation and tumor development nor at the more molecular level of physiological mechanism can we make statements of significant generality. The phenomena are seemingly quite complex, and the research has been quite simple. The data that are available and the conclusions that have been drawn from them make it appear that a thorough understanding of the role of psychological factors in animal tumor development will require

---

[1] This paper is a somewhat altered version of a poster presentation at the first annual meeting of the Academy of Behavioral Medicine Research. The original was a summary of work from our laboratory on the inhibition of DMBA-induced rat mammary tumors by aversive conditions; it presented much of the data from our studies. Because the details are or will be available elsewhere, it seemed reasonable to eliminate most of them from this account and to emphasize instead some of the relatively general issues related to our findings.

PERSPECTIVES ON
BEHAVIORAL MEDICINE

329

integrating the psychology of stimulation, neuroendocrinology, immunology, and tumor biology. This is a formidable task. The results,
however, may be worth the effort; the data which suggest that the problem
is complex also suggest that the effects of psychologically relevant stimulation on tumor development can be profound.

The Human Research Context

Obviously, the possibility that behavioral factors influence human
cancer is the major impetus to interest in the effects of such factors on
animal neoplasms. With this in mind, it should be remembered that there
are two rather distinct ways in which psychological factors may influence
neoplastic disease. The first of these involves overt behavior which exposes
the potential host to exogenous carcinogens, promoters, or, possibly,
tumor-inhibiting agents. The psychological questions in these instances
focus on the reasons for such behavior as smoking or failure to take safety
precautions in workplaces. Understanding and being able to modify
behavior which exposes individuals to relevant exogenous agents could
surely prevent many cancer cases. Hence, the need for research in that area
is clear. However, animal research is only indirectly relevant to
psychological questions of exposure to exogenous agents. The applicable
animal work is that pertaining to basic processes in areas such as motivation, learning, attitudes, and social interaction.

The second type of situation, one to which nearly all animal work on
psychological factors and cancer relates, assumes that any necessary exposure to exogenous initiating or promoting agents has taken place or will
take place. The concern is thus with internal processes which influence host
resistance. The psychological focus in the area of endogenous processes is
on external stimulation which alters the internal milieu so as to alter the
probability or severity of neoplastic disease. The term "psychobiological"
will be used to refer to this second situation.

The case for the importance of psychobiological factors to human cancer
is much weaker than that for behavioral exposure to exogenous agents.
With an exogenous agent, its identification may point directly to behavior
patterns that influence exposure and hence answer the simple question of
whether psychological variables are involved at all. With endogenous influences the long, complex, and problematic series of links between
psychological events and significant neoplasms is an immediate stumbling
block. Even considering simple associations between stimulation (or personality) characteristics and human cancer—without attempting to trace

physiological mediators—presents vexing problems. The latent periods of malignancies and the complexity of human histories make clear data difficult to obtain. When one wishes to go beyond association and consider possible causal influences of psychobiological factors, the complexity of the problem increases dramatically. Confounding of personality or stimulation variables with exposure to exogenous agents and early effects of disease processes on behavior, for example, must be ruled out. Fox [11] and Morrison and Paffenbarger (this volume) have noted these and other difficulties in the course of evaluating human research on behavioral factors in cancer. Their discussions make it clear that, while there are suggestive data and plausible rationales for psychobiological effects on human cancer, there are yet no findings capable of resolving the question.

Problems with obtaining and interpreting human data in this area produce a strong argument for animal research. Obviously, animal studies allow better control and are more convenient for investigating putative links between psychological factors and tumor development. Further, a well-developed body of animal data might suggest methodological points and plausible predictor variables for human studies.

The selection of psychological predictor variables for human research presents problems because of the paucity of firm data and empirically supported theory. Long-term prospective studies with large samples are likely to be essential in getting at psychobiological effects on human cancer, but they will be costly and complex in design. Beyond global measures related to emotional experience and psychosocial history—measures which might not be specific enough to predict intervening physiological events related to a particular type of tumor—there is little guidance for the researcher wishing to select from the multitude of possible predictors.

Animal research could eventually be of value in selecting plausible, specific predictors for human studies. The limited psychological similarity between man and laboratory animals is a real obstacle; yet it should be possible to work from animal tumors to human psychosocial stimulation via neuroendocrine mediators. To take an hypothetical example, difficulty in expressing emotion has been suggested as related to human cancer development [14, 21]. It might make little sense to speak of such a problem in rodents. However, if an abnormality of emotional expression were known to be associated with a particular neuroendocrine pattern in humans, and stimulation producing a similar neuroendocrine pattern influenced tumor development in rodents, then the effort required to assess expressive patterns in large-scale human studies would have an increased justification.

Tying psychological factors in animal and human research together by means of physiological response patterns may seem a roundabout approach to some, and it is certainly not the only approach to be taken. It does have advantages, however. It focuses attention on the internal milieu, where effects on tumor development must ultimately take place. It also avoids the difficulty of attempting to equate the responses of lower animals to verbal reports of human subjective experience and finesses to some extent the problem of finding animal analogues to complex human interpretations of stimulation. It is difficult enough to deal objectively with subtle phenomena like anxiety, depression, object loss, and hostility in the species in which they were originally identified and to which researchers themselves belong. Trying to extend them prematurely to animals could actually obscure important interspecies relationships in psychobiological influences on cancer.

Truly comparative data are needed on neuroendocrine and immunologic responses to a variety of environmental conditions. Mason [30] has stressed the complexity of neuroendocrine responses and has noted differences between organisms given ostensibly similar stimulation. Individual differences in human psychophysiological responding are well known [24]. In a related vein, Solomon and his colleagues [45, 46] have emphasized the complexity of neuroendocrine influences on the immune system. Fox [11] has noted that failure to differentiate among types of human cancers may obscure important relationships between psychological factors and tumor development. Differences between animal tumors and their presumed human counterparts may be expected to provide the same type of impediment. For example, two widely used rodent mammary tumors, the spontaneous mouse tumor induced by the mouse mammary tumor virus (MTV), and the DMBA-induced rat tumor, differ from each other in some respects critical for psychobiological influences and also seem to differ from human mammary cancers in important respects. Smithline, Sherman, and Kolodny [44] suggest that the rodent and human tumors may develop from different cell types, that the mouse and human tumors are preceded by precancerous hyperplasias, unlike the rat tumor [cf.3], that the rat and human tumors are often hormone responsive while only the preneoplastic nodules are responsive in the mouse, that in the rat system prolactin before induction is protective while after induction it promotes tumor development, that the role of estrogens in stimulating prolactin is seemingly much greater in rodents than in humans, that the rodent tumors rarely metastasize. It seems that the two rodent systems could respond quite differently to psychologically relevant stimulation, but it is not clear that either can be embraced as a complete model for psychobiological effects on the human cancer.

General Characteristics of Findings on Psychobiological Factors and Animal Cancer

The simple, general question of whether psychologically relevant stimulation can affect the development of animal neoplasms via endogenous agents has been answered in the affirmative. A sizable number of studies have reported such effects [23]. Moreover, the size of effects as indicated by the magnitude of group differences can be considerable, suggesting·that psychobiological effects on human cancer may be of practical importance.

Animal research in this area has focused on the effects of conditions that can be considered aversive, stressful, or taxing to the potential hosts. The term stress is often used to describe the response to such conditions, but it may be misleading in the present context. As used by Selye [41], the term is to refer to the nonspecific aspects of response to adaptational demands. With regard to tumor development effects, however, we are far from certain that the nonspecific reaction to a demand will be more important than its specific characteristics. Glucocorticoids and catecholamines, the two primary indices of stress, can be decoupled in the sense that they can be secreted in different ratios in response to different arousing or aversive stimuli [17] and can adapt differentially to different types of stimulation [32]. If, as Henry, Stephens, and Watson [18] have suggested, aversive stimulation producing a relatively high ratio of corticoids to catecholamines promotes tumor development, whereas stimulation producing a low ratio inhibits development, the difference may not properly be attributable to nonspecific stress.

Most studies of psychologically relevant stimulation and animal tumors have assessed the major stress response systems crudely if at all. Our research on the DMBA-induced rat mammary tumor has relied chiefly on adrenal and thymus weights taken at sacrifice. Using these measures, we have found little evidence for the stressfulness of the restraint manipulation which consistently inhibits development of the tumor [34, 36]. Adrenal weight and thymus weight do not index sympathomedullary activation and are hardly sensitive measures even of adrenal cortical output. Taking these measures at the end of experiments gives information on animals' status only after tumor effects have occurred and at a time when controls are under demands from greater average tumor mass. Hence, for several reasons it cannot be said that our results are a function of the "stressfulness" of the restraint treatment. Many of the same considerations apply to other studies. In addition, it must be remembered that even when appropriate measures of nonspecific stress are taken, the effects of the eliciting stimuli cannot be attributed to the nonspecific stress response unless specific components have been controlled.

Whether because of the partial independence of the relevant physiological responses, inadequate or incomplete assessments, measures taken at an insufficient number of times, or the failure to find evidence for nonspecific stress, it has usually not been possible to ascribe effects of psychologically relevant stimulation accurately to stress. To encourage recognition of the uncertainties about the independent variables that have been used, a *less* precise term, *presumably stressful stimulation* (PSS), will be substituted for stressor.

Terminology aside, once the existence of psychobiological effects on animal cancers has been noted and given due weight, the outstanding characteristic of the animal PSS–cancer literature is its disarray. A variety of tumors have been shown to be responsive to psychologically relevant stimulation, including viral, transplanted, and chemically induced types. A similar diversity of PSS types has been used, including electric shock, extreme temperatures, infection, restraint, demanding learning tasks, social disruption, exposure to predators, and ordinary laboratory routine. A variety of intensities, durations, and timings of exposure have been included.

Both tumor-enhancing and tumor-inhibiting effects of PSS have been reported in convincing numbers. A partial list of neoplasms reported to have been enhanced by PSS includes Ehrlich carcinoma [20, 28], mammary tumors presumably induced by the mouse mammary tumor virus [18, 37, 40, 50], DMBA-induced rat mammary tumors [20, 38], murine sarcoma virus (MSV)-induced tumors [2], P815 mastocytoma [43], and dibenzpyrine-induced papilloma and subsequent carcinoma [13]. Among those reported to have been inhibited are Ehrlich carcinoma [28, 31], murine leukemia [25], DMBA-induced rat mammary tumors [34–36, 38, 39], and MSV-induced tumors [2]. Numerous other studies are cited by Riley (this volume) and by LaBarba [23]. It is important to note that chemically induced, viral, and transplanted tumors are included among those inhibited by PSS and among those enhanced. The general class of experimental tumor does not seem to predict PSS response.

The sheer diversity of stimulation and tumor types used in these experiments strengthens the case for believing that psychobiological effects occur in human cancer. The larger the number of tumor systems and PSS types related in animal research, the greater the probability of functional similarity to some human cancers and human experiences. However, all of the exploration of PSS and animal cancers has yet to result in a systematic understanding of the effects of host stimulation on tumor development. There are as yet no confirmed general principles capable of predicting even the direction of effect with an untried combination of tumor system and stimulation. We do not know, for example, why restraint [36] and electric shock [35, 38] should inhibit the DMBA rat mammary tumor, whereas forced swimming and handling [38] enhance it; why there is little or no indication that the mouse MTV tumor can be inhibited by PSS; why the Ehrlich tumor may be inhibited by avoidance conditioning or restraint yet enhanced by avoidance conditioning in another experiment [28]; why the progression of chemically induced papillomas is facilitated by skin wounding and laparotomy but inhibited by audiogenic and electric shock [13]. The list could be extended.

Some organizing principles have been suggested and will be mentioned further on in this chapter, but the research which has been reported has not been sufficiently systematic to resolve such disparaties. Relatively little effort has yet been devoted to extensive investigation of differences among tumor types, stimulation characteristics and potential neuroendocrine and immunological mediators *as these variables operate jointly* in psychobiological effects on tumor development. This is not to disparage what has been done. There are reasons for the lack of systematization. The entire area is new and just emerging from the status of a scientific curiosity. The development of a literature with disparate findings has perhaps been needed to demonstrate the complexity of the phenomena. Many laboratories lack ready access to the range of techniques needed to study several mediating variables simultaneously. As data accumulate and the potential importance of psychobiological effects on cancer becomes more widely recognized, this will change.

Tumor System Variables

An animal cancer model necessarily consists of both a host species–strain and a type of neoplasm. Each must be assumed to have a particular set of responsivities, and they must be assumed to interact even apart from stimulation differences. Many animal tumors, of course, require quite specific hosts, and immunologic relationships are surely involved in a large number of those dependencies [16]. It seems probable that psychobiological characteristics of hosts are involved in at least some instances whether the immune system or some other factors mediate the dependency. Differences in neuroendocrine reactivity could influence tumor development either through direct hormonal involvement or via the immune system. Leukemias, for example, may be directly inhibited by adrenal corticosteroids [25]. One could at least imagine a leukemia which is equally immunologically compatible with two host strains differing in pituitary–

adrenal reactivity. Even under the mild, constant stimulation of "normal" laboratory conditions, development of the disease could be quite different in the two strains.

A less problematic example can be found in the response of Sprague–Dawley and Long-Evans rats to DMBA and 7,8,12-trimethylbenz(a)anthracene [19]. Both strains are susceptible to mammary carcinogenesis by these compounds. When single doses were given at a standard age, Sprague–Dawley animals were much more susceptible than Long-Evans; however the strains were much more comparable when multiple doses were given. Among the possible reasons for this difference is the later onset of puberty noted by Huggins, Oka, and Fareed in the Long-Evans strain. Differences in puberty could alter the distribution of the carcinogen over mitotically active periods in mammary development, so that later doses would be required to get a high tumor yield in Long-Evans.

When the basic relationship between tumor or carcinogen and host varies, PSS effects may vary. In the case of the two hypothetical leukemia systems, the effects of PSS on the disease might be greater in the reactive strain unless two relatively intense levels were compared, in which case it might be greater in the nonreactive strain. In the case of the rat mammary tumor, stimulation which alters the time of puberty [27] might have different effects with different host strains and induction procedures.

All tumor systems are not equally relevant for the study of all psychobiological effects. Transplanted cells cannot be used to study PSS effects on early stages of neoplastic cell transformation unless they contain cancer viruses. With viral induction, both early and later stages of tumor development take place in the host, but the virus itself needs to be taken into account. When the virus replicates in the host, initiation and later developmental events may be taking place simultaneously, making it more difficult to interpret PSS effects. In the case of the milk-transmitted MTV, effects of preinitiation PSS—which are known to be significant in at least some systems—are difficult to investigate since the virus must be assumed present shortly after birth. Purely chemically induced tumors allow relatively clear distinctions among preinitiation, initiation, and postinitiation stages, but information on the persistence of the carcinogen and active metabolites is required. Also to be considered with chemical induction is the possibility that the carcinogen interacts with other agents such as latent viruses. Some believe that unremarked viruses are quite common [47]. If they are involved in chemical carcinogenesis, then the tumor development process may not respond to host stimulation as the investigator supposes.

The immunogenicity of neoplastic cells is crucial to PSS effects because it bears directly on the question of the types of mechanisms that can act. If a tumor is not significantly antigenic, if tolerance is induced, or if the inducing agent is strongly immunosuppressive, then presumably PSS effects on the immune system are not going to be crucial to host–tumor balance. It has been suggested [22] that chemically induced tumors may be less antigenic in general than other types. To the extent that this is the case, other mechanisms than acquired immunity must be sought in understanding PSS effects on those tumors. With viruses, the host may be able to respond to viral antigens as well as tumor antigens, possibly enhancing the chance of significant immunological control, particularly when viral antigens are expressed at the neoplastic cell surface.

Development rate is another tumor system variable of importance in studying psychobiological effects. Some tumors progress quite rapidly. The transplanted P815 mastocytoma is detectable within 5–6 days following innoculation [42]. MSV-induced tumors reach their maximum size within 10–15 days after virus injection [2]. In stark contrast, C3H mouse mammary tumors may not reach 50% incidence until 250–550 days of age [40]. DMBA-induced rat mammary tumors are of middling developmental speed, average latency to first palpable tumor being at 1–3 months after DMBA administration at the usual age of 50–60 days.

Clearly, effects of long-term PSS cannot be studied using tumors that develop in a few days. On the other hand, brief stimulation may fail to show an effect on slowly developing tumors, not because no effect occurs, but because it is too small to be detected against the great variability likely to accompany slow development. The development rate factor can make it difficult to draw conclusions from comparisons of tumor systems, particularly if the neuroendocrine response to PSS adapts or changes in some other way as a function of exposure duration. Age is also a potential confounding variable in comparisons of tumors that develop at different rates.

It may be feasible to alter the development rate of some tumors by varying the quantity of cells, carcinogen or virus used, or by altering their administration in some other way. This could facilitate comparisons of tumor system responses to PSS by allowing more comparable durations of exposure to the stimulation. An unpublished experiment in our laboratory investigated the effect of restraint on the DMBA-induced rat mammary tumor when the first carcinogen administration was given at 90 days of age rather than the 50 days of age which has been usual. The experimental group were restrained daily from 30–165 days of age. At 165 days of age, 55% of controls (11 of 20) had palpable tumors, whereas 6% (1 of 16) restrained animals had palpable tumors. These data suggest that the inhibitory effect of restraint survives the age-related changes that reduce mammary susceptibility to the carcinogen. Although tumor incidence was still well above that of the C3H mouse tumor, further adjustments in dose and administration timing might slow DMBA tumor appearance more.

Amkraut and Solomon [2] provided evidence that dose changes will not always alter development greatly. They found that tenfold differences in virus doses had only little effect on the MSV tumor.

Temporal Characteristics of Stimulation

Temporal factors, such as chronicity of stimulation and its application at various stages of tumor development, have been shown to be important in animal tumor response to PSS. As with other variables, no broad generalizations have yet been supported empirically, but it is reasonable to assume that temporal factors interact with other stimulation characteristics such as intensity, and with tumor system characteristics. As pointed out above, the tumor system selected for study will often constrain the values temporal variables may take.

Our research suggests that PSS applied after initiation is necessary and sufficient to inhibit development of the DMBA rat mammary tumor. One series of experiments used our standard induction procedure (2 mg DMBA in emulsion IV at 50, 53, and 56 days of age) and a regimen of 30 strong foot-shocks per day occupying 18 hours of each day. The foot-shock treatment significantly inhibited tumor development when applied from 35–120 days of age or from 35–75 days of age, but not when applied from 35–60 days of age [35]. A more extended set of comparisons was made using forced restraint as PSS [34]. These experiments used the same induction method as the foot-shock experiments. One experiment compared preinduction and induction period restraint with and without extension into the postinduction period, using nonrestrained animals and animals restrained throughout the experiment as comparison groups. All groups receiving long-term restraint (30–120, 50–120, 30–100 days of age) developed fewer tumors than controls, whereas restraint limited to the preinduction period (30–49 days of age) or induction period (50–69 days of age) failed to have a significant effect. A second experiment involved eliminating restraint from most of the induction period. Animals in a gapped restraint condition were restrained from 30 to 44 days of age and again from 62 to 120 days of age. Another group was restrained only from 62 to 120 days of age. Both restrained groups developed fewer tumors than controls. In a third experiment, restraint beginning at 80 days of age—24 days after the last DMBA injection—also inhibited tumor development. These findings indicate that restraint inhibition of the DMBA tumor is largely a postinduction phenomenon, an interference with cell proliferation rather than with initiation of cells by the carcinogen.

Our findings with the DMBA tumor do not represent the only type of relation that can occur between temporal factors and tumor development. In their studies of MSV-induced tumors in mice, Amkraut and Solomon [2] found that both preinoculation and postinoculation shock influenced tumor size, but in opposite directions. Shock prior to virus injection decreased tumor size, whereas shock after injection increased tumor size. Stern, Winokur, Graham, and Lefton [49] found that a 75-day forced exercise regimen increased the incidence of papillomas induced by 3-methylcholanthrene when begun concurrently with skin painting, but the effect was markedly reduced when the 75-day treatment began 15 days before skin painting commenced. The study leaves open the possibility that a preinduction treatment which terminated prior to induction would decrease incidence of the tumor, providing a parallel to the Amkraut and Solomon [2] results. Another study provided somewhat related findings. Minster [33] used celiotomy, performed at various times prior to inoculation of Walker 256 cells. This procedure increased tumor takes relative to controls when performed 1–12 or 20–30 days prior to inoculation. However, it significantly reduced takes when performed 16 or 18 days before inoculation.

The possibility of complex effects of temporal factors, as suggested by the Minster [33] results, is supported by one of our experiments [34]. It was reasoned that, if inhibition of the DMBA rat mammary tumor by restraint is an interference with cell proliferation, then an increase in the appearance of new tumors should follow termination of the restraint regimen. Three groups of rats received daily restraint beginning at 30 days of age but terminating at 60, 75, or 90 days of age. New tumor appearance in those animals was compared to that of continually restrained and control groups. As predicted, an increase in new tumor appearance followed restraint termination. A later, unanticipated decrease also occurred. Thus, although the restraint manipulation appears to render at least some transformed cells permanently incapable of proliferation to palpable tumors, an apparent increase in tumor development can seemingly result from termination of PSS which had been holding tumor growth in check.

Sklar and Anisman [42] also report results possibly due to an effect of PSS offset. They found that 1 and 5 days of shock following injection of mastocytoma cells decreased tumor latency, whereas 10 days of the same shock schedule produced a small, nonsignificant delay of appearance and a significant decrease in tumor size compared to controls. Sklar and Anisman note the possibility that the 10-day shock regimen attenuated tumor-promoting aftereffects of PSS. The (slight) evidence for inhibition with the 10-day regimen opens the possibility that PSS onset effects are tumor-inhibiting in their mastocytoma system.

The need to consider the relationship of PSS to stages of tumor development and to distinguish PSS onset effects from PSS offset effects with animal tumors raises some questions for the optimal design of human studies. The effects observed with humans might depend critically upon the precise relationship between life events and the stage of potential malignancies. If PSS prior to initiation inhibits development while PSS following initiation promotes development, then the average risk of individuals with calm and turbulent histories could be assessed as the same even in a long-term prospective study using adequate predictor variables. The results might therefore mask strong psychobiological effects on cancer. Such findings might be adequate for some purposes, such as advice to the general population, but misleading when applied to more specific situations. If neoplastic development can be held in check by PSS, only to continue with termination of a stressful period [34], then human studies might conclude that PSS promotes tumor development when the opposite is actually the case.

Solomon, Amkraut, and Rubin [46] refer to a relatively brief temporal "window" for enhancement of the immune response by substances influencing cyclic nucleotide levels. At least some agents having such effects are PSS-responsive. Given the number of sequenced components involved in immune responses, it is possible that there are other such "windows." Selye's concept of a multiphasic general adaptation syndrome [41], although not as well documented as could be wished [29], suggests further opportunities for temporal factors to influence tumor response to host stimulation.

In view of the likely temporal complexity of psychobiological influences on cancer, the outcome for a human individual might well rest upon his or her particular environmental situation during a few hours or days around the time of exposure to an exogenous agent or around the time at which a neoplastic clone first appears. This raises the unpleasant possibility that human research to document and trace psychobiological influences will be extremely expensive. Indeed, should simplifying principles not be developed through either animal or human research, one would be tempted to take successful human studies as evidence for a high frequency of cancer cell appearance in human tissues.

Intensity and Related Variables

It is difficult to imagine that PSS intensity—in some meaningful sense of the term—can fail to be related to tumor response. Yet intensity is not necessarily a straightforward variable in terms of the effects it may be expected to have. The psychological intensity of aversive stimulation is not necessarily easy to quantify even with variables such as electric shock whose physical parameters are simple and well known [4]. Qualitatively different conditions such as forced exercise [49], social disruption [2, 18], and exposure to hungry predators [31] cannot be compared in terms of their physical parameters.

Even considering intensity in terms of physiological response can present problems. To the extent that nonspecific stress responses or specific responses adapt with repeated exposure to PSS, "functional" intensity of stimulation may be said to change over time. Pilot work has suggested that rats adapt quickly to our daily restraint manipulation (10–12 hr duration per day), as indicated by adrenal and thymus weights. Adaptation can complicate the interpretation of temporal factors, as indicated above. In the Stern *et al.* [49] exercise–papilloma study, for example, the animals exercised beginning 15 days prior to induction may have adapted considerably by the time of carcinogen administration. The reduced effect in the early exercise group could reflect nothing more than lower levels of neuroendocrine activity in their response to the postinduction exercise. Intense PSS beginning prior to tumor initiation and extending into the initiation and/or postinitiation stages may thus be functionally equivalent to less intense stimulation which begins at the time of initiation. The problem of adaptation, then, extends the number of conditions that must be compared in studies of temporal parameters and increases the need for repeated assessment of presumed physiological mediators.

Riley (this volume) points out numerous stimulation characteristics that may complicate the interpretation of PSS-cancer studies; some of the factors he mentions bear directly on the question of interpreting intensity effects. In particular, Riley [40] has emphasized the need for quiescent baseline laboratory conditions and for investigation of low-intensity PSS. Without such information, it is quite difficult to interpret findings from more severe stimulation, since the lower levels of the intensity continuum are missing. As Riley indicates, given the number of PSS-responsive systems, their intimate interrelations, and known tendencies for different response patterns to appear with different types of PSS, it is reasonable to speculate that differing PSS intensities may produce qualitatively different internal conditions. Such qualitative differences may affect different tumor systems in different ways.

At least as important as any data available on PSS intensity and animal tumors are the general suggestions that have been made regarding intensity and related variables. Turkevich [50] has suggested a J-like function relating severity of PSS to tumor development. The assumption is that mild stimulation will "activate" higher CNS functions and increase host resistance to neoplastic disease. Severe stimulation and/or stimulation that places great coping demands upon the host will enhance tumor development via a "functional derangement" of higher nervous processes. Turkevich cites Soviet experiments in which the presumed severity of experimental stimulation related to the direction of tumor effect.

A related hypothesis offered by Henry, Stephens, and Watson [18] noted that the DMBA-induced rat mammary tumor has tended to be inhibited by PSS, while mouse mammary tumors have tended to be enhanced. They also noted that the rat studies had tended to use predictable aversive stimulation while unpredictable events—or at least events whose termination could not be predicted—often characterized mouse studies. They suggested the possibility that stimulation allowing accurate prediction of offset promotes pituitary–adrenocortical adaptation, while continuing to elicit sympathomedullary response. Less predictable stimulation, in contrast, might produce a sustained adrenocortical response. This suggestion integrates psychological and physiological levels of analysis into the hypothesis that predictability is a potent determinant of the direction of tumor response to PSS. It is not unreasonable to assume that part of the difference between predictable and unpredictable PSS is a matter of functional intensity, given the evidence for greater neuroendocrine response to unpredictability [26, 30, 51].

Evidence consistent with a predictability or coping hypothesis has been obtained by Sklar and Anisman. They found that inescapable shock promotes transplanted mastocytoma; however, when an escapable shock group and yoked controls were compared to nonshock controls, tumor enhancement occurred in the yoked shock group but not in the escape condition [42]. In other experiments, Sklar and Anisman [43] have found that changes in housing conditions can enhance mastocytoma development and that fighting—which they suggest as a coping response—eliminated the tumor enhancing effects of a change to social housing.

The suggestions made by Turkevich [50], Henry, Stephens, and Watson [18], and Sklar and Anisman [42] might be taken to imply some sort of functional intensity continuum involving physical intensity and predictability–controllability components. The virtues of the idea that the direction of PSS effects on tumors varies with such a dimension include encompassing of diverse effects, relation to other findings such as those of Weiss [51] on ulcers, relation to general psychological viewpoints such as the arousal-adaptation level view, and at least a modicum of empirical support.

However, there are data not easily reconciled with an intensity–predictability–controllability hypothesis. Riley, in his comments to this meeting, has referred to tumor facilitation from the presumably mild stimulation of rotation. Our research, although it has involved several types of PSS, has yet to produce facilitation of the DMBA rat mammary tumor (however, see [38]). In one unpublished experiment, mild daily handling had no effect. Restraint has consistently produced inhibition despite daily durations varying from 5–14 hours [34, 36]. Long-term foot-shock at intensities of 5–7 ma has also inhibited tumor development, despite evidence for a sustained adrenocortical response [35].

In a study intended as a preliminary check on the effects of predictability [37], the DMBA rat mammary tumor and the C3H mouse tumor were compared using both predictable and unpredictable stimulation. The predictable stimulation was daily restraint for 12 hr—a procedure which has consistently inhibited the rat tumor. In the unpredictable condition, three types of stimulation were employed—restraint, exposure to a Noble–Collip drum, and exposure to cages of three unfamiliar conspecifics. Each of these had three possible durations (10, 12, 14 hr for restraint and conspecifics; 2, 5, or 8 min for the drum). Schedules generated from Latin squares were used to assign a different subgroup of animals to each stimulation type on each day and to give each animal equal exposure to each duration of each type. In addition, within the constraints of a 16-hr laboratory day, the time of onset was independently randomized for each stimulation type on each day. Thus an animal in the unpredictable condition could accurately predict neither the type of event, nor its duration, nor its time of onset for any day.

In the mouse experiment, restraint and unpredictable stimulation treatments commenced at 59 days of age and continued daily until 445 days of age. In the rat experiment, the treatments began at 38 days of age and continued through 125 days of age. With the mouse system, the unpredictable stimulation significantly increased incidence relative to controls, whereas predictable restraint had no effect; both PSS manipulations produced thymus : adrenal weight ratios significantly lower than that of controls. In the rat experiment, both PSS types inhibited tumor development to an equal degree, but neither affected the organ weight ratio.

The failure of predictable restraint to inhibit the mouse tumor and of the unpredictable treatment to promote the rat tumor is not consistent with a general predictability hypothesis of the sort suggested by Henry, Stephens, and Watson [18]. Our findings suggest rather that tumor system and stimulation characteristics *interact* in influencing tumor development. What enhances one tumor will inhibit another. In addition, the pattern of thymus : adrenal ratios suggests that the degree of adrenocortical reaction may not be crucial for PSS effects on tumor in either system, although the index is not a particularly good one.

It is not reasonable to reject an intensity–predictability–controllability hypothesis on the basis of the available evidence, although at best it would seem to be applicable only under a limited, yet undefined set of boundary conditions with careful account taken of other variables. Rotation may not be a particularly mild stimulus [15]; the functional intensity of stimulation may be different in different species or with widely varying exposure durations even if they are long; the relationships between functional intensity and tumor development might have similar forms but different minima depending on tumor immunogenicity. It is unlikely that all such issues will be resolved in favor of this type of hypothesis. Nonmonotonic hypothesis are difficult to test with complex variables such as predictability. However, the hypothesis seems to have considerable utility at present in organizing thinking about some PSS characteristics.

Physiological Mechanisms

It should be apparent that the physiological links between host experience and tumor cells must be understood if a psychology of cancer is to develop. Even if a purely psychological analysis is possible, the possibility must be demonstrated largely through study of physiological mechanisms. It should also be apparent from the papers in this volume, and from the whole corpus of behavioral medicine research, that large numbers of interacting factors are potentially relevant and that very few can yet be dismissed. That attention will focus on the neuroendocrine and immune responses is self-evident, given that these systems almost exhaust the possibilities. As knowledge has developed, both systems have been recognized as quite complex, and intimately related to each other and to psychologically relevant stimulation [29, 30, 46]. Even an apparently straightforward process such as lymphocytopenia induced by corticosteroids may be deceptive, since some cells are not destroyed but merely altered in their pattern of circulation [48]. The susceptibility of immunosuppression (Ader, this volume), corticosteroid elevation [1], and corticosteroid suppression [6] to classical conditioning adds yet another dimension to our efforts to understand the psychobiological effects on cancer.

There are few cases in which the physiological mechanisms of animal tumor response to PSS are even reasonably clear. Some of the relevant data on the chemically induced rat mammary tumors may serve to illustrate the types of gaps that occur. Modulation of immune response to these tumors by PSS has been little studied and will be made somewhat difficult by the probability that each individual tumor is antigenically distinct [52], and by the fact that outbred hosts have usually been employed.

On the other hand, hormonal influences have been more thoroughly studied. Adrenalectomy promotes development of the rat mammary tumor induced by 3-methylcholanthrene [7]. This finding is consistent with PSS-induced inhibition of the similar DMBA tumor and suggests (weakly) that corticosteroid lymphocytopenia is not a major factor in control of these tumors. However, although the effect of adrenalectomy indicates an involvement of either the pituitary–adrenocortical system or the sympatho-medullary system, it does not permit a distinction between them.

The pituitary–gonadal axis and prolactin have a well-documented relationship with rat mammary tumors [8, 9, 44] and represent a plausible link between PSS and tumor development. However, the proportion of tumors regressing after ovariectomy is not affected by a restraint regimen which reduces overall tumor numbers, suggesting that PSS does not favor either hormone-dependent or hormone-independent tumor types [34]. Gala and Loginsky [12] found that repeated ether anesthesia, which stimulates pro-lactin, inhibited development of the DMBA rat mammary tumor. They also found that etherized animals failing to develop tumors had higher pro-lactin levels after anesthesia than did those animals which did develop tumors. Chan and Cohen [5] found that a high-fat diet enhanced the DMBA tumor, suggesting a role for nutritional factors. More interestingly, they found that this enhancement was abolished by an antiprolactin agent.

Data of the sort reported by Gala and Loginsky and Chan and Cohen suggest prolactin as a mediator of PSS effects on the DMBA tumor, although they do not require it. Indirect evidence against prolactin media-tion derives from studies comparing preinduction and postinduction PSS [34]. Preinduction prolactin protects against DMBA-induced mammary tumors and postinduction prolactin promotes their development [12, 44]. If PSS elevates prolactin levels, the preinduction PSS should retard tumor de-velopment, while postinduction PSS should enhance it. This is not the pat-tern we have found, and so other mechanisms may be involved.

Conclusions

This discussion has not attempted to touch upon all of the questions, all of the findings, or all of the variables which must be dealt with in under-standing the effects of presumably stressful stimulation on experimental cancers. Yet even this selective and rather disjointed collection of issues can serve to indicate the degree to which the literature presents basic problems of interpretation, and the variety of phenomena which seem to be operat-ing.

Despite the confusion, the available data provide a compelling case for psychobiological effects on neoplastic disease (in addition to behavioral in-fluences on exposure to exogenous agents). The animal findings clearly sug-gest the possibility of psychobiological influences on human cancer.

It is equally obvious that no simple or general conclusion concerning the influence of psychologically relevant variables on cancer can now be accepted. Certainly the assumption, implicit in much of the scientific literature and explicit in semipopular literature, that "stress" is somehow constrained only to exacerbate cancer is not tenable. There is ample reason to proceed instead from the assumption that the direction and magnitude of psychological effects on cancer result from the interplay of a number of classes of variables, each of which includes its own subsets of variables. This, in turn, suggests that predicting outcomes must be done on the basis of information about the type of stimulation, its duration, the timing of its onset and offset, host characteristics and tumor characteristics. There seems to be sufficient complexity in the neuroendocrine and immune systems to permit, if not to require, such interactions.

Faced with interactions of such complexity the need is not just for more research, but for research of a somewhat different character from what has gone before. The current animal literature confirms the relevance of psychobiological factors. Further efforts need to address the inconsistencies noted earlier and the underlying mechanisms related to the observed effects. To a degree, answers must wait upon additional information from the fields which combine to constitute the behavioral medicine of cancer, but only to a degree. Investigators can, for example, include more than one tumor system in their studies. They can systematically investigate temporal variables, select types and parameters of stimulation on the basis of those used by others, and include more physiological dependent variables. They can supplement PSS investigations with physiological interventions designed to mimic or prevent observed PSS effects, and thus differentiate between processes which are causal and those which are merely correlated with PSS effects on tumor development.

Of course, all this work may not be necessary. It is always easier to argue that something is complicated than to see an underlying simplicity.

References

1. Ader, R.: Conditioned adrenocortical steroid elevations in the rat. *Journal of Comparative and Physiological Psychology* 60:1156–1163, 1976.
2. Amkraut, A. A.; and Solomon, G. F.: Stress and murine sarcoma virus (moloney)-induced tumors. *Cancer Research,* 32:1428–1433, 1972.
3. Beuving, L. J.; and Bern, H. A.: Hormonal influence upon normal, preneoplastic, and neoplastic mammary gland. In *Estrogen target tissues and neoplasia,* ed. T. L. Dao; pp. 257–273. Chicago: Univ. Chicago Press, 1972.
4. Campbell, B. A.; and Masterson, F. A.: Psychophysics of punishment. In *Punishment and aversive behavior,* eds. B. A. Campbell and R. M. Church. New York: Appleton, 1969.

5. Chan, P.; and Cohen, L. A.: Effect of dietary fat, antiestrogen, and antiprolactin on the development of mammary tumors in rats. *Journal of the National Cancer Institute* 52:25–30, 1974.

6. Coover, G. D.; Sutton, B. R.; and Heybach, J. B.: Conditioning decreases in plasma corticosterone level in rats by pairing stimuli with daily feedings. *Journal of Comparative and Physiological Psychology* 91:716–726, 1977.

7. Daniel, P. M.; and Prichard, M. M. L.: The effect of adrenalectomy on the growth of mammary tumors induced by 3-methylcholanthrene in rats. *International Journal of Cancer* 2:619–627, 1967.

8. Dao, T. L.: Carcinogenesis of mammary gland in rat. *Progress in Experimental Tumor Research* 5:157–216, 1964.

9. Dao, T. L., ed.: *Estrogen target tissues and neoplasia*. Chicago: Univ. Chicago Press, 1972.

10. Fenner, F.; McAuslan, B. R.; Mims, C. A.; Sambrook, J.; and White, D. O.: *The biology of animal viruses* (2nd ed.), New York: Academic Press, 1974.

11. Fox, B. H.: Premorbid psychological factors as related to cancer incidence. *Journal of Behavioral Medicine* 1:45–133, 1978.

12. Gala, R. R.; and Loginsky, S. J.: Correlation between serum prolactin levels and incidence of mammary tumors induced by 7,12-dimethylbenz(a)anthracene. *Journal of the National Cancer Institute* 51:593–597, 1973.

13. Gottfried, B.; and Molomut, N.: Effect of surgical trauma and other external stress agents on tumor growth and healing of cancer. *Proceedings of the Eighth Anti-Cancer Congress* 3:1617–1620, 1963.

14. Greer, S.; and Morris, T.: Psychological attributes of women who develop breast cancer: A controlled study. *Journal of Psychosomatic Research*, 19:147–153, 1975.

15. Haroutunian, V.; Riccio, D. C.; and Gans, D. P.: Suppression of drinking following rotational stimulation as an index of motion sickness in the rat. *Physiological Psychology* 4:467–472, 1976.

16. Hellstrom, K. E.; and Hellstrom, I.: Recent developments indicating homologous effects on cancer cell growth. In *Endogenous factors affecting host-tumor balance*, eds. R. W. Wissler, T. L. Dao, and S. Wood, pp. 177–183. Chicago: Univ. Chicago Press, 1967.

17. Henry, J. P.; Ely, D. L.; Watson, F. M. C.; and Stephens, P. M.: Ethological methods as applied to the measurement of emotions. In *Emotions, their parameters and measurement*, ed. L. Levi, pp. 469–497. New York: Raven Press, 1975.

18. Henry, J. P.; Stephens, P. M.; and Watson, F. M.: Force breeding, social disorder and mammary tumor formation in CBA/USC mouse colonies: A pilot study. *Psychosomatic Medicine* 37:277–283, 1975.

19. Huggins, C. B.; Oka, H.; and Fareed, G.: Induction of mammary cancer in rats of Long and Evans strain. In *Estrogen target tissues and neoplasia*, ed. T. L. Dao, pp. 333–343. Chicago: Univ. Chicago Press, 1972.

20. Kavetsky, R. E.; Turkevich, N. M.; and Balitsky, K. P.: On the psychophysiological mechanism of the organism's resistance to tumor growth. *Annals of the New York Academy of Sciences* 125:933–945, 1966.

21. Kissen, D. M.: The significance of personality in lung cancer in men. *Annals of the New York Academy of Sciences* 125:820–826, 1966.

22. Klein, G.: Immune surveillance and malignant neoplasia. *Program and Abstracts, Third International Symposium on Detection and Prevention of Cancer*, International Study Group for the Detection and Prevention of Cancer. New York, 1976.

23. LaBarba, R. C.: Experiential and environmental factors in cancer: A review of research with animals. *Psychosomatic Medicine* 32:259–276, 1970.

24. Lacey, J. I.; and Lacey, B. C.: Verification and extension of the principle of autonomic response-stereotypy. *American Journal of Psychology* 71:50–73, 1958.

25. Lemonde, P.: Influence of various environmental factors on neoplastic diseases. In *Husbandry of laboratory animals,* ed. M. L. Conalty. New York: Academic Press, 1967.

26. Levine, S.; Goldman, L.; and Coover, G. P.: Expectancy and the pituitary-adrenal system. *Ciba Foundation Symposium 8* (new series). Amsterdam: Associated Scientific Publishers, 1972.

27. Mandl, A. M.; and Zuckerman, S.: Factors influencing onset of puberty in albino rats. *Journal of Endocrinology* 8:357–364, 1952.

28. Marsh, J. T.; Miller, B. E.; and Lamson, B. G.: Effect of repeated brief stress on growth of Ehrlich carcinoma in mice. *Journal of the National Cancer Institute* 22:961–977, 1959.

29. Mason, J. W.: A re-evaluation of the concept of "non-specificity" in stress theory. *Journal of Psychosomatic Research* 8:323–333, 1971.

30. Mason, J. W.: Emotion as reflected in patterns of neuroendocrine integration. In *Emotions: Their parameters and measurement,* ed. L. Levi, pp. 143–181. New York: Raven Press, 1975.

31. Matthes, T.: Experimental contribution to the question of emotional stress reactions on the growth of tumors in animals. *Proceedings of the Eighth Anti-Cancer Congress* 3:471–473, 1963.

32. Mikulaj, L.; and Mitro, A.: Endocrine functions during adaptation to stress. In *Advances in experimental medicine and biology: Neurohumoral and metabolic aspects of injury* (vol. 33), eds. A. G. Kovach, H. B. Stoner, and J. J. Spitzer, pp. 631–638. New York: Plenum, 1973.

33. Minster, J. J.: Decreased resistance to tumor cells after stress, followed by increased resistance. *Proceedings of the Society of Experimental Biology and Medicine* 113:377–379, 1963.

34. Newberry, B. H.: Restraint-induced inhibition of 7,12-dimethylbenz(a)-anthracene-induced mammary tumors: Relation to stages of tumor development. *Journal of the National Cancer Institute* 61:725–729, 1978.

35. Newberry, B. H.; Frankie, G.; Beatty, P. A.; Maloney, B. D.; and Gilchrist, J. C.: Shock stress and DMBA-induced mammary tumors. *Psychosomatic Medicine* 34:295–303, 1972.

36. Newberry, B. H.; Gildow, J.; Wogan, J.; and Reese, R. L.: Inhibition of Huggins tumors by forced restraint. *Psychosomatic medicine* 38:155–162, 1976.

37. Newberry, B. H.; and Mactutus, C. F.: Differential effects of varied and predictable stimulation on two rodent mammary tumors. Manuscript submitted for publication, 1980.

38. Nieburgs, H. E.; Weiss, J.; Navarrete, M.; Grillione, G.; and Siedlecki, B.: Inhibitory and enhancing effects of various stresses on experimental mammary tumorigenesis. *Program and Abstracts, Third International Symposium on Detection and Prevention of Cancer* New York, 1976.

39. Ray, P.; and Pradhan, S. N.: Growth of transplanted and induced tumors in rats under a schedule of punished behavior. *Journal of the National Cancer Institute* 52:575–577, 1974.

40. Riley, V.: Mouse mammary tumors: Alteration of incidence as apparent function of stress. *Science* 189:465–467, 1975.

41. Selye, H.: *Stress in health and disease.* Boston: Butterworth, 1976.

42. Sklar, L. S.; and Anisman, H.: Stress and coping factors influence tumor growth. *Science* 205:513–515, 1979.

43. Sklar, L. S.; and Anisman, H.: Social stress influences tumor growth. Manuscript submitted for publication, 1979.
44. Smithline, F.; Sherman, L.; and Kolodny, H. D.: Prolactin and breast carcinoma. *New England Journal of Medicine* 292:784–792, 1975.
45. Solomon, G. F.; Amkraut, A. A.; and Kaspar, P.: Emotions, stress, and immunity. *Annals of Clinical Research* 6:313–322, 1974.
46. Solomon, G. F.; Amkraut, A. A.; and Rubin, R. T.: Stress and psychoimmunological response. In *Mind and Cancer*. ed. B. A. Stoll, pp. 73–84. London: Wiley, 1979.
47. Spiegelman, S.: Molecular methods for detecting viruses in human cancer. *Program and Abstracts, Third International Symposium on Detection and Prevention of Cancer* International Study Group for the Detection and Prevention of Cancer, New York, 1976.
48. Sprent, J.: Recirculating lymphocytes. In *The lymphocyte: Structure and function* (part I), ed. J. J. Marchalonis. pp. 43–112. New York: Marcel Dekker, 1977.
49. Stern, J. A.; Winokur, G.; Graham, D. T.; and Lefton, R.: Effect of forced activity stress on the development of experimental papillomas in mice. *Journal of the National Cancer Institute* 23:1013–1018, 1959.
50. Turkevich, N. M.: The development of the neoplastic process during functional changes of the higher part of the nervous system. In *The neoplastic process and the nervous system*, ed. R. E. Kavetsky. The State Medical Publishing House, 1958. Translated by the Israel Program for Scientific Translations. Published by NSF, Washington, D.C., 1960.
51. Weiss, J. M.: Effects of coping behavior with and without a feedback signal on stress pathology in rats. *Journal of Comparative and Physiological Psychology* 77:22–30, 1971.
52. Weissman, I. L.; Hood, L. E.; and Wood, W. B.: *Essential concepts in immunology*. Menlo Park: Benjamin/Cummings, 1978.

Beta-adrenergic Hyperreactivity and Behavioral Stress: A Precursor to Established Essential Hypertension? [1]

PAUL A. OBRIST, KATHLEEN C. LIGHT
JANICE L. HASTRUP, AND ALAN W. LANGER

A borderline or labile hypertension observed in a young adult population, has a certain predictive value as a precursor to established essential hypertension later in life [7, 9]. Furthermore, in an appreciable percentage of individuals with a borderline or labile hypertension, the elevation of the blood pressure is attributed to an elevated cardiac output mediated by excessive sympathetic or beta-adrenergic drive on the myocardium [7, 8]. These observations suggest that such excessive beta-adrenergic drive may be a mechanism which evokes a borderline hypertension and, as such, is an early cardiodynamic precursor to an established hypertension. However, there are limitations to these observations. For one thing, a borderline or labile hypertension is far from a perfect predictor of an established hypertension. What is required are longitudinal studies which not only assess the predictability of a borderline hypertension in conjunction with excessive sympathetic drive on the myocardium, but studies which focus on other mechanisms and mediating events that may interact with this aforementioned mechanism. We have in mind changes in vascular compliance due to structural changes or autoregulatory effects, as well as renal mechanisms such as suggested by Guyton [5] and Julius [3]. Also needed are studies which evaluate the relationship between excessive beta-adrenergic drive and these other interacting events, which indicate whether behavioral stress is of significance in the etiology of essential hypertension.

---

[1] This research was supported by the following research grants: MH 07995, National Institute of Mental Health; HL 18976 and HL 23718, National Heart, Lung and Blood Institute; National Service Awards F-32–HL 05531 to Kathleen C. Light and F-32–HL 05671 to Janice L. Hastrup, National Heart, Lung and Blood Institute.

It is a commonly held belief in behavioral biology that the stresses of life hold such significance, yet the available data are not that convincing.[2]

In this paper we will report the results of some of our more recent research, which we believe makes certain limited inroads on these issues and questions, and specifically in respect to the relationship of behavioral stress to beta-adrenergic influences on the myocardium. For some time, we had been evaluating the mechanisms mediating anticipatory heart rate (HR) changes observed in humans using classical aversive conditioning procedures. The results, though in some respects reasonably definitive, were disappointing with regard to the issue of the role of behavioral stress in the pathogenesis of cardiovascular disease. For one thing, we observed primarily vagal control of HR, both decreases and increases [18], which in turn was directionally related to somato-motor activity [16]. We did not view vagal control of HR, perhaps with exception of syncope and possibly certain sudden death phenomena, as of great consequence in the etiological process. For another thing, the observation of a direct relationship between these vagally mediated HR changes and somato-motor events did not strengthen our belief that these behavioral stressors had any significant consequences in the etiological process. We seemed to be dealing with an exerciselike relationship [17] and to our knowledge, no one holds exercise as harmful to one's health—at least in a healthy organism. Finally, we were not particularly impressed with the magnitude of these phasic as well as tonic HR effects. They were from a biological perspective quantitatively trivial. For example, how could a phasic anticipatory HR decrease of 4–5 beats per minute (bpm) extending over a period of 5–6 sec have any great significance to pathophysiological processes? Similarly, on those limited occasions when blood pressure was measured, the phasic anticipatory increases were equally trivial [18].

This situation began to change when the behavioral paradigm was modified and when we began to focus more on tonic levels of myocardial performance as well as the blood pressure. We achieved our first objective, which was demonstrating that a behavioral stressor could evoke a beta-adrenergic influence on the myocardium, by changing the behavioral paradigm from one in which the individual was a passive recipient of the stressors, as in classical aversive conditioning, to one where the individual was given some opportunity to avoid the aversive stressors, contingent on

---

[2] It might be noted that where excessive sympathetic drive has been observed in conjunction with a borderline or labile hypertension, it is not clear whether behavioral stress is of significance. For example, these observations are most commonly made in the "resting state." We say "resting state" in quotes because the individual is not being subjected to common laboratory stressors but is nonetheless being stressed to some extent by the various laboratory procedures (e.g., indwelling catheters).

some aspect of his behavior. This was a shock-avoidance task. We now observed both a sympathetic influence on HR as well as two other indirect measures of myocardial performance, carotid dp/dt and pulse transit time. These sympathetic effects were seen both phasically (i.e., in anticipation of an aversive stimulus) [14], and tonically [12, 13, 15]. The tonic effects, in at least some individuals, were far more pronounced (e.g., HR increases exceeding 40 bpm in some individuals with the average change in one study being 32 bpm). The sympathetic origin of these myocardial events was verified by beta-adrenergic pharmacological blockade. Furthermore, these sympathetic effects were observed to be independent of concurrent somatomotor events. This suggested that once sympathetic influences were clearly evoked, the heart was performing inappropriately or inefficiently from a metabolic perspective. This is a condition which we believe necessary if these behavioral stressors are of significance in the etiology of cardiovascular pathology. A more conclusive demonstration of the metabolic inappropriateness of these myocardial effects is an even more recent effort [10] using chronically prepared dogs. In this study, the relationship between both cardiac output (CO) and HR, and blood oxygen extraction (i.e., the arterial venous blood oxygen content difference) was evaluated, first while the dogs exercised on a treadmill, and then when subjected to a behavioral stressor—namely a shock-avoidance task. The exercise condition consistently produced a linear relationship between both the CO and HR, and the blood oxygen extraction as has been previously observed in exercise studies [1]. The behavioral stressor disrupted this relationship in two respects. In some dogs, the linear relationship was no longer found. That is to say, blood oxygen extraction was no longer predictable from either the CO or HR. Perhaps more importantly, in four of the six dogs during shock avoidance, blood oxygen extraction was observed to be significantly decreased at levels of the CO and HR encountered during exercise. This indicates that relative to exercise, the heart is pumping excessive amounts of blood with respect to metabolic requirements. This is what we mean by metabolically inappropriate or inefficient. A note of caution—we have not as yet evaluated beta-adrenergic influences while measuring blood oxygen extraction, although beta-adrenergic influences have been demonstrated in still another study in chronically prepared dogs during shock avoidance [4].

At this point, we would like to shift gears a bit and now focus on blood pressure effects associated with the evocation of beta-adrenergic influences on the myocardium in humans. The first observation to note is that conditions which evoke the greatest myocardial beta-adrenergic effect also evoke the greatest increase in the systolic blood pressure (SBP) (e.g., average increases of 30 mm Hg). Pharmacological blockade (beta-block) verified that these SBP effects were significantly influenced by beta-adrenergically mediated myocardial effects. On the other hand, conditions which evoke the greatest beta-adrenergic influence on the myocardium, have the least effect on diastolic blood pressure (DBP) (i.e., the DBP increases less under those conditions and in those individuals where beta-adrenergic influences are maximal). This DBP effect is attributable to beta-adrenergically mediated vasodilation, likely in the skeletal muscles. This is indicated by the observation that beta-block, while attenuating SBP increases, results in a greater increase in the DBP. However, this is only observed under those conditions which clearly evoke beta-adrenergic excitation on the myocardium. Therefore, we have moved one more step—namely, the demonstration of a linkage between behavioral stress evoked beta-adrenergic drive and the control of the blood pressure, particularly the evocation of a large tonic increase in the SBP [13].

Such observations only hint as to the relevance of behavioral stress in the etiology of hypertension. They are a necessary first step but do not establish as yet the significance of behaviorally evoked beta-adrenergic activity in the etiological process. More recent experiments provide data that come a little closer to this goal.

First, we observe appreciable individual differences in beta-adrenergic reactivity. This is exemplified in Figures 1 and 2. Figure 1 uses only HR

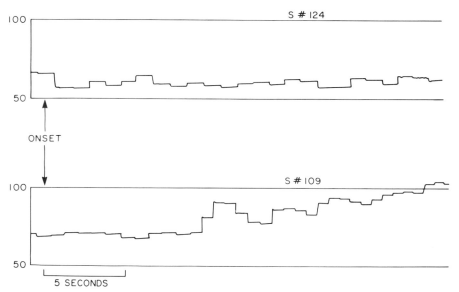

FIGURE 1. *The cardiotachometer write-out illustrates individual differences in reactivity at the onset of an unsignaled reaction time shock-avoidance task.*

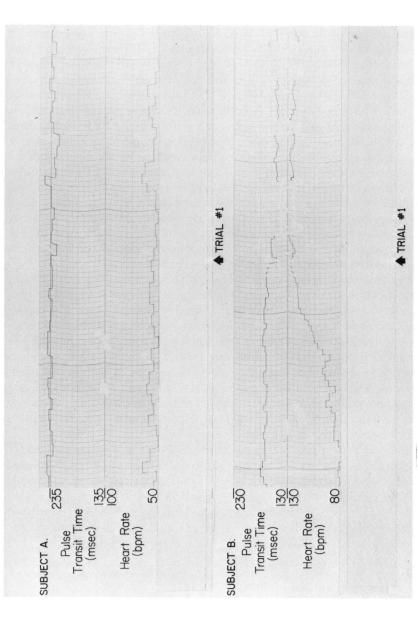

FIGURE 2. *The cardiotachometer and pulse transit time writeout illustrates individual differences in reactivity at the onset of an unsignaled reaction time shock-avoidance task.*

data from a cardiotachometer at the onset of a shock-avoidance task. In the unreactive subject, HR does not change from a baseline value of approximately 65 bpm. In the more reactive subject, HR increases from about 70 bpm to 100 bpm over a period of 30 sec. Figure 2 illustrates under similar circumstances not only individual differences in HR reactivity, but also with pulse transit time (PTT). The latter has been shown [15] to be sensitive to beta-adrenergic influences on the myocardium. In this case we again see essentially no change in either HR or PTT in the one subject at the onset of the shock avoidance task. In the other subject, we see an increase in HR from about 80 bpm to 130 bpm within a 1 min period. PTT time decreases from about 180 msec to 150 msec in the same period. The latter, by our standards, is an appreciable effect.[3] The magnitude of the changes in the two reactive subjects is underestimated since the HR and PTT values at the onset of the tracing is elevated for HR and decreased for PTT relative to a minimal stress baseline—a matter we shall discuss shortly. With such a baseline we have observed HR changes at the onset of a shock avoidance task in one study using 56 subjects to range from − 11 to + 103 bpm. These are extremes, but nonetheless such individual differences are not dependent on one or two subjects as should become apparent shortly.

These individual differences are important for two reasons. First, if such individual differences did not exist and individuals reacted in a similar quantitative manner, then we would be hard pressed to argue that stress-evoked increases in beta-adrenergic reactivity are relevant in the etiology of pathophysiological conditions. Since only a limited percentage of the population become hypertensive, one would expect a similar limited percentage to display hyperresponsiveness if the latter is of relevance. Second, these individual differences raise the question of whether stress-induced hyperresponsiveness is an early manifestation and thus a predictor of the eventual development of essential hypertension or, for that matter, of other aspects of heart disease.

Definitive answers to the latter question await a longitudinal study. Nonetheless, we do have three lines of evidence which suggest that beta-adrenergic hyperresponsiveness is of significance in this young adult population and which encourage us to consider such a longitudinal study. For one thing, myocardial beta-adrenergic responsiveness is directly related to SBP responsiveness. For example, those individuals demonstrating the greater HR increases also demonstrate the greater SBP increases.[4]

---

[3] Note that part of the record is obliterated in the reactive subject by the polygraph pens colliding during the period of peak reactivity.

[4] DBP tends to be inversely related to myocardial beta-adrenergic responsiveness. This, it could be argued, is embarrassing to any position implicating beta-adrenergic responsiveness in the etiological process, because the DBP has been considered by some as the more reliable in-

Secondly, individuals demonstrating greater beta-adrenergic and SBP responsiveness to the avoidance condition also demonstrate greater beta-adrenergic and SBP changes to other laboratory conditions, though not as great. The data we wish to discuss are presented in Table 1 for HR and Table 2 for SBP. These tables were derived as follows. There are two baseline conditions. One is referred to as a relaxation session baseline and it is this baseline from which the range of individual differences previously alluded to (i.e., +103 to −11 bpm) was derived [11]. Data for this baseline were obtained by having the subjects return to the laboratory on two occasions, usually 1–2 weeks after first being exposed to the stressors. On each occasion they were told just to relax for 15 min and that they would not be exposed to any stressors. The second baseline referred to as stress day baseline was a resting period, which occurred on the first occasion they came to the laboratory and just prior to being stressed. In Experiment 1 of Table 1A, three stressors were used, the cold pressor, a pornographic movie, and the unsignaled shock avoidance task previously alluded to. The 56 subjects were divided into quartiles on the basis of their HR reactivity at the onset of the shock-avoidance task (i.e., first 2 min) using the relaxation baseline as the reference point.

There are several notable aspects of this HR data from Experiment 1. The individual differences in HR reactivity during the shock avoidance task are pronounced. With respect to the relaxation baseline, the 14 more reactive subjects demonstrate an average 57 bpm increase (i.e., a 90% change) while the 14 least reactive demonstrate an average increase of 9 bpm (i.e., a 13% change). Second, the two baselines, not too surprisingly, differ with the prestress baselines being the higher. However, the magnitude of this difference is a function of HR reactivity to the shock avoidance task, with the most reactive subjects showing the greatest difference between baselines, whereas the least reactive subjects demonstrate no difference. Also, with respect to the two other stressors (i.e., the cold pressor and film), the more reactive subjects, as defined by the difference between the relaxation baseline and shock-avoidance task, also demonstrate greater HR

---

dicator of an established hypertension. However, it can be argued that in the early phases of the etiological process, increases in the SBP should preceed increases in the DBP. First, elevations in the DBP should lag because the development of a fixed hypertension is dependent on vascular changes (i.e., an increase in the TPR which is secondary to myocardial influences through mechanisms which may involve structural vascular changes and/or autoregulatory influences on the vasculature or possibly even renal influences). Second, in young adults (i.e., < 30 years of age), considered to be borderline hypertensives, it is commonly observed that only the SBP is elevated (i.e., > 140 mm Hg). The DBP is within commonly accepted normotensive levels (i.e., < 90 mm Hg) [20]. To the extent that a borderline hypertensive is the precursor of a fixed hypertension—then such data suggest that the SBP should be the first to be elevated.

TABLE 1A

Mean Heart Rate (bpm) Using Two Types of Baselines and Stress and Quartiled on Basis of HR Reactivity during Shock Avoidance—Percentage Change in Parentheses

HR reactivity	Baseline (relaxation)	Baseline (stress day)	Cold pressor	Film	Shock avoidance
Experiment 1 ($N = 56$)					
Most	63	80 (26)	96 (51)	86 (35)	120 (90)
↓	65	78 (20)	92 (40)	80 (23)	103 (57)
	68	75 (11)	88 (29)	80 (18)	93 (37)
Least	67	66 (−2)	80 (19)	72 (7)	76 (13)
	$\overline{X} = 66$	75	89	79	98
Experiment 2 ($N = 90$)					
Most	69	90 (30)			107 (55)
↓	65	75 (15)			90 (38)
	62	69 (11)			79 (27)
Least	68	65 (−4)			73 (7)
	$\overline{X} = 66$	75			87

reactivity than the subjects in the remaining three quartiles. Therefore, the picture that emerges is that the condition (i.e., the shock avoidance task) which evokes the greatest beta-adrenergic effect as indexed by HR, does so selectively among subjects. These more reactive subjects also generalize their reactivity to all other conditions on that first occasion they come to the laboratory, including a rest period which occurs just prior to being stressed.

It is also important to emphasize the necessity to obtain a relaxation baseline. If one uses only the prestress baseline, HR reactivity during the avoidance task in the more reactive subjects is attenuated and their reactivity to the other stressors is more or less comparable to that of the other subjects. This is most obvious when one looks at the response to the cold pressor using the prestress rest as the baseline. The difference here in the four subgroups is 16, 14, 13, and 14 bpm, but when the relaxation values are used as the baseline, it is 33, 27, 20, and 13 bpm (ordered with respect to HR reactivity to the shock avoidance task).

In a follow-up study (Experiment 2 of Table 1A), we also obtained two baselines in the same manner as in Experiment 1. These subjects were exposed only to the unsignaled reaction time task.[5] The data as presented in

---

[5] We refer to the unsignaled reaction time task in this study as a shock avoidance task in order to simplify communications. This is only the case for 36 of the 90 subjects. Another 36 received the aversive stressors, but their receipt was not contingent on their performance (i.e., they were yoked controls [12]. Another 18 received no exposure to shock. These differing pro-

Table 1A, Experiment 2, were ordered in the same manner as in the first study (i.e., quartiled on the basis of the relaxation baseline shock-avoidance difference). As is apparent, very similar baseline differences were again observed, and the ordering of mean HR values during the stress day baseline is a function of the difference between the relaxation baseline and the tonic levels of HR observed during the onset of the avoidance task.

Finally, one additional study with 20 naive subjects further indicates that these HR effects, particularly in the more reactive subjects, are appreciably influenced by beta-adrenergic drive. They were exposed to the cold pressor, film, and shock-avoidance task (similar to Experiment 1) following beta-adrenergic blockade with IV propranolol. Their average HR values during prestress rest, and each of the three stressors are presented in Table 1B. It should be noted that prestress resting HR after blockade is comparable to relaxation values when the sympathetic innervation is intact (i.e., 67 versus 66 bpm), suggesting that the relaxation values with an intact innervation reflect very little sympathetic drive. With blockade, reactivity to the stressors is noticeably attenuated particularly with the shock-avoidance task (i.e., average differences with an intact innervation using relaxation baseline is 32 bpm in contrast to 5 bpm with a blocked innervation).

There are many parallels in the SBP data from experiments 1 and 2. The SBP data as presented in Table 2 are ordered for both experiments in the same manner as the HR data in Table 1. That is to say, the data was quartiled on the basis of the subjects HR rather than SBP reactivity between the relaxation baseline and the shock-avoidance task. Thus, the HR and SBP quartiles include the same subjects. This was done because of our interest in the influence of myocardial beta-adrenergic activity on SBP. Inspections of Table 2 reveals for both experiments comparable differences among the two baselines as was seen with HR as well as with respect to reactivity. For example, subjects who are the more reactive in terms of HR during the onset of the shock avoidance task demonstrate greater prestress baseline SBP values, as well as high levels of SBP during all the stressors. On the relaxation baseline, however, their values are comparable to the remaining subjects. This holds in both experiments. Also, the importance of obtaining a relaxation baseline in order to assess SBP reactivity is apparent, as it was for HR.

There is one other aspect of the data from these two experiments to note. As just indicated, the more reactive HR subjects show an appreciable labil-

---

cedures likely account for the observation that as a group, these subjects were not as reactive. However, this is immaterial with respect to the baseline differences and the current discussion. The ability to have control of shock delivery or the presence or absence of this aversive stimulus had no effect on the prestress baseline.

TABLE 1-B

Mean HR during Stress Day Baseline and Three Stressors—with Beta-adrenergic Blockade ($N = 20$)—Percentage Change in Parentheses

Baseline (stress day) $\overline{X} = 67$	Cold pressor 72 (7)	Film 68 (1)	Shock avoidance 72 (7)

ity in their SBP values between prestress and relaxation baseline. One can argue that the conditions under which the prestress SBP values were collected have similarities to clinical studies evaluating hemodynamics in borderline hypertension. Both situations are usually novel and inherently stressful. Therefore, it would not seem unrealistic to propose that subjects in our two studies who demonstrate an elevated prestress resting SBP could be considered borderline hypertensive, which is stress induced, and are in principal no different from those individuals considered borderline hypertensive in the clinical studies. Such a possibility is supported by the following: Of the 146 subjects in these two experiments, 33 demonstrated a prestress resting SBP of 140 mm Hg or more, a value commonly considered to be borderline hypertensive, and the incidence of this was directly related to HR reactivity. Table 3 presents the frequency with which pre-stress SBP values were 140 mm Hg or more in each quartile of HR reactivity. As can be seen, the greatest incidence of SBP values of 140 or more occurred in the upper quartiles of HR reactivity, with 24 of the 33 elevations occurring in

TABLE 2

Mean SBP during Two Types of Baseline and Stress. Note: Quartiled on Basis of HR Reactivity during Shock Avoidance (see Table 1). Percentage change in parentheses

HR reactivity	Baseline (relaxation)	Baseline (stress day)	Cold pressor	Film	Shock avoidance
Experiment 1 ($N = 56$)					
Most	124	137 (10)	157 (26)	149 (20)	170 (37)
↓	121	130 (7)	142 (17)	137 (13)	154 (27)
	124	126 (2)	137 (11)	137 (11)	150 (22)
Least	121	124 (2)	141 (17)	133 (9)	137 (13)
	$\overline{X} = 123$	129	144	139	153
Experiment 2 ($N = 90$)					
Most	124	138 (11)			152 (23)
↓	124	133 (7)			146 (18)
	122	130 (7)			140 (15)
Least	126	129 (2)			139 (10)
	$\overline{X} = 124$	133			144

TABLE 3
The Frequency with Which Stress Day Resting SBP Values Are 140 mm Hg or More as a Function of HR Reactivity[a]

		HR reactivity				
	Most	– – – – – – – – – – – – – – – – – – ➔				Least
HR quartile		1	2	3	4	
No. SBP values 140 mm Hg or greater		15	9	4	5	
		$X^2 p < .05$				

[a] Defined as the difference between mean HR during the relaxation session baseline and mean HR during the first 2 min of the avoidance task.

the upper two quartiles. The normotensive values observed in most of these same subjects during the relaxation baseline indicates that these hypertensive values are due to stress. In effect, we are proposing that when borderline hypertensive values are observed with our paradigm, they are no different in significance than those observed in clinical studies, they are stress-induced, and mediated in large part by excessive beta-adrenergic reactivity.

Summarizing these two studies, we find appreciable individual differences in beta-adrenergic reactivity as assessed by HR. Such HR reactivity is clearly related to the individual being exposed to our experimental conditions. They are minimized once the individual is acclimated to our procedures and surroundings and is no longer stressed. They are not only elicited by the various stressors we use but are observable in the resting state when the individual is first exposed to the laboratory procedures. HR reactivity is highly related to SBP reactivity with individuals who demonstrate excessive HR reactivity commonly demonstrating borderline hypertensive SBP values while resting prior to being stressed.

A third and final line of evidence that we have just collected indicates that in young adult males, beta-adrenergic hyper-responsiveness, as indexed by HR, is directly related to the incidence of essential hypertension in the parents. This study was undertaken because of the evidence of familial trends in the occurrence of hypertension [19]. It was hypothesized, in the light of this familial trend, that if beta-adrenergic reactivity is an early indicator of an eventual sustained hypertension, then a greater incidence of hypertension should be observed in the parents of higher as opposed to lower reactivity subjects.

A reasonably detailed medical health questionnaire was sent to the parents of 137 young adult males. Of these 137 questionnaires, 117 were returned—a return rate of 85%. Thirteen of the questionnaires were not used for various reasons, such as ambiguous data, kidney disease, or data were available on only one parent. This left us with 104 pairs of parents (208 parents) with usable data. Of these 208 parents, we considered 34, or 16%, to have primary hypertension. Thirty of these indicated that they were told they were hypertensive by their physicians; of these, 26 indicated they were on some sort of antihypertensive regimen. Four other parents were considered hypertensive because they reported recent BP readings of 135/90 or greater, although they did not indicate they were on medication or that their physicians had informed them that they were hypertensive. The remaining 174 parents we considered normotensive. This included 10 parents who reported episodic elevations of blood pressure associated with some discrete life event like taking oral contraceptives.

We evaluated the relationship between the reactivity of the sons[6] (see Note 5) and the parental history in two ways. First, since our primary interest was in whether beta-adrenergic hyperreactivity in the sons is predictive of hypertension in the parents, we looked at the incidence of hypertension in the parents as a function of HR. We had available six ways to evaluate the HR effects, restricting our conditions to the prestress and relaxation session HR values and HR values during the shock-avoidance task. These six procedures included the mean HR for each of the two rest periods and the avoidance task, and the differences between each of these conditions.

In four of the six analyses, there was a clear association between either HR level or reactivity and parental history. In the remaining two, there was no consistent trend (see Figure 3). Subjects were quartiled on the basis of their absolute level of HR during the shock avoidance-task and the difference between each base period and shock-avoidance. The absolute level of HR during shock-avoidance provided the best predictor of parental history. Eighteen of the 34 hypertensive parents had sons in the upper quartile while 12 of the remaining 16 had sons in the next highest quartile. This provides a median split of 30–4. A similar effect although not as pronounced, was seen with the HR difference scores. In all three cases, the effects were significant.

---

[6] These included subjects who participated in experiment 2, Tables 1-a and 2, some of whom were either yoked controls for the shock-avoidance subjects or never were exposed to the aversive stimuli. In such subjects we might be underestimating their reactivity which in turn would influence any relationship between reactivity and parental history, particularly in parents we considered hypertensive. In order to evaluate this possibility, we selected only subjects whose parents we considered hypertensive and compared those from experiment 1 to those from experiment 2 with respect to HR and SBP reactivity. There was a trend for the experiment 2 subjects to be less reactive, but these yoked subjects with parental histories of hypertension were as reactive as the avoidance subjects with similar parental history, and there were no hypertensive parents among the subjects not exposed to the aversive stimulus.

This analysis was repeated with SBP, using the same six methods to quantify the data. The quartile analysis revealed the same trend in five of the analyses with either higher SBP values or greater SBP differences between conditions being associated with a greater incidence of parental hypertension. These data are presented in Figure 4 for four of the methods of analysis. The differences between quartiles are not quite as sharp as with HR, but the trend is obvious and significant, with respect to both base levels and SBP level during the shock-avoidance task.

A second method of analysis reversed procedures in that it evaluated whether the level of either HR or SBP during the relaxation baseline, prestress rest, and the shock avoidance task was a function of whether there was a parent with hypertension. We had 9 subjects with both parents considered hypertensive and 16 subjects with one parent considered hypertensive. These were evaluated separately and in comparison to the 79 subjects with no parent considered hypertensive.[7] Figures 5 and 6 depict the average HR and SBP values during the relaxation baseline (referred to as *base*), the prestress rest and the shock avoidance task. In both instances, the levels of HR and SBP tended to be higher under all conditions if at least one parent was hypertensive. With SBP, the values were consistently higher if both parents were hypertensive. With both measures, the differences between subjects with hypertensive parents are greatest during the shock avoidance task and least during the relaxation baseline. This trend is significant with both measures, as indicated by the interaction between conditions and parental history. Finally, it should be noted that with SBP, there is a nonsignificant trend for subjects with two hypertensive parents to have higher levels of SBP at all three measurement points, an effect which is most pronounced during the shock-avoidance task.

In passing, there are several other facets of these data to note. We have HR and SBP data during the cold pressor and pornographic movie on 45 subjects and thus family health questionnaires on 90 parents. The cold pressor has been used on and off over the years as a prognostic tool in the hope that it would identify prehypertensives. It is likely fair to state in the light of available evidence from several long-term follow-up studies [2, 6], that this expectation has not been fulfilled. This is not surprising in the light of two considerations. One, if beta-adrenergic hyperreactivity is one of the early or prehypertensive conditions, and in the light of our own evidence indicating that the cold pressor does not evoke as large or as consistently a beta-adrenergic effect, then one would not expect the cold pressor to be as

---

[7] With SBP, the number of parents considered hypertensive was one less than with HR, because SBP during prestress rest and shock avoidance was not available for one subject with a hypertensive parent.

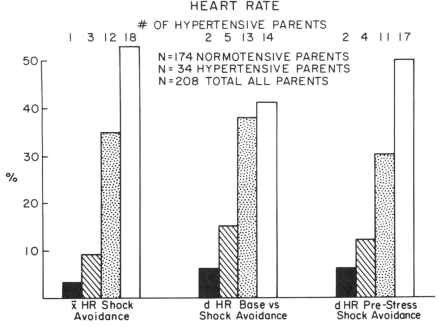

FIGURE 3. *The graph shows number of hypertensive parents in each quartile as a function of subjects mean HR at the onset of the shock-avoidance task and the mean difference in HR between each baseline and the onset of the shock avoidance task.*

effective a predictor as, for example, the shock-avoidance task. Second, if a prestress baseline is used to assess reactivity to the cold pressor, then the magnitude of the effect may be underestimated if the prestress baseline is elevated. We did evaluate in this subsample of 45 subjects the relationship between HR and SBP effects associated with the cold pressor to parental history. With HR, there were no significant effects or even trends, whether looking at the absolute level of HR or the difference from relaxation baseline. We repeated the analysis using the shock-avoidance data on this subsample and found the same trends as with the entire sample, with the effect being significant in a couple of instances (e.g., mean HR during shock avoidance).

With SBP there were also no significant effects, but there were some trends consistent with the observations made with the shock avoidance data and associated baselines using the entire sample. These were seen with the level of SBP during the cold pressor and difference from relaxation session baseline. For example, if one dichotomizes the sample into the largest and smallest SBP levels or differences, we find the incidence of hyperten-

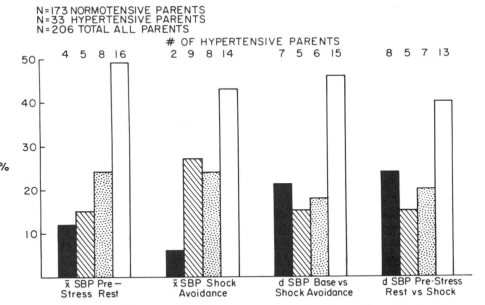

FIGURE 4. *The graph shows number of hypertensive parents in each quartile as a function of subjects mean SBP during prestress rest and the onset of the shock avoidance task, and the mean difference in SBP between each baseline and the onset of the shock-avoidance task.*

sion in the parents as a 13–7 split for the mean level during the cold pressor and a 14–6 split for the difference from relaxation baseline. Because of the small N, it is likely unwise to pursue this discussion further. In any case, it would seem necessary if one were to pursue the use of the cold pressor that they keep in mind the points raised at the beginning of this particular discussion.

There are three other matters to consider in regard to this family history data. Because the incidence of hypertension increases with age, it is possible that the greater incidence of parental hypertension in our more reactive subjects was simply due to these parents being older and not associated with the subjects reactivity. Not surprisingly, we found the hypertensive parents to be on the average approximately 4 years older than the normotensive parents (i.e., 54 years, 3 months versus 50 years, 4 months). This is a significant effect. However, if one determines the average age in each quartile of the analysis using mean HR during the shock avoidance task, where the relationship to parental history of hypertension was most pronounced, there are no significant age differences among quartiles. For example, 18 of the 52 parents in the highest quartile were hypertensive,

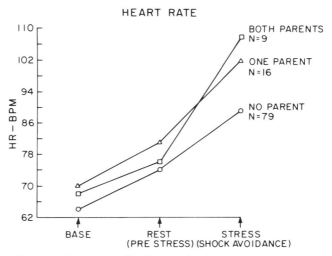

FIGURE 5. *The graph shows mean HR during relaxation rest (base), prestress rest, and the onset of the shock-avoidance task as a function of whether no parent, or both parents are hypertensive.*

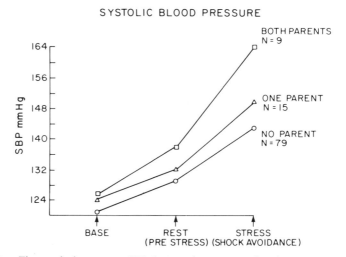

FIGURE 6. *The graph shows mean SBP during relaxation rest (base), prestress rest, and the onset of the shock-avoidance task as a function of whether no parent, one parent, or both parents are hypertensive.*

whereas only 1 of 52 parents in the lowest quartile were hypertensive, yet the mean age of both quartiles were similar (i.e., 50 years, 4 months in the upper quartile versus 50 years, 8 months in the lower quartile). The intermediate quartiles show similar mean ages. Therefore, although there is an overall age difference, it does not appear to influence the distribution of hypertensive parents among the quartiles. Also, the age effect may be working against us. This could occur in the more reactive subjects with younger parents of which there are an appreciable number. Such parents, in the light of the relationship between age and the incidence of hypertension, may not have yet evidenced hypertensive values, in part because they are less likely to have had their BP checked if they were as yet asymptomatic. In any case, any influence of relationship with age will likely prove to be a complex matter which a study of this nature cannot resolve.

We are reasonably confident in the accuracy of the parental reports at least in regard to those parents we consider hypertensive. Nonetheless, we have recently contacted the parents' physicians to verify the information the parents provided. The physician reports are just being returned. We also requested the parents to provide us information on the health history of their parents (our subjects' grandparents). These data appear inconclusive, with, at best, trends toward relationships between the grandparents' history of heart or hypertensive disease, and the grandsons cardiovascular responses. This could be for any number of reasons, such as lack of, or inaccurate, information on the parents' part. Also, heart disease, including hypertension, if it manifests itself only later in life, may have an etiological basis different from hypertension seen earlier in life. Finally, one other matter to note concerns the observation that seven of the fathers of our subjects were reported to have myocardial infarctions, four of whom were deceased. Their sons most commonly were among the more reactive individuals with regard to mean HR but not SBP. For example, using a simple median split we found all seven subjects to be in the upper half of the relaxation baseline distribution and six of the seven to be in the upper half of the shock-avoidance distribution.

While we are encouraged by family history data, we do want to expand our data base. We now routinely obtain family health information from subjects and plan to follow this up with information provided directly by the parents. Also, it is important to emphasize that the purpose of this work is not to evaluate the basis of any familial trend, but only to provide additional evidence that beta-adrenergic hyperreactivity in young adults may have some significance with regard to eventual pathophysiology. Such evidence encourages us to consider a longitudinal study. But additional evidence is needed before one can justify such an effort. One question we are now actively seeking answers to is whether beta-adrenergic hyperreactivity to our contrived laboratory stressors is characteristic of the reactivity of such subjects to more natural laboratory as well as field stressors.

In summary, our current research is primarily focusing on the significance of beta-adrenergic mechanisms in mediating the influence of behavioral stress in the etiology of hypertension. Our focus is not on the symptoms (i.e., and elevated BP, per se) but on a potentially significant mediating event. It is very likely that there are multiple interacting processes involved in the etiological process of which beta-adrenergic reactivity may prove to be but one. We believe available clinical data suggests its potential significance. In this chapter, we have provided data which we feel further implicates beta-adrenergic influences in the pathogenic process, but in this case, they are clearly related to behavioral stress, a situation which is not definitive with the clinical data. Several points should be reemphasized. Stressors where the individual is given some opportunity to cope actively, produce a greater beta-adrenergic effect on the myocardium than stressors where the individual is only passively involved (i.e., cannot actively cope). Associated with these more pronounced beta-adrenergic effects are more pronounced changes in SBP. Three lines of evidence indicate that these events may be of significance in the pathogenic process: (1) there are appreciable individual differences in beta-adrenergic reactivity; (2) individuals who demonstrate a greater degree of beta-adrenergic reactivity tend to generalize this reactivity and their SBP responsiveness to other conditions, and they also tend to more frequently evidence prestress rest SBP values that could be considered borderline hypertensive; and (3) the incidence of hypertension in the parents is significantly greater in young adult males who demonstrate greater beta-adrenergic reactivity as indexed by HR.

References

1. Barger, A. C.; Richards, V.; Metcalfe, J.; and Gunther, B.: Regulation of the circulation during exercise—cardiac output (direct Fick) and metabolic adjustments in the normal dog. *American Journal of Physiology* 184:613–623, 1956.
2. Barnett, P. H.; Hines, E. A.; Schirger, A.; and Gage, R. P.: Blood pressure and vascular reactivity to the cold pressor test: restudy of 207 subjects 27 years later. *Journal of the American Medical Association* 183:845–848, 1963.
3. Esler, M.; Julius, J.; Zweifler, A.; Randall, O.; Harburg, E.; Gardiner, H.; and DeQuattro, V.: Mild high-renin essential hypertension—neurogenic hypertension? *New England Journal of Medicine* 296:405–411, 1977.
4. Grignolo, A.; Light, K. C.; and Obrist, P. A.: Beta-adrenergic influences on the canine myocardium: A behavioral and pharmacological study. *Pharmacology, Biochemistry, and Behavior*, 5, 1981. In press.

5. Guyton, A. C.: Personal views on mechanisms of hypertension. In *Hypertension— Physiopathology and Treatment*, eds. J. Genest, E. Koiw, and O. Kuchel, pp. 566-575. New York: McGraw-Hill, 1977.
6. Harlan, W. R., Jr.; Osborne, R. K.; and Graybiel, A.: Prognostic value of the cold pressor test and the basal blood pressure based on an eighteen-year follow-up study. *American Journal of Cardiology* 13:683-687, 1964.
7. Julius, S.: Borderline hypertension: Epidemiological and clinical implications. In *Hypertension-Physiopathology and Treatment*, eds. J. Genest, E. Koiw, and O. Kuchel, pp. 630-640. New York: McGraw-Hill, 1977.
8. Julius, S. and Esler, M.: Autonomic nervous cardiovascular regulation in borderline hypertension. *The American Journal of Cardiology*, 36:685-696, 1975.
9. Julius, S. and Schork, M. A.: Borderline hypertension—A critical review. *Journal of Chronic Disease* 23:723-754, 1971.
10. Langer, A. W.: Obrist, P. A.; and McCubbin, J. A.: Hemodynamic and metabolic adjustments during exercise and shock avoidance in dogs. *American Journal of Physiology: Heart and Circulatory Physiology* 5:H225-H230, 1979.
11. Light, K. C.; and Obrist, P.A.: Cardiovascular Reactivity to Behavioral Stress in Young Males With and Without Marginally Elevated Casual Systolic Pressure: A Comparison of Clinic, Home and Laboratory Measures. *Hypertension*, 2:802-808, 1980.
12. Light, K. C.; and Obrist, P.A.: Cardiovascular response to stress: Effects of opportunity to avoid, shock experience and performance feedback. *Psychophysiology* 17:243-252, 1980.
13. Obrist, P. A.; Gaebelein, C. J.; Teller, E. S.: Langer, A. W.; Grignolo, A.; Light, K. C.; and McCubbin, J. A.: The relationship among heart rate, carotid dP/dt and blood pressure in humans as a function of the type of stress. *Psychophysiology* 15:102-115, 1978.
14. Obrist, P. A.; Lawler, J. E.; Howard, J. L.; Smithson, K. W.; Martin, P. L.; and Manning, J.: Sympathetic influences on the heart in humans: Effects on contractility and heart rate of acute stress. *Psychophysiology* 11:405-427, 1974.
15. Obrist, P. A.; Light, K. C.; McCubbin, J. A.; Hutcheson, J. S.; and Hoffer, J. L.: Pulse transit time: Relationship to blood pressure and myocardial performance. *Psychophysiology* 16:292-301, 1979.
16. Obrist, P. A.; Webb, R. A.; and Sutterer, J. R.: Heart rate and somatic changes during aversive conditioning and a simple reaction time task. *Psychophysiology* 5:696-723, 1969.
17. Obrist, P. A.; Webb, R. A.; Sutterer, J. R.; and Howard, J. L.: The cardiac-somatic relationship: Some reformulations. *Psychophysiology* 6:569-587, 1970.
18. Obrist, P. A.; Wood, D. M.; and Perez-Reyes, M.: Heart rate during conditioning in humans: Effects of UCS intensity, vagal blockade, and adrenergic block of vasomotor activity. *Journal of Experimental Psychology* 70:32-42, 1965.
19. Paul, O.: Epidemiology of hypertension. In *Hypertension: Physiopathology and Treatment*, eds. J. Genest, E. Koiw, and O. Kutchel, pp. 613-629. New York: McGraw-Hill, 1977.
20. Safar, M. E.; Weiss, Y. A.; Levenson, J. A.; London, G. M.; and Milliez, P. L.: Hemodynamic study of 85 patients with borderline hypertension. *The American Journal of Cardiology* 31:315-319, 1973.

Animal Models in Biobehavioral Research: Effects of Anxiety Stress on Immunocompetence and Neoplasia

VERNON RILEY
M. A. FITZMAURICE
DARREL H. SPACKMAN

Introduction

Prior to the initiation of these studies, it was observed in our laboratory, and by others, that a number of uncontrolled environmental circumstances and technical procedures produced physiological alterations in experimental and control animals, and that these uncontrolled stress-associated changes interferred with or distorted various experimental parameters that cancer researchers, immunologists, and other investigators were attempting to measure with accuracy. As a consequence, these findings provided disquieting evidence that the most carefully done studies using animal models were subject to misinterpretation, or could yield erroneous data unless such stress-inducing environmental and animal-handling factors could be identified and controlled.

To minimize these experimental problems, certain modified animal handling procedures and animal housing have been established in our laboratories, which are now considered essential prerequisites for animal experimentation. These improved techniques allow the investigator to distinguish between truly quiescent and chronically stressed mice, as well as to determine the authentic consequences of experimentally imposed stress [27, 28, 29, 39, 43].

Another experimental factor that is essential to the control and detection of inadvertent stress is the elimination of the generally unrecognized LDH-virus contamination from experimental mice, tumors, and oncogenic virus preparations [30-32, 36]. In mice infected by this ubiquitously distributed murine virus, changes occur in plasma corticosterone levels, the thymus, spleen, lymph nodes, macrophages, T-cells and B-cells, as well as functional components of various enzyme systems.

These improved experimental conditions and procedures permit the use of more reliable experimental designs for the detection and quantitation of mild stress by facilitating accurate and sensitive measurements of a variety of relevant parameters [31a, 34, 39–41]. These include plasma corticosterone (CSR) elevation, T-cell and B-cell depletion, adrenal hypertrophy, and weight loss of the thymus, spleen, and nodes. It has been confirmed, under more controlled experimental conditions, that the previously observed stress-mediated physiological changes in mice, such as thymus involution, lymphocytopenia, etc., quickly follow and are undoubtedly caused by the rapid and profound elevations of plasma corticosterone [7, 27, 29, 31, 34, 36].

One of the more important products of these basic protective techniques has been an experimental documentation of the rapid and exquisitely sensitive physiological response of mice to the mild stress that is associated with conventional housing and animal handling procedures employed in most laboratories [26, 27, 29, 39, 41, 43].

In order to carefully control the intensity of experimentally induced stressful stimuli, a simple device has been designed and tested for inducing mild, nontraumatic anxiety–stress [31a]. The manifestations of such stress are quantitative, predictable, and readily reproducible.

As a result of these technical developments, the specific hormonal and cellular changes that occur as a consequence of stress can now be studied with confidence. Of special relevance is the consequential ability to obtain reproducible alterations of some neoplastic processes by either emotionally induced or chemically simulated stress.

The Biochemical Nature of Stress

Anxiety or other varieties of psychosocial stresses in experimental animals produce a series of biochemical events that are mediated through the neuroendocrine system. These biochemical responses have demonstrable destructive effects upon specific cells and tissues that are required for immunological defense. As a consequence, the stress-compromised animal is less capable of defending itself against cancer cells, infectious agents, and certain other disease processes. Thus, uncontrolled stress factors are important components to be reckoned with in designing and carrying out experiments.

There are, of course, many varieties of stress which may activate separate physiological systems, either singly or as complexes. For purposes of simplification in this report we shall restrict our discussion and data presentation to the effects of uncomplicated anxiety involving emotionally aroused stress, which is associated with the activation of the adrenal cortex.

A characteristic expression of such stress is an abrupt and dramatic increase in circulating plasma glucocorticoids. In rodents, this is corticosterone; in man it is cortisol. Such stress-induced hormone elevations produce secondary stress effects involving T-cells and thymic components, and thus elements of the immunological apparatus [15, 31a, 44]. Relevant metabolic and related biochemical alterations also occur through the influences of increased glucocorticoid action [47, 51].

Within the framework of this limited definition of stress, it is assumed that the adrenal medulla is either not significantly activated by mild stress, or does not greatly alter the effects of the adrenal cortex. However, activation of the adrenal medulla system occurs in rodents under more drastic stressful conditions where fear or rage is the inciter [2, 16, 20].

The rationale of stress-induced or stress-mediated disease follows logically from a series of known physiological events. Although the overall biochemical phenomena associated with stress are complex and have many subtle consequences, the primary events relevant to disease processes appear to be straightforward, at least those involving the adrenal cortex, as depicted in the abbreviated pathway diagram of Figure 1.

Critical experimental studies cannot be carried out with confidence using conventional animal housing facilities, since they are not suitable for the maintenance of normal quiescent baseline values of stress-associated hormonal and cellular elements that influence or control physiological and pathological processes. We have therefore designed animal facilities that not only serve the experimental needs of our physiological stress research, but in addition, provide safer facilities for working with infectious or allergenic agents. Prototypes of low-stress animal facilities are shown in Figure 2.

From the standpoint of the low stress that is essential for reliable biological research, these individually ventilated shelf units offer several beneficial features [26, 28–31]. For example, the enclosed shelves provide a substantial amount of soundproofing, which is of special significance, since it has been established that animals are stressed by a wide variety of noises that stimulate immunologically adverse neuroendocrine reactions. Stressful noises and cage motion are prevalent in most conventional animal rooms, particularly where there are rolling metal racks, metal cages, radios, shouting, frequent cage cleaning with rough handling, and other noisy and stressful operations.

The most essential features required for protective low-stress animal housing are as follows: (a) no recirculation of noxious air that has been in

ABBREVIATED SEQUENCE OF EVENTS RELATING STRESS AND NEOPLASIA

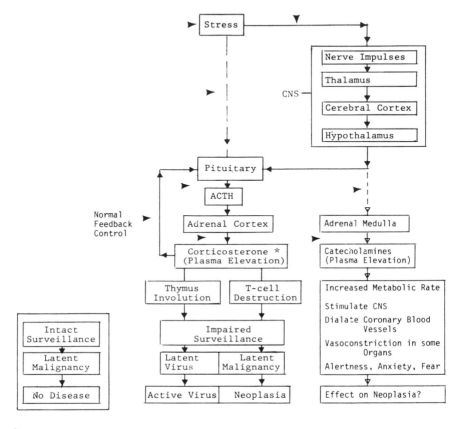

► Possible blocking by specific compounds on hormone feedback for potential therapeutic applications. The upper arrows indicate the therapeutic effects observed in mice by reducing environmental stress.

*Although cortisol is the primary glucocorticoid in man, corticosterone is the principal C21 steroid secreted by adrenocortical tissue in birds, mice and rats.

FIGURE 1.   *The chart illustrates physiological pathways involved in the response to anxiety stress resulting in immunological impairment.*

previous contact with the animals; (*b*) partial soundproofing of storage shelves to protect the animals from stressful noises; (*c*) elimination of vibrations and high-pitched sounds of centrifuges, vacuum cleaners, and heavy equipment; (*d*) elimination of drafts and air turbulence; (*e*) light control to stabilize circadian rhythms; (*f*) segregation of males and females with respect to transmissible odors, pheromones, and other signals; (*g*)

DISPOSABLE FILTER DETAIL AT
AIR-INTAKE END OF SHELVES

FILTERS IN POSITION AT AIR
INTAKE END OF ENCLOSED SHELVES

AIR CONTROL LOUVERS AT
EXHAUST END OF SHELVES

ENCLOSED SHELVES READY
TO RECEIVE MOUSE CAGES

SHELVES IN OPERATION WITH
VIRUS COLOR CODE CARDS

SLIDING SHELF AND DOUBLE
DOOR PASS-THRU BETWEEN
CLEAN AND VIRUS ROOMS

FIGURE 2. *These are various views of a low-stress protective animal facility showing the disposable air filter system and the exhaust louvers that control airflow. This is a prototype unit in which the shelves were individually attached to wall standards, and sliding plexiglas doors were employed. Also shown is the sliding shelf and airlock, whereby normal animals are transferred from their quarantine holding area to the experimental quarters. Air pressure is slightly higher in the "clean" room, so that any air exchange which may occur flows from the clean area to the experimental area.*

segregation of experimental animals that are experiencing stress from normal or experimental control animals; and (*h*) introduction of special minimal-stress animal handling techniques and cage cleaning procedures.

Materials and Methods

ANIMAL CAGING AND ENVIRONMENT

Standard plastic cages, 28 × 18 × 13 cm (11 × 7 × 5 in.), containing about 2 cm of San-I-Cel ground corncob bedding, were employed in all experiments unless otherwise indicated. In our experience, plastic cages are superior to metal cages in terms of general insulation, resistance to temperature changes, cold conductivity, and minimization of sound as well as thermal stress factors. Inasmuch as endocrine and various circadian effects are related to light and dark exposures, the plastic cages are also preferable over metal for controlling admittance of diffuse light to the animals. Standard 12-hr intervals of light and dark were controlled by automatic clock-controlled switches. Temperature was maintained at 75°F (±3).

HOUSING

All animals, including both stock and experimental groups, except those in special environmental experiments, were protected by a special barrier system consisting of ventilated enclosed shelves provided with filtered laminar air-flow vented outside of the building following contact with the mice and their released aerosols [26]. When the doors of these facilities are closed, each shelf becomes a separate, independent and isolated unit within a larger protected facility. The only cross-contamination that is theoretically possible would occur in those cages that are "downwind" from infected animals in the airflow of a given shelf. However, by appropriate segregation, this possibility is readily avoided.

MICE

Two C3H mouse substrains were employed in most studies: C3H/Bi, harboring from birth the milk-borne mammary tumor virus (MTV), and C3H/He, derived from cesarean, foster-nursed animals and thus free of high titers of the milk-passaged virus. In certain experiments, BDF hybrid mice (C57BL/6 × DBA/2) were used. All mice were obtained from commercial breeders as weanlings weighing 18–22 gm. Upon arrival in our laboratory they were randomly segregated into groups of 10, and housed in standard plastic holding cages. These cage groupings, or further subdivisions into smaller or recombination into larger groups, were maintained throughout the experimental periods. To minimize psychosocial stress, remixing of mice following their social equilibration was avoided. Experiments were usually initiated when the animals were 8–12 weeks of age, weighing 20–30 gm, and were fully quiescent and equilibrated with respect to acquired transportation-induced stress.

EXPERIMENTAL GROUPS

Mice used in a given experiment were from uniform groups in terms of age, weight, sex, strain, and origin. Mice were received from reliable commercial breeders in batches of 50 or 100, with their age range limited to about 5 days. Upon receipt, the animals were held in protective facilities for a minimum of 2 weeks equilibration prior to use, usually longer. Any abnormal-appearing mice, or those departing from our weight and other specifications, were discarded. The establishment of mouse social order equilibration is of importance in maintaining animals under conditions of minimum stress in order to avoid elevated adrenocortical concentrations with their attending effects on the thymus, T-cells, and immunological competence.

MOUSE DIET AND SANITATION

The mouse diet consisted of Wayne Lab Blox pellets supplied through the cagetop food hopper, unless otherwise indicated. This nutritionally complete diet was available to the mice ad libitum. Clean water was available through the use of pint glass bottles and stainless steel drinking tubes. High standards of sanitation were employed in the routine changing and sterilization of drinking bottles, tubes, and cages. Cages and bedding were changed once a week with a minimum of animal disturbance.

ASSAY FOR PLASMA CORTICOSTERONE IN MICE

A microfluorimetric assay was developed in our laboratories [39], based on the procedure described by Glick *et al.* [14]. Our assay requires only 50 μl of plasma obtained from individual mice by the nonharmful orbital bleeding procedure [27]; repetitive assays were carried out on plasma from individual mice or samples pooled from several mice, depending upon individual experimental requirements.

CORTICOID INJECTIONS

Fluocinolone acetonide (FCA), a synthetic corticoid, was administered intraperitoneally (ip) as a freshly prepared saline suspension. Because of limited solubility, the FCA is absorbed slowly to give a long-lasting effect from a single dose of 50 mg/kg. The same applies to dexamethasone (DMS).

ORGAN WEIGHTS

The thymus weight responses of mice exposed to environmental or experimental stress were compared with those of appropriate control animals. The control mice were sham-injected with saline in those experiments where treatment injections were given. At autopsy, the weights of the thymus, spleen, adrenals, and pooled inguinal and axillary lymph nodes were determined for each animal. Similar measurements were made following administration of synthetic corticoids, or of any other stress-inducing experimental procedure such as rotational-induced anxiety [29].

TUMOR IMPLANTATION AND MEASUREMENTS

The Gardner lymphosarcoma (6C3HED) grows as a solid tumor mass when implanted subcutaneously (sc). The donor tumors were harvested aseptically and injected into recipient mice as a 20–50% suspension of free cells and small fragments of tumor tissue in .9% NaCl solution [30]. In order to follow the tumor growth and regression quantitatively, the tumor mass was measured in three dimensions by calipers [30]. The 6C3HED lymphosarcoma has been maintained in our laboratory for about 8 years by intermittent passage in C3H female mice.

ELIMINATION OF A COMMON TUMOR CONTAMINENT

Without special processing, most transplantable tumors carry the LDH-virus as a perpetual contamination [30–32]. Since the hazards that this virus may cause in the interpretation of data have been discussed and in some cases demonstrated [30–32], all tumors utilized in these studies were processed to remove the LDH-virus. For certain experimental purposes involving biological stress, the virus was intentionally introduced into specific mouse groups as appropriate. Such infected mice and noninfected controls were housed and handled so as to avoid subsequent cross-contamination. Critical monitoring of our mice for absence of the virus in the controls was a standard procedure.

AMINO ACID DETERMINATIONS

Analyses of free plasma and urine amino acids were carried out on a Beckman Model 120 B amino acid analyzer modified to provide accelerated, semiautomatic runs of high sensitivity [42]. Recently revised and improved methods of analysis were employed [38]. An improved sodium citrate buffer system for basic amino acids allows the routine analysis of E-N-monomethyllysine along with all other basic amino acids. Lithium citrate buffers were used for the acidic and neutral amino acids.

Results

Corticosterone Elevation by Stress

Figure 3 illustrates several relevant facts. First that an extremely mild "handling" stress is capable of inducing anxiety in mice which, in turn, produces an immediate and substantial increase in plasma corticosterone. The cluster of unconnected points at the bottom left hand corner of the chart are "normal", quiescent plasma corticosterone values of individual mice obtained when a group of 10 animals was removed from protective storage and all 10 bled by the rapid orbital bleeding technique within 3.5 min. This short time period is insufficient for the overt expression of any stress or anxiety to be manifested biochemically by an elevation of plasma cor-

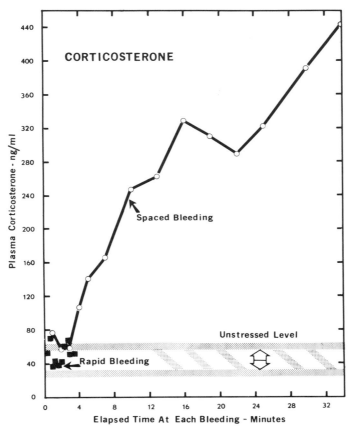

FIGURE 3. *This chart shows the influence of normal laboratory manipulation upon the production of stress-induced corticosterone levels in normal mice. The cluster of unconnected points at the unstressed level of corticosterone represents 10 animals whose blood samples were taken rapidly within a 3.5 min period. The ascending curve shows the systematic increase in corticosterone with time following removal of the mice from their storage shelf, followed by capturing individual animals in the cage and bleeding at periodic intervals as indicated in the Figure. This demonstrates the rapidity of physiological response to stress as measured by the corticosterone parameter. Mice were BAF females.*

ticosterone. However, when analogous cages of mice were similarly removed from protective storage, and 1 animal was captured and bled every 2 or 3 min, so that the total elapsed handling time was about 30 min between the first and last animal captured, the ascending curve shows the rate at which corticosterone becomes elevated in the blood plasma of such mildly stressed animals. Similar results have been obtained from each of four different strains tested (BDF, BAF, C3H, and CBA).

These experimental results further demonstrate the need for quiescent, protective housing facilities, and the necessity to employ special animal handling techniques in studies on biochemical and biological effects of stress.

Benign Stress Machine

Previous studies have demonstrated the need for a simple, nontraumatic and reproducible means for inducing controlled stress in experimental animals. Such stress should be produced without activating other hormonal systems, significantly altering the metabolism of the host, or changing caloric intake. Figure 4 shows a simple stress-inducing device that provides a controlled quantitative form of stress which is readily reproducible, and lends itself to automation with a wide variety of intermittent stress–rest programming. This machine is a modified phonograph turntable

FIGURE 4. *The picture shows a new programmable stress machine. Entire cages of mice are slowly rotated at predetermined speeds and for various periods of intermittent rotation and rest. Automatic timers control the rotation/rest ratios, which permits the mice to be stressed in their cages without depriving them of food or water, or employing physical restraint. The machine can be programmed for any time and periodicity that the experimental design requires.*

that has the four standard speeds of 16, 33, 45, and 78 rpm. The instrument has been designed so that an entire cage of animals can be placed on the machine for rotation without changing the established arrangement of their living facilities. With this device it is not necessary to alter the availability of their food and water, inasmuch as the slow rotational speeds and intermittent on–off cycles permit the animals to move about their cage and to continue eating and drinking. It may also be noted that the lateral gravitational force involved is less than 1 G. This stress-inducing instrument is thus not a centrifuge device, but merely a mechanical means for inducing mild spatial disorientation, and possibly virtigo or dizziness, with its associated anxiety.

Stress-Induced Corticosterone Quantitation

The ability of this instrument to induce variable intensities of stress is shown in Figure 5, where plasma corticosterone values are plotted against the various rotational speeds. It may be seen that following the rotation of separate groups of mice for 20 min at each of the four speeds, that a systematic increase in plasma corticosterone was observed [31a, 39]. For most stress-inducing purposes, the intermediate speed of 45 rpm has been employed, and the animals are usually rotated for 10 min followed by a 50-min rest. This, or other cycles, can be repeated for any desired period of time by employing programmed automation.

Rotational Stress and Cellular Changes

Figure 6 shows the effect of such programmed rotation on the white blood cell count. It is relevant to note that this stress-induced leucocytopenia immediately follows and is a consequence of the elevated plasma corticosterone levels induced by the anxiety stress.

Enhancement of Tumor Growth by Rotational Stress

Figure 7 (p. 384) shows the influence of intermittent rotational stress on the subsequent growth rate of the Gardner lymphosarcoma (6C3HED) in C3H/He mice. In this experiment the tumor-bearing mice were exposed to intermittent rotational stress (45 rpm) for 10 min out of each hour during the first 6 days following subcutaneous implantation of the transplantable lymphosarcoma. A logical interpretation of these observations suggests that those animals receiving rotational stress had some elements of their cell-mediated immunological competence compromised [3, 8, 17, 37], which permitted this sensitive tumor to grow at a more rapid rate than occurred in the control animals, who possessed the immunological capability

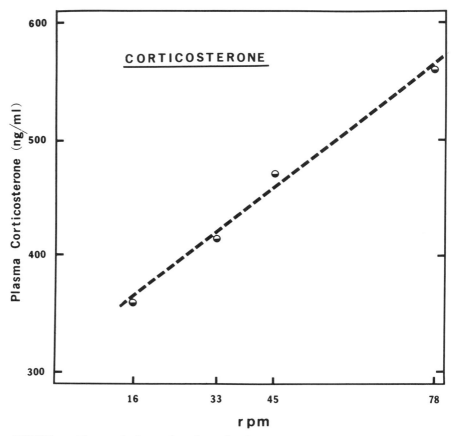

FIGURE 5. *The graph shows the relationship between speed of rotation (rpm) and the resulting corticosterone levels in the mouse plasma following 20 min of cage rotation. It should be noted that the maximum speed employed generates less than one G at the maximum radius at the cage corners. Thus, this is not a centrifugal-induced stress, but merely a spatial disorientation, which produces anxiety with a consequential corticosterone increase, probably via the hypothalamus, pituitary, and ACTH pathways, which activate the adrenal cortex.*

to restrain the optimal growth of this tumor. Such a stress-induced decrease in immunological competence is a natural consequence of the corticosterone elevation induced by anxiety stress.

Effects of Stress on Thymus Involution

Figure 8 illustrates and compares the influence of three distinct stress factors on the induction of thymus involution. Figure 8a shows the effect of

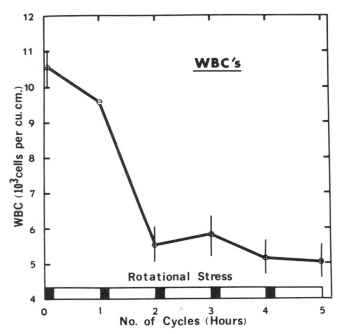

FIGURE 6. *In this experiment lymphocytopenia induced by mild, nontraumatic rotational stress at 45 rpm during five 60-min cycles consisting of 10 min rotation followed by 50 min rest. An approximate 50% lymphocytopenia is produced by the end of the second cycle, and is maintained throughout the 5 hr of intermittent stress. Standard errors for each point are represented by vertical lines.*

the LDH-virus on the loss of thymus weight as a function of time following infection, whereas Figure 8b indicates that a similar effect can be induced by the administration of a single dose of dexamethasone. In Figure 8c similar effects were obtained by the induction of anxiety–stress through the slow rotation of mice at 45 rpm.

Rotational Stress and Amino Acids

Figure 9 (p. 386) illustrates some of the physiological consequences of a mild rotation-induced anxiety stress [31a], as indicated by significant alterations in the amino acid profile of the urine of normal mice compared with analogous stressed animals. Some of the more conspicuous changes which may be noted are the decreased concentration of lysine, and in contrast, the elevations of glutamic acid, alanine, valine, leucine, tryptophan, phenylalanine, tyrosine, proline, and isoleucine.

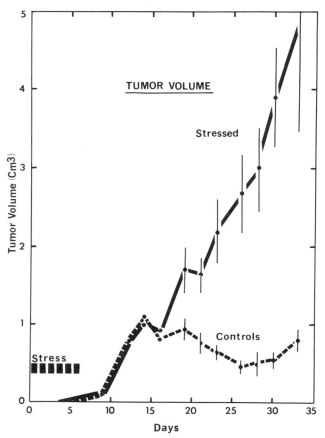

FIGURE 7.   *This graph shows the results of stress-associated influences on tumor growth in a host exposed to an intermittent course of mild anxiety stress. The stress was induced by slow rotation at 45 rpm for 10 min out of each hour during the first 6 days following tumor implantation. The tumor was the 6C3HED ascites lymphosarcoma inoculated subcutaneously into C3H/He female mice about 10 weeks old. Food and water were available at all times during the course of the experiment.*

These observations demonstrate the sensitivity of the collocated, concentration-prioritized amino acid profiles for detecting subtle physiological changes [43]. Of equal importance, the combined data illustrate the remarkable sensitivity of the organism in responding to both its internal and external environments.

Although there is no direct experimental evidence that the observed stress-induced changes in amino acid concentrations are related to the

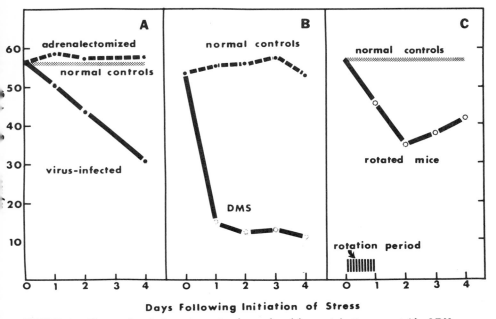

Days Following Initiation of Stress

FIGURE 8. *Thymus involution was variously produced by an infectious agent (the LDH-virus), a biochemical substance (DMS, a synthetic corticoid), and anxiety-stress associated with the disorienting effects of slow rotation of an entire cage of mice following their removal from protective storage. (a) The LDH-virus was injected on Day 0 into both intact and adrenalectomized female BAF mice; as shown by the left-hand panel, the thymus involution in the intact mice contrasts with the lack of response of the adrenalectomized animals. (b) The thymus involution produced by a single injection of an insoluble suspension of DMS, which was absorbed over an extended period, is shown in the middle panel. (c) The thymus destruction resulting from stress associated with rotation at 45 rpm for 10 min out of each hour for a 24-hr period is shown in the right-hand panel. During this mild stress period the plasma corticosterone was elevated approximately fivefold.*

observed tumor growth enhancement, it has been reported that changes in certain amino acid levels have been associated with a reduction of immunological competence [21].

Simulated "Stress" by a Synthetic Corticoid

Figure 10 provides further experimental evidence concerning the effects of stress on neoplastic behavior. In this experiment, the neuroendocrine pathways were intentionally bypassed, and physiological "stress" was simulated by the introduction into the animals of a highly potent synthetic corticoid. In this case, a single injection of fluocinolone acetonide (FCA), which is closely related chemically to dexamethasone, was administered at

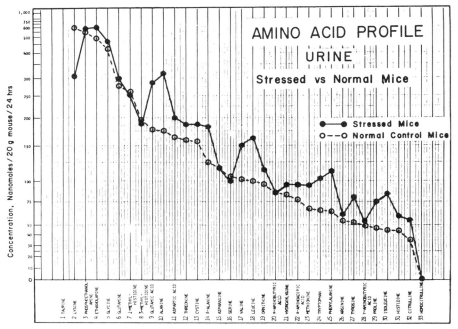

FIGURE 9. *The graph shows amino acid concentration profiles of the urine of mildly stressed mice as compared with normal, quiescent control animals. The anxiety stress was quantitatively induced under highly controlled experimental conditions using a slow-speed rotational device at 45 rpm intermittently for 24 hr. The urine was a 24-hour sample collected during the rotation period. The rotational intermittence was controlled automatically and was programmed for 10 min rotation and 50 min rest each hour. Food and water were available at all times during the 24-hr period. The centrifugal force of the rotation was less than one G, which permitted the mice to move about their cage at will.*

various times following transplantation of the Gardner lymphosarcoma. When this corticoid was administered seven days following implantation of the tumor, no tumor regressions occurred, in contrast to 70% regressions observed in the untreated control C3H/He mice. However, this corticoid effect was systematically diminished when the compound was administered at later times in the course of tumor growth. These data may be interpreted as a demonstration of the damage inflicted upon the host immunological apparatus by glucocorticoids, whether endogenous or administered. The expression of this damage by a decrease in tumor regressions, however, is dependent upon the stage of tumor development at the time of glucocorticoid administration.

This is indicated by Figure 11, which shows the tumor growth enhancement resulting from FCA injections at the various times following tumor

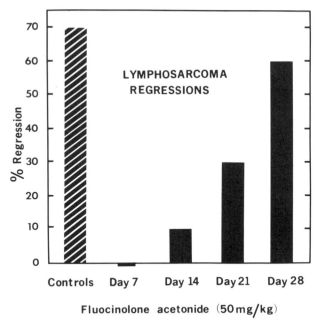

FIGURE 10. *The graph shows the influence of a synthetic glucocorticoid in inhibiting the regression of established tumors. The synthetic glucocorticoid was fluocinolone acetonide (FCA) and was injected intraperitoneally at a dose of 50 mg/kg suspended in physiological saline, at the times indicated following tumor implantation. The tumor was the Gardner lymphosarcoma (6C3HED), implanted subcutaneously in the hip of C3H/He female mice. Ten mice were used for each group.*

implantation. In this experiment, maximum tumor growth enhancement occurred following FCA administration 7 days after implantation. Lesser effects were observed when the compound was injected on the fourteenth and twenty-first day postimplantation, while the FCA had no effect on tumor growth when injected 28 days after implantation.

Population Density Experiments

It is important for the investigator to know what effects various numbers of animals housed in a standard cage will have upon the results of an experiment. In order to minimize animal fighting, or for other reasons, some investigators house their mice or rats 1 per cage, while others engaged in similar studies may have various numbers ranging from 2–10 per cage.

Several publications have described the stressful effects of "cage-crowding", and the alleged consequential influences on the growth or in-

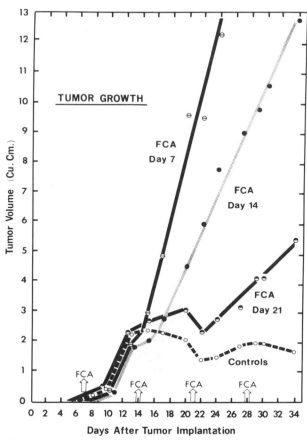

FIGURE 11. *These data show the different tumor growth rates resulting from the injection of a synthetic corticosteroid at various times in respect to tumor implantation. The groups of mice were the same as those shown in Figure 10. Those mice receiving FCA on the twenty eighth day postimplantation exhibited a tumor growth rate that was indistinguishable from that of the untreated tumor-bearing controls.*

cidence of various tumors, or other disease processes, presumably due to alterations in the immunological competence of the hosts [5, 6, 13, 15]. The adverse psychosocial effects associated with isolation-rearing in contrast to standard rearing have also been reported [1, 18–20, 23, 24, 35].

We have undertaken experiments to reexamine this question utilizing protective, minimal-stress facilities and low-stress handling techniques, in order to control a maximum of the known forms of stress in carrying out experiments concerned with various biological processes. Experiments were designed to determine the different levels of anxiety stress among mice caged in groups of 1, 2, 3, 5, 10, 15, or 20, and held for relatively long periods in standard plastic cages. There were no mice of the opposite sex either in the cages or in the immediate vicinity, and thus there were no obvious pheromones which could provide uncontrolled stress-inducing circumstances.

Effects of Population Density upon Plasma Corticosterone Levels

It has been established in these studies that various population densities of caged female mice do not constitute, in themselves, a basis for "cage crowding stress". This was determined by a failure to detect differential levels of plasma corticosterone (CSR) in mice caged either 1, 2, 3, 5, 10, 15, or 20 per standard plastic cage. It was expected, however, that quite different effects would be observed when employing competitive male mice under analogous experimental circumstances. It was thus surprising to observe that various cage-population densities of males also failed to demonstrate elevated plasma corticosterone. Figure 12 illustrates the similarity of plasma corticosterone levels in male C3H/He mice when housed in various population densities, as compared with females under similar circumstances.

Effects of Population Density upon Relative Food Consumption

In addition to the CSR data, Figure 12 also shows that the differences in food consumption observed with females maintained under conditions of various population densities, also apply to male mice. These data also show an unexpected systematic difference in individual daily food consumption, which is expressed as a concave curvilinear function of population density. Mouse weight was taken into consideration in the plotting of these data.

Our interpretation of these observations is that the low-stress animal facilities, in conjunction with our experimental design, have permitted a sensitive quantitative detection of the homeostatic thermal regulatory mechanism that controls caloric intake as a function of body-temperature maintenance requirements.

It is obvious that body heat-loss occurs more rapidly in mice residing alone, or in small numbers, as compared with the loss in high density populations where huddling and multiple body contact occurs. Other possible explanations for these observations have been considered and experimentally examined; however, the constant body-weight data shown in

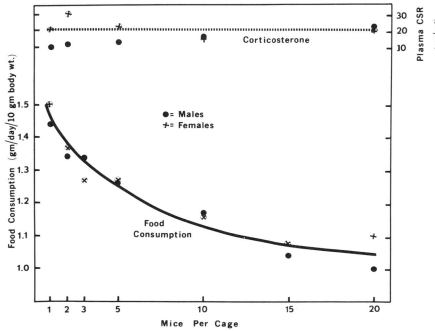

FIGURE 12.   *The graph compares the effects of population density upon the food consumption and daytime plasma corticosterone levels of male and female mice. Food consumption is plotted per 10 gm of body weight, to correct for body-weight differences in male and female mice. Food consumption was determined by weighing the food three times per week; each food consumption point represents the mean over a 4-week period. Corticosterone levels were determined at the end of the experiments. Each corticosterone point represents a plasma pool from five mice. C3H/He mice were employed.*

Figure 13 and the absence of hierarchial imposed weight differences are all consistent with the caloric requirement hypothesis.

Irrespective of the mechanism, these observations are relevant to the experimental design of nutritional, neoplastic, and related experiments in which caloric intake is of importance. In this respect, it is appropriate to recall the influences that have been reported, of varying caloric intakes [33, 45, 46] and temperature conditions [9, 49, 50] upon carcinogenic processes.

Effects of Population Density on Adrenal Weights

In contrast to the absence of any influence of cage population density upon plasma corticosterone, there does seem to be a systematic increase in adrenal weight as a function of the number of animals per cage. This is

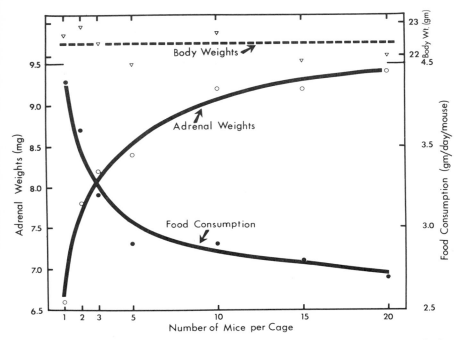

FIGURE 13.   *The graph shows the effects of population density upon food consumption, body weights, and adrenal weights of the C3H/He female mice. When calculated by the chi-square method, the combined adrenal weight data of 1, 2, and 3 mice per cage (32 animals) compared with 10, 15, and 20 mice per cage (45 animals) gave a p < .05.*

shown in Figure 13. We have considered several hypotheses to rationalize these findings. One possibility is that changes in adrenal weight under these circumstances may be a more sensitive parameter of stress than plasma corticosterone levels. However, based upon previous experiments, this seems somewhat unlikely. Another possibility that we have considered is that the increase in adrenal weight is an expression of adrenal medulla hyperplasia rather than adrenal cortex hyperplasia. The adrenal cortex is, of course, the tissue involved in the production of corticosterone, whereas the adrenal medulla is concerned with the production of catecholamines, the most conspicuous being epinephrine and norepinephrine.

James Henry, a "stress physiologist" at the University of California, has evidence that the stress function can be divided into two separate categories, with anxiety–stress being primarily associated with the adrenal cortex, whereas stress involving fright or fury as in fighting animals, or in the establishment of social hierarchy, involves the adrenal medulla and its catecholamines, rather than, or in addition to, the adrenal cortex and glucocorticoid elevation [18]. Histological examination of the adrenals is obviously required to determine which elements show either cellular depletion or tissue hyperplasia. Another possible explanation is that the daytime plasma samples which were employed do not accurately reflect the relative CSR levels at night during the competitive feeding period.

Effects of Population Density upon Tumor Growth

A part of the testing procedure on possible effects of cage crowding included monitoring the animals for tumor incidence, tumor latent periods, tumor growth rates, and survival times following the implantation of various transplantable tumors. One of the tumor types that was reported to be responsive to "cage crowding" was a transplantable B-16 mouse melanoma [5, 6].

On Day 29, following initiation of a population density experiment involving 1, 2, 3, 5, 10, 15, or 20 mice per cage, all of the BDF female mice that were in the experiment were implanted with the B-16 melanoma. Tumor measurements were carried out twice a week in order to determine relative tumor growth rates. Tumor-latent periods were also determined, as well as the survival times of the hosts.

In contrast to the previous reports of Dechambre and Gosse [5, 6], we were unable to detect any significant influence on the tumor growth rate, or the survival times of the hosts, as a function of the number of animals per cage. Thus, the behavior of this particular tumor was essentially the same in those animals that were housed one to a cage as those mice that were housed 20 to a cage, as well as in the other intermediate population densities.

In contrast to this observation of a lack of effect of cage-population density upon the B-16 melanoma, Figure 14, nevertheless, shows the effects of population density upon the growth of the Gardner 6C3HED lymphosarcoma, as indicated by differences in the maximum tumor volumes that were attained in the various groups. This illustration also shows the effects of population density upon food consumption prior to tumor implantation. It is unclear whether the effects of population density upon the growth of this tumor may be related to the earlier differences in food consumption, or to the observed differences in adrenal size shown in Figure 13, or other factors.

Effects of Population Density upon Tumor Regressions

Since tumor regression is a good index of immune competence, we used that parameter as one means for determining the optimal population of

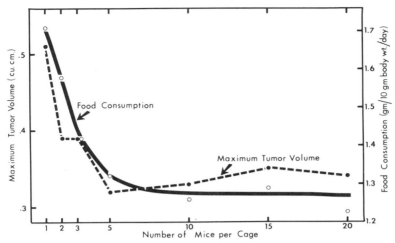

FIGURE 14. *The graph shows effects of population density upon food consumption and subsequent maximum tumor volumes in female C3H/He mice. Each food consumption point represents the mean of determinations made at 3- or 4-day intervals during the period between 3 and 36 days following the initiation of the various population densities. Subsequently, on day 56 of the experiment, all mice were implanted with the Gardner lymphosarcoma. Each maximum tumor volume point represents the average of 10 to 20 values.*

mice per cage in respect to this parameter. The results of these experiments were unexpected. The tumor regression rate of the Gardner 6C3HED lymphosarcoma in C3H/He female mice, where there was only one animal per cage, was 60%. This was in contrast to other population densities of 2, 3, 5, 10, 15, or 20 mice per cage, which had an average of 93% regressions, with a range of 80–100% ($p < .001$). Thus, based upon ability of female mice to reject a tumor challenge, all tested densities of group housing were preferable to that of single animal isolation. (See Table 1.) As shown in Table 2, male C3H/He mice housed one or two per cage had a lesser ability to reject the Gardner 6C3HED lymphosarcoma that did those housed 3, 5, 10, 15 or 20 per cage. Unlike female mice, male mice housed 2 per cage exhibited no advantage over isolated mice with respect to tumor growth. It therefore appears that male mice should not be housed 1 or 2 per cage. However, any number over 2 per cage, up to 20 per cage, yielded similar results; no optimum number per cage in this range was exhibited. Despite the differences in tumor regressions, the effects of housing male mice 1 or 2 per cage had no observable influence upon daytime plasma corticosterone levels. It was noted, however, that male mice housed 2 per cage exhibited lower food consumption and somewhat lighter body weights that those housed 1 or 3 per cage.

These and related data demonstrate the importance of recognizing and

TABLE 1
Effects of Population Density upon Tumor Regressions in Female Mice

No. per Cage	Percentage of tumor regressions[a]
1	60
2, 3, 5, 10, 15, or 20	93
$p < .001^b$	

[a] Tumor regressions were determined on day 25 after tumor implantation. The Gardner 6C3HED lymphosarcoma was implanted into C3H/He female mice 56 days after initiation of the various population densities.

[b] p value was determined by the chi-square method, comparing the data from 1 mouse per cage with the combined data from 2, 3, 5, 10, 15, or 20 per cage.

controlling experimental circumstances that produce stress, and its inevitable accompaniment of immunological impairment, which in turn, may alter tumor growth rates and subsequent tumor regressions [11, 22, 40, 41].

TABLE 2
Effects of Population Density upon Tumor Regressions in Male Mice

No. per cage	Percentage of tumor regressions[a]
1	70
2	65
1 or 2 (combined data)	67.5
3, 5, 10, 15, or 19 (combined data)	84.6
$p < .01^b$	

[a] Tumor regressions were determined on day 25 after tumor implantation. The Gardner 6C3HED lymphosarcoma was implanted into C3H/He male mice 56 days after initiation of the various population densities.

[b] p value was determined by the chi-square method, comparing the combined data from 1 or 2 per cage with the combined data from 3, 5, 10, 15, or 19 per cage.

Discussion

Corticosterone Levels

As a consequence of several interrelated developments, it has been established that experiments using mouse models for the study of immunological and neoplastic problems are undoubtedly complicated, and in some cases compromised, by the inadvertent and unappreciated stress that is present in mice maintained in conventional housing facilities and handled in the usual manner. The anxiety–stress of such mice is readily demonstrated by a determination of their plasma corticosterone. The quiescent corticosterone level of unstressed animals in our protective animal rooms is 0–35 ng/ml during the morning hours, whereas in mice housed in conventional animal rooms, the plasma corticosterone levels are usually elevated and have been shown to be in the range of 150–500 ng/ml for those tested.

Stress-induced Cellular and Tissue Lysis

When such glucocorticoids are present in the blood at concentrations above normal and for extended periods, they have lytic effects on lymphocytes and upon lymphatic tissues such as the thymus, nodes and spleen. Since these cellular elements are important components in immunological defense, the potential consequences of their depletion on latent pathological processes seem obvious. There thus appears to be a logical sequence of biochemical and cellular events that lead from stressful stimuli to the enhancement of various pathological processes, including that of cancer.

However, not all neoplastic processes exhibit enhancement following exposure of the host to stress. Rapidly growing tumors that are syngeneic with their host have not responded to the moderate stress which has been effective with slowly growing tumors that are partially under host control. These observations suggest that stress may have potentiating effects only on those malignancies that are usually under control of the host's defense mechanisms, such as the 6C3HED lymphosarcoma when grown in C3H/He mice.

Population Density

It is important for the investigator to know the caging conditions that are optimum for his experimental requirements; or, more specifically, to know what effects various numbers of animals per standard cage will have upon the results of an experiment. In order to minimize animal fighting, or other unwanted animal interaction, some investigators house their mice or rats 1 per cage, while other laboratories engaged in similar studies may have various numbers ranging from 2 to 10 per cage. We have carried out a series of experiments to examine this question in some depth. A useful approach is to employ an appropriate tumor–host relationship as a sensitive means for determining the immunological status of experimental animals as a function of population density. Since the host-induction of tumor regression is a good index of immune competence, that parameter was employed as one of several means for determining the optimal cage population.

The results of these experiments were unexpected. The tumor regression rate of the 6C3HED Gardner lymphosarcoma where there was only 1 animal per cage was 60%. This was in contrast to the other population densities of 2, 3, 5, 10, 15, or 20 mice per cage, which had an average of 93% regressions, with a range of 80–100% ($p < .001$). Thus, based upon host ability to reject a tumor challenge, all tested densities of group housing were preferable to that of single animal isolation. When the maximum tumor volume attained was employed as an indicator of immunological competence, the greatest 6C3HED tumor growth was observed in the isolated female mice, held 1 per cage, while the smallest tumors were found in the female mice housed 5 per cage ($p < .005$). However, when the same tumor was implanted into male C3H/He mice, the greatest tumor growth was observed in those housed 2 per cage, and no clear-cut optimum number per cage, in the case of male mice, was determined. It was concluded that both male and female mice were stressed by isolation, and in addition, male mice housed 2 per cage exhibited the effects of greater stress.

In contrast to the results obtained using the 6C3HED lymphosarcoma, no effects of cage crowding on the B-16 tumor were observed, presumedly because of the lack of host immunological control over this rapidly growing pigmented tumor.

These data demonstrate the importance of recognizing and controlling experimental circumstances that produce stress and its inevitable accompaniment of immunological impairment, which in turn, may alter the growth rate and subsequent tumor regression of sensitive tumors.

Summary

Experimentally or environmentally induced psychosocial stress produces increased levels of adrenal corticoids through well-known neuroendocrine pathways involving the cerebral cortex, the hypothalamus, the pituitary, and the adrenal cortex. A direct consequence of such stress-induced plasma corticoid elevation is injury to important elements of the immunological apparatus, which may leave the subject vulnerable to the action of latent oncogenic viruses, newly transformed cancer cells, or other incipient pathological processes that are normally held in check by an intact immunological surveillance apparatus.

In order to establish the potential pathological influence of alterations in adrenal corticoid levels, we have compared the biochemical and cellular effects resulting from experimental and environmental stress with those which occur following the imitation of "stress" through the direct administration of natural or synthetic corticoids. Both naturally occurring and chemically induced elevations of "stress" hormones produce similar physiological effects. In both cases, there is a lymphocytopenia, as well as a decrease in the weight of various immunological organs including the thymus, spleen, and peripheral lymph nodes.

The biochemical and physiological details of these processes have been examined in our laboratories using rodent models, with the expectation that the biological principles which apply to mice may be relevant in some respects to humans. Our attention is thus directed to an examination of the adverse influences that stress-induced elevated concentrations of circulating adrenal corticoids have upon thymus and thymus-dependent T-cells, as well as their effects upon various neoplastic processes, including those involving viruses and transplantable malignant cells.

Psychosocial stress can be quantitatively measured by both biochemical and cellular parameters, providing that truly quiescent baselines can be obtained in the control and experimental animals by the use of appropriate protective housing, modified handling procedures, and the elimination of common infectious contaminants.

Acknowledgments

These studies were supported in part by the National Cancer Institute, NIH, The National Science Foundation, The American Cancer Society, The Eagles Cancer Fund, The Alexander Foundation, The Hewitt Fund, The Glenn Foundation for Medical Research, and the Schulte Fund.

References

1. Andervont, H. B.: The influence of environment on mammary cancer in mice. *Journal of the National Cancer Institute* 4:579–581, 1944.
2. Cannon, Walter B.: *Bodily Changes in Pain, Hunger, Fear, And Rage.* (2nd ed) Appleton, New York, 1929.
3. Cochran, A. J.; John, U. W.; and Gothoskar, B. P.: Cell mediated immunity in malignant melanoma. *Lancet* i:1340–1341, 1972.
4. Comsa, J. and Hook, R. R., Jr.: Thymectomy, In *Thymic Hormones*, ed. T. D. Luckey, pp. 1–18, Baltimore: University Park Press, 1973.
5. Dechambre, R. P. and Gosse, C.: Influence of population density on mortality in mice bearing transplanted tumors. *Comptes Rendus Hebdomadaires des Seances de l'Academie des Sciences. D: Sciences Naturalles* (Paris) 267:2200–2202, 1968.
6. Dechambre, R. P. and Gosse, C.: Influence of an isolation stress on the development of transplanted ascites tumors in mice. Role of the adrenals. *Comptes Rendus Hebdomadaires des Seances de l'Academie des Sciences. D: Sciences Naturalles* (Paris). 272:2720–2722, 1971.
7. Dougherty, T. F.; Berliner, M. D.; Schneebeli, G. L.; and Berliner, D. L.: Hormonal control of lymphatic structure and function. *Annals of the New York Academy of Sciences* 113:825–843, 1964.

8. Fossati, G.; Colnaghi, M. I.; Della Porta, G.; Cascinelli, N.; and Veronesi, U.: Cellular and humoral immunity against human malignant melanoma, *International Journal of Cancer* 8:344–351, 1971.

9. Fuller, R. H., Brown, E., and Mills, C. A.: Environmental temperatures and spontaneous tumors in mice. *Cancer Research* 1:130–133, 1941.

10. Gisler, R. H.; Bussar, A. E.; Mazie, J. C.; Hess, R.: Hormonal regulation of the immune response. I. Induction of an immune response in vitro with lymphoid cells from mice exposed to acute systematic stress. *Cellular Immunology* 2:634–645, 1971.

11. Gisler, R. H. and Schenkel-Hullinger, L.: Hormonal regulation of the immune response. II. Influence of pituitary and adrenal activity on immune responsiveness in vitro. *Cellular Immunology* 2:646–657, 1971.

12. Gleason, K. K.: The behavioral significance of pheromones in vertebrates. *Psychological Bulletin* 71:58–73, 1969.

13. Glenn, W. G. and Becker, R. E.: Individual vs. group housing in mice: Immunological response to time and phase injections. *Physiological Reviews* 42:411–416, 1969.

14. Glick, D.; Von Redlick, D.; and Levine, S.: Fluorometric determination of corticosterone and cortisol in 0.02–0.05 milliliters of plasma or submilligram samples of adrenal tissue. *Endocrinology* 74:653–655, 1964.

15. Green, S.; Diefenbach, D.; and Santisteban, G. A.: Comparison of the adrenocortical responses to the stressing effects of crowding and life in a complex environment in CBA mice. *Anatomical Record* 157:2, 1967.

16. Harlow, C. M. and Selye, H.: The blood picture in the alarm reaction, *Proceedings of the Society for Experimental Biology and Medicine* 36:141–144, 1937.

17. Hellstrom, I.; Sjogren, H. O.; Warner, G.; and Hellstrom, K. E.: Blocking of cell-mediated tumor immunity by sera from patients with growing neoplasms. *International Journal of Cancer* 7:226–237, 1971.

18. Henry, J. P.; and Meehan, J. P.: Psychosocial stimuli, physiological specificity, and cardiovascular disease. In *Brain, Behavior, and Bodily Disease*, eds. H. Weiner, M. A. Hofer, and A. J. Stunkard. New York: Raven Press.

19. Henry, J. P., and Santisteban, G. A.: The induction of arteriosclerosis by psychosocial factors in CBA mice: Observations on the heart, aorta, and kidneys. *Arteriosclerosis* 14:203–218, 1971.

20. Henry, J. P.; Stephens, P. M.; and Watson, F. M. C.: Force breeding, social disorder, and mammary tumor formation in CBA/USC mouse colonies. A pilot study. *Psychosomatic Medicine* 37:277–283, 1975.

21. Jose, D. G. and Good, R. A.: Quantitative effects of nutritional essential amino acid deficiencies upon immune responses to tumors in mice. *Journal of Experimental Medicine* 137:1–9, 1973.

22. Marsh, J. T. and Rasmussen, A. F., Jr.: Response of adrenals, thymus, spleen, and leucocytes to shuttle box and confinement stress. *Proceedings of the Society for Experimental Biology and Medicine* 104:180–183, 1960.

23. Muhlbock, O.: Effect of environment on development of cancer: Studies on mammary cancer in mice. *Nederlands Tijdschrift voor Geneeskunde* 94:3747–3752, Amsterdam, 1950.

24. Muhlbock, O.: Influence of environment on the incidence of mammary tumors in mice. *ACTA International Union Against Cancer* 7:351, 1951.

25. Riley, V.: Adaptation of orbital bleeding technique to rapid serial blood studies. *Proceedings of the Society for Experimental Biology and Medicine* 104:751–754, 1960.

26. Riley, V.: Protective ventilated shelves for experimental animal storage. *Proceedings of the 23rd Session of the American Association of Laboratory Animal Sciences* 1972.

27. Riley, V.: Cancer and stress: Overview and critique. *Cancer Detection and Prevention* 2:163–195, 1979a.

27a. Riley, V.: Introduction: Stress–cancer contradictions: A continuing puzzlement. *Cancer Detection and Prevention* 2:159–162, 1979b.

28. Riley, V.: Unpublished data.

29. Riley, V. and Spackman, D. H.: Housing stress. *Lab Animal*, 6:16–21, 1977.

30. Riley, V. and Spackman, D. H.: Modifying effects of a benign virus on the malignant process and the role of physiological stress on tumor incidence. In *Fogarty International Cancer Proceedings*, ed. M. A. Ciragos no. 28, pp. 319–336. Washington, D.C.: U.S. Government Printing Office, 1977.

31. Riley, V.; Spackman, D. H.; Hellstrom, K. E., and Hellstrom, I.: Growth enhancement of murine sarcoma by LDH-virus, adrenocorticoids, and anxiety stress, *Proceedings of the American Association for Cancer Research* 19:57, 1978.

31a. Riley, V.; Spackman, D.; McClanahan, H.; and Santisteban, G. A.: The role of stress in malignancy. *Cancer Detection and Prevention*, 2:235–255, 1979.

32. Riley, V.; Spackman, D. H.; Santisteban, G. A.; Dalldorf, G.; Hellstrom, I.; Hellstrom, K. E.; Lance, E. M.; Rowson, K. E. K.; Mahy, B. W. J.; Alexander, P,; Stock, C. C.; Sjogren, H. O.; Hollander, V. P.; and Horzinck, M. C.: The LDH-virus: An interfering biological contaminant. *Science* 200:124–126, 1978.

33. Rusch, H. P.: Extrinsic factors that influence carcinogenesis. *Physiological Reviews* 24:177–204, 1944.

34. Santisteban, G. A., and Dougherty, T. F.: Comparison of the influences of adrenocortical hormones on the growth and involution of lymphatic organs. *Endocrinology* 54:130–146, 1954.

35. Santisteban, G. A. and Henry, J. P.: The induction of arteriosclerosis by psychosocial factors in CBA mice: Observations on the heart, aorta, and kidneys. *Anatomical Record* 169:2, 1971.

36. Santisteban, G. A.; Riley, V.; and Fitzmaurice, M. A.: Thymolytic and adrenal cortical responses to the LDH-elevating virus. *Proceedings of the Society for Experimental Biology and Medicine* 139:202–206, 1972.

37. Solomon, G. F., and Amkraut, A. A.: Emotions, stress, and immunity. In *Frontiers of Radiation Therapy and Oncology* 7:84–96, ed. J. M. Vaeth, Baltimore: University Park Press, 1972.

38. Spackman, D. H.: Improved resolution in amino acid analysis in cancer therapy studies. *Federation Proceedings* 28:898, 1969.

39. Spackman, D. H. and Riley, V.: True adrenal glucocorticoid values in experimental animals: Implications for cancer research, *Abstracts of the XIIth International Cancer Congress*, vol. 2. p. 26, 1978.

40. Spackman, D. H. and Riley, V.: The modification of cancer by stress: Effects of plasma corticosterone elevation on immunological system components in mice. *Federation Proceedings* 35:1693, 1976.

41. Spackman, D. H.; Riley, V.; Santisteban, G. A.; Kirk, W.; and Bredberg, L.: The role of stress in producing elevated corticosterone levels and thymus involution in mice. *Abstracts of the XIth International Cancer Congress* 3:382–383, 1974.

42. Spackman, D. H.; Stein, W. H.; and Moore, S.: Automatic recording apparatus for use in the chromatography of amino acids. *Analytical Chemistry* 30:1190–1206, 1958.

43. Spackman, D. H. and Riley, V.: Unpublished data.

44. Sundberg, R. D.: Lymphocytes and plasma cells. *Annals of the New York Academy of Science* 59:671–689, 1955.

45. Tannenbaum, A.: The initiation and growth of tumors. I. The effects of underfeeding. *American Journal of Cancer* 38:335–350, 1940.
46. Tannenbaum, A. and Silverstone, H.: Nutrition in Relation to Cancer. *Advances in Cancer Research* 1:451–501, 1953.
47. Turner, C. O. and Hagnara, J. T.: *General Endocrinology*, 5th edition, pp. 382–383, Philadelphia: Sanders, 1971.
48. Voss, W. A. G.: Personal communication (Ultrasonic communication in mice). 1979.
49. Wallace, E. W.; Wallace, H. M.; and Mills, C. A.: Effect of climatic environment upon the genesis of subcutaneous tumors induced by methylcholanthrene and upon the growth of a transplantable sarcoma in C3H mice. *Journal of the National Cancer Institute* 3:99–110, 1942.
50. Wallace, E. W.; Wallace, H. M.; and Mills, C. A.: Influence of environmental temperature upon the incidence and course of spontaneous tumors in C3H mice, *Cancer Research* 4:279–281, 1944.
51. White, A.; Handler, P.; and Smith, E. L.: *Principles of Biochemistry*. 4th Edition, pp. 936–964, New York: McGraw-Hill, 1968.

Psychological and Physiological Correlates of Type A Behavior Pattern [1]

REDFORD B. WILLIAMS, JR.
THOMAS HANEY
JAMES A. BLUMENTHAL

The purpose of this brief paper is to describe the latest results in two ongoing research programs relating to the psychological and psychophysiological correlates of Type A behavior pattern. The first area concerns the joint relationship of Type A behavior pattern and other psychological characteristics to coronary atherosclerosis in patients undergoing coronary arteriography with chest pain as the indication. The second area relates to differential physiological responding of Type A persons under laboratory tasks where the motivation is manipulated using a monetary incentive.

Type A, Hostility, and Coronary Atherosclerosis

We have previously reported that Type A patients undergoing diagnostic coronary arteriography have increased levels of coronary atherosclerosis in comparison to non-Type A patients [2]. Whereas Type A and non-Type A patients are about equally represented in the group of patients with minimal levels of coronary atherosclerosis, Type A patients constitute 71% of the group of patients with moderate levels and 93% of the group of patients with severe levels of coronary atherosclerosis. Since that study, we have been systematically collecting data pertaining to a wide variety of psychosocial characteristics of patients undergoing diagnostic coronary arteriography at Duke University Medical Center, including such measures as the Minnesota Multiphasic Personality Inventory (MMPI), life change

[1] Supported by NIH HL 18589 and HL 22740 and NIMH Research Scientist Development Award (RBW) MH-70482.

401

stress, Type A behavior pattern, quality of life, and social support networks. In this paper, we report on the replication of the earlier finding of relationship between Type A behavior pattern and coronary atherosclerosis and the extension of those earlier findings to include an evaluation of the composite relationship of gender, Type A behavior pattern, and hostility to levels of coronary atherosclerosis.

As a measure of hostility we used the 50-item scale from the MMPI originally described by Cook and Medley [3]. The psychosocial data and the assessment of coronary anatomy were carried out independently of one another, as described in our previous study [2]. Significant coronary atherosclerosis was defined as at least one of the major coronary arteries having a stenosis of at least 75% decrease in luminal diameter. The findings reported here are derived from a sample of 424 patients (307 males and 117 females).

As before, we find that the Type A behavior pattern continues to be significantly associated with increased levels of significant coronary atherosclerosis. Among the 319 Type A patients, 71% were found to have at least one significant coronary occlusion of at least 75%, whereas among the 105 non-Type A patients only 56% were found to have significant occlusions ($p < .01$, chi-square).

In addition, scores on the hostility scale were also found related to severity of coronary atherosclerosis, but in a nonlinear fashion. Patients with scores of 10 or less (maximum possible score = 50) on the hostility scale were found to have at least one artery significantly occluded at the rate of 48%. In contrast, patients in any of the other five higher sextiles of hostility scores exhibited a 70% rate of significant occlusions ($p < .02$, chi-square).

To evaluate simultaneously the relationships of hostility scores, Type A behavior pattern, and gender we employed methods of categorical linear models analysis according to Cox [5]. As shown in Table 1, there is a striking progression in severity of coronary atherosclerosis, from 12.5% with at least one significant occlusion among non-Type A women with low (≤ 10) hostility scores, to 82% among Type A men with high (> 10) hostility scores. Interestingly, there were no significant interactions among the three descriptors in relating to level of coronary atherosclerosis, and all three were significantly and independently related to severity of disease. Sex showed the strongest ($p < .0001$) relationship to coronary atherosclerosis, followed by hostility score ($p < .008$) and Type A behavior pattern ($p < .05$).

These findings replicate our earlier finding [2] of a significant relationship between Type A behavior pattern and extent and severity of coronary atherosclerosis. It is interesting, however, that when adjustment is made

TABLE 1
Relationship of Hostility Scores, Type A Behavior Pattern, and Gender to Levels of Coronary
Atherosclerosis

	Females				Males			
	Low hostility score		High hostility score		Low hostility score		High hostility score	
Behavior pattern	non-A	A	non-A	A	non-A	A	non-A	A
Percentage of subjects with at least one occlusion >75%	12.5	25	29	46	57	68	74	82

for hostility scores, the strength of the relationship between Type A behavior pattern and level of coronary atherosclerosis is diminished, though it remains statistically significant. To the best of our knowledge, the present finding of a relationship between hostility score and coronary atherosclerosis represents the first example of a psychometrically determined characteristic more strongly related to an index of coronary heart disease than Type A behavior pattern as measured using the Structured Interview. Further studies along the lines of the present one will, it is hoped, help to identify other psychological characteristics of patients, which account more completely for the variance in coronary atherosclerosis univariately explained by Type A behavior pattern. Such characteristics could aid greatly in identifying underlying psychological and physiological mechanisms accounting for the relationship between Type A behavior pattern and various manifestations of coronary heart disease.

Psychophysiological Correlates of Type A Behavior Pattern

We have previously reported that in comparison to Type B persons Type A subjects respond earlier and with a greater absolute number of responses on a task of inductive reasoning when a monetary incentive is provided for subjects who achieve the correct solution on the earlier among five clues [1]. Since the task employed was essentially a "mental work" task, we hypothesized, based on earlier research [6] that the usual physiological response during such a task would be a muscle vasodilatation as indexed by changes in forearm vascular resistance. To the extent that subjects were engaged in attending to the experimenter who presented the clues, previous research [6] also suggested that the expected muscle vasodilatation would be masked by a vasoconstriction associated with the behavior of sensory intake.

Subjects were 44 university undergraduates, half of whom were Type A and half of whom were Type B, based on the student version of the Jenkins Activity Survey [4]. Forearm blood flow (FBF) was measured at 1-min intervals, using venous occlusion plethysmography and a mercury-in-silastic strain gauge. Blood pressure was determined concomitantly with each FBF determination. Forearm vascular resistance (FVR) was calculated by dividing the mean BP (diastolic BP plus one-third of the pulse pressure) by the FBF. After a 10-min baseline period during which subjects were instructed to sit quietly and relax, half the subjects in the Type A group and half in the Type B group were instructed that they would be presented with a series of sets of five clues and that their task was to guess the meaning of a nonsense word (*grobnik*) from the context of the sentence. Clues were in the form *The grobnik is round, The grobnik is very far from earth, The grobnik is very hot,* etc. No penalties were imposed for incorrect guesses, and subjects were instructed that they might give as many responses as they cared. The other half of the subjects in each group received these same basic instructions, but were also told that if they got the correct answer on the very first clue they would win 25¢; 10¢ if they got the right answer on the second clue; 5¢ with the third clue; 2¢ with the fourth clue; and 1¢ on the last clue. The experimenter was unaware of each subject's behavior pattern.

During the baseline period, the Type A subjects (both monetary incentive and nonincentive) exhibited a significantly higher ($p < .05$, t-test) FBF than both Type B groups, indicating a more vasodilated state to begin with for the Type A subjects. During the task the Type B subjects with or without a monetary incentive showed no change in FBF, as did the nonpaid Type A subjects. In contrast to the other groups, the Type A subjects with monetary incentive showed a significant *increase* in FBF during the task, despite their initially more vasodilated state.

This differential cardiovascular response of Type A subjects under the condition of monetary incentive is consistent with the earlier and more frequent behavioral responding reported under similar conditions in our prior study [1]. Insofar as our prior work has shown a tendency toward increased FBF to occur in association with mental work behaviors [6], we interpret the tendency of Type A subjects with monetary incentive in the present study to show vasodilatation during a mental work task to be a reflection of their greater specific vasomotor arousal during the task. Further analyses of the data of this study are currently under way to more fully evaluate the differential cardiovascular responsivity of Type A subjects suggested by the preliminary results reported above. To the extent that these further analyses bear out the preliminary findings, we will be in a better position to increase our understanding of psychophysiological mechanisms whereby Type A persons subject their arterial system to greater wear and tear, hence explaining the increased coronary atherosclerosis reported in the first section of this chapter.

References

1. Blumenthal, J. A.; McKee, D. L.; Haney, T.; and Williams, R. B.: Incentives and Type A behavior. *Journal of Applied Social Psychology* 1979.
2. Blumenthal, J. A.; Williams, R. B.; Kong, Y.; Schanberg, S. M.; and Thompson, L. W.: Type A behavior pattern and coronary atherosclerosis. *Circulation* 58:634–639, 1978.
3. Cook, W. W.; and Medley, D. M.: Proposed hostility and pharisaicvirtue scales for the MMPI. *Journal of Applied Psychology* 39:414–418, 1954.
4. Glass, D. C.: *Behavior patterns, stress, and coronary disease.* Hillsdale, N.J: Lawrence Erlbaum, 1977.
5. Lox, D. R.: Regression models and life tables. *Journal of the Royal Statistical Society* 34:187–196, 1972.
6. Williams, R. B.; Bittker, T. E.; Buchsbaum, M. S.; and Wynne, L. C.: Cardiovascular and neurophysiologic correlates of sensory intake and rejection: I. Effect of cognitive tasks. *Psychophysiology* 12:427–433, 1975.

SUBJECT INDEX